Access to European Justice for Environmental
Civil Society Organizations

European University Studies
Europäische Hochschulschriften
Publications Universitaires Européennes

Series XXXI
Political Science

Reihe XXXI Série XXXI
Politikwissenschaft
Sciences politiques

Vol./Bd. 604

PETER LANG
Frankfurt am Main · Berlin · Bern · Bruxelles · New York · Oxford · Wien

Inga Immel

Access to European Justice for Environmental Civil Society Organizations

PETER LANG
Internationaler Verlag der Wissenschaften

Bibliographic Information published by the Deutsche Nationalbibliothek
The Deutsche Nationalbibliothek lists this publication in the Deutsche Nationalbibliografie; detailed bibliographic data is available in the internet at http://dnb.d-nb.de.

Zugl.: Münster (Westfalen), Univ., Diss., 2011

D 6
ISSN 0721-3654
ISBN 978-3-631-61979-7

Internationaler Verlag der Wissenschaften
Frankfurt am Main 2011

www.peterlang.de

Vorwort und Dank

Diese Arbeit wurde der Philosophischen Fakultät der Westfälischen Wilhelms–Universität Münster vorgelegt und als Dissertation angenommen.

Für die Unterstützung meiner Arbeit möchte ich mich bei einigen Menschen besonders bedanken.

Professor em. Dr. iur. Dr. h.c. Gerhard W. Wittkämper sei überaus für die gute Betreuung meiner Dissertation an der Graduate School of Politics gedankt. Ebenfalls danke ich Professorin Doris Fuchs Ph.D. für die Anfertigung des Zweitgutachtens.
Hervorheben möchte ich auch die engagierten Professoren und Dozenten der Universiteit Maastricht, die den Grundstein für mein wissenschaftliches Interesse an der Europäischen Union gelegt haben; insbesondere: Professorin Dr. Hildegard Schneider, Dr. Andrea Ott und Dr. René Gabriëls. Auch meinem ehemaligen Deutsch– und Geschichtslehrer, Dr. Rolf Kauffeldt, danke ich herzlich, dass er mich schon früh zum Schreiben ermutigt hat.

Dem Evangelischen Studienwerk e.V. Villigst und allen „Villigstern“ gilt großer Dank für die Förderung meiner Promotion und die Aufnahme in ihre Promo–Gemeinschaft.

Darüber hinaus danke ich all denen, die mich in meinem Leben begleitet, Wissensdurst in mir geweckt und so manches Mal durch angeregte Diskussionen gestillt haben.

Meinen ganz persönlichen Dank richte ich an meine Eltern, Michaela und Georg, meine Geschwister, Jessica und Clemens, sowie Jan Rauch und James und Sharyn Moore.
Ohne euch wäre diese Arbeit nicht möglich gewesen!

Contents

List of Figures

List of Tables

Abbreviations

AC	Aarhus Convention
ACHPR	African Court on Human and Peoples' Rights
AEUV	Vertrag über die Arbeitsweise der Europäischen Union
appropr.	appropriate
Art.	Article
ASEAN	Association of Southeast Asian Nations
CEE	Central & Eastern Europe
CFI	Court of First Instance
CoE	Council of Europe
Council	Council of the European Union
CONNECS	Consultation, the European Commission and Civil Society
CoR	Committee of Regions
CSOs	Civil Society Organizations
CT	Constitutional Treaty
def.	definition
DG	Directorate–General
diff.	different
Dir.	Directive
DSU	Dispute Settlement Understanding
EAP	Environmental Action Plan
EBRD	European Bank for Reconstruction and Development
EC	European Communities; also in combination with articles: Treaty establishing the European Community
ECB	European Central Bank
ECHR	(European Convention on Human Rights) Convention for the Protection of Human Rights and Fundamental Freedoms
ECJ	(European Court of Justice) Court of the European Union (formerly: Communities)
ECOSOC	Economic and Social Council
ECSC	European Coal and Steel Community
ECtHR	European Court of Human Rights
EEB	European Environmental Bureau
EEC	European Economic Community
EESC	European Economic and Social Committee
EIA	Environmental Impact Assessment
EIB	European Investment Bank
env.	environmental
EP	European Parliament
EU	European Union
ext.	extension
G10	Green Ten = ten environmental CSOs
GC	General Court
IACHR	Inter–American Court of Human Rights

ICC	International Criminal Court
ICJ	International Court of Justice
ICSID	International Center for the Settlement of Investment Disputes
iCSO System	integrated Civil Society System
ICTR	International Criminal Tribunal for Rwanda
ICTY	International Criminal Tribunal for the former Yugoslavia
INGO	International Non–Governmental Organization
in conj. with	in conjunction with
incl.	including
info	information
IO	International Organization
IPPC	Integrated Pollution Prevention and Control
IR	International Relations
ITLOS	International Tribunal for the Law of the Sea
LT	Lisbon Treaty
ltd.	limited
MEP	Member of European Parliament
Mercosur	Mercado Común del Sur
MLG	Multi–Level–Governance
MOP	Meeting of the Parties
nat.	national
NAFTA	North American Free Trade Area
NATO	North Atlantic Treaty Organization
NGO	Non–Governmental Organization
OSCP	opportunity structure for citizens' participation
particip.	participation
POS	political opportunity structure
poss.	possible
P & P	Plans and Programs
Reg.	Regulation
SEA	Single European Act
sent.	sentence
subpara.	subparagraph
TEU	Treaty on European Union
TEU LT	Treaty on European Union after the Lisbon Treaty
TFEU	Treaty on the Functioning of the European Union
UNECE	United Nations Economic Commission for Europe
UNEP	United Nations Environment Programme
UNFCC	United Nations Framework Convention on Climate Change
UNO	United Nations Organization
w/in	within
WPG	White Paper on European Governance
WTO	World Trade Organization
EU	Europäische Union
EuG	Europäisches Gericht
EuGH	Europäischer Gerichtshof
ZGOs	Zivilgesellschaftsorganisationen

Introduction

The preceding two decades have revealed a steady growth in depth and width of civil society organizations (CSOs) throughout western democracies. Particularly within the institutional framework of the European Union (EU), civil society has distinctly gained in importance throughout the development process of new policies. Civil society organizations provide the necessary information and particular expertise on specific policy issues that civil servants lack within the administrative apparatus. This form of participatory democracy is intended by politicians to compensate for the democratic deficit of the EU, which is characterized by an insufficient representative democracy and a lacking democratic legitimization of some of its institutions[1]. Strategic lobbying of Commission officials, who are assigned to initiate specific legislation, as well as of members of the two legislative institutions, the European Parliament (EP) and the Council, is only one of the many tactics employed by such organizations. While lobbying and other methods of participatory democracy have become subject to an ever expanding scope of political studies, the relationship between judiciary and participatory governance has been subjected to a significant lesser degree of research. The latter is the focus of this dissertation.

Central Claim

This dissertation delves into the relations of European civil society engaged in the protection of the environment and the European Court of Justice (ECJ) including its first instance, the General Court (GC). It is guided by the research question on how access to the ECJ could be improved for environmental civil society organizations. This question is based on three basic assumptions that finally result in the below stated claim.

Assumption 1: Participation by civil society organizations is of benefit to EU environmental governance.

Assumption 2: Access and participation opportunities for these actors are comparatively well established at the political institutions of the EU.

1 This trend has not least been supported by the publication of the Commission's White Paper on European Governance in 2001 (COM(2001) 428 final, *European Governance. A White Paper*) and the thereof resulting institutionalization of civil society influence on the preparation of legislative proposals.

Assumption 3: Access to the ECJ is hampered for civil society associations acting in the general interest area of environmental protection.

Assumption 4: The premises of political participation can to a certain extent be transferred to the rules on *locus standi* for environmental CSOs to improve access to the European Court of Justice.

Claim: Access and participation opportunities should be comprehensively given to environmental civil society organizations throughout the policy cycle as a whole, i.e. to all institutions, bodies, offices and agencies responsible for European Union governance.

Comprehensive participation refers to the ability of organizations acting in the public interest to participate at each EU Institution at any given stage of the policy cycle, rather than a selective striving for valuable input by CSOs in few instances only. It is important to note, however, that these participation opportunities should be granted freely, fairly, without discrimination and, most importantly, with an open end. Yet, influence in the final outcome of a decision cannot be guaranteed to all participants. To the contrary, the opportunity to take part in deliberations and the consideration of valid arguments of qualified, credible, and legitimatized non-governmental actors should ideally result in a final decision that considers the concerns of all stakeholders involved and arrives at the best solution. These standards should be applied by the administration of political institutions as much as by the judges of the ECJ.

It is the judiciary's task in any government to safeguard the institutional system of checks and balances, to interpret the law under its jurisdiction, and to control the legality of the other two branches' actions. It is thereby indispensable for judges to be independent of any external influence in order to perform their duties with complete impartiality. Other than the political institutions of the EU, however, the ECJ is in no need to justify its decisions on grounds of democratic input legitimacy. The need for external expertise is therefore necessary, not to legitimatize the Court's own position, but to ensure that concerns for environmental protection are safeguarded. It is the aim of this dissertation to offer an alternative means to ensure that external expertise on environmental matters is provided to the Court without paving the way for 'judicial lobbying'. The introduction of briefs submitted by an *amicus curiae* is thus found to offer an innovative and appropriate solution to provide access to European justice for environmental civil society organizations.

Outline

The dissertation is structured as follows.

Part I „European Environmental Policy and Civil Society“ justifies the choice of the three subjects under study. Chapter 1 introduces the political and legal system of the European Union and places it between the international legal order and the national legal systems of the Member States. Chapter 2 discusses the need for political action in environmental protection. Chapter 3 then identifies civil society organizations as valuable contributors to environmental policy and presents the specific features of environmental interest representation at the EU level.

Part II „Participatory Governance at the EU & Recourse to Litigation" introduces the methodological approach of this work against the background of European integration theories in political science. Chapter 4 discusses political theories on participatory and deliberative democracy with an eye to the theoretical benefits arising out of greater inclusion of non-state actors into the political process and using the Aarhus Convention as a practical example. Chapter 5 then outlines the academic debate on the existence of a *democratic deficit* in the EU, including the concepts of legitimacy, transparency and governance, and awards special attention to the existing opportunity structures for CSOs at the respective EU Institutions. The model utilized to underline methodologically the above-declared claim on the necessity of comprehensive participation is the policy cycle, introduced and discussed in chapter 6. This model is modified to take into account the specificities of the multi-level and multi-institutional governance of the European Union and is supplemented by a participatory component. The role of the European Court of Justice in furthering European integration and particularly in strengthening citizens' rights is considered in chapter 7 with the help of the neofunctionalist theory. In addition, a brief overview on the Court's jurisdiction and its methods of interpretation leads over to chapter 8, in which the conditions that determine whether potential litigants initiate cases before the ECJ as well as the circumstances for potential benefits and costs and the likelihood of success are highlighted.

Part III „The Aarhus Convention at the EU" assesses the compliance of EU law with the three pillars of the *Aarhus Convention on Access to Information, Public Participation in Decision-making and Access to Justice in Environmental Matters* (*AC*) to which the EU and 26 of its Member States are parties. Chapter 9 compares the requirements of Article 4 AC with the respective legislation regulating access to information and documents at the EU Institutions and Member State authorities respectively. The compatibility of EU legislation addressing the Member States with the provisions of the Aarhus Convention on public participation in decision-making is assessed in chapter 10. Finally, chapter 11 introduces the requirements of the Aarhus Convention on access to justice and then offers a detailed overview on the review procedures available to and the standing requirements for environmental CSOs applied within the EU legal system. These include preliminary and administrative review undertaken by the European Commission and the European Ombudsman, as well as the direct actions for annulment and failure to act before the General Court, and the preliminary reference procedure before the ECJ. Given the latter's origin in disputes adjudicated by national courts, a study executed by Milieu Ltd. under the order of the Commission offers considerable insights into the rules and regulations governing *locus standi* for associations in the Member States.

The current rules on standing and the interpretation of an applicant's individual concern by the ECJ is critically examined in Part IV „Critical Assessment of the Status Quo". Particularly chapter 12 offers an in–depth discussion on the Court's position, the criticism of academics and practitioners, as well as a number of proposals for a reformulation of the test by, *inter alia*, the former Court of First Instance and Advocate-General

Jacobs. Arguments for and against such a modification are presented below. Chapter 13 then responds to the nature of environmental legal disputes and provides an overview on environmental case-law of the ECJ and particularly the *Greenpeace* cases. Finally, proposals specifically designed to address the paradox that, the more persons affected, the greater potentially the environmental harm, yet the less likely a complaint will be admitted to the Court, are discussed.

Given that a change in the rules on *locus standi* does not appear very likely, an alternative tool, borrowed from U.S. litigation and several international arbitration systems, is introduced in chapter 14. The concept of *amicus curiae* participation in legal proceedings of other legal systems is analyzed and its potential benefits and costs are assessed for both, the governance system, as well as the potential *amicus*. The title of Part V „Complementing Participation" finds its fulfillment in chapter 15, where the introduction of *amicus curiae* submissions to EU litigation is proposed for cases affecting the state of the environment. The proposal is accompanied by a cost-benefit-analysis as well as a suggested amendment to the rules of procedure of the Court of Justice.

Finally, the conclusion amends the EU participatory policy cycle introduced in chapter 6 with the participation of *amici curiae* and emphasizes the resemblance of participation rights in political decision-making processes with those in legal proceedings. The conclusion further summarizes the significance of this study for political science as well as practice within the EU and provides an outlook on potential studies that could be undertaken in this area.

Part I.

European Environmental Policy and Civil Society

Part I

1. The Political and Legal System of the European Union: Multi–Level Governance

1.1. Introduction

This chapter is guided by the question of why the examination of participatory governance in environmental policy is of particular interest within the context of the European Union. It therefore shortly introduces the European political and legal system and presents its specific characteristics that distinguish it as one of a kind from national legal orders embedded in a state structure or the realm of international law.

1.1.1. European Integration: Competences of the Union

At the time of this writing, the European Union consists of twenty–seven Member States[1] that, although having transferred specific competences to the EU, retain their national sovereignty. The Union has developed successfully over the past fifty years and serves as a model for other regional integration organizations. While the original intention of the founders of the then European Coal and Steel Community (ECSC) in 1952 and the succeeding European Economic Community (EEC), namely peace, regional security and economic prosperity among the participating countries, can still be mentioned as primary goals of the European Union, today, other aspirations have developed as well. These goals are formulated in Article 2 of the Treaty on the Functioning of the European Union (TFEU). The Lisbon Treaty furthermore introduced a list on the exclusive competences of the Union and those shared with the Member States in Articles 3 and 4 TFEU respectively. Further co–ordination is provided for in Articles 5 and 6 TFEU. Those competences that are not listed in the two provisions of the Treaty and do not fall under the cooperation in economic policies under Article 5 TEU LT, remain under the exclusive sovereignty of the Member States. Environmental policy, the field under study, falls under the category of shared competences as Article 4(2)(e) TEU LT stipulates.

The number of policy areas covered by the so–called supranational governance mode has steadily grown, though to a differing degree, from purely economic fields, including the creation of a single market with a common customs and a monetary union, to those

1 For updated information, cf. http://europa.eu/about–eu/27–member–countries/index_en.htm

that are attached to a lesser degree to economic considerations such as the environment[2], public health[3], culture[4] and civil protection[5]. The depth of inter–state co–operation has been augmented as well in policy areas that have traditionally been reserved to state sovereignty, for instance security and defense matters (formerly second EU pillar) or justice and home affairs (formerly third EU pillar) in order to achieve the general aims of the organization.

It is relevant to examine the legal framework and institutional setting given that the EU is authorized to develop action plans, adopt legislation and take decisions regarding particular activities relating to the field of environmental policy that are binding upon the Member States.

The Institutions

Not only the policy areas in which the EU has become active have increased in number and deepened in detail, but also the institutions and their powers have undergone substantial development over the past five decades. The European Council comprising the Heads of State and Government is an exception. Its task to determine the general course of further European integration twice a year during the summits has changed comparatively little. The European Commission (Commission of the European Union), on the other hand, has transformed from a comparatively weak High Authority to an influential administrative office that incorporates powers ranging from the initiation and drafting of new legislation to acting as a 'guardian of the Treaties' and ensuring the correct application of the Treaties' obligations by the institutions and the Member States[6]. It disposes of the widest powers in competition policy, where the Commission takes acts as legislator (takes binding decisions), executor (implements and enforces them) and as judiciary (imposes fines and other penalties). The European Parliament demonstrates the greatest development within the institutional framework of the EU. Despite the primarily advisory function of the early Parliamentary Assembly, the EP has steadily gained greater competences and a right to substantially co–determine European policies. Since its first direct election in 1979, it is furthermore the only institution that is democratically legitimatized on EU level. Corresponding to the increase in influence of the EP, the power of the Council has declined, though not dramatically. Today, co–decision has superseded consultation and cooperation as the "ordinary legislative procedure"[7] and reduced the latter two to legislative decisions in few policy areas. For the sake of completeness, the Parliament's assent is still required regarding, *inter alia*, some decisions concerning the European Central Bank, the accession of new Member States to the Union, and the approval of the College of Commissioners and its President. Accordingly, the style of

---

2 Title XX, Articles 191–193 TFEU
3 Title XIV, Article 168 TFEU
4 Title XVIII, Article 167 TFEU
5 Newly introduced: Title XXIII, Article 196 TFEU
6 Article 17(1) TEU LT
7 Articles 294 TFEU et seq.

policy–making has shifted from an intergovernmental approach, where representatives of Member State governments bargain for compromises purely based on national interests to supranational decision–making, which regards the overall effects on European integration.

Whereas the institutional framework of the EU does not provide for a strict delimitation of the legislature and the executive within the meaning of the traditional doctrine of the separation of powers, the judiciary is exclusively occupied by the Court of Justice of the European Union (ECJ) and the General Court (GC; renamed from "Court of First Instance", CFI by the Lisbon Treaty, now: Article 19(1) TEU). The jurisdictions of the respective courts are outlined in further detail in part III. For the purposes of a short overview, the following shall suffice. The tasks of the Court have hardly changed over the decades; yet, its role in the integration process has gained in importance. Through its case–law, the ECJ was able to heavily determine the course of European legal integration and thereby put political decision–makers under pressure. Critics therefore condemn the Court for law–making and accuse the judges of intervening in politics. It is, however, true that the jurisprudence of the ECJ has, for instance, defined and strengthened the transformation of the treatment of Member State nationals from market participants[8] to Union citizens, who may enjoy specific rights and must perform certain duties. Other examples among many include the creation of the doctrines of the supremacy of EU primary[9] and secondary[10] law over national law (the former prevails over the latter in case of conflict) and its direct effect (litigants can rely on EU law before national courts)[11] or the *ERTA* doctrine on the implied powers (powers that have been transferred to the EU internally can also be executed by Union Institutions externally, i.e. with regard to relations with third countries or organizations without having to be explicitly confirmed in the Treaties)[12].

The General Court was established as the 'Court of First Instance' in 1989 in order to distribute the growing case applications among the two instances and relieve the workload of the ECJ. The GC is competent to adjudicate at first instance direct actions[13] and disagreements concerning contracts concluded by the EU pursuant to clauses of the contract[14]. Amendments of the Nice Treaty further provide for the GC to declare preliminary rulings under specific circumstances. In practice, however, the ECJ remains the sole authority in preliminary reference proceedings[15]. The ECJ thus functions as an appeal court and reviews the decisions of the GC on points of law.

---

8 e.g. employers, employees, manufacturers, producers, importers, exporters and consumers

9 ECJ, Case 26/62 *NV Algemene Transport– en Expeditie Onderneming van Gend & Loos v Netherlands Inland Revenue Administration* [1963] ECR 1, para.1, last sentence

10 ECJ, Case 14/68 *Walt Wilhelm and Others v Bundeskartellamt* [1969] ECR 1, para.7

11 ECJ, Case 6/64 *Flaminio Costa v E.N.E.L.* [1964] ECR 585, sent. 15

12 ECJ, Case 22/70 *Commission of the European Communities v Council of the European Communities (ERTA)* [1971] ECR 263, para.19; cf. Bieber, Epiney & Haag, 2005, p.603

13 Article 263 TFEU (action for annulment); Article 265 TFEU (action for failure to act)

14 Article 272 TFEU

15 Article 267 TFEU

Next to these institutions, the institutional framework of the EU includes two advisory bodies and numerous agencies. Subject to the provisions of the relevant policy area and the legislative act, the legislating institutions are either obliged to or may consult the European Economic and Social Committee (EESC) or the Committee of Regions (CoR) within a predetermined period of time[16]. While the EC Treaty left it to the discretion of the EP to decide whether or not to invite the committees to facultative consultation[17], the Lisbon Treaty, probably owing to its new position as influential co–legislator, makes these consultations mandatory under the same conditions as for Council and Commission[18]. In addition, the two advisory committees[19] may also deliver their opinion on their own initiative whenever they deem appropriate[20]. The EESC comprises of "representatives of organisations of employers, of the employed and of other parties representative of civil society, notably in socioeconomic, civic, professional and cultural areas"[21] divided into three groups representing employers (group I), employees (group II) and various other interests related to or affected by the market economy (group III)[22]. The degree of influence of the committees' opinions is, overall, comparatively small, even though it varies of course according to the policy area and the respective action. As will be elaborately shown in chapter 5, the EESC has strongly contributed to the debate on the conceptualization, as well as the inclusion, of organized civil society into the EU policy process. Other institutions, e.g. the European Central Bank (ECB), or bodies such as the European Investment Bank, or offices and agencies[23] are not subject to this study and therefore left out of the discussion.

It follows from the above that the EU, as a governance system, is a valuable framework of investigation because supranational decision–makers, e.g. the EP and the Commission, commonly determine the course of integration and adopt legislation with representatives of national governments in the Council. In addition, regional and other sub–national public authorities attempt to exert influence as well and are, due to the fact that they are the prime executors of EU law, indispensable for its implementation. The legality of these actions and the compliance with procedural rules is controlled by the ECJ on the basis of the Treaties. These three 'levels of governance' are connected in sincere cooperation, yet also mutually dependent on each other and individually attempt to exert the greatest influence possible. The following section introduces a theoretical framework that attempts to acknowledge the role played by all public authorities involved in European decision–making at the respective levels of governance.

16 EESC: Article 304(1) & (2) TFEU; CoR: Article 307(1) & (2) TFEU
17 EESC: Article 262(4) EC; CoR Article 265(4) EC
18 EESC: Article 304(1) & (2) TFEU; CoR: Article 307(1) & (2) TFEU
19 EESC: Article 300(1)TFEU; CoR: Article 300(1) TFEU
20 EESC: Article 304(1) TFEU; CoR: Article 307(4) TFEU
21 Article 300(2) TFEU
22 European Economic and Social Committee, 2002, Rule 27(1), Rules of Procedure
23 Europa, *Agencies of the European Union, Community Agencies*, Website

Multi–Level Governance

The need to go beyond traditional International Relations (IR) theories, for instance realism and liberalism, in order to explain the specific dynamic of European integration became evident early on. Yet, most approaches have been built upon the basic assumptions of specific categories of IR theories and were then further developed. This is the case for instance with Haas' *neofunctionalism* or Moravcik's *liberal intergovernmentalism*. Still, most theories are only capable of explaining the state of integration at a specific and delimitable period of time. Thus, at the latest, the reform brought about by the Maastricht Treaty (1993) and subsequent Treaty revisions manifested the need to develop a new theory to account for the newly established, comprehensive political system of the European Union. The multi–level governance (MLG) approach, developed in the 1990s by Liesbet Hooghe and Gary Marks, leaves the discourse on pure (liberal) intergovernmentalism as opposed to neofunctional assumptions of supranationalism. One important point needs to be made here. MLG is not capable of explaining enhanced political integration among European states and therefore does not amount to a grand theory as it emphasizes the unpredictability of further integration[24]. Rather, as a middle–range theoretical approach[25], it illustrates the specificities of European policy–making and is best suitable for policy network analyses[26].

The central claim of MLG results from three basic assumptions. First, political authority and competences are dispersed between different levels and among different governmental as well as non–governmental actors. This does not only include the general separation of powers in terms of legislature, executive and judiciary but extends to the varying degrees of power in different policy areas[27]. MLG neither exclusively focuses on the Member States as sole actors nor assumes that supranational institutions develop their own dynamic and completely disempower the formerly sovereign nation states. Rather, MLG considers the various levels of supranational governance. States are not, as is the case in the rationalist opinion, viewed as black boxes, whose internal political system is irrelevant, but quite to the contrary, it is of utmost importance.

In sum, the European Union consists of three governance levels, each comprising a multitude of governmental authorities as well as non–state actors. The sub–national level includes the jurisdiction of local authorities and, in countries with a federated structure, parliaments and governments of the constituent parts. The national level consists of the central or federal government including all public administrations and authorities that fall under its responsibility. The supranational level circumscribes the EU Institutions within their areas of competence except for the European Council and the Council of Ministers, in which national interests are represented and which may therefore be regarded as intergovernmental. Agreements concluded with other regional or international

24 Knodt & Große Hüttmann, 2006, p.229

25 Rosamond, 2000, p.126

26 Knodt & Große Hüttmann, 2006, p.229; Rosamond, 2000, p.111

27 Rosamond, 2000, p.110; Knodt & Große Hüttmann, 2006, pp.223, 228

organizations and third countries are also binding on both the European Union and its Member States and might be added as a fourth level, if not governance, then at least one of influence. Representatives of these governmental organizations are not directly involved in the decision–making process at European level but the legal obligations arising out of international cooperation may, to a varying degree, determine certain rules and standards to which the Union Institutions and national governments must adhere. This matter is outlined in more detail in the subsection on the hierarchy of norms.

The supranational method of decision–making within the EU leads to a significant decrease in the relative power on part of the Member States. Yet, important decisions may now be adopted even against the will of large Member States even though, in practice, consent is usually striven for. This is partly the consequence of the increased use of qualified majority voting in the Council in more and more policy areas. Overall, the pressure for finding a compromise that amounts to the lowest common denominator is substantially reduced[28]. MLG therefore leaves the state–centric discussion and rather focuses on multiple actors, including supranational institutions and external public and private groups. Member State governments remain important, yet not the sole politically relevant decision–makers[29].

Moreover, the different levels of political decision–making are not clearly distinguishable. Quite to the contrary, they are assumed to be interconnected and to some degree even interdependent[30].

Owing to these characteristics of European policy–making, Hooghe and Marks do not refer to the EU as 'government' but as 'governance'. This postmodern term in political theory does not restrict the competence to determine a society's formal rules and to formulate the content of its policies to the 'government' as the peak of a political hierarchy but rather extends the inclusiveness to other political authorities at lower levels of the hierarchy, as well as to non–governmental actors[31].

1.2. The European Legal System

The European Union is a community based on the rule of law[32] that respects democratic principles[33] and strives for 'good governance'[34]. The adherence to written law and general legal principles of international law, as well as those originating from Member States' traditions, is for these purposes an indispensable prerequisite[35]. The ECJ has continuously confirmed the position of general legal principles within European law in

28 Knodt & Große Hüttmann, 2006, p.228

29 Knodt & Große Hüttmann, 2006, pp.226–227

30 Knodt & Große Hüttmann, 2006, p.229

31 Rosamond, 2000, p.111; Knodt & Große Hüttmann, 2006, pp.223 & 224

32 Kwanka, 2006, p.1; Lenaerts & van Nuffel, 2005, p.712

33 cf. Article 6 & Title II TEU LT; cf. Lenaerts & van Nuffel, 2005, p.712

34 Definition given in: European Commission, 2001, COM(2001) 428 final, *European Governance. A White Paper*, pp.10–11

35 Harratsch, Koenig & Pechstein, 2009, pp.179; Lenaerts & van Nuffel, 2005, p.711

its jurisprudence. Particularly its decision in *Internationale Handelsgesellschaft*[36] illustrates the fact that general principles of law are an inherent part of the EU legal order as the Court declared that "[r]espect for fundamental rights forms an integral part of the general principles of law protected by the Court of Justice. The protection of such rights [...], must be ensured within the framework of the structure and objectives of the Community"[37].

These principles include those relating to human rights and fundamental freedoms[38], as well as principles of administrative law[39]. In particular, the principles of the right to be heard for applicants[40], the duty to state reasons by the institutions when issuing a decision or another act[41], as well as general principles relating to sound administration[42], are indispensable for the relations of environmental interest groups with the supranational administration.

European law disposes of its own very specific principles, distinguishing EU law from general international law. A substantial number of these principles have been formulated and enforced by the ECJ, as for example the above–outlined principles of supremacy of European law, including the duty to interpret national law in conformity with the former, as well as direct effect of EU law in national courts[43]. Both the principle of proportionality[44] and the principle of subsidiarity[45] are not only enshrined in the EU Treaty but must be carefully observed in all actions undertaken by any EU Institution[46].

1.2.1. Hierarchy of Norms

Similar to the multiple layers of governance that characterize the political system of the Union, the EU is furthermore confronted with a hierarchy of different levels of law. The mutual influence and spillovers of three legal systems, namely international law, including international customary law, European law and national law, becomes increasingly important regarding globalization. Roughly categorized, one could place EU law in a "*position en sandwich*" between international law on the one and national law on the other side, which results in an interconnection of the legal orders[47]. However, the

---

36 ECJ, Case 11/70 [1970] ECR 1125

37 ECJ, Case 11/70 *Internationale Handelsgesellschaft* [1970] ECR 1125, para.3 of the summary

38 Article 6 and Title II TEU LT

39 Lenaerts & van Nuffel, 2005, p.711

40 ECJ, Case 32/62 *M. Maurice Alvis v Council* [1963] ECR 49, para. A–1, last sentence; Lenaerts & van Nuffel, 2005, p.717

41 ECJ, Case 125/77 *Koninklijke Scholten–Honig NV and De Verenigde Zetmeelbedrijven "De Bijenkorf" BV v Hoofdproduktschap voor Akkerbouwprodukten* [1978] ECR 1991, para.1

42 ECJ, Joined Cases 33 & 75/79, *Richard Kuhner v Commission* [1980] ECR 1677, para.5; Lenaerts & van Nuffel, 2005, pp.713–714

43 Lenaerts & van Nuffel, 2005, pp.666–667

44 Article 5 TEU LT; e.g. ECJ, Case C–359/92 *Germany v Council* [1994] ECR I–3681, para.44

45 Article 5 TEU LT

46 Oppermann, Classen & Nettesheim, 2009, p.169; cf. also Harratsch, Koenig & Pechstein, 2009, pp.181, 182

47 Tohidipur, 2008, p.103

hierarchy of legal norms in the European system, though not explicitly stipulated, yet assumed in the Treaties on the basis of Article 263 TFEU, displays a different order and is one in its own right[48].

At the top ranks primary EU law adjacent to general principles of law, including those originating from international law[49] or international customary law[50]. Agreements concluded with one or more third parties, i.e. countries or international organizations, rank below the Treaties given that their compatibility with the latter may be reviewed by the Court of Justice on the basis of Article 218(11) TFEU; yet they rank above EU legislation[51]. Secondary law adopted by the EU Institutions follows at a lower rank because their legality is scrutinized on the basis of their conformity with primary EU and international law, including agreements concluded with third parties[52]. Still, secondary European law enjoys primacy over national law, although it should also be mentioned that many principles of law, as well as administrative practices, are retrieved from the traditions of the Member States[53].

The general rules apply in case of collusion, i.e. specialized law is to be exercised preferably to general law (*lex specialis derogat legi generali*) and later enacted law supersedes its predecessors (*lex posterior derogat legi priori*). Yet, more recent but general law is always inferior to specialized law, even if the latter is older[54]. It follows from all the above that the European legal order is defined as *sui generis*, one of a kind.

1.2.2. Treaties: European primary law

The notion of primary EU law comprises first and foremost the founding treaties adopted by the Member States according to their respective constitutional principles. Yet, it also includes general legal principles[55]. The treaties establish the legal basis for the existence and continuity of the European Union. They determine the legal rules, assign the areas of competences to the Union, allocate the powers and functions among the institutions and bodies, and stipulate the formal procedures etc.

The basis of European integration has not been static and fixed but rather dynamic and has been subjected to a number of new treaty adoptions and amendments. The Treaty of Paris in 1952[56] established the ECSC and was followed six years later by the Treaties of

48 Lenaerts & van Nuffel, 2005, pp.14, 703

49 cf. Article 216(2)TFEU; Harratsch, Koenig & Pechstein, 2009, p.182

50 Lenaerts & van Nuffel, 2005, pp.704, 711; Oppermann, Classen & Nettesheim, 2009, pp.166–170

51 Harratsch, Koenig & Pechstein, 2009, p.185; Bieber, Epiney & Haag, 2005, p.610; European Commission, 2008, SEC(2008) 556, *Aarhus Convention Implementation Report – European Community*, p.3

52 ECJ, Joined Cases 21–24/72 *International Fruit Company* [1972] ECR 1219, para.3 of summary; Lenaerts & van Nuffel, 2005, pp.703, 704 & 740–741; Bieber, Epiney & Haag, 2005, p.610

53 Lenaerts & van Nuffel, 2005, p.705

54 Harratsch, Koenig & Pechstein, 2009, pp.155; Lenaerts & van Nuffel, 2005, p.704

55 Lenaerts & van Nuffel, 2005, pp.705 & 706

56 The dates refer to the year in which the Treaties entered into force. The signature by the State parties precedes that date usually by two years. Cf. Lenaerts & van Nuffel, 2005, p.4

Rome that marked the legal foundation of the Euratom and the then European Economic Community (EEC)[57]. The contemporary legal framework is governed by the Treaty on the Functioning of the European Union (TFEU) as created by the Lisbon Treaty [formerly EC Treaty] after the Merger Treaty of 1967, the Single European Act (SEA) of 1987[58], and the revisions undertaken in Maastricht (1993), Amsterdam (1999)[59], Nice (2003)[60] and the failure to bring the Constitutional Treaty (2004)[61] into force as well as the Treaty on European Union (TEU) as established by the Maastricht Treaty in 1993[62] and subsequent amendments in Amsterdam (1999), Nice (2003)[63] and Lisbon (2009). Even though the term as such is avoided[64], the Treaties function *de facto* as a constitution.

1.2.3. International law

International agreements whose content affects competences that are internal, i.e. concerning the adoption of legislation, shared between the EU and its Member States, are concluded as mixed agreements on the basis of Article 218 TFEU and the respective clauses in national constitutions. On grounds of the principle of legitimate expectations on part of the other contracting parties, the agreement is binding upon the Union and Member States as a whole (cf. Article 216(2) TFEU)[65] and constitutes an integral part of the European legal order[66]. As a consequence, EU Institutions must carefully obey the rules and duties of international law when carrying out their actions[67] given that they are otherwise vulnerable to liability claims[68].

The ECJ has confirmed that provisions of international agreements may entail direct effect (cf. below) and direct applicability provided that certain conditions are fulfilled. These are namely that wording, nature and purpose of the agreement as a whole already reveal the indication of the drafters to grant direct effect as well as that an obligation must be clear and precise, while not being subjected to the adoption of any subsequent

57 Lenaerts & van Nuffel, 2005, pp.6–7

58 Lenaerts & van Nuffel, 2005, p.43

59 Lenaerts & van Nuffel, 2005, p.58

60 Lenaerts & van Nuffel, 2005, p.64

61 The date annexed to the Constitutional Treaty is the date of its signature, given that the negative referendums in France and The Netherlands in May and June 2005 have prematurely terminated its ratification process.

62 Lenaerts & van Nuffel, 2005, p.47

63 Lenaerts & van Nuffel, 2005, pp.58–65

64 especially after the misery with negative referendums on the *Treaty Establishing a Constitution for Europe* in The Netherlands and France in May and June 2005.

65 Harratsch, Koenig & Pechstein, 2009, p.184; Lenaerts & van Nuffel, 2005, p.739; Bieber, Epiney & Haag, 2005, p.609

66 cf. ECJ, Case 181/73 *Haegemann* [1974] ECR 449, para.1 of the summary; Bieber, Epiney & Haag, 2005, p.609

67 Bieber, Epiney & Haag, 2005, pp.600–601

68 ECJ, Case C–61/94 *Commission v Germany* [1996] ECR I–3989, para.30; cf. Bieber, Epiney & Haag, 2005, pp.600–601

measure[69]. It would therefore have to be assessed for each provision of the agreement under study, the *Aarhus Convention on access to information, public participation in decision–making and access to justice in environmental matters*, whether individuals as well as environmental interest groups may rely on the rights or duties enshrined therein before national or EU courts.

1.2.4. European law

European legislation, i.e. secondary law, takes five forms, each of which are listed in Article 288 TFEU. The type of the legislative act is defined by its aim, content and circle of addressees rather than simply its label[70]. Regulations are generally applicable, i.e. they are not designed to address a very specific situation but rather comprise a general scope and stipulate all–embracing rules within a policy area. They are furthermore directly applicable in all Member States and to the EU Institutions. The regulation is thus automatically incorporated into the legal system for which no transposition act is required, although national governments are not precluded from enacting further measures to facilitate implementation where appropriate. Finally, regulations are binding in their entirety and do not leave room for discretionary implementation measures[71].

Directives, by far the most utilized pieces of legislation for reasons of subsidiarity, are "binding as to the result to be achieved [...] but shall leave to the national authorities the choice of form and methods"[72]. Contrary to regulations, directives need to be transposed into national law before becoming legally effective. The Treaties grant Member States discretion in the form of implementation as long as the provisions have been transposed before the expiration of the stipulated deadline. Otherwise, infringement proceedings may be initiated against the respective Member State that has failed to implement the directive's requirements correctly, in a timely manner, or at all. The principle of legal certainty and the obligation that European legislation must be applied homogeneously in all Member States require unconditional clarity and precision of the directive's provisions. Directives are usually addressed to all Member States; they may however, also specify a closed list of addressees as well[73].

Decisions taken by one or more EU Institutions identify their addressees and thus dispose of an individual as opposed to the regulations' general scope and therefore usually cover very specific and definable circumstances. While regulations and directives are only directed at a number or all Member States or Union Institutions, decisions are frequently also taken with regard to (groups of) private individuals[74]. A decision is furthermore "binding in its entirety upon those to whom it is addressed"[75].

69 cf. ECJ, Case 12/86 *Demirel* [1987] ECR 3719, para.14; Harratsch, Koenig & Pechstein, 2009, p.185; Lenaerts & van Nuffel, 2005, p.742; Bieber, Epiney & Haag, 2005, p.611
70 Lenaerts & van Nuffel, 2005, p.763
71 Article 288(2) TFEU; Lenaerts & van Nuffel, 2005, pp.763–765
72 Article 288(3) TFEU
73 Lenaerts & van Nuffel, 2005, pp.766–768
74 Lenaerts & van Nuffel, 2005, pp.780–781
75 Article 288(4) TFEU

Recommendations and opinions fall under the category of 'soft law' are not discussed because they do not produce legal effects.

Common to all pieces of legislation is that they are binding on all authorities within a Member State and all subdivisions of the EU Institutions unless they provide otherwise[76]. It is required for all legally binding acts to refer to the respective provision(s) of the Treaty that serve as a legal basis, as well as to state the reasons on which they are based and to have acted in accordance with the principle of subsidiarity[77]. Regulations and directives enter into force either on the date of their publication in the Official Journal or at the date stipulated therein. Directives or decisions addressed to one or more persons or Member States become legally effective upon notification to the addressee[78]. As mentioned above, the ECJ is competent to review the legality of all pieces of legally binding legislation under a direct action for annulment[79] or via a preliminary reference from a national court[80].

Following its jurisprudence on directly effective Treaty articles in 1964, the Court also formulated conditions under which provisions of secondary law entail direct effect. The direct effect of an act is an indispensable precondition for individuals to challenge acts and actions of the EU before national courts. Common to all acts is the condition that provisions must be "unconditional and sufficiently precise"[81] when levying duties or rights upon individuals. Regulations are usually held to be directly effective given that they do not "leave any margin of discretion to the authorities"[82] as a consequence of a regulation's direct applicability[83]. The ECJ further confirmed[84] that decisions directed at the Member States may be also directly effective[85]. Directives that have been properly transposed into national law are most obviously directly effective, if they fulfill the above–mentioned criteria. Those, however, that have been implemented incorrectly or not within due time, were held by the ECJ to contain direct effect provided that first, the deadline had already expired and second, individuals enact the provisions vis–á–vis state bodies. Thus, the Court limited the range of direct effect to vertical relations, i.e. private individuals against the state[86]. It thereby excluded horizontal direct effect, i.e. actions taken between individuals[87]; a possibility that exists for specific Treaty provisions.

---

76 Lenaerts & van Nuffel, 2005, p.781

77 Lenaerts & van Nuffel, 2005, p.759

78 Lenaerts & van Nuffel, 2005, pp.760–761

79 Article 263 TFEU

80 Article 267 TFEU

81 e.g. ECJ, Case 8/81 *Becker v Finanzamt Münster–Innenstadt* [1982] ECR 53, para.25 for directives; "clear and precise": ECJ, Case 9/73 *Schlüter* [1973] ECR 1135, para.32 for regulations

82 ECJ, Case 9/73 *Schlüter* [1973] ECR 1135, para.32

83 Lenaerts & van Nuffel, 2005, p.765; Bieber, Epiney & Haag, 2005, p.205

84 ECJ, Case 9/70 *Franz Grad v Finanzamt Traunstein* [1970] ECR 825, para.1 of the summary

85 Bieber, Epiney & Haag, 2005, pp.205–206

86 ECJ, Case 8/81 *Becker v Finanzamt Münster–Innenstadt* [1982] ECR 53; cf. also ECJ, Case 41/74 *Yvonne Van Duyn v Home Office* [1974] ECR 1337, para.2 of the summary; cf. Lenaerts & van Nuffel, 2005, pp.770–771; Bieber, Epiney & Haag, 2005, pp.205–206

87 Lenaerts & van Nuffel, 2005, p.772

1.3. The incorporation of international law into the European legal framework using the example of the Aarhus Convention

The EU is a party to the *Aarhus Convention on access to information, public participation in decision–making and access to justice in environmental matters*. The signature dates from 25 June 1998 and the approval has been formalized on 17 February 2005 by Council Decision 2005/370/EC[88]. As any international agreement relating to environmental protection, the Convention was signed as a mixed agreement on the basis of then Article 175(1) EC in conjunction with the first sentence of the first subparagraph of Article 300(2) and the first subparagraph of Article 300(3) EC separating the competences of the EU and its Member States respectively[89]. As a consequence of paragraph 2 of Article 216 TFEU, the EU is under a duty not only to ensure that the Member States but also its Institutions abide by the provisions of the Convention[90].

The EU is highly committed to a proper implementation of the Aarhus Convention. This ambition is reflected in the declaration accompanying the then EC's signature of the Convention[91]: "[...] [I]t was felt important not only to sign up to the Convention at Community level but also to cover its own institutions, alongside national public authorities". Furthermore, "the Community also declares that the Community institutions will apply the Convention within the framework of their existing and future rules on access to documents and other relevant rules of Community law in the field covered by the Convention"[92]. In addition, there has been a shift of style in EU legislation from the central and homogenized determination of substantive criteria to the emphasis on proceduralization that is compatible with the Aarhus Convention[93].

The provisions of the Aarhus Convention relating to distributing information, providing participation channels to the public, and adjudicating disputes of law are addressed to 'public authorities' as defined in Article (2)(2)(a) and (d) AC. Given the lack of a clearly defined government at European level, the definition in Article 2(2)(a) on "[g]overnment at national, regional and other level" may at least be controversially applied to the EU. Yet, the latter definition in subparagraph (d) explicitly refers to the "institutions of any

88 Council of the European Union, 2005, Council Decision of 17 February 2005 *on the conclusion, on behalf of the European Community, of the Convention on access to information, public participation in decision–making and access to justice in environmental matters*

89 The Lisbon Treaty adds an explicit provision in Article 216 TFEU that transfers the power to "conclude agreements with one or more third countries or international organisations where the Treaties so provide or where the conclusion of an agreement is necessary in order to achieve, within the framework of the Union's policies, one of the objectives referred to in the Treaties, or is provided for in a legally binding Union act or is likely to affect common rules or alter their scope".

90 Rodenhoff, 2002, p.343

91 Lee & Abbott, 2003, p.82

92 Rodenhoff, 2002, p.350; cf. United Nations Treaty Collection, 1998, *Aarhus Convention, Parties & Declarations*, Website.

93 Lee & Abbott, 2003, p.82

regional economic integration organization referred to in article 17 which is a Party to this Convention"[94]. Quite obviously, this definition includes the EU Institutions. However, there is uncertainty about the definition of 'institutions' within the European legal system itself. There is no coherent approach concerning the organs established by law and their classification as 'institutions'[95]. The TFEU elaborately introduces the institutions[96] in Part Six, Title 1, Chapter 1 of the Treaty[97]; namely the European Parliament, the European Council, the Council, the Commission, the Court of Justice, the European Central Bank and the Court of Auditors.

Separated from the afore–mentioned institutions, the Economic and Social Committee[98], the Committee of Regions[99] and the European Investment Bank (EIB)[100] are listed. On the official website of the European Union, these organs are classified as 'bodies' that exist in addition to the institutions . These bodies also include the European Ombudsman[101]. Furthermore, 22 specialized agencies, the most prominent among them being the European Environment Agency (EEA)[102], are explicitly distinguished from the institutions. Hence, from this perspective, it appears that solely the EP, Council, Commission, ECJ, and Court of Auditors, and possibly the ECB, could be considered as 'public authorities' as defined in Article 2(2)(d)AC. However, with regard to the ability of the ECJ to review EU acts under Article 263 TFEU, the bodies, offices, or agencies are equated with the other institutions of the Union[103]. To further add to this confusion, Article 2(2) second subparagraph AC unequivocally excludes "bodies or institutions acting in a judicial or legislative capacity". Accordingly, the GC and ECJ would no longer fall under the provisions of the Aarhus Convention as would the Council and EP when legislating. As an interim conclusion, the definition of public authorities in Article 2(2)(a)AC cannot be applied to the EU Institutions, bodies and agencies without difficulty.

However, when considering the definitions spelled out in the two middle paragraphs of Article 2(2) AC, the list of potential addressees of the Convention's provisions becomes considerably longer. Article 2(2)(b) AC refers to "[n]atural or legal persons performing public administrative functions under national law, including specific duties, activities, or services in relation to the environment" as public authorities, while the definition in Article 2(2)(c) AC includes "[a]ny other natural or legal persons having public responsibilities or functions, or providing public services, in relation to the environment, under the control of a body or person falling within subparagraphs (a) or (b) above". Thus,

94 Article 2(2)(d) Aarhus Convention
95 Rodenhoff, 2002, p.350
96 also mentioned in Title III Provisions on the Institutions, Article 13 TEU LT
97 Sections 1 –7
98 Part Six, Chapter 3, Section 1
99 Section 2
100 Chapter 4
101 Article 228 TFEU
102 established by Council Regulation (EEC) No 1210/90 of 7 May 1990 *on the establishment of the European Environment Agency and the European Environment Information and Observation Network*
103 Rodenhoff, 2002, p.355

whenever performing "duties, activities or services in relation to the environment", any of the EU Institutions, bodies or agencies (provided they do not act as judiciary or legislator) is to be defined as public authorities for the purposes of the Aarhus Convention[104].

1.4. The EU as governance system under study

Some noteworthy arguments may justify the EU governance system as a valuable study subject. First, environmental policy is not part of the exclusive sovereignty of national governments but the competence is shared between Member States' authorities and EU Institutions. European countries are not able to act in pure isolation with regard to the adoption of internal laws as well as the conclusion of international agreements. Second, EU law is both influenced by general principles of international law and bound to the provisions of international agreements to which it is a party, while at the same time, it determines the laws and legislation relating to environmental protection that are applied by national authorities within the Member States.

Third, the hierarchy of legal norms reveals the close connectedness between the three regimes of international, supranational and national legal systems. Fourth, the institutional framework within the EU and the dispersed powers among the institutions in legislating and executing European law offer various opportunity structures for environmental CSOs to exert influence on decision–makers. Fifth, these opportunities are not only given on the supranational level of governance but are also provided at national and regional level on the basis of the multiple governance levels within the European system.

Sixth, in order to ensure a homogeneous interpretation, as well as application of EU law despite the allocation of powers at the various governance levels, the Union is characterized by a very strong judiciary. The ECJ's jurisprudence is accordingly crucial in the verification of the legality of the institutions' and Member States' actions and legislation. In addition, through the interpretation of the Treaties, the Court substantially determines the path of future European integration. Finally, the fact that the Aarhus Convention contains provisions that explicitly address regional economic integration organizations[105], including their institutions[106], and provides for their accession to the convention reveals not only acceptance but rather acknowledgment of the influential role played by the EU in the field of environmental protection in international relations.

104 Rodenhoff, 2002, p.343, p.351
105 Article 17 Aarhus Convention
106 Article 2(2)(d) Aarhus Convention

2. European Environmental Policy

2.1. The need for political action regarding the protection of the environment

Nature, climate, flora and fauna are ubiquitous, while at the same time unique and irrecoverable once they have been harmed or even destroyed. Even a simple and perfunctory examination of the interrelations of environmental policy with other policy fields and the potential side–effects of one policy towards the other reveals a convincing picture and justifies the prioritization of environmental protection on the political agenda.

Among the most obvious subdivisions of environmental policy are the preservation of the diversity in flora and fauna; i.e. the protection of natural habitats and the creatures living therein in order to maintain ecological balance. It, however, also includes the protection of pets and farm as well as other useful animals or fish stocks in the oceans and therefore touches upon agricultural and fisheries policies. Both policy areas have traditionally been very important at the European level and particularly the former regularly requires one of the largest shares of the Union's budget [1]. Moreover, related to agriculture, as well as consumer protection, is the production and marketing of genetically modified food whose long–term effects on nature and human health remain scientifically uncertain. Public health may furthermore be affected by, *inter alia*, poor air and drinking water quality. The causal links between environmental pollution and chronic illnesses, for example allergies including asthma or neurodermatitis and cardiovascular diseases, are widely acknowledged.

Market–related and business–oriented policies, the original policy areas in which the EEC was competent to take actions, also affect the state of the environment and must therefore consider potential ramifications for nature and climate. Perhaps most prominent are the areas of transport and energy policies. The emissions of planes, trucks and ships result in air and water pollution, as well as the destruction of water habitats.

With regard to the energy sector, politicians have already reacted to the scientific evidence for the, at times fatal, repercussions on the environment provoked by the use of nuclear energy and the extraction and exploitation of non–renewable energy resources, e.g. fossil fuels, including coal resources, or oil[2] and natural gas, and promote the uti-

---

1 Agricultural expenditure today falls under the title "preservation and management of natural resources"; European Commission, 2009, *General budget of the European Union for the financial year 2009*, pp.8, 9, 14–15; particularly pp.19 & 20

2 An unfortunate example is the accident on the oil platform "Deepwater Horizon" on April 20th 2010 and the resulting spill of oil for three months into the Gulf of Mexico.

lization of alternative, renewable energy resources such as wind or solar energy, water power, or biofuels for automobiles and electric cars. The existence of scientific evidence and the development of environmental–friendly technologies for business and private use owes much to technological research and innovation that may in turn also be subsidized through the state. Finally, all these problems, in some cases even more severe, are also prevalent in other, mostly non–industrial countries. Thus, development aid as a policy must also take into consideration the unbearable living and farming conditions caused by natural disasters and other consequences of worldwide climate change.

Environmental problems and disasters do not stop at national borders. Environmental protection is therefore of concern to all people and should consequently be part of the political agenda of all governments[3]. Climate change is a worldwide phenomenon, as its synonym 'global warming' already indicates. In addition, those countries, whose industry and lifestyle are primarily responsible for climate change and those, whose population will suffer the most, do not coincide. It is for the above–mentioned reasons that the protection of the environment and the mitigation of global warming cannot be achieved by national policies in complete isolation but rather through a combined effort in an international context including as many states as possible.

This awareness rose first in the 1970s and was triggered by the oil crises. The nuclear catastrophe of Chernobyl in 1986, the more frequent occurrence of extreme weather events and natural disasters such as floods or earthquakes are just randomly selected examples that further indicated dramatic environmental change. International activism by interest groups further raised the pressure on governments to take action.

The scenarios developed by science suggest that action needs to be taken soon. This is particularly important with regard to the concept of intergenerational equity concerning future generations. Climate change, the elimination of the diversity of flora and fauna, and their above–mentioned potential ramifications may not drastically affect those generations that were primarily, although possibly unwittingly, responsible; namely past and current generations, yet all the more the unborn generations of the future. Hence, national governments and regional and international organizations have prioritized environmental protection on their agenda and are providing the path for future action.

2.1.1. Environmental co–operation at international level concerning procedural rights: The Aarhus Convention

Most of these actions in form of international agreements relate to material concessions, for instance, the fixing of emission rates or the development of specific rules and standards for the industry etc. Yet, as early as the 1970s, attempts had been undertaken to establish procedural rights for individuals regarding the formulation of environmental policy. These efforts were based on the presumption that, although administrations

3 Spagnuolo, 2009, p.49

take decisions that may adversely affect the environment, affected individuals should be placed in a position to influence these decisions in order to guarantee a compromise. As a precondition, information relating to the environment should be easily accessible in order for all those involved to form a well–informed and reasoned opinion. As a consequence, potential disagreements between all stakeholders involved should be settled by an impartial body of law[4]. For instance, an annexation of a Protocol to the European Convention on Human Rights (ECHR)[5] would have added the right to a clean environment to those rights protected under the Convention and, consequently, by the Strasbourg Court. However, despite broad consensus on the existence of such a right, agreement could not be reached regarding its form and scope (cf. chapter 11)[6]. Hence, none of these efforts resulted in a legally binding agreement of comparable significance for the European region as the *Convention on access to information, public participation in decision–making and access to justice in environmental matters* did two decades later[7].

The Aarhus Convention was adopted within the framework of the United Nations Economic Commission for Europe (UNECE) on 25 June 1998 in Århus, Denmark[8]. The convention entered into force on 30 October 2001[9] and disposes to date[10] of forty signatories and forty–four parties[11]. Although adopted under the auspices of the UNECE, the agreement is open for ratification not only to European states but as well to countries in Central and West Asia and Northern America[12]. The European Union and all EU Member States with the exception of Ireland have ratified the Aarhus Convention so far[13].

The Convention is embedded in a period of time when politicians began to realize that action was needed in order to attenuate the negative effects of ecological destruction, environmental pollution and climate change. They further acknowledged that it was necessary to tackle these global problems at international level. Thus, the agreement on the Aarhus Convention followed only six months after the adoption of the Kyoto Pro-

4 Milieu, 2007, pp.21–22

5 Council of Europe, 1950, *Convention for the Protection of Human Rights and Fundamental Freedoms*

6 Milieu, 2007, p.21

7 Morgera, 2005, p.138

8 Morgera, 2005, p.138

9 Article 20(1) of the Aarhus Convention: "This Convention shall enter into force on the ninetieth day after the date of deposit of the sixteenth instrument of ratification, acceptance, approval or accession".

10 July 17th, 2010

11 For updated information on the state of the Aarhus Convention, cf.: http://treaties.un.org/Pages/ViewDetails.aspx?src=TREATY& mtdsg_no=XXVII–13& chapter =27& lang=en

12 Central Asia: Kazakhstan, Kyrgyzstan, Tajikistan, Turkmenistan and Uzbekistan; Western Asia: Israel; Northern America: Canada and USA

13 July 17th, 2010; cf. also Milieu, 2007, p.1

tocol[14], an environmental treaty under the auspices of the United Nations Framework Convention on Climate Change (UNFCCC) for the worldwide reduction in the emission of greenhouse gases. The Kyoto Protocol will not be discussed here but simply serves as a concrete illustration of the political environment in which the Aarhus Convention was drafted. This is quite crucial given the fact that the Aarhus Convention is only one of many international initiatives that aim at committing national governments to environmental protection. However, it distinguishes itself from other international agreements insofar as most regulate the substantive requirements for environmental protection (i.e. cf. Kyoto Protocol), while the Aarhus Convention is concerned with procedural aspects[15]. These procedural rights guaranteed in the Convention relate first, to the possibility for the public, i.e. private individuals including environmental interest groups, to gain access to environmental information held by state authorities (Article 4 AC). Second, the participating countries undertake to offer opportunities to the public to participate in decision–making relating to environmental policy or activities that may have adverse effects on the environment (Articles 6 – 8 AC). Third, the Convention requires adequate judicial remedies which the public may enforce in front of courts (Article 9 AC).

The urgent need for an international treaty establishing procedural rights regarding the development of policies aiming at environmental protection was already notably formulated in Principle 10 of the 1992 Rio Declaration on Environment and Development (Rio Declaration) by the United Nations Environment Programme (UNEP):

> Environmental issues are best handled with participation of *all concerned citizens*, at the relevant level. At national level, *each individual shall have appropriate access to information concerning the environment that is held by public authorities*, including information on hazardous materials and activities in their communities, and the opportunity to participate in decision–making processes. States shall facilitate and encourage public awareness and participation by making information widely available. *Effective access to judicial and administrative proceedings*, including redress and remedy, shall be provided [emphases added][16].

Inspired by the Rio Declaration, an UNECE Task Force on 'Environmental Rights and Obligations' drafted guidelines on the safeguard of procedural rights relating to the protection of the environment on international level that were adopted by the *Third Ministerial Conference* "Environment for Europe" in Sofia, 1995. The ministers further stated that an "appropriate involvement of NGOs" should be instigated[17].

14 December 1997. No follow–up agreement was reached in Copenhagen, Denmark in Dec/2009.
15 Rose–Ackermann & Halpaap, 2001, p.1
16 United Nations Environment Programme, 1992
17 Wates, 2005, p.7

2.1.2. Right to a healthy environment

The general appraisal of the Aarhus Convention was exceedingly positive. The then UN Secretary–General Kofi Annan emphasized the Convention's global significance[18] and some scholars even termed it "by far the most impressive elaboration of Principle 10 of the Rio Declaration" and consequently "[the] perhaps [...] most significant international innovation in this area"[19]. Particularly Article 1 of the Convention is perceived to be one of the clearest formulations in international legal texts of the acknowledgement of a "right of every person of present and future generations to live in an environment adequate to his or her health [...]" [20].

This 'right to a healthy environment' serves as a foundation upon which the procedural rights guaranteed by the Convention are built. This is an important development given the fact that most Western democratic systems have not yet recognized the existence of such a right. In general terms, Central and Eastern European (CEE) countries are more receptive to the recognition of a right to a healthy environment than their Western neighbors. In some countries, such as Belgium, Slovenia, Hungary and Georgia, as well as in several non–European states, judges of high courts have already interpreted the right to a healthy environment affirmatively[21]. Also, the European Court of Human Rights (ECtHR) has considered the failure by a State party to protect the environment in its case–law, even though the Convention formulates no such obligation[22]. While the Court to date avoids to interpret Article 2 ECHR on the right to life[23], in the context of matters concerning environmental protection, it has done so with regard to procedural errors as spelled out in Article 6 on the right to a fair trial (cf. ECtHR, *Zander v. Sweden*[24]), Article 8 on the right to a private and family life, and finally, Article 10 guaranteeing the right to freedom of expression[25]. Claiming violations of Article 8 on the right to a private and family life, however, has turned out to be most promising to have the right to a healthy environment adjudicated upon in the context of the ECHR[26]. In para.51 of its judgment in *López Ostra v. Spain*[27] the ECtHR ruled that "[n]aturally, severe environmental pollution may affect individuals' well–being and prevent them from enjoying their homes in such a way as to affect their private and family life adversely, without, however, seriously endangering their health".

---

18 Morgera, 2005, p.138

19 Lee & Abbott, 2003, p.80

20 Rodenhoff, 2002, p.344

21 Stec, 2003, p.73

22 Andrusevych, 2003, p.77

23 e.g. ECtHR, *Guerra and Others v. Italy*, application 14967/89 (case 116/1996/735/932) [19.02.1998], para. 62. "Having regard to its conclusion that there has been a violation of Article 8, the Court finds it unnecessary to consider the case under Article 2 also". Cf. also: Andrusevych, 2003, p.78

24 application 14282/88 (case 45/1992/390/468) [25.11.1993], e.g. paras.16, 27 – 29

25 Andrusevych, 2003, p.77

26 Stec, 2003, p.74

27 application 16798/90 (case 41/1993/436/515) [9.12.1994]

The approaches in legislation and judgments worldwide and even among the parties to the Aarhus Convention vary considerably. Stephen Sec classified the current views prevalent in this debate into the following three categories. The first view places the right to a healthy environment in line with general human rights and insists upon its fundamental character. Representatives of the second category recognize the existence of such a right but instead of equalizing it with basic human rights, they argue that it can rather be derived from the latter. Scholars and politicians falling into the third category vehemently negate the mere existence of this kind of right. However, even among the proponents of a right to a healthy environment, disagreement concerning the owner of this right prevails. It is highly disputed, whether individuals can exclusively rely upon this right, whether it can be extended to groups, or whether it is merely a 'third–generation' right[28].

The drafters of the Aarhus Convention made a great move towards linking the right to a healthy environment to the enjoyment of basic human rights. In their first meeting, the parties to the Convention further emphasized the connection between the exercise of basic human rights and the right to a healthy environment[29]. Not only can the whole Convention be construed to combine essential principles of environmental protection with elements traditionally characteristic of international agreements on human rights protection[30], but also specific provisions explicitly point towards a direct link[31]. Paragraph 6 of the preamble recognizes "that adequate protection of the environment is essential to human well–being and the enjoyment of basic human rights, including the right to life itself". Here, direct reference is made to the elementary condition that a healthy environment constitutes for every human being to be able to rely on his or her right to life, which is indisputably a basic human right. The right to life is enshrined in several national constitutions[32]. It is furthermore guaranteed by Article 2 of the ECHR of the Council of Europe to which all EU Member States are parties as well as Article 2 of the Charter of Fundamental Human Rights of the European Union, which is incorporated into EU law and "shall have the same legal value as the Treaties"[33].

Paragraph 7 of the preamble recognizes "also that every person has the right to live in an environment adequate to his or her health and well–being, and the duty, both individually and in association with others, to protect and improve the environment for the benefit of present and future generations". This formulation clearly indicates that the drafters of the Aarhus Convention not only acknowledged a "right to live in an envi-

28 Stec, 2003, p.73

29 Morgera, 2005, p.139

30 Rodenhoff, 2002, p.343; Morgera, 2005, p.139

31 Morgera, 2005, p.139

32 e.g. Article 2(2) Basic Law, Germany (Deutscher Bundestag, 2010); Article 15 Constitution of Spain (Senado de España, 1992); Article 17 Constitution of Slovenia (Ustavno sodišče, 2006); Article 38 Constitution of Poland (Seijm Rzeczypospolitej Polskiej, 1997) even stipulates that "[t]he Republic of Poland shall ensure the legal protection of the life of every human being".

33 Art. 6(1) TEU LT

ronment adequate" to every person's health but, even more importantly, refer to a duty imposed upon individuals as well as organizations to protect that environment. If one considers that the duty can only be executed, if these persons are given broad access to information, democratic participation opportunities and justice, it could be interpreted as connoting the substantive character of the procedural right to a healthy environment to be collective (a group right).

Finally, Article 1 of the Aarhus Convention spells out the objective of this treaty:

> In order to contribute to the protection of the right of every person of present and future generations to live in an environment adequate to his or her health and well–being, each Party shall guarantee the rights of access to information, public participation in decision–making, and access to justice in environmental matters in accordance with the provisions of this Convention.

It establishes not only the existence of a right to a healthy environment but also grants this right to "present and future generations" and obliges every party to "guarantee" the provisions of the convention. It clearly is an innovative step that the Aarhus Convention is the first transnationally legally binding instrument that acknowledges the right of future generations to a healthy environment. Thus, taking Preamble para.7 and Article 1 AC together, states shall establish the legal and administrative framework so that unrestricted opportunities for individuals as well as associations are established to ensure the protection of the environment for their own as well as future generations[34].

The claim that the Aarhus Convention connects environmental protection with fundamental human rights, may be supported by a comparative look at the countries that are parties to the respective regional agreements. All members of the Council of Europe, i.e. forty–seven European states[35], have ratified the *European Convention on the Protection of Human Rights and Fundamental Freedoms*, while the Aarhus Convention counts forty–four parties. Even though some countries have committed themselves to the legal obligations of only one convention, most countries are parties to both agreements. This is the case for all EU Member States except for Ireland, which, although the country signed the Aarhus Convention, has not yet become a full–fletched party to it. This fact places Ireland into a special position. Although the country itself is not yet legally bound by the provisions of the convention as such, it is obliged to implement and adhere to all acts passed by the EU in order to comply with the requirements of the Aarhus Convention.

Furthermore, the European Union stands out as well. Articles 17 and 19(1)AC explicitly enable "regional economic integration organizations constituted by sovereign states members of the Economic Commission for Europe to which their member States have transferred competence over matters governed by this Convention, including the competence to enter into treaties in respect of these matters", to become a party to the

34 Stec, 2003, p.75
35 incl. Eurasian countries

convention on procedural rights in environmental matters. The EU shares competences with its Member States in the area of environmental protection policy (cf. chapter 1). Yet, accession to the ECHR by the European Union is at present retarded given that Protocol No.14 to the ECHR and its Article 17[36] have not yet entered into force due to Russia's ratification refusal.

2.2. Evolution of European environmental policy

Even though the European Union is today one of the most ecologically concerned supranational organizations that pressures for a high level of international protection of the environment[37], such concerns have not formed part of the foundation of the former European Economic Community. The original Treaty of Rome neither provided a legal basis nor made any reference to the environment in other policies. Priority was clearly put on cooperation between Member States in order to achieve economic goals, which was also reflected by interest representation at European level. Exceptions constituted animal rights groups, which settled comparatively early in Brussels. Slowly, in the 1970s, the awareness rose that environmental protection could not be ensured by national measures in isolation but rather through a combined effort on supranational and international level[38].

In light of this awareness, the Heads of State and Government created the first Environmental Action Program (EAP) at the 1972 summit in Paris[39] and formulated leading principles, including the precautionary principle, principle of prevention, subsidiarity, correction at source, and the polluter–pays principle, which have formally been incorporated into the EC Treaty by the SEA and the Maastricht Treaty[40]. As a consequence of the missing explicit provision for environmental action and the overlap of matters relating to the protection of the environment with other policy areas, early legislation was based on the rather general provisions of ex Article 100 EC (now Article 115 TFEU) and ex Article 235 EC (now Article 352 TFEU)[41]. In addition, the Commission initiated several directives and programs vaguely based on a Council Directive of 1973[42].

Activists proclaiming environmental protection in general, and nature and species conservation in particular, had been crucial for the evolution of environmental policy in the absence of a clear legal basis. Still, economic interests striving to establish a common market without any barriers to trade enjoyed priority over environmental or other

36 Council of Europe, 2004, *Protocol No. 14 to the Convention for the Protection of Human Rights and Fundamental Freedoms, amending the control system of the Convention*
37 Oppermann, Classen & Nettesheim, 2009, p.600
38 Cichowski, 2007, p.57; Oppermann, Classen & Nettesheim, 2009, pp.599, 600
39 Greenwood, 2007a, p.129; Senior Nello, 2005, p.257
40 Oppermann, Classen & Nettesheim, 2009, p.601; Senior Nello, 2005, pp.258–259
41 Oppermann, Classen & Nettesheim, 2009, p.600
42 Harlow, 1992, p.432

non–economic considerations[43]. Thus, it was not until 1985 that the ECJ declared environmental protection to be "one of the [then] Community's essential objectives" on whose basis restrictions on free trade could be justified[44]. Hence, the early years of environmental legislation primarily resulted from pressure executed by environmental activists, as well as the judicial interpretation of the overall aims of the Union by the European Court of Justice.

Corresponding to the extension of then 'Community' competences through Treaty amendments into other non–purely economic policy areas, such as social policy, consumer protection and culture, the number of citizen interest groups that turned to the EU since the 1970s increased substantially. With regard to environmental CSOs, the vast majority established outreach offices in Brussels in the late 1980s to early 1990s[45]. From the mid–1990s onwards, the most dramatic growth of environmental interest activity was mainly due to the reforms brought about by the amendments of the EC Treaty in Maastricht (1993), Amsterdam (1997) and Nice (2000)[46].

Further innovations were initiated by the Environmental Action Programs that have been adopted by the European Council for the duration of several years since the 1972 Paris Summit. Particularly the Fifth EAP (1993–2000) introduced the notion of *sustainable development*, which was emphasized by the Gothenburg Summit in 2001 and has been included into the EC Treaty by the Treaty of Amsterdam[47]. The EAP furthermore introduced a shift in policy approach from a correction of the damage already occurred to the prevention of possible harm, as well as from regulatory policy tools to market–based instruments[48]. The aforementioned summit also put specific aims concerning environmental protection on the agenda of the Lisbon Strategy that was originally intended to be achieved until 2010[49].

In addition, the establishment of the European Environment Agency in 1993 ensured a reliable and persisting source of expert information and scientific evidence for the evaluation of environmental risks and benefits of new legislation projects[50]. With regard to civil society participation, the signature of the Aarhus Convention triggered high expectations on part of environmental interest groups, which were, however, not completely met[51].

The European Court of Justice regularly confirms in its case–law the high level of protection demanded by the Treaties, which even justifies restrictions on the free movement of goods – one of the first and greatly valued among the four freedoms within the single

43 Cichowski, 2007, p.57
44 Cichowski, 2007, p.57; cf. ECJ, Case 240/83 *ADBHU* [1985] ECR 531, para.13
45 Greenwood, 2007a, p.133
46 Cichowski, 2007, p.57
47 Greenwood, 2007a, p.129; today: Article 3(3) & (5) TEU LT and Article 11 TFEU
48 Senior Nello, 2005, p.258
49 Greenwood, 2007a, pp.129–130
50 Greenwood, 2007a, p.129
51 Greenwood, 2007a, p.129; Cichowski, 2007, p.58; cf. Part IV

market[52]. Thus today, EU policies have the reputation of being some of the world's most advanced in environmental protection[53]. The EU's conceptualization of 'the environment' is capacious and adaptive and includes the socio–economic context of a person[54]. Current estimations state that about eighty to ninety percent of national environmental law within the Member States originates from European legislation, which covers all areas of environmental protection[55].

2.2.1. Legal basis for environmental policy at European level

As stated previously, Member States and Union share the competences in environmental policy, including the adoption of legislation and conclusion of agreements with third parties. This is formally confirmed in an explicit provision in Article 4(2)(e) TEU LT.

It was, however, not until the Single European Act in 1986, shortly after the *ADBHU* decision[56] of the ECJ, that environmental protection was officially incorporated into the EC Treaty with a distinct Title (now: Articles 191ff TFEU). The explicit provision fulfilled the demands for, amongst others, ensuring "a high level of protection and improvement of the quality of the environment" as stated in Article 3(3) TEU LT[57]. Article 191(1) TFEU lists the general goals of first, "preserving, protecting and improving the quality of the environment"; second, "protecting human health"; and third, utilizing natural resources in a prudent and rational manner, which EU environmental policy should pursue. In order to meet the fourth objective listed in this paragraph, namely the promotion of "measures at international level to deal with regional or worldwide environmental problems" as added by the Maastricht Treaty[58], Article 191(4) TFEU provides the legal basis for the conclusion of mixed agreements with third countries and international organizations under the procedure laid out in Article by 218 TFEU[59]. Member States are therefore enjoined from concluding agreements that have opposing objectives to those concluded jointly with the EU[60]. Article 191(2) TFEU emphasizes that the Union should aim in its activities at preventing environmental damage and prioritizing the precautionary principle.

The SEA furthermore added the horizontal clause on environmental mainstreaming of contemporary's Article 11 TFEU according to which potential effects on the environment and particularly on sustainable development must be considered in the execution of

52 Weber, 2008, p.414; cf. ECJ, Case 302/86 *Commission v Denmark* [1988] ECR 4607, paras.6 & 9; ECJ, Case C–463/01 *Commission v Germany* [2004], para.75; Oppermann, Classen & Nettesheim, 2009, p.603

53 Greenwood, 2007a, p.128

54 Oppermann, Classen & Nettesheim, 2009, p.602

55 Meyer–Ohlendorf, 2004, p.97

56 ECJ, Case 240/83 *Procureur de la République v Association de défense des brûleurs d'huiles usagées (ADBHU)* [1985] ECR 531, paras.15, 25 & 29

57 Oppermann, Classen & Nettesheim, 2009, p.603

58 Senior Nello, 2005, p.259

59 Oppermann, Classen & Nettesheim, 2009, p.615

60 Oppermann, Classen & Nettesheim, 2009, pp.605–606

other policies[61]. On the other hand, Article 5(4) TEU LT demands from environmental policy to be proportionate in comparison with the other objectives of the Treaty and to not "exceed what is necessary to achieve the objectives of the Treaties"[62]. In a similar manner, Article 114(3) TFEU places Commission, Parliament and Council under the obligation to base new legislation on the most recent scientific evidence for ensuring a high level of protection[63]. The Maastricht Treaty also introduced the obligation for the Commission to undertake environmental impact assessments when drafting legislation proposals[64]. Paragraph 3 of that article obliges decision–makers to consider regional variations in economic and social terms when drafting policies in addition to the evaluation of the available scientific and technical data[65].

The procedures for the actions that are taken in order to achieve the above–listed objectives are outlined in the first three paragraphs of Article 192 TFEU. Paragraphs four and five determine the financial aspects of the implementation of environmental policy. The multi–level character of the EU becomes hereby visible as the institutions adopt the appropriate action, while it is incumbent on the Member States to implement environmental policy as well as to provide the finances for its execution[66]. Decisions are taken by an extended use of the ordinary legislative procedure (co–decision)[67], in which the Parliament is set on an equal footing with the Council and the latter decides by qualified majority voting[68]. Important to note is also the obligatory consultation of EESC and CoR before a decision is to be taken. Exceptions are provided for in a closed list of activities in paragraph 2 of the article.

The second paragraph of Article 191 TFEU also acknowledges that, despite the fact that environmental problems are of a global nature, regions may be confronted with different environmental challenges or at least with varying degrees of the same incident. In this context, the highest level of protection possible is striven for[69]. This aspired level is, however, as a consequence of qualified majority voting, mitigated to a compromise at average level. Yet, this "shall not prevent any Member State from maintaining or introducing more stringent protective measures"[70] provided that these are in line with the Treaty and are notified to the Commission[71].

---

61 Oppermann, Classen & Nettesheim, 2009, pp.600, 602, 604; Senior Nello, 2005, p.259; Cichowski, 2007, p.58

62 quote: Article 5(4) TEU LT; Oppermann, Classen & Nettesheim, 2009, p.604

63 Oppermann, Classen & Nettesheim, 2009, p.604

64 Senior Nello, 2005, p.260

65 Article 191(3) TFEU

66 Oppermann, Classen & Nettesheim, 2009, p.604; Cichowski, 2007, p.59

67 Article 192 TFEU

68 Greenwood, 2007a, p.126; Senior Nello, 2005, p.260; Cichowski, 2007, p.58

69 Oppermann, Classen & Nettesheim, 2009, p.603

70 Article 193 TFEU

71 Oppermann, Classen & Nettesheim, 2009, p.607

3. European Environmental Civil Society

3.1. The Concept of Civil Society

Despite the growing awareness of the increasingly important political role of civil society in democratic governance systems, neither political practitioners nor academic scholars have developed a single, all–embracing definition of what actually constitutes 'civil society' in general and 'civil society organizations' in particular. The difficulty lies in the details. A general definition must be broad enough to comprise as many characteristics as are represented within such a heterogeneous concept. A definition that is too narrow and stiff can obviously not provide such flexible applicability. To the contrary, a definition that is phrased too broadly may fail to distinguish the object from 'outsiders' and consequently also fall short of drawing conclusions that are specific only to the object of analysis.

3.1.1. Historical Overview

After having pointed out the difficulty in achieving an all–embracing definition of civil society, one may attempt to approach the concept from a historical perspective. The concept as such is not a new invention of the post–modernity but, to the contrary, has existed in the jargon of political philosophers since ancient times. The meaning of the term, even though always having been defined very broadly, has undergone significant development. While the concept is nowadays seceded from the state as a political institution, it was commonly perceived by Aristotle and his fellow philosophers that *politike koinonia* was to be understood as the aspiration of political decision–makers to rule for the common good instead of their own private interests[1]. The emphasis is thereby placed upon the receivers of political action as opposed to those who conduct it[2]. Summarized, the comparison reveals a reversion of the meaning from civilization as the passive receivers of political services in the past as opposed to contemporary civil society organizations that actively seek to become involved into the policy process.

Yet, throughout the two millennia of social change and political development, the concept has been interpreted corresponding to the socio–historical environment by the dominant political school of thought. Following the above–mentioned interpretation of

1 Anheier, Glasius & Kaldor, 2001, p.12; Armstrong, 2002, p.107
2 Cf. the distinction between input and output legitimacy of present political discussions.

ancient Greek philosophers, whose views were shared by ancient Roman scholars, it was not until the 17th century that the debate on the nature and function of civil society regained momentum in the context of the creation of nation states[3]. Citizens on the European continent then strove to define their role within the political system[4].
In the 18th century, Hegel was one of the first scholars to dissociate civil society institutionally from the government; while on the other hand, he attributed social and public functions to civil society itself[5]. In line with Hegel's assumptions, de Tocqueville considered the activities of civil society as a necessary mechanism of checks and balances of state power for the redistribution of wealth[6]. Civil society then functioned as a mediator between the individual and the state, primarily in the struggle for social security and a stable standard of living[7]. While Marx defined civil society in purely economic terms in the middle of the 19th century[8], less than a century later, political scientists painted a fairly different picture and emphasized the political and cultural value of CSOs. Civil society then was linked to principles of popular participation and civic mindedness[9], civility[10], or the community[11]. Others re–attached civil society to the public sphere[12] thereby blurring the strict distinction between the state and civil society. Putnam[13] introduced the idea that civil society contributes to the 'social capital' of a state, whereas Gramsci[14] emphasized the role of promoting culture and values through organizations such as the church, schools and trade unions, thereby diminishing the importance of social and economic functions[15]. Recent academic scholarship further divides civil society into branches such as *third* and *voluntary sector*, which correlates to the primary focus of the respective organizations.

Summarizing, it is important to point out that it is common to all definitions from any historical epoch, except ancient Greece, that the most decisive characteristic is the clear separation of civil society from the state as such. Although civil society has always been engaged in mutual relations with governments, it could never be equated with state actors but was rather viewed as complementing state activities. There were also first indications for the emphasis on the functions of today's civil society as mediators between governments and their citizens.

---

3 Anheier, Glasius & Kaldor, 2001, p.12
4 Anheier, 2004, p.20
5 Anheier, Glasius & Kaldor, 2001, pp.12–13; Armstrong, 2002, p.107
6 Anheier, Glasius & Kaldor, 2001, p.13
7 Warleigh, 2001, p.620
8 Armstrong, 2002, p.108
9 cf. Verba, 1995; as cited in: Anheier, 2004, p.21
10 cf. Elias, 1994; as cited in: Anheier, 2004, p.21
11 cf. Etzioni, 1971; as cited in: Anheier, 2004, p.21
12 Habermann, 1992; as cited in: Anheier, 2004, p.21
13 2000; as cited in: Anheier, 2004, p.21
14 1971; as cited in: Anheier, 2004, p.21
15 Anheier, 2004, p.21; Anheier, Glasius & Kaldor, 2001, p.13

3.1.2. Practitioners' Views

Aside from political theorists, practitioners have since the end of the Second World War observed the development of civil society with increased attention and awareness. The statutes of the former League of Nations did not grant NGOs an official status, which reduced their role to informal lobbying activities. Its successor, the United Nations Organization (UNO), was the first international organization (IO) that not only formally recognized the additional input by non–governmental organizations but also regulated consultative relations with the Economic and Social Council (ECOSOC) in Article 71 of the UN Charter[16]. Today, the UN homepage offers a separate website on an integrated Civil Society Organization (iCSO) System that provides for, *inter alia*, the accreditation of civil society organizations for gaining consultative status with the ECOSOC provided that they meet specific criteria[17]. A similar approach has been taken by the Council of Europe (CoE) in 1949. Since the beginning, NGOs have been informally engaged until their 'consultative status' had been officially recognized in 1952 and was widened into a 'participatory status' for international NGOs by Resolution (2003)8[18] and even a 'partnership status' for national NGOs by Resolution (2003)9[19]. In addition, an INGO Liaison Committee was set up in 1967 that facilitates relations between the CoE Secretariat and civil society organizations. Most remarkable is the fact that NGOs are able to rely on Article 34 Convention for the Protection of Human Rights and Fundamental Freedoms in case of infringements of their own rights[20].

Although the European Union (then European Economic Community) could have relied on the example of the two aforementioned international organizations, it failed to do so. The founding Treaties of Rome of 1957 neither specifically referred to NGOs nor provided for officially recognized consultative relations[21]. Thus, it was not until the 1980s that civil society became sporadically mentioned in official documents[22]. Furthermore, only in the mid–1990s, it entered the sphere of EU terminology that was actively promoted by several EU Institutions[23]. However, the 'civil dialogue' still lacked a legal basis given that neither Treaty revisions in Maastricht nor Amsterdam changed this. Only Declaration 23 on the 'cooperation with charitable associations', added to the Maastricht Treaty, was a first basis for the institutionalization of relations with civil society[24].

16 Rust, 2004, p.47
17 United Nations Department of Economic and Social Affairs, *NGO Branch. Consultative Status*, Website; cf. also Rust, 2004, p.48
18 Council of Europe, 2003a, *Participatory status for international non–governmental organizations with the Council of Europe*
19 Council of Europe, 2003b, *Status of partnership between the Council of Europe and national non–governmental organisations*
20 Rust, 2004, p.49
21 Rust, 2004, p.49
22 Zimmer & Sittermann, 2004, p.16
23 Zimmer & Sittermann, 2004, p.21
24 Rust, 2004, p.52

Particularly in the EU context, it can be observed that definitions of civil society correspond to the aspirations that politicians and civil servants attach to such organizations in order to enhance their own position in the political context. This will be discussed more extensively in the following parts. Those differences in the position towards civil society originating from the intentions of those, who utilize such definitions, amount to the great difficulties in arriving at one comprehensive but clear–cut definition[25]. The connotation, however, attributed to this concept is without exception positive and "fashionable"[26]. The political aims of a practitioner may stand in stark contrast to that of an academic or a member of 'civil society' itself. Even within the same category of profession, the differences are almost more visible than the similarities. A further obstacle to clarification has resulted from the, at the moment, twenty–three official languages within the European Union. Translation problems have already revealed that particularly the term 'civil' may connote different meanings in several languages[27] and resulted in much confusion among those affected.

3.1.3. Working Definition

Within the sphere of academic research, relative consensus has emerged on some of the key characteristics that uniquely distinguish 'civil society' from other actors in the political arena. The features listed below are to be kept in mind, when reference is made to civil society organizations in the remaining parts of the text.

Intermediary. First, the sphere that civil society populates is independent from that of the state, the market, as well as that of the family[28], and is therefore defined as 'intermediary'[29]. Even though civil society can be explicitly distinguished from the other three concepts, it also has specific points of contact with each of them. While civil society must be independent from the state, it may nonetheless receive funding from public authorities, let alone that its primary targets are state institutions. Likewise, the market cannot be isolated from civil activities given that, often, economic interests trigger action by such organizations. In addition, the internal structure of an organization must be economically efficient in order to persist in a highly competitive environment; particularly regarding 'organized' civil society. It must also not be forgotten that business players originating from the market may form interest groups that may be included into the broader notion of civil society and that the market can at least be involved in activities of CSOs, if not being the target of action itself. Last but not least, the family as such is distinguishable from civil society insofar as it is the environment in which individuals live and who may form such groups in order to have their personal priorities represented.

---

25 Anheier, Glasius & Kaldor, 2001, p.11

26 Kohler–Koch, 2010, p.102

27 Freise, 2008b, p.2

28 e.g. Freise, 2008a, p.11, Hilger, 2008, p.182; Anheier, 2004, p.22; Zimmer & Sittermann, 2004, pp.17–18

29 Zimmer & Freise, 2008, p.21

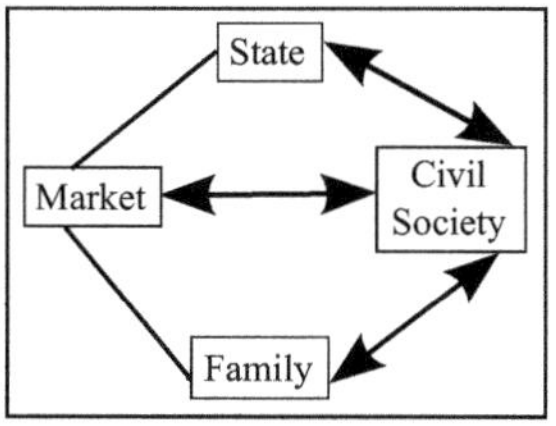

Figure 1: Civil Society as mediator between family, market and state

Voluntary. Second, socio–political scientists strongly emphasize the voluntary character of civil society [30]. Membership in such organizations is, by definition, always "voluntary and non–coercive"[31] and can therefore quickly be entered into but may as easily be terminated as well. Not only passive membership but also active participation in the activities of CSOs is purely based upon the notion of "voluntary support"[32]. An exception may be the advised donation or fixed membership fee that members may have to pay.

Organized. Third, civil society is comprised not of a diffuse and chaotic assembly of individual actors but consists of groups that each are internally organized and well–structured, that are able to strategize their actions and mobilize their members. Several of these groups with similar goals may form coalitions or networks in order to execute a greater impact on political decision–makers.

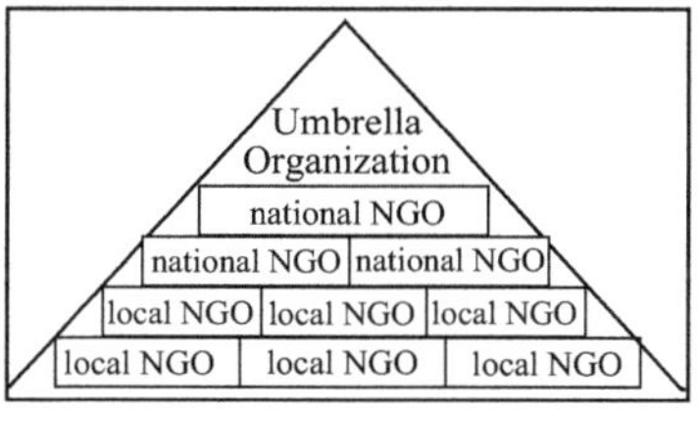

Figure 2: Transnational Umbrella Organization of Civil Society

Borderless. Fourth, the structured organization of civil society referred to in point three is not confined to the national territory. Quite to the contrary, it may be either embedded into the specific local, regional, transnational, or even global contexts[33]. In many cases, local and regional organizations form associations or umbrella organizations in order to leave a visible impact in the trans– and international political arena[34]. All of the local and national CSOs maintain their sovereignty and the control over the most important decisions. This may result in the fact that different emphases of local CSOs may compete

30 Hilger, 2008, p.182; Anheier, 2004, p.23; Armstrong, 2002, p.110

31 Zimmer & Freise, 2008, p.30

32 Zimmer & Freise, 2008, p.28; Hilger, 2008, p.182; Anheier, 2004, pp.23–25; Armstrong, 2002, p.110

33 Anheier, Glasius & Kaldor, 2001, p.3; Anheier & Themudo, 2002, p.193

34 cf. Kohler–Koch, 2010, p.111

for setting priorities on the respective umbrella agenda. On EU level, most transnational organizations have established a seat in Brussels, which serves as a contact point for the various national member organizations as well as allowing them to gain direct access to the EU Institutions[35].

Overall, one may conclude that the definition of civil society must always be placed into its relevant context. This is composed of the respective historical epoch, the geographical territory and the political systems as well as a society's cultural values[36]. Applied to the civil society that is of interest to the dissertation project, this results in the following. The time era covers roughly two decades from the 1990s to 2010. The place is the jurisdiction of the European Union and only CSOs that represent the populations of at least three Member States are considered. The political system will be more discussed in more depth in the following sections. At this stage, it may suffice to describe the system as a weakly developed representative democratic federation of sovereign states, including a first attempt at including participatory structures. Lastly, the cultural values that include, at the EU level, freedom, accessibility and publicity are considered.

With regard to the branch of civil society[37] that is analyzed in this research project, it is generally referred to CSOs as 'civil society organizations' in the context of European environmental policy. As will be seen in the context of the participatory policy cycle, it is of vital importance that the relevant organizations represent the interests of individuals, who would not be able to make their voice heard by themselves but need a collective approach.

3.2. Environmental Interest Representation to the EU

Environmental interest representation at European level with nine groups in total had been rather low and incidental up until the 1970s[38]. Although Treaty amendments and Court decisions slowly provided for a more ecological friendly policy atmosphere in Brussels, it was not until the late 1980s to mid–1990s onwards that the majority of environmental interest groups established themselves in the EU capital. While current assessments estimate that overall up to five thousand organizations with about 10.000 staff members have established offices in Brussels[39], 77 groups employing well over one hundred staff members[40] have been classified as environmental groups by 2003[41]. One of the first among these was the European Environmental Bureau (EEB), a federation of more than 140 national and local environmental protection groups within the Member States and candidate countries when it was established in 1974. The establishment of

35 Harlow, 1992, p.341
36 Freise, 2008a, p.25
37 Chandhoke, 2002, p.46
38 Cichowski, 2007, p.64
39 Greenwood, 2007a, p.12 & p.117; Randzio–Plath, 2004, p.3
40 Greenwood, 2007a, p.132
41 Cichowski, 2007, p.64

the EEB was highly supported – both financially and ideologically – by the Commission to which the EEB remains one of the most important contact points in environmental matters[42].

3.2.1. Features Specific to European Interest Representation

Civil Society is embraced by the European Union for the reasons outlined in chapters 4 and 5. The EU not only heavily relies on the input offered by these organizations internally but also highlighted the contribution of organized civil society to the democratic development of the Central and Eastern European countries throughout the late 1980s and 1990s and supported this fact in its external relations[43]. A noteworthy characteristic that distinguishes CSOs organized at EU level from those being active in other political structures is their high degree of institutionalization[44]. Thus, it is not exaggerated to assume that the institutional structure of the EU and especially the allocation of powers and responsibilities taken together with the multiple levels of governance (supra, sub– and national) heavily influence the organizational structure of those groups that most successfully represent their respective interests. One feature of the multi–level governance (MLG) is the consensual style of policy–making, which results in pluralist outcomes and thereby offers various access points for civil society[45]. In short, these organizations should ideally be European federations of a number of national interest groups that are established in the majority of the Member States. Moreover, they must be internally democratically structured and well–organized, have a visible membership status, be in the possession of stable financial resources, and provide for accountability and transparency in their activities[46]. However, these requirements are not easy to meet and sectoral discrepancies are quite obvious with business organizations having a clear advantage over citizen interest representatives[47]. Tensions have particularly arisen between EU registration systems and CSOs with regard to the criteria on geographical and thematic representativeness as well as on accountability towards their own members[48]. From the perspective of the EU Institutions [particularly the Commission and the EESC], such representativeness is an indispensable prerequisite for the participation in the making of EU policies[49].

In order to help diminishing the asymmetries in interest representation at European level, the EU provides funding in a total amount of one billion Euros, which equals approximately one percent of the total budget, to eligible CSOs[50]. Estimates list up

42 Greenwood, 2007a, p.125
43 Kohler–Koch, 2008, p.269
44 Greenwood, 2007a, p.1; Greenwood, 2007b, p.179
45 Greenwood, 2007b, p.185
46 Greenwood, 2007a, pp.1, 14, 16 & 23; Maloney & Van Deth, 2008, pp.4–5; Mahoney, 2008, pp.172–173; Hilger, 2008, pp.185, 194–195; Smismans, 2003, p.484
47 Knill, 2005, p.188
48 Armstrong, 2002, p.127; Kohler–Koch, 2010, p.111
49 Kohler–Koch, 2010, pp.101 & 110
50 Greenwood, 2007a, pp.1 & 117; Greenwood, 2007c, p.344; Maloney & Van Deth 2008, p.8

to 300 CSOs as recipients of Commission funding, of which 28 groups are dedicated to the protection of the environment[51]. However, two crucial points of criticism have been put forward in the debate on providing financial support to organized interests. First, it is greatly doubted that the funding reaches its aim in diminishing the levels of asymmetries among those groups[52]. It is rather expected that the same actors that are preferred in the consultation process, i.e. large, well–organized European umbrella organizations, may also receive greater monetary support[53]. Second, the allocation of financial resources by governmental actors (i.e. the Commission) raises serious concerns about the independence of CSOs and their ability to perform their roles as mediators between the state and the individual and about intrusion of the political sector into civil society[54]. Interestingly enough, the beneficiaries argue to the contrary, namely that this source of funding actually guarantees their independence insofar as they are not in need to seek financial support elsewhere, for instance in business sectors[55]. In the general context of transparency within EU consultation procedures, also the rules and receivers of funding were reformed after an ECJ decision[56] annulled a funding decision of the Commission in 1998, which resulted in a severe financial crisis of many CSOs. In this situation, various actors from civil society merged their forces and brought the issue to the attention not only of the Commission, EP and Council but also to the public through the use of the media[57].

51 Maloney & Van Deth, 2008, p.9; Greenwood, 2007a, p.132

52 Greenwood, 2007a, pp.18–19

53 Maloney & Van Deth, 2008, p.249

54 Saurugger, 2008, p.1284

55 Greenwood, 2007a, pp.18–19; Greenwood, 2007b, p.182

56 ECJ, Case C–106/96 United *Kingdom v Commission* [1998] ECR I–2729, point 1 of operative part

57 Smismans, 2003, p.478

Part II.

Participatory Governance at the EU & Recourse to Litigation

4. The Need for Political Participation

Most scholars studying European politics have observed that the notion of 'civil society' has been increasingly used by practitioners as an idealized "panacea" to account for the democratic deficit of the European Union[1]. As mediators between the state, in this case the EU and its institutions, on the one side, and individuals, i.e. European citizens, on the other, civil society is very receptive to the concerns and demands of the population and channels these interests to those responsible for policy–making. In turn, it is expected that the consideration of those interests will increase the acceptance of policies by the population in the Member States and facilitate the implementation of European law on national and local level[2]. It is further desired that the EU as a supranational system will become more appraised by its citizens.
This chapter therefore presents the alleged benefits of an inclusive policy–style that offers various political opportunity structures to citizens from a practical perspective. It further provides the theoretical background underlying these assumptions.

4.1. Practical Example: The Aarhus Convention

The concept of participation and inclusion of non–governmental actors should be applied in all areas of political decision–making. This argument, although it may be controversially perceived, is supported by the basic assumptions of several international agreements. The Aarhus Convention therefore will be used as an example illustrating this claim from practical politics.

The convention refers to three interrelated, so–called, pillars on procedural rights for the public, upon which the right of every person "to live in an environment adequate to his or her health and well–being"[3] depends. These are first, the guaranteed access to information relating to environmental activities, plans, programs and policies; second, the right to participation in environmental decision–making for the public; and third, to gain access to justice in environmental disputes. The overall predication, however, is that the effectiveness of political processes depends upon the number of actors involved and the range of interests that they represent. The Aarhus Convention thereby inseparably links the guarantee of these procedural rights to the enjoyment of substantial rights, as the discussion about the link between the right to a healthy environment with fundamental human rights has shown.

1 Freise, 2008a, p.23; cf. also Heinrich, 2008, p.48; Maloney & Van Deth, 2008, p.4
2 Finke, 2007, p.6
3 Preamble para.7 of the Aarhus Convention

4.1.1. Participation by the public – special role assigned to environmental NGOs

The 'public', by definition of Article 2(4)AC, natural or legal persons "and, in accordance with national legislation or practice, their associations, organizations or groups" of the participating countries is the primary beneficiary of the Convention. NGOs promoting the protection of the environment are even placed in a better position as they fall under the definition of the "public concerned" in Article 2(5)AC and shall "for the purposes of this definition, [...] [when] meeting any requirements under national law [,] [...] be deemed to have an interest". It is quite remarkable that those NGOs only have to fulfill the requirements under national law but are not obliged to prove an interest at stake when relying on the provisions of the Aarhus Convention[4]. This is in line with the general provision in Article 3(4) AC on the "appropriate recognition of and support to associations, organizations or groups promoting environmental protection and [the reassurance] [...] that its national legal system is consistent with this obligation" of each party to the convention respectively. The drafters of the Aarhus Convention therefore acknowledged the importance of non–state actors representing general interests and referred to these definitions in the provisions of each respective pillar of the convention.

These privileged procedural rights of environmental NGOs may well be the result of the latter's heavy involvement in and contribution to the drafting and negotiation processes of the Aarhus Convention[5]. Such groups were admitted to participate in plenary meetings of working groups, as well as most drafting committees and were able to intervene in the discussion if the chair allowed them to do so[6]. In addition, environmental CSOs remained involved in the development of the convention when observing the meetings of the parties (MOP). Their observation status can only be withheld, if objections are expressed by more than one–third of the parties present at the respective meeting[7]. Finally, NGOs may furthermore suggest nominees for the compliance committee, a body that monitors implementation errors by participating countries. Indeed, nominees by NGOs have already sat on that committee[8].

Some observers regard the emphasis on NGOs as a welcoming counterbalance to existing industrial lobbyists. While it is appreciable to achieve equilibrium of industrial, environmental and other interests, primarily in the area of participation in decision–making procedures, one should not confuse this with enhanced democratic legitimacy due to the fact that associations promoting environmental protection only represent one particular branch of public opinion but most certainly not the views of the general public[9]. It is furthermore not ensured that participation of environmental NGOs will automatically

4 Morgera, 2005, pp.139–140
5 Hallo, 2007, p.6
6 Morgera, 2005, p.139
7 Article 10(5) of the Aarhus Convention; cf. also Morgera, 2005, p.140
8 Morgera, 2005, p.140
9 Lee & Abbott, 2003, pp.86–87 & 108

result in improved substance of environmental policy decisions, even though the great variety of actors will reflect public opinion as well as scientific research[10]. Lee and Abbott conclude that, for the purposes of the Aarhus Convention, improved environmental policy is equalized with more protection resulting out of increased public participation. Yet, the general public does not automatically prioritize long–term environmental protection over short–term economic gains[11]. This reluctance about the actual gains from public participation are to be found in the, at times, vague formulation of the provisions in the convention that may be inferior to already existing laws in some legal systems[12].

Many of those benefits, as well as critical remarks found in this practical example, are incorporated into political theories that produced models for democracy that may be improved by introducing participatory elements.

4.2. Political Theories on Democracy

This section is devoted to the description and discussion of general political and democratic theories that acknowledge the participation of non–state actors in the political process. The author shares most of the basic assumptions regarding the benefits of a greater inclusiveness in political decision–making procedures and has developed an EU Participatory Policy Cycle (cf. chapter 6) on the basis of –and greatly owing to– the authors of grand democratic theories discussed below.

4.2.1. Participatory and Deliberative Democracy

Both participatory and deliberative democracy theories focus on the input–side of political decision–making and expect that greater inclusiveness through access to information and other resources, rights to participate in decision–making, and an open and fair discourse held by citizens will lead to more democratic governance by enhancing a system's effectiveness as well as the legitimacy of the decisions taken[13]. Thus, the society as a whole benefits from the inclusion of stakeholders in the decision–making process[14]. The theories criticize the liberalist perception of democracy as "a competition for political power among responsible elites"[15].

Jürgen Habermas, a reputable proponent, defines deliberative democracy as a style of politics, in which consultancy and decision–making in matters that affect the general public are jointly taken[16]. The general public and individuals are thereby able to submit their concerns into the political debate and politicians will have their decisions assessed

10 Lee & Abbott, 2003, p.82
11 Lee & Abbott, 2003, p.86
12 Rose–Ackermann & Halpaap, 2001, p.3
13 Saurugger, 2008, p.1276; Greenwood, 2007c, p.341
14 Schmidt, 2008, pp.237–238; Zittel, 2007, p.9
15 Zittel, 2007, p.9
16 Schmidt, 2008, pp.242–243

in light of the previous discussions[17]. The deliberative style thereby requires higher legitimacy as other modes of decision–making. Habermas formulated the following conditions for the functioning of deliberative democracy. Deliberation must be publicly accessible and, above all, this access should be equally given to all interested individuals and groups and guarantee exchange of information and arguments[18]. Furthermore, participation must be free of any coercion and should be nothing but voluntary. Public consultation should, in general, be unrestricted in time; yet, if suspended, the opportunity to continue must be offered at any time. Additionally, deliberation should comprise all materials that are in the general interest of the public. It is furthermore indispensable for the basic rights to be protected. Finally, the concrete consultation and inclusion of as many stakeholders as possible should be reflected in the final decision[19]. Overall, one could conclude that participatory democracy is not necessarily seen as a bottom–up approach, in which masses of ordinary citizens foregather and pressure for greater participation within political processes. Rather, from a top–down perspective, governments establish formal channels and other incentives in order to encourage citizens to become involved in the policy process[20].

However, this work slightly departs in the appraisal of the ordinary citizen from participatory and deliberative democracy theories. The latter regard citizens optimistically as already well–informed and skilled and in the possession of "the necessary cognitive, motivational and organizational capacities"[21] to directly participate in political processes, and are assumed to strive for a greater common good. Although deliberationists are aware of the fact that these capabilities may also have to be learned and acquired through a targeted education process[22], critics rightly point out that individuals usually prefer personal gains in the short– or medium–term that may contradict positive overall long–term effects[23]. Direct democracy, in which citizens take politically relevant decisions that may concern very technical details, is accordingly not advocated. Rather, citizens should be given the opportunity to make their qualified and sophisticated opinion heard in a deliberative process. The final decision should then reflect a compromise of all relevant arguments heard. There is a real danger that ordinary citizens may vote for or against a certain bill not on the basis of the latter's content but to simply use their vote to make a general political statement concerning their overall (dis–)satisfaction with their government.

---

17 Finke, 2007, p.15
18 Schmidt, 2008, pp.242–243; Kohler–Koch & Finke, 2007, p.213
19 Schmidt, 2008, pp.242–243
20 Zittel, 2007, p.9
21 Kohler–Koch & Finke, 2007, p.214
22 Zittel, 2007, p.11
23 Schmidt, 2008, pp.240–241 & 246–247

Hence, the approach of expansive democratization is supported. Inclusion is thereby not only measured with regard to the actual number of citizens that gain access to information and political decision–making processes but rather the quality of the outcome of participation. In other words, participatory democracy is only beneficial, if political decisions reflect a compromise of all interests affected by the decision. By installing such consultation schemes, governments may further legitimatize their political authority[24].

These assumptions are shared by proponents of associative democracy from which this work finds its theoretical approach. Associative democracy recognizes the potential pitfalls of mere citizen involvement mentioned above and promotes the inclusion of "membership–based" groups in political decision–making processes. The involvement, it is assumed, creates a win–win situation for politicians and administrative decision–makers as well as for the citizens whose interests are represented by such groups. Organized interests still retain contact with their members at the grassroots level, while at the same time, they are able to offer valuable information and expert knowledge to officials, which the bureaucracy would otherwise lack[25].

One could summarize that CSOs expect that, in exchange for the provision of valuable information to administrative and political bodies they, in return, will not only have access to decision–making procedures but also that their position will be effectively reflected in the policies[26].

While it is true that access opportunities should not be equated with influence, the degree of the latter is assumed to depend upon the quality of the facts and arguments provided by the deliberating stakeholder. CSOs are viewed to be better equipped and capable of providing such information than individual citizens[27]. Although proponents admit that the representation of citizens' interests through organized groups "is certainly neither perfect nor without bias", they emphasize the ability of diverse interests in a pluralistic society to be represented on equal terms as well as the benefits gained from competition but as well cooperation among these groups [28].

4.2.2. Opportunity structures for citizen participation

In order to allow for organized interests to become involved in political decision–making, it is indispensable for state institutions and public administrations to set up political opportunity structures (POS). POS, as a concept, was first developed by scholars in the 1960s and 1970s[29] and circumscribes the aggregated conditions under which formal schemes of consultation enable citizens to form collective action and to gain access to

24 Zittel, 2007, pp.16–17
25 Saurugger, 2008, p.1276
26 Princen & Kerremans, 2008, p.1135
27 Kohler–Koch, 2010, p.107
28 Saurugger, 2008, p.1277
29 Nentwich, 1996, p.1

political institutions[30]. These opportunity structures and those that are encouraged to become active and make use of them mutually adapt to each other and are closely linked to a society's structure[31]. In the beginning, POS was usually referred to as being one opportunity structure of civic influence per polity. The notion of opportunity structures for citizens' participation (OSCP) today reflects the multiple access possibilities for private individuals within the whole political system[32].

In the context of this dissertation, policy–related OSCPs are of particular interest because they aim at providing access for stakeholders to the policy– and decision–making processes and enable them to execute influence upon these[33]. It is, however, important to emphasize that access to these processes is essential but in itself insufficient given that the success of participation is reflected in the final policy outcome and thus dependent on the willingness to acknowledge the added value by CSOs on part of political actors[34].

Within the EU, almost each institution[35] has established its own system of OSCPs with a varying degree of development. They range from participation in elections and petitions to the EP or direct contacts with Members of Parliament, over White and Green Papers published by the Commission, in order to receive valuable feedback on their agenda by everyone, who is interested to do so, hearings and stakeholder conferences organized by the Commission, the EESC and Parliamentary committees respectively, to the official Internet registers for public interest organizations (e.g. CONECCS)[36]. Active membership in political parties, business federations or interest groups may furthermore provide an alternative mode for indirect influence on internal decision–making processes within the EU Institutions. In addition, the use of mass media to increase public awareness and even trigger public debates constitutes a powerful tool whose effects may be reflected in public opinion polls undertaken by *Eurobarometer* or comparable institutes[37].

4.2.3. Political Opportunity Structure and Litigation Strategies

Insufficiently developed or appreciated political opportunity structures may encourage stakeholders to return to litigation strategies as the last resort in protesting against political actors. Recourse to courts may therefore be used either complementary, i.e. in addition to political strategies e.g. lobbying, or alternatively[38]. Litigation as a complementary method of citizen participation is reasonable given that the evaluation of policies and interpretation of the Treaties are undertaken by the ECJ at the very last stage of the policy cycle (cf. chapter 6).

30 Nentwich, 1998, pp.126–127
31 Nentwich, 1996, p.1
32 Nentwich, 1996, p.2
33 Nentwich, 1996, p.2
34 Hilson, 2002, p.242
35 The opportunity structures at each EU Institution are elaborated on in chapter 5.
36 Nentwich, 1998, p.130
37 Nentwich, 1996, p.7
38 Hilson, 2002, p.239 & p.250

However, these forms of judicial evaluation can also mark the start of a new policy, trigger subsequent amendments to existing legislation, or create new rights which private and legal individuals, as well as accumulated interest representatives, can invoke before national courts. In these instances, the ECJ is involved in judicial law–making, i.e. creating new rules or defining the scope and meaning of legislation[39].

It is for the above–mentioned reasons that citizen participation in the democratic process increasingly also includes the ability to have recourse to judicial dispute settlement mechanisms. A parallel change in the role of the courts and the fact that citizens, and increasingly their representatives, are empowered to set in force this type of judicial control can be observed on national, supranational as well as on international level[40]. It should, however, be emphasized at this point that the ability of groups to employ either a lobbying or litigation strategy or both depends on the organization's resources, specialization of policy area, as well as the involvement in wider networks[41].

4.3. Benefits of public participation

In sum, CSOs are regarded as citizen–initiated and representing a broader range of sectoral interests than governmental institutions[42]. As described earlier, one of the commonly agreed key characteristics of civil society is its role as a mediator between the citizen and the state[43]. Once civil society has gained access to political institutions, it becomes an additional controlling force that checks whether institutions and other interest groups behave according to established rules[44]. In cases of maladministration or improper policy–making, CSOs are close enough to recognize the misconduct and are in a position to inform and mobilize the public[45]. In so doing, they increase the political awareness of the individual and may potentially provoke civic engagement on the one hand and, on the other hand, provide an incentive for politicians and civil servants to conform to the rules. This may again increase the citizens' trust and confidence in the political system and at the same time provide an additional tool for public accountability. Hence, direct accountability is improved by allowing representatives of citizens to become involved in internal working processes and by exposing administrative organs to the potential risk of being caught by conducting an intentional or accidental error[46].

In addition, from the perspective of the individual, democracy is enhanced insofar as a particular concern is brought forward to political decision–makers. The individual may either choose to become actively involved by participating in campaigns of a specific CSO (e.g. serve as a member of the board, recruit new members) or simply passively

39 Cichowski, 2006, p.62
40 Cichowski, 2006, pp.50–51
41 Princen & Kerremans, 2008, pp.1131–1132
42 Kohler–Koch, 2008, p.270
43 e.g. Freise, 2008a, p.26
44 Greenwood, 2007c, p.356
45 Mahoney, 2008, p.171
46 Lovan, Murray & Shaffer, 2004, p.7; Greenwood, 2007a, p.3; Kohler–Koch, 2008, p.280

support such activities through donations. Thus, he or she is offered an alternative way to participate in the political process in addition to casting a vote in parliamentary elections. Furthermore, this way of representation may be more appealing than voting for a political party given that party programs encompass a wide variety of issues some of which may find the approval of the individual, while others at the same time do not. In short, for some voters, it results in choosing the best out of a number of bad and worse alternatives[47].

While representation by Members of Parliaments is of a geographical and territorial nature[48], representation by interest groups is first and foremost issue–specific and pluralistic. Despite the fact that there are groups that represent more than one particular matter, in the majority of the cases, one general concern is represented. In addition, concern for, for example, the environment can be expressed with various emphases (protecting the diversity of plants and animals on the local area or preserving the flora and fauna on another continent; impeding the clearing of tropical rain forests or bringing global warming to the attention of the public and politics etc.) from which the individual may again select. Hence, an individual may support as many different organizations as he or she wishes in order for the total of his or her concerns to be represented at political level in the best suitable manner. Consequently, the advantage of CSO representation in contemporary pluralistic society as opposed to parliamentary representation, is that the individual must not be satisfied with one alternative but rather has his or her strongest concerns directly and actively promoted with political decision–makers through multiple actors.

Overall, the advantages for individuals appear fairly obvious. Also politicians and civil servants are becoming increasingly aware of the additional gains that civil society may deliver. Again, the first point might seem a little trivial considering the discussion above, but the opportunity that organized civil society provides for individuals to be heard in the political arena should not be underestimated. In short, such groups are expected to foster political deliberation by, on the one hand, informing the public and bringing topical problems on the policy agenda and, on the other hand, proposing alternative or supplementary solutions to them[49]. The variety of interests and the internal organizational structure of CSOs are expected to reflect the populations' pluralism of societal interests and to provide a balance to business, market–driven and state interests[50]. It is, however, assumed that interest groups are more influential in policies concerning technical issues rather than in problems relating to "high politics"[51]. The linkage of interest groups to the needs and concerns of the population (or at least that specific part of the population that it represents) facilitates the formulation of policies and the delivery of services that

47 Cf. Saurugger, 2008, pp.1275–1276 on the connection of people's abstention in democratic elections and the creation of alternative means for political action.

48 Smismans, 2003, p.473

49 Glasius, 2002, p.162; similar: Kohler–Koch, 2010, p.106

50 Maloney & Van Deth, 2008, pp.13–14; Armstrong, 2002, p.105; Kohler–Koch, 2010, p.106

51 Dür, 2008, p.1217

reflect the citizens' priorities[52]. In particular, monitoring and reporting mechanisms are prepared to provide feedback on cooperative relations. Through their participation in the political process and direct contacts with decision–makers, civil society is expected to redound to increasing the transparency of the political business and enhancing public accountability of political and administrative institutions[53]. Furthermore, practitioners hope that the inclusion of CSOs in the formulation of policies may have positive effects on a fluent implementation of policies on the national and local level by informing the public of the aim and usefulness of the law[54].

An additional, very crucial, argument for practitioners is the fact that CSOs may have a greater variety of resources (financial and political), more time and specialized staff to provide expert knowledge; for instance research studies, statistics, surveys, calculations etc. CSOs therefore not only contribute to the democratic legitimization of EU Institutions but also provide valuable input into the pre–legislative working processes[55]. Overall, the increased inclusion of organized interests into the policy process would ideally result in decreasing the distance between European citizens and EU decision–makers and may additionally aid in the population's acceptance and appraisal of European politics and institutions[56], provided that access is granted upon the principle of equality[57].

4.3.1. Critical Voices

It is not a secret that the benefits of participatory democracy are questioned by some in the literature and the concepts and instruments applied within the EU are – at times – heavily criticized[58].

Contrary to the ideal theory, participatory democracy within the EU is not a process initiated from the bottom upwards but rather instigated by the institutions[59]. The democratic quality of CSOs' internal structure is, at least for some associations, greatly doubted[60] given that, *inter alia*, resources and capacities for self–organization are distributed unevenly among the wide spectrum of 'public interests'[61]. Those organizations that have specialized themselves might turn themselves into elite actors, thereby lose their close links to the grassroots level and thus their character of having been citizen–initiated. Accordingly their capability of enhancing the legitimacy of EU policy–making becomes disputable. As has been said, particularly the Commission indeed treats such associations preferentially[62].

52 Lovan, Murray & Shaffer, 2004, p.5; Maloney & Van Deth, 2008, p.6
53 Glasius, 2002, p.162
54 Finke, 2007, p.6
55 Maloney & Van Deth, 2008, pp.13–14; Greenwood, 2007c, p.341; Dür, 2008, pp.1213–1214
56 Lovan, Murray & Shaffer, 2004, p.5; Maloney & Van Deth, 2008, p.6
57 Wainwright, 2004–5, p.95
58 Finke, 2007, pp.14–15; Kohler-Koch, 2010, p.107
59 Saurugger, 2008, p.1286
60 Saurugger, 2008, p.1278 & 1285; Greenwood, 2007c, p.347
61 Saurugger, 2008, pp.1278–1279
62 Saurugger, 2008, p.1275 & 1279

It has been stated in chapter 3 that a comprehensive definition of 'civil society' does not (yet) exist. Political scientists have pointed at this flaw, criticizing that not only the EU Institutions differ in their definition but also many researchers attribute different groups comprising various features to this concept in their respective studies. Questions concerning the voluntary character or the degree of professionalization of these groups arise regularly[63]. The various political cultures and the many official languages at the EU[64] further add to the transaction costs of CSOs to become involved in European politics. Those asymmetries in interest representation in the dominance of business over citizens' interests as well as the larger number of organizations originating from the "old" Member States are pointed out[65]; however, governmental funding – with all its negative effects – has been installed to adjust the level of resources and consequently the ability to influence[66].

Overall, the attempts to provide for improved opportunity structures for citizens and their representatives have been criticized as insufficient and unregulated; thus again privileging those actors that already obtain established relations and dispose of sufficient resources[67]. This applies, once more, particularly to the Commission. One staff member was cited, who found that the Commission could better "link with the citizens [...] by more effective results", whereas direct inputs are rather "for speeches and the rhetoric"[68]. Similarly, Warleigh examined opportunities for direct citizen participation in environmental policy and cited an interviewee, who stated that he would prefer "to get people involved", however, limited time necessitated him to rather "get on with advocacy" given that he had to "ensure the best results for the environment"[69].

However, opposite opinions have been cited also in the area of environmental policy. Particularly members of the G–10[70] group have been able to establish settled and regular relations with Directorate–General (DG) Environment. A staff member even declared that DG Environment could not have "survived" "without NGO support"[71].

Thus, whereas the benefits of participatory and deliberative democracy apply almost universally, the criticism voiced by political researchers concerns the (so far) implementation deficiencies at EU level; yet does not question the overall gains of complementing representative democracy with participation opportunities for citizens and their functional representatives.

---

63 Saurugger, 2008, p.1282
64 Kohler–Koch, 2008, p.271
65 Kohler–Koch, 2008, p.280; Kohler-Koch, 2010, p.111
66 Saurugger, 2008, pp.1282 & 1286
67 Saurugger, 2008, pp.1282–1283
68 Greenwood, 2007c, p.356
69 Greenwood, 2007c, p.348
70 Birdlife International, Climate Action Network Europe, CEE Bankwatch Network, European Environmental Bureau, European Federation for Transport and Environment, Friends of the Earth Europe, Greenpeace Europe, Health and Environment Alliance, International Friends of Nature, World Wildlife Fund
71 Greenwood, 2007c, p.346

5. Participatory Democracy within the European Union

5.1. The Democratic Deficit of the European Union

The democratic deficit has emerged in the political discourse in the aftermath of the Treaty establishing European Union (TEU, 1993) and the negative referendum of the Danish population[1]. The Treaty transferred a great number of sensitive policy competences from the national level to the EU. Not only the quantitative increase in competences was criticized but even more so the qualitative nature of the type of competences[2]. Areas including foreign affairs, defense, as well as matters concerning police cooperation and judicial prosecution that have traditionally fallen within the sole authority of a nation state, have then partly been delegated to the intergovernmental arena of decision–making. While these competences at least remained shared between national and European political institutions, other policy areas have even become the exclusive competence of the EU Institutions under the former 'Community pillar'[3].

Critics argue that the lack of a common identity by the population of the Member States amounts to a structural deficit that renders the creation of a European demos impossible even in the medium–term[4]. Without such a demos, however, it is not viable to establish a well–functioning democracy at supranational level within the Union. This alienation between the public and the governing staff in the EU[5] is considerably furthered by the unequal integration processes and velocities in the economic and legal sector, as opposed to political and cultural integration. The latter include not only the already claimed lack of a common demos but also extend to the missing Union–wide mass media, political parties and leisure groups[6]. Others more optimistically identify deficiencies in the representation of and participation by citizens that can, however, be corrected[7]. Over-

1 Saurugger, 2008, p.1277; Knodt & Große Hüttmann, 2006, p.234

2 Finke, 2007, p.6

3 *Inter alia* argument of the claimant in the judgment of the Federal Constitutional Court of Germany on the Maastricht Treaty: BVerfG, BVerfGE 89, 155 vom 12. Oktober 1993 (2 BvR 2134, 2159/92), II.1.a)

4 Schmidt, 2008, p.402; p.282; Saurugger, 2008, p.1278

5 This trend, however, is not exclusively observed with regard to EU politics. Political researchers have identified a general alienation by citizens of the political class. Cf. Saurugger, 2008, pp.1275 & 1278

6 Schmidt, 2008, p.405

7 Schmidt, 2008, pp.402–403

all, participation opportunities for citizens to the EU Institutions are considered to be problematic. Access is still hampered, unequal, and participation leads to unsatisfactory results as output is comparatively low[8]. Great differences, however, exist between policy areas and institutions (cf. below).

With regard to the shortcomings in citizen representation, the argument is as follows. The removal of powers of national parliaments, and thereby the disempowerment of the people, was not adequately compensated for by a comparable increase of powers and responsibilities of the European Parliament[9], although the Parliament has come a long way. For instance, the EP still does neither, as is common for national parliaments, enjoy full scrutiny over the budget, nor does it fill the high positions within the EU's executive. Furthermore, even though co–decision became the 'ordinary' decision–making procedure, in which the Council of Ministers and the EP take decisions as equitable partners, the latter has less shaping powers than the Council. Inequality in the representation within the EU Institutions adds to the problem. The number of seats per nationality in the Parliament, as well as the votes distributed within the Council, result in an over–representation of small Member States, while countries with larger population sizes are under–represented[10].

Other arguments put forward in the substantiation of the democratic deficit include the fact that decisions are merely the result of a long, non–transparent negotiation process between the EU Institutions in which an unidentifiable range of actors is involved. It is accordingly not feasible to retrace the arguments and the process of developing specific decisions. It further exacerbates the problem of holding specific actors accountable for their (mis–)behavior. The dense net of comitology and other committee networks within the European administrative system thereby neglects rulings of the ECJ that emphasize the judicial responsibility and political accountability of the EU Institutions. The non–transparent bargaining method 'behind closed doors' is therefore another point of criticism of the EU's democratic deficit[11].

The above–indicated problem that the composition of the supranational executive and the judiciary is determined in negotiation processes far out of reach of the citizens relates to a similar point of criticism. In addition, the difficulty in controlling other organs such as the ECB and the high dependency on the Commission as the executor of EU policies and politics are suggested. Together with the high utility of externalization of executive functions by the establishment of agencies or the private sector, as well as the general weak, long and non–transparent chains of delegation, these arguments add substantially to the legitimacy problem of the European Union[12]. These deficiencies can, under certain circumstances, lead to dramatic negative effects on the political systems

8 Schmidt, 2008, p.403

9 Holzinger, 2005, pp.90–91; cf. also claimant in Federal Constitutional Court of Germany on the Maastricht Treaty: BVerfG, BVerfGE 89, 155 vom 12. Oktober 1993 (2 BvR 2134, 2159/92), II.1.a)

10 Schmidt, 2008, p.403

11 Kohler–Koch, 1997, p.54

12 Schmidt, 2008, p.404

of the Member States, which, in the worst case, could undermine their own democratic legitimacy[13]. The strength of all of these arguments, again, varies according to the respective policy area[14].

Overall, low turnouts in elections to the European Parliament, as well as the negative referendums on the Treaty establishing a Constitution for Europe (Constitutional Treaty, CT, 2004) in The Netherlands and France, and the rejection of the Lisbon Treaty (LT, 2007) by the Irish population have illustrated the long apparent fact that the EU has so far failed its goal to connect Europe closer to its citizens, which was boldly declared at the 1996 Summit in Turin[15]. The key arguments on the democratic deficit may be summarized as follows. Deficiencies in the structure of representative democracy in combination with insufficiently developed participation opportunities and non–transparent administrative habits lead to a great legitimacy deficit within supranational governance. The EU appears to citizens as a bureau– and technocratic apparatus that is characterized by informal and non–transparent procedures, non–public decision–making, as well as insufficient access to documents[16]. Empirically, the conception of the EU as a "government of governments" has been created. "Legitimatized expertocracy" has furthermore been developed as a term based on the fact that only experts are capable of entering a European–wide communication community, while the vast majority of the population is excluded[17]. Thus, direct confrontation between the staff of EU Institutions and ordinary citizens remains a rare exception to the rule[18].

5.2. Alleviating the EU's Democratic Deficit

There are, however, also political scholars, who have intensely studied the EU governance system and conclude that the Union does indeed dispose of adequate democratic legitimacy. If one speaks of a democratic deficit, it would concern a revisable formal deficiency or a deficit that may nevertheless be democratically legitimatized[19].

Strong proponents claim that the EU is, as a regional organization, sufficiently legitimatized on the basis of the high quality of democracy prevalent in all its constituent parts, i.e. the Member States and the chains of legitimacy between EU Institutions and national ministries[20]. This assumption may be compatible with a liberal intergovernmentalist view with regard to European integration, in which the Member States are considered to be the 'masters of the Treaties' that retain the overall control over the

13 Schmidt, 2008, p.283
14 Schmidt, 2008, p.282
15 cf. e.g Commission, 2001, COM(2001) 428 final; *European Governance – A White Paper*, p.8; also: Saurugger, 2008, pp.1275–1276; Kohler–Koch & Finke, 2007, p.210
16 amongst others: Armstrong, 2002, p.106
17 Schmidt, 2008, pp.284 & 406
18 Schmidt, 2008, p.284
19 Schmidt, 2008, p.401
20 Schmidt, 2008, pp.284 & 399

integration process including the possibility to revise certain steps[21]. This work, however, is based on assumptions originating from the multi–level governance approach and supranationalism and considers that the integration process has developed its own dynamic and transferred important competences to supranational institutions in the EU framework of governance. An exclusive legitimatization based on the democratic system within the Member States is therefore deemed insufficient.

This opinion may also be shared by those, who admit the existence of a severe democratic deficit on European level, yet identified first attempts to increase legitimacy through a strengthening of the EP, additional transparency and flexibility in deliberation processes, and who propose further modifications. Those proponents argue with the existence of a dual legitimacy originating from national parliaments and the EP, which should guarantee sustained chains of legitimacy from the demos over its elected representatives to those responsible in EU governance. In their view, also the other institutions next to the EP are legitimatized in an effectual manner. The Council obtains its legitimacy through the national governments that have been constituted by national parliaments according to the respective constitutional settings. Those legitimatized members of the Council determine the composition of the College of Commissioners that is liable to disclose information to[22] and is subjected to the control of the EP. While the appointment of the Commission was interpreted undemocratic by the skeptics of EU democracy, it is now deemed sufficient by their scholarly counterparts.

Furthermore, the institutional framework of the EU is regarded as providing a secure system of checks and balances. As additional indications of the positive democratic progress, the rights to cast votes in municipal elections (Article 22(1)TFEU) and elections to the EP (Article 22(2) TFEU) for Union citizens residing in a Member State other than their country of nationality are mentioned as examples[23]. Other approaches with which this work is associated point to the multiple levels of governance of the EU governance system and the fact that the sum of the shared sovereignty and the combination of the respective decision–making procedures add up to a valid legitimatization[24]. In addition, the introduction of a citizens' legislation initiative based on the signatures of one million EU citizens originating from a specified minimum number of Member States in Article TEU 11(4) TEU illustrates the aspired co–existence of representative and participatory democracy[25] that should complement rather than replace each other[26]. Yet, some observers do not consider the citizen–initiative to be sufficient as it is merely a *"invitation"* – not an obligation – for the Commission to consider the content for a legislative proposal[27].

21 Schmidt, 2008, p.401
22 Schmidt, 2008, p.400
23 Schmidt, 2008, p.401
24 Schmidt, 2008, p.402
25 Articles 10 & 11 TEU; Saurugger, 2008, p.1282; Finke, 2007, pp.4 & 21; Kohler–Koch, 2008, p.265 & 268
26 Saurugger, 2008, p.1281; Greenwood, 2007c, p.341
27 Kohler–Koch, 2008, p.266; Nentwich, 1996, p.1

In this context, civil society serves as an idealized mechanism to overcome the democratic deficit or at least to provide an alternative approach towards government by and for the people (cf. chapter 3)[28]. Participatory democracy "overcomes the 'no demos - no democracy'–thesis" on the basis of the argument that citizens are organized in groups which represent their interests at the political level and thereby are able to directly participate in political decision–making[29].

5.2.1. Legitimacy

Regarding the appraisal and classification of democratic quality within the European Union, much reference has been made to the concept of legitimacy. It indeed occupies a prominent place in the debate on the democratic deficit and its possible cures and should therefore be more closely defined.

The lack of an appropriate accountability scheme is closely intertwined with the insufficiently developed democratic legitimization of the EU Institutions. The opposing opinions have already been presented above. Beetham formulated the following conditions for legitimacy of governmental action. First, *legality* must be ensured; i.e. political power should be obtained and executed according to pre–established rules and regulations. Second, *normative justifiability* refers to the necessity that all rules are justifiable on grounds of the "rightful source of authority" as well as the "proper ends and standards of government". Last but not least, the recognition by other authorities that are legitimatized themselves, as well as the approval of the population are important prerequisites for *legitimatization*[30].

Hence, important preconditions for democratic legitimacy are 'demos', i.e. a people that approves those who take political decisions on their behalf, and a government that conducts its work according to the will and in the best interest of its people. However, legitimacy as a concept can further be divided into two component parts. *Input* legitimacy can be equated with "government *by* the people", while *output* legitimacy depicts "government *for* the people" [emphases added][31]. The former mode of governance requires the direct and concrete participation or at least approval of the population of the conduct of the government. The latter evaluates the effectiveness and efficiency of governmental action with regard to the common benefit[32]. While the European Union seemed to have legitimatized itself comparatively successfully through its output for decades and received broad approval by the population until the changes brought by the Maastricht Treaty[33], today, the emphasis is placed upon achieving input legitimacy. This is best achieved by providing political opportunity structures to all citizens or their representa-

28 Maloney & Van Deth, 2008, p.4; Armstrong, 2002, p.106; Warleigh, 2001, p.620
29 Smismans, 2003, p.474
30 Beetham & Lord, 1998, p.15
31 Wolf, 2002, p.39
32 Wolf, 2002, p.39; Heinrich, 2008, pp.45–46; Holzinger, 2005, pp.92–93; Freise, 2008a, p.10
33 Holzinger, 2005, pp.92 & 94

tives under equal and fair conditions[34]. Proclaiming to fulfill this condition, the European Commission in particular strives to legitimatize its political function by providing for the equal inclusion of a broad range of interests into decision–making and offering CSOs the opportunity to propose alternative solutions to policy problems and thereby to contribute to policy bargaining resulting in an enhanced political deliberation process[35]. However, through the reliance on external expertise provided by civil society as technical input into policy–formulation and with the goal of developing the best–researched and resourced policy outcome for the European population, the EU also still seeks some elements of output–related legitimacy[36].

Both input and output legitimacy have also been put forward in the academic discourse on the EU's democratic conditions. It is argued that the success in the area of output legitimacy – transnational cooperation in policy areas that exceed the abilities of nation states, for instance environmental protection – fully compensates for the deficiencies that are currently prevalent in terms of input legitimacy[37]. Proponents of this approach point to the undeniable success in e.g. the safeguarding of peace and stability, abiding by the rule of law, as well as economic prosperity, including the elimination of barriers to trade as examples of the EU's output record[38]. At the same time, input legitimacy is greatly improved through the consideration of the EU's pluralism of interests by increasing and formalizing consultation with national civil servants, as well as non–governmental experts and civil society organizations[39]. This process is still in need of perfection and will be discussed in more detail further on.

5.2.2. Transparency

Another concept that is widely utilized and inseparably connected to the legitimacy and accountability of political institutions is the notion of transparency, i.e. the visibility of internal working processes and the opportunity of the public to access non–confidential documents. As early as 1997, transparency clauses were introduced into the Treaty of Amsterdam (Article 255 EC) and the Charter on Fundamental Rights (Article 43). However, in the context of promoting 'good governance' within the EU, these efforts accelerated in speed as well as in width. Even though Regulation 1049/2001/EC regulates access of outsiders to documents released by the Commission, Council and Parliament through online search engines and registers, many exceptions to the rule are possible and therefore, it does not establish a comprehensive system of transparency[40]. Furthermore, in addition to the open systems of consultation in, as for instance, advisory committees,

34 Wolf, 2002, p.39
35 Holzinger, 2005, p.93; Heinrich, 2008, p.46; Hilger, 2008, p.189; Greenwood, 2007a, p.116
36 Heinrich, 2008, pp.45–46; Holzinger, 2005, p.92
37 Schmidt, 2008, p.402
38 Schmidt, 2008, pp.283–284
39 Schmidt, 2008, pp.284 & 401
40 Friedrich, 2008, p.75; Greenwood, 2007b, p.186; Greenwood, 2007c, p.352

some Commission DGs have also turned to a less transparent, unstructured and ad hoc consultation of specific interests[41].

In recent years, the Commission has launched the European Transparency Initiative, under which the Green Paper (2006) also demands transparency in the Commission's consultation procedures of lobbyists, defined as "persons carrying out [...] activities [aimed at shaping the processes of European policy–making], working in a variety of organisations such as public affairs consultancies, law firms, NGOs, think tanks, corporate lobby units or trade associations"[42]. It is, however, a precondition that the latter must also be willing to disclose information about their outside relations, as well as their internal working procedures, which is regulated in the codes of conduct by the relevant EU Institution[43]. The Commission for its part is obliged to state the reasons for considering some positions and denying others, to undertake impact assessments of the measure on other policy areas, and to release "road maps" that make consultation modes traceable. The practice, however, differs among the respective Commission DGs. While some regularly publish synthesis reports, others only inform those that had been involved in a particular proceeding. This is primarily due to the fact that Commission officials are not legally committed to such transparent working procedures but rather do so on grounds of promoting the institution's own legitimacy[44].

5.2.3. The EU – a complex and multi–layered governance construct

Supranationalism

The general assumptions of this work are furthermore linked to supranationalism as a European integration theory. It was developed in the 1990s most prominently by Stone Sweet and Sandholtz in opposition to Moravciks liberal intergovernmentalism. Supranationalism aims at providing an explanation for the unequal speed and mode of integration in different policy areas[45]. The theory draws from items of Haas' neofunctionalism, Deutsch's transaction theory[46], as well as historical institutionalism[47] and is compatible with Hooghe's and Mark's multi–level governance approach.

Stone Sweet and Sandholtz developed a continuum with intergovernmental decision–making at the one and supranational governance at the other end[48]. The degree of supranational governance depends on the interaction of three separate, yet, co–existing, dimensions. First, formal and informal relations between the various actors at European level constitute 'EU norms'. Second, EU organizations are institutionalized governance

41 Nentwich, 1998, p.131
42 European Commission, 2006, 2006, COM(2006) 194 final *Green Paper. European Transparency Initiative*, p.5
43 Greenwood, 2007b, pp.186, 190
44 Kohler–Koch, 2008, p.281
45 Nölke, 2006, p.145
46 Nölke, 2006, p.146; Rosamond, 2000, p.127
47 Nölke, 2006, p.146
48 Rosamond, 2000, p.127

structures that produce, execute and interpret those EU norms. Obviously, as their influence increases, the continuum moves closer to the supranational end. Finally, supranationalists also award great attention to the potential role of furthering European integration by transnational society[49]. They understand transnational society as those non–state actors that take influence on European decision–making through the exchange of opinions and deliberation processes. In intergovernmental decision–making modes, transnational actors are attributed a mediating role between governments and those, whose interests they represent. At the supranational end of the continuum, a variety of formal access channels are offered to interest groups and external experts, in which the input of such groups is sought and greatly appreciated by the EU Institutions[50].

The formation of a transnational society and its development is the starting point of greater supranational governance. The existence of transnational interest groups that seek modes of influence necessitates the creation of formal rules of conduct and a structured system of collaboration[51]. Due to the transaction costs of lobbying each (at least of the larger) Member State separately and potential impediments at national level, direct access to EU Institutions is gaining momentum[52]. The strategic and combined action of interest groups in specific sections furthermore provides an understandable explanation for the fact that these policy areas are decided according to the supranational decision–making mode. Primary addressees of augmented initiatives are the European Commission and the Court of Justice[53]. The most supranational institutions and their civil servants, commissioners and judges neglect their nationality and commit themselves to 'European' interests. The process continues and develops its own dynamic, if EU organizations have an interest in strengthening integration and interactions that are regulated by EU norms[54].

Supranationalists also attribute the supranationalization of policy areas that have originally not been included in the Treaties to the activities of transnational civil society and particularly to litigation before the ECJ. Once the process is triggered, it is difficult to be put on hold or even to be reversed. This dynamic is explained by a transaction logic and the 'path dependency' of institutions as proclaimed by historical institutionalists. Those norms that have been created in order to extend transactions lead to an adaptation in behavior by all actors involved and practically impede a reversal of the newly achieved supranational competences and governance modes[55]. European secondary law might then touch upon other policy areas and necessitate supranational action again. This is a modification of Ernst B. Haas' neofunctionalist concept of 'spillovers'[56].

49 Rosamond, 2000, pp.126–127
50 Nölke, 2006, pp.151–152
51 Nölke, 2006, pp.151–152; Rosamond, 2000, p.128; Wessels, 1997, p.19
52 Nölke, 2006, pp.151–152; Rosamond, 2000, p.128
53 Nölke, 2006, pp.154–155
54 Nölke, 2006, pp.155–156
55 Nölke, 2006, p.156
56 Nölke, 2006, p.157

Critics, for instance Kohler–Koch, disagree and argue that "[t]heoretical reasoning and empirical evidence confirm the proposition that the European organizations of interests grew in response to, and not, in advance of, integrative steps, and that European interest groups, in particular, were not the driving forces of regional integration"[57]. However, she also admits that, if not providing a theoretical tool of explanation for the overall political process of European integration, organized interest representatives are nonetheless taking considerable influence in shaping former EC and nowadays EU policies[58]. As the work is not concerned with the analysis of overall regional integration in Europe, the agreement among political scientists regarding the indispensability of organized interests in EU policy–making, including civil society organizations, shall suffice.

A final remark concerns the role of the Court of Justice in the development of supranational governance. It is, indeed, a very important one. As soon as EU norms are in force, individual actors strive to oppose or clarify them. The ECJ, as well as the legislature, are therefore under the obligation to specify the content of the norms, which may even lead to a change of their original meaning[59].

Multi–Level Governance and policy networks

The multi–level governance approach has already been introduced to describe the specificities of the EU political system. It further offers theoretical scope for an alleviation of the EU's democratic deficit in general and the legitimacy problem in particular. MLG introduces a new form of governance that includes, in addition to governmental elites, also other actors from the public as well as private sector. It overcomes the intergovernmental vs. supranational debate and rather attracts notice to the specific national, European and substantive interests that are represented in EU decision–making[60].

The participation of CSOs that have expert knowledge but are also sensitive to the wider implications of the policy areas, in which the Union has at least shared competence, is particularly suitable to address the technocratic character as well as multi–level and multi–institutional governance of EU decision–making[61]. Thus, MLG is of interest in the context of participatory democracy insofar as the multiple layers of governance and the diffusion of legislative and executive powers theoretically offer a number of access points for interested parties[62]. The approach offers participation and inclusion of non–state actors[63]. Such private associations have accustomed to the characteristics of EU governance and follow a dual, if not triple, strategy as they attempt to gain influential access to the supranational Commission and EP as well as to national and subnational political and administrative authorities[64].

---

57 Kohler–Koch, 1997, p.46
58 Kohler–Koch, 1997, pp.45–46
59 Nölke, 2006, p.157
60 Knodt & Große Hüttmann, 2006, p.234
61 Saurugger, 2008, p.1276; Kohler–Koch, 2010, p.103
62 Greenwood, 2007a, p.2; Randzio–Plath, 2004, p.5; Kohler–Koch, 2010, p.111
63 Knodt & Große Hüttmann, 2006, p.235
64 cf. Finke, 2007, p.8

Given that simultaneous lobbying at different levels is not automatically promising[65], CSOs also vary in their strategies to persuade political decision–makers to support their interest because they have adapted to the different POS offered by the various political organs. Sub–national authorities are more open to those interest groups that represent concerns that coincide with those of their electorate; i.e. region–specific problems. However, these interests may be of little importance for European integration and therefore receive less attention by EU Institutions. Thus, on the one hand, the multiple levels of governance within the European Union provide an opportunity for CSOs given that, even if governmental bodies of one level of governance may not be convinced by the represented interests, there are still two levels that might potentially support them. On the other hand, this demands great effort from CSOs to adapt their lobby strategies to the relevant institution at the respective level, as well as to increase their staff, time and financial resources. Neglecting to address all levels may entail the risk of failing to effectively incorporate the organization's interest into European law and legislation[66]. Moreover, the multiple access points at the various governance levels and institutions or bodies within the European Union might be a guarantee that no single interest can exclusively dominate the political agenda[67].

The measurement and classification of participation opportunities may be comparatively manageable, whereas the relative power of all actors involved is difficult to assess; particularly in general terms. Degrees of the respective influence of state and civic actors may substantially vary among policy areas[68]. Wessels, however, argues that the likelihood of achieving satisfactory policy results increases, if interest representatives are able to use the EU's multi–level governance system for their own benefit. Not only should they be permanently established in Brussels and maintain close links with civil servants of the EU Institutions and Members of European Parliament but furthermore, should remain active also at governmental authorities at national and subnational actors. Otherwise, Wessels predicts the emergence of a vicious cycle: "[W]ithout a reputation for being able to sell a compromise at home, players lose influence in Brussels, which in turn reduces their capacity to act for their ministry of interest group; a factor which then further reduces their reputable credit in Brussels"[69].

5.2.4. Governance vs. Government

As outlined above, civil society is expected to have the potential to contribute to the democratic development of a political system. The theory surrounding the concept of participatory democracy identifies civil society organizations as key actors in contemporary aspirations of democratic governance. It is indispensable to define the meaning of

65 Dür, 2008, p.1220
66 Kohler–Koch, 1997, p.47
67 Greenwood, 2007c, p.337
68 e.g. Kohler–Koch & Finke, 2007, p.209
69 Wessels, 1997, pp.35–36

'governance' before discussing the assumptions of participatory democracy because the latter can only be executed in a modern system of governance as opposed to government.

A government is a constitutionally fixed institution of political actors that has the delegated authority to take important decisions for the population living in the respective territorial jurisdiction. The concept of governance, however, has emerged only recently (roughly since the 1980s) in the language of political scholarship[70]. It circumscribes a more open and flexible mode of political decision–making by focusing on the interdependent and steadily changing sets of relations between governmental and non–state actors[71]. Decisions are therefore not made in an instant but arrived at as a result of a deliberative process aimed at problem–solving through achieving compromises of the various interests and opinions involved[72]. In this pluralistic environment, the government takes the position of managing the "level playing field"; i.e. determining which actors are eligible to participate, establishing the general rules of consultation systems, and coordinating the proposals of the various stakeholders[73]. Hence, present conceptualizations of governance amount to an adequate mixture of a well–functioning representative democracy complemented by elements of equal participation rights for all potential stakeholders within the political community[74].

5.3. Citizen Opportunity Structures at the EU Institutions

This section outlines the formal access opportunities for influence that are provided by the respective EU Institutions to the numerous civil society organizations within the EU[75]. The next chapter then separates the participation opportunities according to the relevant stage of a policy[76]. It is very important to keep the findings on the individual institutions in mind when following their respective roles and power throughout the policy cycle. For reasons of a clearer structure and comprehensibility, the discussion on the institutions and the policy cycle have been separated on purpose.

Princen and Kerremans argue that the opportunity structures at the political institutions of the EU encourage direct lobby and litigation activities rather than public protest and thus are distinguishable from those existing at national level. They base their argument on, *inter alia*, the following reasons. First, with the exception of the EP, the institutions and European political parties are much less sensitive to elections than Member State

70 Finke, 2007, p.5
71 Finke, 2007, p.5; Lovan, Murray & Shaffer, 2004, pp. xv, xvi & 3
72 Greenwood, 2007a, p.3; Michalowitz, 2005, p.3; Richardson, 2006, p.9
73 Gbikpi & Grote, 2002, pp.20–21; Lovan, Murray & Shaffer, 2004, pp.3, 7–8
74 Friedrich, 2008, p.69; Weale, 1998, p.51; Maloney & Van Deth, 2008, p.5
75 Bouwen & McCown, 2007, p.422
76 The Policy Cycle is explained in chapter 6.

governments. Second, the lack of a common sense of European identity[77] as well as transnational media broadcasting renders the mobilization of the *European* public a difficult task[78]. Finally, as the institutions are themselves "diverse", the support of diffuse interests aids the strengthening of their position vis–á–vis the Member States[79].

As has been shown in chapter 3, the type of definition employed as well as the appraisal of CSO inclusion in policy development depends on the intentions of the relevant person. This particularly applies to the EU Institutions as these - despite their close cooperation during the policy process - are inherently independent from each other in their respective functions. Obviously, as a general rule of thumb, it can be stated that those institutions that have the highest degree of CSO inclusion in their working processes, need civil society for their own purposes, i.e. mainly for legitimacy reasons, which is in turn reflected in their working definition of civil society in general. As will be elaborated on below, the European Commission is not only the primary target of CSO action but also in the greatest need of sustaining such relations. For similar reasons, the European Economic and Social Committee ranks second place in their position towards civil society. The EP, although being target of a massive form of lobbying itself, maintains rather ambiguous relations with interest groups. The Committee of Regions (CoR) as well as the Council of Ministers, though due to different reasons, both neither warmly welcome nor nourish fruitful relations with CSOs[80]. Given that the relations between the ECJ and environmental civil society is the core of this dissertation, they will be discussed thoroughly in subsequent chapters. Other bodies of the EU institutional system do not fall within the scope of this research project and are therefore not covered here.

5.3.1. Commission of the European Union

The Commission only slowly entered the discourse on participatory opportunity structures and the role of civil society within a democratic governance system in the mid–1990s in response to the uprising criticism on the EU's democratic deficit. It was not until the end of the decade that structured and institutionalized relations with CSOs were positively considered by the officials. Before, an accreditation system that would have disclosed the Commission's consultation practices was declined with the argument that the Commission intends neither to build new bureaucratic hurdles, nor to privilege specific interest representatives over others[81]. The gradual development in the attitude towards civil society has been reflected in the language used in official Commission documents ranging from "consultation" in the 1960s and 70s over "partnership" in the 1980s to "participation" from the last two decades onwards[82].

77 cf. e.g. Greenwood, 2007c, p.334
78 Princen & Kerremans, 2008, p.1133
79 Princen & Kerremans, 2008, p.1134
80 cf. Bouwen & McCown, 2007, p.424
81 Greenwood, 2007b, pp.188–189
82 Kohler–Koch & Finke, 2007, p.209; cf. also Zimmer & Sittermann, 2004, p.30; Smismans, 2003, pp.480–481

The intensification of the co–operation between public administration and civil society only gained speed after the scandal of the Santer Commission that resulted in the resignation of the whole College in 1999 and offset the EU's goal of defining and applying 'principles of good governance'[83]. In this context, the White Paper on European Governance (WPG)[84] marked the turning point in the Commission's approach towards the inclusion of civil society in the European policy process. The paper does not offer its own definition of civil society, but instead refers to the one developed by the EESC in 1999 (cf. below).

As such, the WPG aimed at reforming European policy from scratch. It identified the principles of good governance as: openness, participation, accountability, effectiveness and coherence; all of which can be placed in relation to a more inclusive policy style and offering political opportunity structures to actors from civil society. However, as described before, the most important role attached to CSOs is to act as mediators between the EU and the citizens[85]. In this function, civil society would help to forward positive as well as negative feedback on policy decisions to the responsible EU Institution, which is essential for the preparation of subsequent legislation and the overall improvement of democratic principles[86]. In order to achieve a greater inclusion of a variety of interests into the policy process, a number of measures were introduced under the heading of enhancing a 'civic dialogue' in the immediate post–WPG era[87]. One of the most important of these was the establishment of CONECCS, an Internet register for those organizations and experts that are eligible to be consulted by the Commission in order to provide for more transparency[88]. In order to be registered in CONECCS, groups have to provide proof of their existence in at least three Member States and their ability to represent their members[89]. After DG Environment was the first to install such an online consultation scheme in 2000, almost all Directorates-General regularly do so by now in the agenda–setting and formulation stages of the policy cycle (cf. chapter 6)[90]. In subsequent stages, however, meetings of advisory and expert groups are still the rule and CSO influence is less visible. Overall, consultation platforms on the Internet of the Commission have accumulated throughout the last decade, although differences still exist among the DGs and the respective policy areas[91]. In addition, a code of conduct was released, which prohibits experts from abusing the privilege of receiving information or documents of the Commission and requires the disclosure of other contacts, as well as the avoidance

83 Kohler–Koch, 2010, p.102
84 European Commission, 2001, COM(2001) 428 final
85 Zimmer & Freise, 2008, p.33; Zimmer & Sittermann, 2004, p.27; Kohler–Koch & Finke, 2007, p.211
86 Zimmer & Sittermann, 2004, pp.27–28; Greenwood, 2007a, p.6
87 e.g. Kohler–Koch & Finke, 2007, p.209
88 Greenwood, 2007a, p.34; Greenwood, 2007b, pp.187–188; Greenwood, 2007c, p.354; Hilger, 2008, pp.188–189; Friedrich, 2008, p.76
89 Greenwood, 2007c, p.350
90 Kohler–Koch & Finke, 2007, p.211; Kohler–Koch, 2008, p.279
91 Kohler–Koch, 2008, p.279

of a conflict of interests[92]. Through the use of external and grassroots expertise, facilitated access to official documents, and increasing overall transparency of the policy process, the Commission seeks to improve its input legitimacy and to achieve greater acceptance for its policy proposals by civil society and citizens[93]. The need for external expertise is not only explainable by reasons of refining its institutional identity[94], but also by the fact that, as a public administration, the Commission is highly understaffed, when compared with its national counterparts and therefore dependent on the external provision of data, facts and information[95]. In addition, the reliance on well–researched and reputable information in form of input–legitimacy[96] enhances the role of the Commission in inter–institutional bargaining during the legislating process[97].

Influenced by the debate on the principles of 'good governance', the Commission has attempted to embrace a more open, inclusive and transparent policy style, which dramatically facilitates the opportunities for organized interests to grant citizens a voice[98]. Yet, even though the variety of interests that are considered by the respective DG have been augmented, the Commission has been criticized for privileging well–established European federations or associations of national interest groups over small, independent and local or national CSOs and thereby encouraging elite groups that are detached from citizens' interests[99]. The practicality of this preference is fairly obvious. Civil servants assume that the position of "Euro–feds" equals the compromised sum of all national positions. Thus, consulting groups that fulfill the criteria of representativeness (for instance, existing in a specified number of Member States and representing a considerable part of the European population) is time– and stress–reducing for the civil servants who undertake the consultations[100]. In addition, these transnational associations may also be better equipped with financial resources, not in the least thanks to the funding by the Commission, which amounts up to one percent of the entire EU budget (approximately 1bn ECU)[101], are well–staffed and, most importantly, have their own office in Brussels and are therefore able to quickly adapt to new situations. This approach has provoked much criticism not only by those CSOs that do not have easy access to the consultation processes of the Commission but also by a considerable number of political scholars, who argue that this selective promotion is not capable of reducing the democratic deficit of the Union.

---

92 Greenwood, 2007a, p.34; Randzio–Plath, 2004, p.7
93 Greenwood, 2007b, pp.180 & 183; Greenwood, 2007a, p.35; Zimmer & Freise, 2008, p.32
94 Hilger, 2008, p.186
95 Zimmer & Freise, 2008, p.32; Greenwood, 2007a, pp.1, 3 & 7; Greenwood, 2007b, pp.179–180; Finke, 2007, p.6; Dür, 2008, p.1215
96 Greenwood, 2007c, p.343
97 Saurugger, 2008, p.1281
98 Kohler–Koch & Finke, 2007, pp.211–212
99 Zimmer & Sittermann, 2004, p.30; Greenwood, 2007a, pp.14 & 35; Friedrich, 2008, p.78; Finke, 2007, p.18
100 Greenwood, 2007b, p.188
101 Maloney & Van Deth, 2008, pp.8–9; Greenwood, 2007a, p.1

On part of the stakeholders, the Commission has become an attractive venue - and the primary target among EU Institutions - for lobbying activities for several reasons. Not only is the Commission the main initiator of legislation and therefore determines the policy agenda and is heavily involved in the formulation of legislative acts, but it also formulates priorities and action plans that have a validity for several years[102]. Overall, the Commission has recognized the role of civil society as a source of information, support for further European integration, as well as a source of democratic legitimacy for its own position[103].

5.3.2. European Economic and Social Committee

Among all EU Institutions, the European Economic and Social Committee seeks the most to maintain well–established relations with CSOs[104]. The EESC even regards itself to "[speak] on behalf of civil society organisations"[105]. As an institution, the committee provides an excellent forum for the exchange of opinions among economic and industrial representatives and complementary as well as competing social interests[106]. Indeed, the EESC has actively contributed to the inclusion of civil society into the debate on European governance and has actually introduced the notion of 'organized civil society' as "the sum of all organisational structures whose members have objectives and responsibilities that are of general interest and who also act as mediators between the public authorities and citizens"[107]. These broadly include all kinds of social activities of a non–state character, which can take a variety of interests. Those autonomous organizations intend to participate in political affairs in a spirit of solidarity and thereby take responsibility for their actions and increase public awareness[108]. When compared with the definition that is commonly agreed upon by many political scientists, it is important to note that both, theorists and practitioners, emphasize the mediating role of CSOs and underline their organized structure, meaning that these are to a greater or lesser degree institutionalized. However, while academics fiercely point to the indispensability of the voluntary nature of these organizations, the EESC silently neglects this. It is additionally important that the committee demands "objectives and responsibilities that are of general interest" as a criterion, while the EESC itself represents rather sectoral interests.

Not only has the EESC introduced the term into "Eurospeak" and nourished the debate on participatory opportunity structures but it has also established certain criteria on the representativeness of civil society since 2006. The EESC suggests admitting those

102 Greenwood, 2007a, p.24; Greenwood, 2007b, p.183

103 Mazey & Richardson, 2006, p.249; Smismans, 2003, p.481

104 e.g. Eisele, 2008, p.88; Zimmer & Sittermann, 2004, p.24

105 European Economic and Social Committee, 1999, *Opinion of the Economic and Social Committee on The Role and Contribution of Civil Society Organisations in the building of Europe*, p.11

106 Smismans, 2003, p.483

107 European Economic and Social Committee, 1999, p.7; cf. Zimmer & Freise, 2008, p.33; Zimmer & Sittermann, 2004, p.24

108 Smismans, 2003, p.482

CSOs that fulfill the following criteria to a more exclusive level of close institutionalized relations. Such organizations must exist permanently at EU level and should additionally have member or sub–organizations in the majority of the Member States. They shall furthermore have the authority to represent interests to the EU Institutions that are already recognized by their national governments. Most importantly, the type of interest must be of general concern to contemporary society. Finally, those organizations should be transparent in their financial resources and internal decision–making procedures, must be independent from any other state or non–state body, and should ensure that their members are accountable internally as well as to the public. Ideally, CSOs should also provide expert knowledge and supplementary information[109].

In its relations with CSOs, the EESC established in 2004, in addition to a number of stakeholder forums, a Liaison Group, which, despite the fact that high–rank officials of the EESC were present, lagged behind its expectations and is fairly weakly institutionalized[110]. Taken as a whole, the EESC fails to meet its own aspiration as constituting a bridge between Europe and organized civil society. Its membership does not represent the whole range of sectoral interests as are reflected by CSOs and especially citizen interest groups are comparatively under–represented and are only included informally in hearings and conventions[111]. In addition, the committee's own role in the EU policy process is fairly weak. Although, in some cases, the Council and EP may not take a legislative decision before having received the opinion of the EESC within a specified time period, there is no duty for the legislators to abide by the suggestions made by the committee. In addition, these opinions are not only delivered at a fairly late stage in the legislation process but also sometimes belated so that decisions are taken without even considering the working effort of the committee[112]. It is for these reasons that CSOs may find it more efficient for the realization of their aims to seek participatory opportunity structures of other EU Institutions.

5.3.3. European Parliament

The EP treats civil society – or more precisely, the various approaches towards participatory democracy – with ambiguity[113]. Obviously, a parliament is by its very nature, a traditional target of lobbying practices by interest groups, since it is a venue of deliberation and a holder of the powers necessary to take final legislative decisions[114]. This is not surprising given that Members of Parliament generally enjoy close links to their constituency, including those organizations that represent interests that are particularly at stake in that region[115]. Due to their democratic credentials, CSOs have created stable

---

109 Eisele, 2008, pp.96–97
110 Eisele, 2008, pp.98 & 102
111 Greenwood, 2007a, p.40; Eisele, 2008, p.104
112 Eisele, 2008, p.89
113 Greenwood, 2007b, p.184
114 Greenwood, 2007a, p.24; Greenwood, 2007b, p.179
115 Greenwood, 2007a, p.24

and long–lasting relationships with Parliamentarians[116]. In addition, the provision of expert knowledge and information complementing the limited resources of the EP's staff is probably to be classified as important in the decision–making process as in the pre–legislative phase in the Commission[117]. Regarding Members of the European Parliament (MEP), over ninety percent admit to have regular monthly meetings with representatives of organized civil society[118]. Particularly environmental interest groups are on an easier footing with Parliamentarians given that those concerns are quite widespread among the electorate[119].

However, the crucial difference between the Commission, and to a lesser extent also the EESC, and the EP is the degree of institutionalization of these relations with civil society. Contacts between MEPs and interest groups are of a far more informal nature. Although the Parliament has established a system of issuing a maximum number of four permanent entrance permits per organization (irrelevant of the size or nature of that organization) since 1997[120], the codes of conduct for interest representatives as well as staff working in the EP are not very elaborated. These codes are annexed to the EP's rules of procedure[121] and primarily inhibit the acquisition of information under false pretenses, as well as to invoke relations to the Parliament with regard to third parties, and the duty to disclose the nature of their represented interests to MEPs, their staff, or civil servants. In case of violation of these rules, the permanent entrance permit will be withdrawn automatically; yet this has, to date, not occurred. In addition to informal contacts at the level of the MEP's constituency or outside the parliamentary buildings, a member of an interest group may even officially work as an assistant to a MEP for one year[122].

Yet, there is also silent unease prevalent in the treatment of the EP towards civil society[123]. The enthusiastic embrace of participatory democracy by other EU Institutions invokes the fear of the EP that it may be bypassed in important decisions. The Parliament has come a long way since its relatively little importance as an assembly and finally evolved into a legislator on an equal footing with the Council under the ordinary co–decision procedure. The EP, as the sole directly elected EU Institution, represents the populations of the EU Member States "indiscriminately" and may be the only one to be democratic accountable to its people and therefore legitimatized[124]. In addition, it still challenges the representativity of those organizations with regard to the actual concerns and needs of the citizens and regards itself, since the first direct elections in 1979,

116 Greenwood, 2007a, p.38
117 Meyer–Ohlendorf, 2004, p.99
118 Greenwood, 2007a, p.38
119 Greenwood, 2007a, p.137
120 Friedrich, 2008, p.77; Randzio–Plath, 2004, p.6
121 European Parliament, 2010, *Rules of Procedure of the European Parliament*, Rule 9(4) and Annex X; Randzio–Plath, 2004, p.6
122 Randzio–Plath, 2004, p.7
123 Kohler–Koch, 2010, p.108
124 Kohler–Koch, 2010, p.108

as the sole democratically legitimatized institution on European level[125]. The attempts by the Commission and the EESC to improve their democratic ties to the population and enhance their legitimacy through civil society as the intermediary sphere are observed with great skepticism. Thus, the EP was eager to emphasize in its reaction to the White Paper on European Governance that "organised civil society [...] whilst important, [...] [is] inevitably sectoral and cannot be regarded as having its own democratic legitimacy"[126] and that merely to the contrary, the sole "basis for a European system with democratic legitimacy" would be "the involvement of both the European and national parliaments[127].

Moreover, for individual MEPs, exclusive reliance on interest group contacts may endanger their re–election. Politicians are usually elected on grounds of a prior publicly announced stance towards a specific issue. Given that they are accountable to their electorate in their respective constituency, a change of position or unpopular decisions taken during a legislative period may be punished in the follow–up elections[128].
It is consequently not surprising that the EP regards the inclusion of CSOs into the policy process only as an additional source of information and expert input as opposed to participatory structures reducing the democratic deficit. The latter should, in its view, be tackled by an increase in the quality of parliamentary powers and the quantity of policies in which these powers are executed[129].

5.3.4. Council of Ministers

The Council of Ministers maintains only weakly developed relations with civil society[130]. While the other EU Institutions have been supranationalized to varying degrees, the Council still strictly represents the intergovernmental mode of international relations. National positions are represented by national delegates, who have to abide by the defined statement of their governments. Accordingly, European federations or umbrella organizations would have difficulty in accessing the responsible person. It is far more efficient for national CSOs to lobby governments that formulate national positions.

Yet, nonetheless, the Council has also undertaken a small number of efforts to increase the inclusiveness and transparency of its political processes, such as a decision that established an action program to promote active European citizenship[131]. However, the implementation of these efforts, both formally and informally, is unfortunately lagging behind the envisaged aims, which currently results in the situation that consultation of external actors appears to be "by grace and favour"[132].

---

125 Greenwood, 2007b, p.184
126 European Parliament, 2001, *European Parliament resolution on the Commission White Paper on European Governance*, Point 11(a)
127 European Parliament, 2001, Point 8
128 Dür, 2008, pp.1216–1217
129 Smismans, 2003, pp.484–485
130 Kohler–Koch, 2010, p.108
131 Maloney & Van Deth, 2008, p.5
132 Friedrich, 2008, p.77

5.3.5. Committee of Regions

The Committee of Regions could offer an exceptional opportunity for local and regional CSOs to be included in the policy process and to contribute to a more balanced interest representation by outweighing the predominance of European umbrella organizations. This would be particularly important for those interests that may not be included in such transnational associations or are ranking in the lower area of priorities of the group's agenda.

Yet, most local and regional public authorities already have close relations with CSOs on–site, so that the positions defended in the committee might already be influenced by the lobbying of civil society. The CoR also stresses the importance of the principle of subsidiarity and the fact that democratic legitimacy can best be achieved through directly elected representatives and not through participatory mechanisms for external actors. The committee would thus rather view civil society as a source of grassroots information rather than one of legitimacy[133]. Furthermore, although it recognizes the potential of CSOs to contribute to political deliberation, it firmly states that the Committee itself bears the "exclusive legitimacy as an institutional discussion partner for the local and regional authorities of the Union"[134]. Of course, it should be kept in mind that the CoR may not be a very attractive target of interest lobbying given its simple consultative status in the EU legislative process. CSOs might find it more efficient to allocate their resources to more profitable political players.

133 cf. Greenwood, 2007a, p.41
134 Smismans, 2003, p.485

6. The EU Participatory Policy Cycle

6.1. Participatory Policy Cycle – A Model outlining Opportunity Structures within the EU

Policy Analysis has emerged prominently within political science in the 1970s and 1980s and intended to explain how policies come into being and, in particular, to determine why certain decisions are taken by which actors involved.

The Model

The model is based on the assumptions and findings formulated by Howlett and Ramesh in *Studying Public Policy. Policy Cycles and Policy Subsystems*[1] and the image created by Jann and Wegrich in their article *Phasenmodelle und Politikprozesse: Der Policy Cycle* in the book "Lehrbuch der Politikfeldanalyse" edited by Schubert and Bandelow[2].

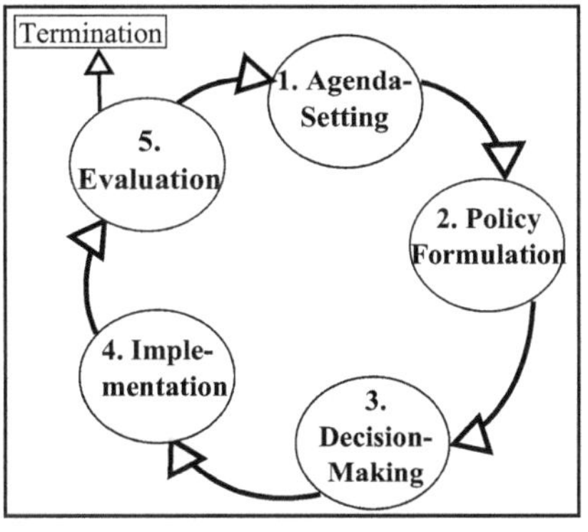

Figure 3: General Policy Cycle, based on Jann & Wegrich, 2003

Policy analysts assume that policies loosely follow a number of subsequent, so–called, 'stages' in which first, a problem is identified and placed on the political agenda and for which secondly, a response is formulated and selected among a number of alternatives. At the third stage, a formal decision is taken and the chosen policy is implemented at the respective governance level by the relevant authority. The outcome of the preceding

1 2003, 2nd edition, Oxford University Press

2 2003, Oldenbourg Wissenschaftsverlag, pp.71–104

stages is then evaluated at the fifth stage of the policy cycle, which either results in the continuation of a successful policy, its termination, or revision. Its circular illustration delineates the ideal evolution of policies that do not develop in a strict linear manner having a clear and determinable starting and ending point, but rather evolve out of earlier policies and the motivation to improve the status quo[3].

The model does not illustrate two obvious truths. Of course, the policy cycle can be stalled or terminated within or between any of the stages. It is similarly possible to go back to a stage already passed and repeat and improve specific steps.

Criticism

The theoretical model of the policy cycle is not undisputed among political scientists. Particularly with regard to the working habits in some states, this mode of analysis is considered useless to grasp the complexity of policy–making. Yet, scholars of EU policies find policy cycle analysis useful and illustrative in terms of separating the respective institutions' functions and identifying all stakeholders involved in the process.

The policy cycle is heavily criticized for its "*heuristic*"[4] illustration of policy–making, which ignores the complexity and neglects its individual dynamic. Policy–making appears "too easy, too unproblematic"[5], as it implies that policies merely need to pass through each stage consecutively in order to be classified as successful[6]. Doubts have further been raised about its claim to provide a generally valid description of how policies come into existence. Some assume that, instead of describing the typical evolutionary process, it rather defines the exception to the rule[7]. It is, thus, not possible to formulate generally applicable explanations suitable for the creation, execution and termination of *any* policy that could empirically be tested[8]. Critics, therefore, declare that the single stages cannot as easily be distinguished from one another and rather intermingle or vanish completely[9].

At the same time, this simplification may be one of the model's greatest strengths. It enables political scientists to structure and reduce the complexity of policy–making processes and thereby offers the opportunity to examine each phase individually, as well as the development of the whole policy[10]. The model extends the actor–centered research and places their specific behavior and influence in the context of the respective policy stages[11]. This is particularly relevant for democracy and administrative research[12].

---

3 Jann & Wegrich, 2003, p.81
4 Blum & Schubert, 2009, p.130; Jann & Wegrich, 2003, p.96
5 translated from German: Blum & Schubert, 2009, p.132
6 Blum & Schubert, 2009, p.132; Jann & Wegrich, 2003, p.97
7 Blum & Schubert, 2009, p.130
8 Blum & Schubert, 2009, p.130; Jann & Wegrich, 2003, pp.63, 96 & 99
9 Blum & Schubert, 2009, p.130; Jann & Wegrich, 2003, pp.63 & 96
10 Blum & Schubert, 2009, p.131
11 cf. Blum & Schubert, 2009, p.130; Schneider & Janning, 2006, pp.62–63
12 Jann & Wegrich, 2003, p.99

Its simple structure, therefore, merely provides the basic framework and is flexible enough to be supplemented and revised according to the author's preferences[13] as has bee done at the end of this chapter.

Another point of criticism refers to the inability to explain causalities in policy–making. The formulation of theoretical assumptions and hypotheses that may be tested empirically already fails, given that it is hardly possible to define the necessary variables. Questions, for instance, of why specific policies succeed and others fail, when one policy stage ends and another begins, or which actors are particularly influential, cannot be answered when solely relying on the policy cycle model[14]. A related concern has been raised about the strict separation of the individual stages. As stated above, the oversimplification neglects the fact that the transition between the stages is blurred and fluid. Moreover, the graphic illustration of the policy cycle model does not account for the time aspect. Stages do not follow each other in a linear and timely evenly dispersed manner but may run parallel to and mutually influence each other or include long pauses until new action is initiated[15]. Yet, most stages have been analyzed by political scientists in isolation and with the utilization of various theoretical approaches, each distinct for a specific policy stage[16].

These points add up to true and valid arguments against the exclusive use of the policy cycle model as a theoretical framework of a policy scientific work. However, this has never been disputed by proponents of the model, simply because the model does not aim at providing this type of solution. To the contrary, it is intended to complement the stage–model with theoretical approaches that aim at explaining causalities. The policy cycle merely *structures* the framework, in which theories are applied to answer scientific questions and confirm or refute hypotheses[17].

Although policy analysis is said to contain a top–down bias and to take the perspective of the legislator[18], the combination of top–down and bottom–up approaches throughout the cycle, thereby taking account of the various stakeholders involved in the policy–process, has nourished rather than impeded academic debate and empirical findings on policy–making[19].

Participation during the cyclical Policy Process

However, most of the points of criticism raised above are not of great importance with regard to this project. The aim of the dissertation is not to reconstruct the process of a specific environmental policy at EU level, beginning with the recognition of the problem and ending with its evaluation. Rather, it is intended to identify the relevant EU

13 Blum & Schubert, 2009, p.133
14 Blum & Schubert, 2009, p.131; Jann & Wegrich, 2003, pp.64 & 97
15 Blum & Schubert, 2009, p.133; Jann & Wegrich, 2003, p.63
16 Blum & Schubert, 2009, p.131; Jann & Wegrich, 2003, p.96
17 cf. Blum & Schubert, 2009, p.131; Jann & Wegrich, 2003, p.96
18 Jann & Wegrich, 2003, p.96
19 cf. Blum & Schubert, 2009, p.132; Jann & Wegrich, 2003, p.95

Institutions active during the policy–making process and to find possible access and participation opportunities for civil society organizations.

The policy cycle thereby aids to structure the process and to identify the particular function of a given institution. Depending on the role that an institution is attributed at a specific policy stage, potential stakeholders adapt strategies that take due account of the relevant structural circumstances within the institution and the specific phase of the policy development[20].

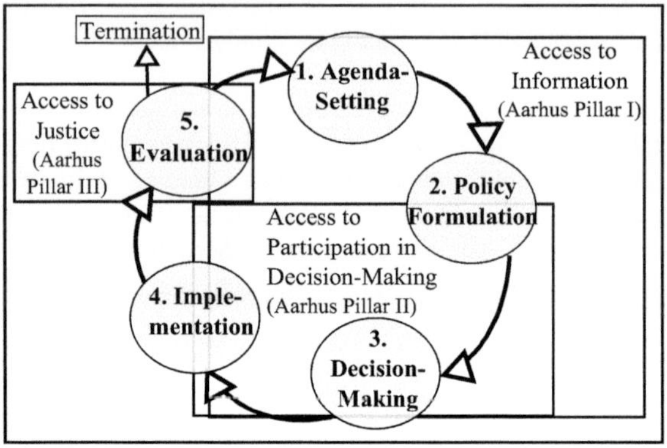

Figure 4: The Policy Cycle and the three Pillars of the Aarhus Convention

The model above shows the simplified policy cycle and the corresponding pillars of the Aarhus Convention that are made visible by the shaded squares. According to these assumptions, the call of the Aarhus Convention for more involvement of the public concerned in policy–making can be distributed as follows. Access to information (largest area of the shaded squares) is undeniably important at any stage of the policy cycle; even at the evaluation stage, if governmental authorities are in the possession of information that are not publicly available. However, it may possibly be most important at setting the political agenda and the first drafts during the policy formulation stage. The latter also corresponds to the right for CSOs to participate in decision–making as these organizations may be well suited to propose alternative policy solutions. The right guaranteed under the second Aarhus pillar, of course, extends to the third stage of the policy cycle. The implementation phase of a policy is already occupied by assisting and monitoring civil society organizations. Finally, the evaluation stage of the policy cycle corresponds to the third pillar of the Aarhus Convention that aims at providing improved access to courts for the concerned public. The emphasis is here placed on the legal evaluation of policies (cf. 6.2.5).

20 For a critical examination of participatory or post–positivist policy analysis, cf. Schneider & Janning, 2006, pp.212–214.

6.2. The Policy Stages

6.2.1. Agenda–Setting

As indicated before, one explicit starting point for a particular policy decision cannot be determined. Yet, it is, nonetheless, the most common approach to begin the description of the policy cycle with the stage of agenda–setting[21]. This is considered to be a decisive phase given that this moment determines what is to be regarded as a serious problem by those, who are politically responsible and which requires political efforts in order to be solved[22]. Thus, the recognition of a problem and its placement on the agenda are of course subsequent steps, yet interlinked, and can be included into the same policy stage[23].

The recognition of a problem and agenda–setting are genuine political processes. It must be selected, which of the social problems that affect the citizens of a state, are to be put on the political agenda[24]. Interest groups and public media are crucial actors in turning the attention of political decision–makers to a given problem[25]. It is therefore indispensable to identify current problems and to bring them to the attention of governmental actors and finally to persuade the latter that political action is needed and suitable by putting forward systematic arguments that are both specific to the given problem and relate to the overall objectives of the EU at one time[26].

The decision to place a problem on the political agenda and to put the policy cycle into operation is neither automatic[27] nor a rational one that can easily be either comprehended or foreseen on the basis of fixed explanatory variables. It is rather determined by a coincidental constellation of the actors and stakeholders involved, their internal capabilities and the influence of external agendas and events[28].

At EU level, Kohler–Koch mentions the conceptualization of the "greenhouse" as an illustrative example for the success of, in this case environmental interest groups, to define a specific problem, to win allies in DG Environment of the Commission, and to reformulate the issue insofar as to convince staff in other primarily economic Directorates–General of the necessity to act. The public debate that was further initiated by activists and Commission alike at both global as well as national levels ensured Member States' support for the proposal submitted by the Commission[29].

---

21 cf. Jann & Wegrich, 2003, p.83; Blum & Schubert, 2009, p.105
22 Howlett & Ramesh, 2003, p.120; Jann & Wegrich, 2003, p.83; Schneider & Janning, 2006, p.50
23 Blum & Schubert, 2009, p.105
24 Jann & Wegrich, 2003, p.83; Blum & Schubert, 2009, p.106
25 Jann & Wegrich, 2003, p.84; Blum & Schubert, 2009, pp.106 & 108
26 Knodt & Große Hüttmann, 2006, p.230; Kohler–Koch, 1997, p.64
27 Howlett & Ramesh, 2003, p.141
28 Jann & Wegrich, 2003, pp.84–85; Blum & Schubert, 2009, p.109
29 Kohler–Koch, 1997, p.63

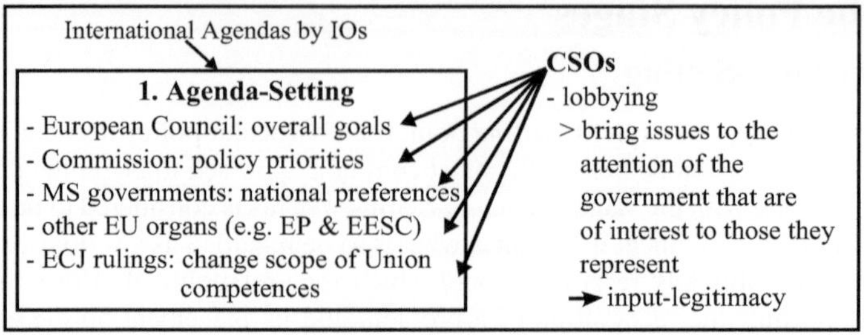

Figure 5: Agenda–Setting

The overall agenda, stipulating specific goals for further European integration, is determined by the Heads of State and Government in the European Council at their semi–annual summits. Particularly the country that holds the presidency introduces a, mostly ambitious, agenda of strategic political decisions or policy aims that should be achieved within its term of office. However, these goals usually simply describe the general direction in and the pace at which cooperation among European states should be pursued. Hence, the Commission, which is detached from national governments' interests, also publishes an agenda including the policy goals that are to be achieved. The Commission's schedule, although usually covering a period of several years, stipulates already in much detail the policy instruments and tools with which these goals are intended to be achieved. In the area of environmental protection, the Environmental Action Programs, published by the Commission, serve as one example.

Of course, national governments also have their domestic policy objectives that they cannot implement effectively without the combined effort on the supranational level of governance. National cabinets and parliaments accordingly formulate policy programs that they want to press through on European level and will therefore try to influence the supranational political agenda according to domestic policy preferences. Influences on the supranational agenda are also executed by other EU Institutions, including, of course, the European Parliament as the co–legislator and, for instance, the Economic and Social Committee. In addition, the aforementioned citizen initiative may also add topics and policy proposals to the supranational agenda.

Re–emphasizing the primary focus of this dissertation, the potential of ECJ rulings for setting the policy agenda cannot be ignored. In general, there are three ways, in which the Court can formulate rulings that may influence the legal scope of subsequent legislation. However, only the first possibility can be categorized at the agenda–setting stage; the other two refer to the formulation of polices (cf. below). The judges may interpret articles of the Treaties in a manner that extends the scope of competences and hence, may provide a new basis for legislation or an extension of law–making competences on EU level.

All agenda–setting institutions mentioned so far are governmental organs and therefore politically authorized to determine the road map of European integration. Yet, external actors also execute considerable influence on the formulation of policy goals. International obligations to which individual Member States (e.g. UNO, NATO) or even the European Union (WTO) are bound and the preferences of IOs for strategic action may be reflected in the policy goals of the EU. Hence, there is interplay between the policy priorities placed by national, supra– and international systems of governance. This is quite logical given that, in times of liberalization of economic markets, global problems affect all countries, connect states with one another, and may force them to find appropriate responses through interstate cooperation.

Hence, CSOs do not only attempt to lobby one sphere of the multiple levels of governance but rather employ a distinct strategy with regard to local and national governments, to EU Institutions, and the secretaries and representatives of IOs. Thus, CSOs have a variety of access points to which they can try to bring specific issues to the attention of members of government and elaborate on the problem in order for it to be put on the political agenda.

The model also indicates the type of legitimacy that is expected from the inclusion of CSOs. The description of prevalent theories on political participation has already distinguished between *input* ('government *by* the people') and *output* legitimacy ('government *for* the people'). With regard to the first stage of the policy cycle, it is fairly obvious that agenda–setting is attributed to input legitimacy, as the interests of the respective parts of the population may be placed on the political agenda through the efforts of CSOs.

6.2.2. Policy Formulation

After politicians have become aware of a problem and placed it on the political agenda[30], the nature of the problem and its effects need to be precisely identified in order to formulate an adequate response that should ideally solve the apparent problems[31]. Thus, the second stage is termed 'policy formulation', given that alternative proposals are suggested, discussed, amended, dismissed, optimized, and prepared for adoption; sometimes on the basis of cost–benefit analyses. This concerns not only the content of the decision but, as importantly, also the legal form of the policy instrument[32]. Throughout the process, mere ideas and opinions are structured into concrete policy instruments and programs[33]. Such instruments range from broad programs over general action plans to legislation with very specific provisions. These policy instruments are increasingly formulated by civil servants in ministries and comparable administrative bureaucracies[34]. Still, this stage offers several participation opportunities for non–state actors, i.e. civil society groups, which may insist on their interests and achieve an adequate bargaining position by providing technical expertise and factual knowledge[35]. Scholars of policy analysis have described the interplay between state and private actors as "policy net-

30 Howlett & Ramesh, 2003, p.143
31 Blum & Schubert, 2009, p.113
32 Howlett & Ramesh, 2003, pp.143–144; Blum & Schubert, 2009, pp.114, 120; Schneider & Janning, 2006, pp.56 & 57
33 Jann & Wegrich, 2003, p.85
34 Jann & Wegrich, 2003, p.86
35 Jann & Wegrich, 2003, pp.87 & 88; Blum & Schubert, 2009, pp.113–114

works"[36], "policy communities"[37], or "advocacy coalitions"[38], depending on the degree of involvement and mutual dependencies.

Again, no rational or objectively 'correct' solution can be offered to a given problem at hand. Rather, as at the agenda–stage, the formulated policy solution is a compromise resulting from bargaining of all interests that were able to participate in the process[39].

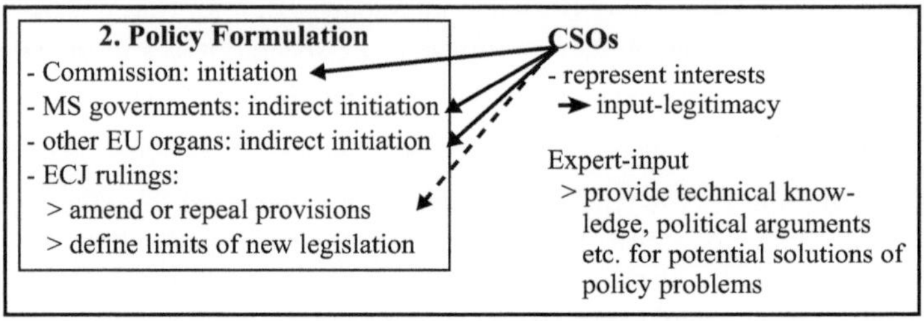

Figure 6: Policy Formulation

Under the former EC Treaty, the Commission had the exclusive power to prepare draft legislation and Council and Parliament mainly amended the legislative text. The Lisbon Treaty qualified this *monopoly of initiation* on part of the Commission. Next to the EP and the Council, also national parliaments, as well as initiatives supported by "no less than one million citizens"[40] may request the Commission to prepare such proposals. Still, however, much of the preparation and formulation work will be done within the Directorates–General of the Commission. Civil servants working in the responsible DGs cannot work in complete isolation from the interests of the other institutions, let alone those of national governments. Keeping in mind that Council and Parliament must adopt legislation, i.e. approve the proposals initiated by the Commission, their opinions will already be taken into account in the early stage of drafting. If either institution refuses to adopt a new piece of legislation, all efforts and work invested by Commission officials and other actors will have been of no use but rather a waste of time. In addition, the consultative bodies of the EU, CoR and EESC, have the opportunity to deliver their opinions and propose amendments. Still, the Commission is considered by most, including the proponents of the multi–level governance approach, to be the most important EU Institution at this stage of the policy cycle. It is quite reasonable therefore, that private actors have focused their lobbying activities at this policy stage towards the respective DG within the Commission that is responsible for the formulation of the draft legislation at issue[41].

36 Katzenstein, 1977; cf. Howlett & Ramesh, 2003, p.150
37 Wilks and Wright, 1987; cf. Howlett & Ramesh, 2003, p.151
38 Jenkin–Smith and Sabatier, 1993; cf. Howlett & Ramesh, 2003, pp.151–152
39 Blum & Schubert, 2009, p.115
40 Article 11(4) TEU LT
41 Knodt & Große Hüttmann, 2006, p.230

Again, the Court of Justice may exert some degree of influence on the legislative branch of government. The first possibility was already discussed within the circumstances of agenda–setting; however, the remaining two are directly related to the formulation stage of the policy cycle. Thus, in cases where a specific piece of legislation is reviewed, the Court can also stipulate in its decisions that an existing legislative act is annulled in total or, more commonly, that parts should be repealed or amended. In many instances, the judgment will lay down the limits to which the amendments of the legislation must abide, i.e. the judges determine the scope of the reformed law. Alternatively, the judges may also state general or more specific requirements that future legislation must adhere to. The ECJ then employs judicial rulemaking. The legislative branch of government, i.e. Commission, Council, and EP, is required to abide by the decisions of the Court and the limitations set therein.

Although the Commission was identified as the primary target of lobby activism, CSOs will nevertheless attempt to exert influence at different levels of governance and employ distinctive strategies to persuade state actors of the benefits of their positions when pursuing their arguments. While at the first stage, transnational civil society and other private actors mainly concentrate on bringing up a specific problem, i.e. focusing on the existence of such a problem and the possible, in most cases negative, effects on polities. Here, the focal point is placed upon potential solutions to the declared problem. Arguments will then not rely on the mere existence and effects but rather suggest policy instruments and tools that may be able to at least reduce or even abolish any negative effects on the population within the respective system of governance.

The Commission has proven to be the primary target not only given its status as provided for in the Treaties but also because it offers one of the most institutionalized opportunity structures. The publication of Green and White Papers prior to the official initiation of specific legislation has enabled external actors to respond to policy projects. It is even the case that the Commission not only welcomes external opinions but actively seeks them for several reasons. Commission staff in the Directorates–General is accustomed to balancing the interests of various stakeholders. Rather than being overwhelmed, the additional scientific expertise and technical input is greatly appreciated[42]. This may not least be the result of the fact that the Commission is highly understaffed, lacks specific expertise, and wants to avoid having to rely completely on national administrations. Hence, while separating themselves from Member States' officials, the Commission strives to receive the relevant information from other, primarily non–governmental sources[43]. Yet, the multiple levels of governance are also prevalent in this regard as national and subnational civil servants are seconded to the Commission either on a temporary basis or to fill permanent posts[44]. National officials regularly participate in meetings at European level and are thus familiarized with the ordinary practice in Brussels. Also a great number

42 Bellier, 1997, pp.110–111
43 Bellier, 1997, p.112; Kohler–Koch, 1997, p.56
44 Bellier, 1997, p.112; Kohler–Koch, 1997, p.48

of national and local administrative staff is involved in the implementation process of European legislation[45].

Official hearings and formalized and transparent consultation schemes have facilitated the dialog with all stakeholders and enabled equal treatment of all groups[46]. A positive side–effect is certainly the greater impediment for larger, well–resourced lobbyists to exert unlawful pressure upon Commission staff to secure the adherence to their respective interests in the legislation[47].

This stage of the policy cycle is very crucial for external actors given that they may be able to determine the content of future legislation. Practical experience has revealed that the exertion of influence will be most successful, if interest groups already enter the preparation of legislative texts at the earliest stage possible. Roughly eighty percent of the substantive demands within the original legislative act remain unmodified after having passed the adoption stage. This is quite impressive. Still, only an estimated five percent of all interest groups follow this strategy, whereas the vast majority of lobbyists only becomes active, once the Commission has published its intentions and officially started consultation proceedings. Overall, interest groups have adapted their own structure to the institutional system of the EU as well as their lobbying tactics[48]. They, thus, not only represent the general intentions and opinions of their members but must also provide convincing arguments, technical information, and expert knowledge in order to successfully persuade decision–makers. In sum, a combination of "expert knowledge, political insight and bargaining experience" counts to the capabilities of the most successful interest representative organizations[49].

6.2.3. Decision–Making

At the third stage of the policy cycle, "authorized public authorities" select one from numerous policy alternatives and issue a "formal or informal statement of intent [...] to undertake, or refrain from undertaking, some action"[50]. It thus ends the process of exploring alternative proposals and settles in a (constitutionally) prescribed formal procedure on one final decision[51]. As indicated before, binding policy (non–)decisions are only taken by governmental actors that have the authority to have a *vote*, whereas private actors may merely make their *voice* heard by "engag[ing] in various kinds of 'lobbying' activities aimed at persuading, encouraging and sometimes even coercing" the former[52]. Most models outlining the policy cycle combine the actual adoption of a decision with the formulation process of a policy. This is quite reasonable, given that, in most gover-

45 Wessels, 1997, pp.28–29
46 Bellier, 1997, p.111; Kohler–Koch, 1997, p.48
47 Bellier, 1997, p.111
48 Bellier, 1997, pp.110 & 113
49 Kohler–Koch, 1997, p.48
50 Howlett & Ramesh, 2003, p.162
51 Howlett & Ramesh, 2003, pp.162 & 164
52 Howlett & Ramesh, 2003, p.163

nance systems, the same political actors formulate, amend and adopt policies [53]. However, for the purposes of this project, it is more suitable to follow the example of Howlett and Ramesh[54] and to thus distinguish these two sequent stages based on the different main actors involved and the different participation opportunities. Strictly speaking, the third stage of the policy cycle on European level formally only involves the Council and the European Parliament as co–legislators. They are the sole institutions that are empowered by the Treaties to adopt legislation and propose amendments. Yet, the Commission, if considering that its proposal has been weakened by numerous amendments by any or both institutions, may withdraw legislation at any stage of the decision–making process. In addition, Commission officials are also present at conciliation committees that facilitate a compromise, where Council and EP have opposing opinions on specific provisions of the legislative act that is to be adopted. As Marks put it, the Commission at this stage "holds the pen" when clarifying or redrafting the initial legislative text[55].

It should further be mentioned that also the Commission and other bodies or even agencies of the EU may adopt decisions or undertake action themselves without the Council and EP being involved. In these circumstances, participation opportunities must, of course, be sought with the responsible authority. The MLG approach has pointed out that the power of single, particularly larger, Member States is reduced by the use of qualified majority voting and the power of the EP as co–legislator. The positions of national governments may furthermore previously be determined by the interests of specific sub-national actors, for instance regional or municipal governments[56]. Thus, interest groups may have to focus their lobbying activities on more than one national ministry in order to gain support of as many members of the Council as possible. Again, the multiple layers of governance become apparent as national and local administrations need to be addressed as much by interest representatives as the permanent representations in Brussels as well as the Council Secretariat[57].

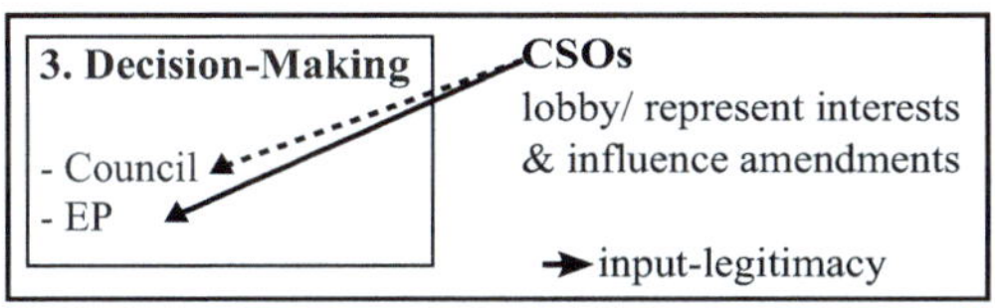

Figure 7: Decision–Making

Overall, however, national governments, as well as Members of the European Parliament, are the primary target of lobbying tactics by interest groups at this stage of the policy process. Their intentions are twofold. First, they aim at influencing possible amendments either positively by encouraging a specific wording or negatively by try-

53 Jann & Wegrich, 2003, p.84; Blum & Schubert, 2009, pp.117–118
54 2003, p.162
55 as cited by: Knodt & Große Hüttmann, 2006, p.232
56 Knodt & Große Hüttmann, 2006, pp.231–232
57 Kohler–Koch, 1997, p.60

ing to leave the original text untouched. Second, they try to persuade as many MEPs and representatives of national governments as possible to vote in their favor either by approving or rejecting the draft legislation. A rejection strategy is most likely to be followed only, once the lobbying in the first two stages has proven to have been unsuccessful. The decision–making stage is clearly an example of input legitimacy.

6.2.4. Implementation

At the fourth stage, an adopted policy is implemented, i.e. set into practice by the relevant administrative actors at the respective level, i.e. supranational, federal, sub–national or local[58]. The choice of the implementation instrument determines, whether civil servants are granted a certain extent of discretion in the execution as long as the predetermined aims are achieved, or whether specific behavior and modes are prescribed[59]. Although the administrative staff in governmental authorities and agencies are primarily responsible for the implementation of policies, the support of non–state actors may greatly facilitate the acceptance and execution of specific rules at grassroots level. In the same manner, their opposition may hamper and delay a smooth implementation process[60].

With the exception of competition policy, the European Commission, although declared executive of the EU, does not implement policies itself. Yet it remains the 'guardian of the Treaties' and monitors Member States' compliance with their legal obligations. Implementation occurs on national level according to the constitutional settings of each Member State. Directives even have to be transposed into national law before being implemented into the domestic legal system. Thus, it is more or less an internal matter for national (or even sub–national) governments to implement EU legislation as long as they do so within the stipulated time period and without breaching their obligations under the Treaties. The Commission and the responsible national authorities remain in sporadic contact throughout the implementation process. This may again spread over all levels of governance, as it not only concerns federal or central institutions, such as national parliaments that adopt transposition measures in order to incorporate EU law into the national legal system, but also extends to regional and local authorities. This is particularly the case in countries with a federal structure, where the relevant legislation affects the competences of the subnational level of governance[61].

---

58 Howlett & Ramesh, 2003, pp.185 & 187; Jann & Wegrich, 2003, p.89
59 cf. Jann & Wegrich, 2003, p.91; Blum & Schubert, 2009, p.125
60 Howlett & Ramesh, 2003, p.189; Greenwood, 2007c, p.431
61 Knodt & Große Hüttmann, 2006, p.232

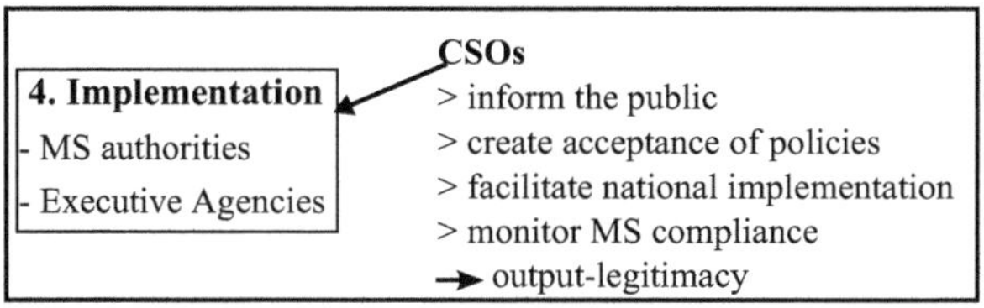

Figure 8: Implementation

Depending on the policy area concerned, executive agencies may also be involved in the implementation process. These agencies were developed as part of the New Public Management approach, under which specific responsibilities and tasks are delegated to lower levels and mostly non–state bodies. This of course affects both the transparency and legitimacy of administrations because the chain of delegation can hardly be retraced by the public. Direct opportunity structures for civil society are therefore not very likely to be prevalent.

Yet, transnational civil society, but particularly interest groups that are active at the local level, are of great value at this stage of the policy process with regard to output legitimacy. Increasing public awareness, e.g. through the use of mass media or public campaigns, which they could use to pressure governments during the first stages of the policy process, will then be of benefit to governments. By turning public attention to the political problems at hand and by promoting their own input into the new law, interest groups not only inform citizens about the newly enacted rules but also enhance public acceptance. If actors other than governmental bodies promote a specific piece of legislation, the population may be more willing to believe that it will bring about positive changes. This in turn may decrease the number of violations of the new law and even avoid non–compliance. Thus, CSOs may facilitate the implementation process for governments through informing the public and promoting the latter's approval[62], provided that the law corresponds with the group's interests.

Overall, the Commission even depends on the monitoring control of local interest groups and their willingness to employ law enforcement mechanisms, e.g. the complainant procedure, which may finally lead to infringement procedures before the ECJ under Article 258 TFEU[63]. The fourth stage thus leans more towards output legitimacy.

6.2.5. Evaluation

The final stage that one specific legislative act needs to undergo is its evaluation, i.e. the assessment on whether it has been correctly implemented and whether it actually brings about the expected change or development within one or more policy areas. The key question to be answered here is whether the policy instrument (legislation) has been capable of providing a workable solution to the problem that was identified on the

62 cf. Schneider & Janning, 2006, p.61
63 Harlow, 1992, pp.343 & 344

agenda[64]. It assesses its actual effectiveness, i.e. the consequences to the policy problem, as well as connected policy areas and persons affected and its financial and otherwise economic efficiency[65]. In short, "policy evaluation assesses the effectiveness of a public policy in terms of its perceived intentions and results"[66]. Evaluation describes not only the political or administrative process of comparing aims with results[67] but extends to public evaluations by the media or the electorate before important elections, and as well to scientific discourses and control instances, such as courts of the judiciary and those of auditors[68]. It further extends to informal modes of examination and "involves most of the key actors arrayed in policy subsystems"[69]. The criteria for the assessment are hence countless and undefined[70].

It is important to note that the final stage for one piece of legislation does not automatically correspond to the final step for a whole policy. Quite the contrary, evaluation may not only lead to the approval of the existing legislation – and the termination of the policy cycle – but in some instances also results in modifications or even the preparation of subsequent legislation[71]. Moreover, negative evaluations may also lead to a termination of the policy cycle based on the fact that the efforts had been disproportionate to the problem and accordingly disappointing given that a practical solution does not seem very realistic at a given time[72].

There are two types of formal evaluation within the EU framework. The administrative assessment is carried out by the Commission, whereas the European Court of Justice is engaged in judicial review. The former assesses the efficiency of the policy in terms of its financial aspects, yet while recognizing the principles of democracy and due administration[73]. Thus, in the words of Howlett and Ramesh, administrative evaluation shall "ensure that policies, are accomplishing their expected goals at the least possible cost and with the least possible burden on the individual"[74]. Judicial evaluation goes even further and examines whether the constitutionally protected rights of the individual had been infringed by the policy. This control includes procedural, as well as substantive rights and extends to the review of legislation and governmental (in–)action on the basis of general principles of law, those enshrined in the constitutional documents, or principles of administrative practice[75].

---

64 Jann & Wegrich, 2003, p.92
65 Blum & Schubert, 2009, pp.126 & 127; Schneider & Janning, 2006, pp.61 & 62
66 Larry Gerston, 1997, p.120 as cited in: Howlett & Ramesh, 2003, p.207
67 Jann & Wegrich, 2003, p.92
68 Howlett & Ramesh, 2003, p.210; Jann & Wegrich, 2003, p.93; Blum & Schubert, 2009, pp.126 & 128
69 Howlett & Ramesh, 2003, p.209
70 Howlett & Ramesh, 2003, p.208; Schneider & Janning, 2006, p.62
71 Howlett & Ramesh, 2003, p.216; Jann & Wegrich, 2003, pp.93 & 94; Blum & Schubert, 2009, pp.128–129; Schneider & Janning, 2006, p.62
72 cf. Blum & Schubert, 2009, p.129
73 Howlett & Ramesh, 2003, p.210
74 2003, p.211
75 cf. Howlett & Ramesh, 2003, p.214

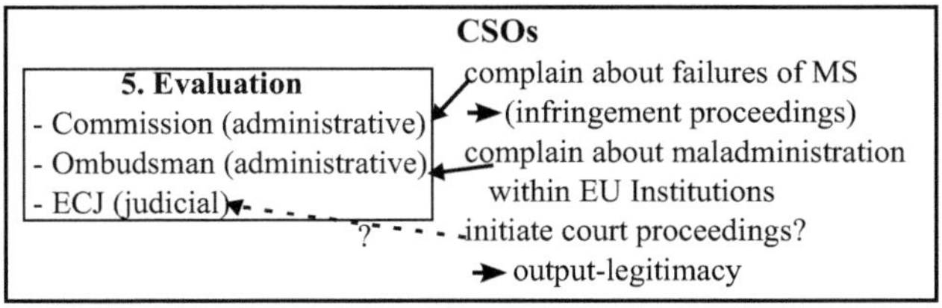

Figure 9: Evaluation

As the 'guardian of the Treaties', the Commission is responsible to ensure that national governments meet their obligations. It thus primarily controls the implementation record of Member States. Incorrect, incomplete, or a complete lack of transposition of EU directives into national legislation will entail infringement proceedings, which may ultimately result before the ECJ under Article 258 TFEU. CSOs may thereby possess a crucial function[76] to make Commission officials aware of the fact that Member States have failed to implement a Union act on environmental protection into national law. As before–mentioned, most CSOs active at the EU level consist of a pyramid structure with many small groups present at local and municipal level, which are combined in a transnational umbrella organization.

Hence, given that the Commission does not have enough staff members to critically observe the implementation of all pieces of legislation in all Member States according to their constitutional specifications, it is even dependent on external observers. Obviously, CSOs have a personal interest at stake when monitoring Member States' compliance with legislation to which the former may have helped to draft. They may accordingly inform the Commission of implementation delays or incorrect transposition. They may furthermore provide evidence that, even in instances in which implementation occurred without any problems, but where the EU act fails to meet its hoped for result. This in turn may either motivate the Commission to initiate new legislation or at least partially influence subsequent legislative proposals.

Yet, whereas access by external actors to methods of administrative evaluation is welcomed by civil servants, it is impeded with regard to judicial review. *Locus standi* concerning European adjudication, i.e. standing rules before the GC and the ECJ, almost entirely exclude private litigants represented by an association. The actual impact of CSOs on judicial rulemaking is therefore clearly limited. Not only are those groups deprived of the opportunity to file new cases to the ECJ (or the GC respectively). Moreover, they are also not able to submit observations regarding cases that are indeed already adjudicated by the Court.

This is quite disappointing, considering that the ECJ is an autonomous, supranational institution, independent from direct Member States' influence and exclusively dedicated

76 cf. Greenwood, 2007c, p.431

to the overall European interest. The pro–integrationist stance of the ECJ has substantially supported further European integration in the past and would accordingly constitute a welcoming venue for civil society activism[77].

However, the above described inclusion of civil society into the other stages of the policy cycle and the appreciation of its participation in the administrative process of legislative evaluation, evokes the question of whether the input provided by CSOs in judicial review could not be enhanced as well. Hence, while presently, the actual ability of influence is heavily restricted, in theory, this may become subject to institutional development and is accordingly the focus of the assessment in the remaining parts of the dissertation.

6.3. Model of the EU Participatory Policy Cycle

As has been discussed above in detail, it is assumed that policies follow a more or less formalized sequence of stages. 'Policy' in this context is defined as the *sum of all decisions by any of the competent EU Institutions or bodies that have an impact on the process of European integration; here: environmental governance.* The main criterion is that the decision must have been taken by a competent organ that had the authority to do so, irrespective of whether the nature of the decision was political, administrative, or judicial. Even more importantly, the decision must be legally binding upon those to whom it was addressed.

The multi–level governance approach as developed by Hooghe and Marks has been introduced. MLG appears to be particularly suitable for the policy cycle analysis on EU level. Recalling that the theoretical framework assumes that European governance disperses political authority among various governmental bodies and non–governmental stakeholders in European policy–making at multiple governance levels, the model further indicates, which actors possess influential positions at each stage of the policy cycle. The range of actors involved includes supranational institutions such as the Commission, the EP, or the ECJ, the intergovernmental Council comprising of the respective national ministry's representatives, as well as national parliaments, political and administrative institutions at subnational level and the whole spectrum of private stakeholders reaching from interest groups from the economic and business sectors to civil society groups or think tanks, research institutes, and other experts[78].

77 Knodt & Große Hüttmann, 2006, p.232

78 Knodt & Große Hüttmann, 2006, pp.229–230; Howlett & Ramesh, 2003, pp.77–79 & 83–84

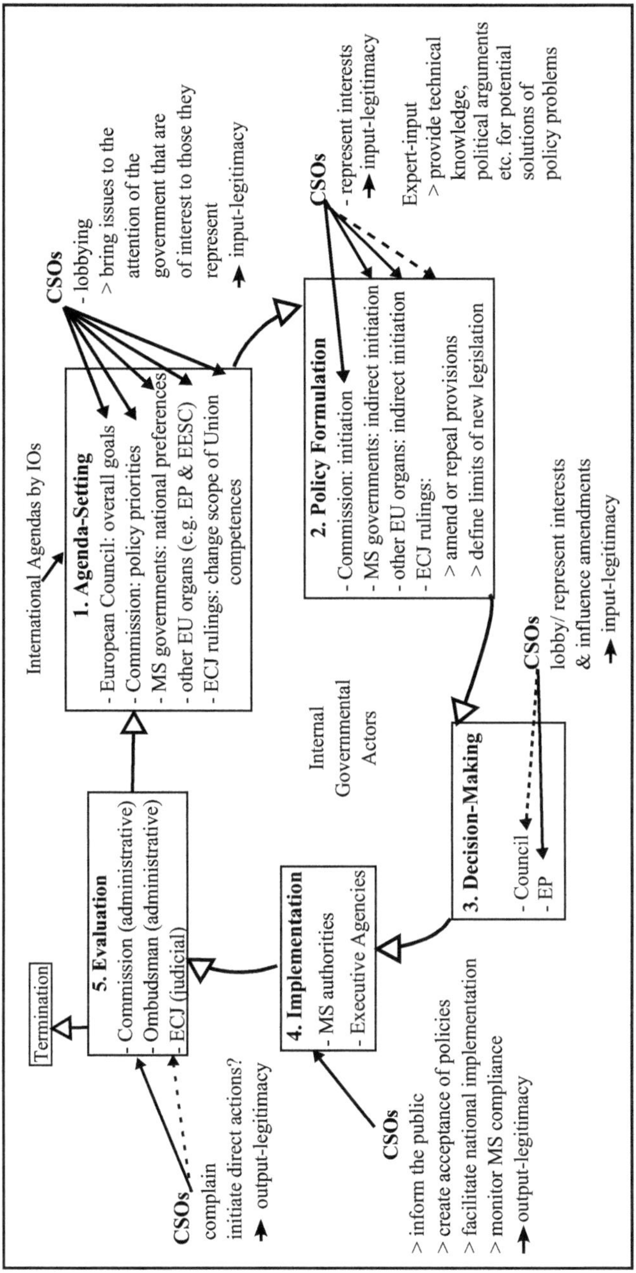

Figure 10: EU Participatory Policy Cycle

By now, these interest groups have become successful and needed policy actors; successful insofar as they have been able to open policy windows and occupy participation opportunities, and needed by the administrative staff and politicians on the basis of the special knowledge in their respective fields of expertise[79]. The reliance on the additional information provided by interest groups is particularly owed to a number of recent developments in public policy, which have been illustrated by Howlett and Ramesh using the example of think tanks and similar research institutes[80]. The transnational nature of many policy problems and the increased competition for influence by the various stakeholders have substantially added to the complexity of the policy–making process[81].

Internal, i.e. governmental actors, and access, as well as influence opportunities have already been identified for each stage of the policy cycle separately. In order to grasp the differences in the opportunity structures offered to CSOs at the stages of the policy cycle, it is advisable to put them together in a comprehensive model on the *participatory policy cycle* (cf. above).

The model acknowledges the dominant position exercised by governmental institutions that are listed within the inner circle of the cycle. EU Institutions and national governments, though to a varying degree, have the ultimate power to take decisions. Yet, the model also draws particular attention to potential and actual participation opportunities provided for external actors, here CSOs.

The numbered boxes illustrate the consecutive stages of the policy process that, taken together, constitute a circle without any clearly demarcated beginning or ending. Although the stages may vary in duration and degree of power on side of state organizations, as well as private actors, no stage can be skipped or neglected. The influence by civil society is graphically illustrated by the black arrows. Differences in thickness symbolize the availability of opportunity structures, i.e. the potential of accessing and influencing governmental institutions.

79 Howlett & Ramesh, 2003, p.83
80 2003, p.79
81 Howlett & Ramesh, 2003, p.79

7. The European Court of Justice as Opportunity Structure

The Court of Justice of the European Union is the judiciary in the vaguely defined separation of powers within the institutional system of the EU. A role, which the Court has fulfilled with a pro–integrationist stance making it indispensable to the unique system of governance[1]. Throughout the decades, the ECJ has issued a number of landmark decisions that dramatically changed the EU legal system. However, the ECJ – as any other court – cannot rule upon the legality of governmental action or omission or interpret the founding legal documents by itself. Litigants, private or public, need to call upon the Court for clarification or the settlement of a legal dispute. The judiciary of any government is dependent upon litigants to initiate cases and upon its authority and the willingness of the parties to the dispute to comply with its reasoned judgment[2]. There is thus great interdependency among the actors at the various levels of EU governance.

7.1. Theory and the European Court of Justice

Political science has very closely observed the project of integrating Europe from its establishment onwards. The varying pace of European integration has been attentively analyzed by scholars since the early 1960s. The institutions, in particular the powerful Commission (formerly 'High Authority'), the Council of Ministers, and the evolution of responsibilities and competences of the European Parliament (ex–Parliamentary Assembly) have been examined separately. However, although the European Court of Justice has been very active and supportive of enhanced cooperation and expanded the scope and depth of European law[3] already during the first decade of its existence, it was not until the 1980s that interdisciplinary studies acknowledged the political significance of the Court's law–making powers[4]. Today, the amount of social science research on the ECJ ranks second only behind the one conducted on the Supreme Court of the United States and is far greater than that on any other high court. Consensus has emerged that the role of the ECJ and the impact of its jurisprudence cannot be neglected in any study on European integration or supranational governance[5].

---

1 Stone Sweet, 2010, pp.2 & 5
2 Stone Sweet, 2010, pp.6 & 19
3 Cichowski, 2007, p.39
4 Mattli & Burley, 1993, p.42; Dyevre, 2008/2009, p.3
5 Stone Sweet, 2010, p.2

7.1.1. Neofunctionalism

Referring to the legacy of Haas' neofunctionalism, Slaughter[6] and Mattli are reputable representatives of scholars applying modified neofunctionalist assumptions to European legal integration. While neofunctionalism was the dominant theory explaining the early years of economic and political integration within the European Economic Community, the 'empty chair' crisis marked the shift to Moravcsik's liberal intergovernmentalism. However, new institutionalism, the multi–level governance approach developed by Hooghe and Marks after the creation of the Union, and other attempts to theorize European integration consist of features of both intergovernmentalism and neofunctionalism. Still, while neofunctionalism is less employed by academics to explain developments within the political sphere of integration, it enjoys a renaissance within the legal scholarship, having become the dominant theory employed to analyze the ECJ and its jurisprudence[7]. This dominance owes much to the combination of aspects of rational choice theory and sociological–constructivism to offer explanations for the flexibility and evolutionary character of European integration.[8].

The primary purpose of neofunctionalism is the examination of the conditions under which states are willing to disperse their sovereignty and pool specific competences with other states in order to collaborate on an equal footing. These states sacrifice sovereignty for the benefit of inter–state cooperation to achieve greater goals, e.g. the preservation of peace and stability[9]. With regard to the European Union[10], governments of the member countries have created institutions with an identity and dynamic of their own and which can operate independently without the Member States' day–to–day interference[11]. Even though governments at the national level have decided to trigger off the integration process, it is largely actors on supranational (the EU Institutions), transnational (primarily CSOs and business federations) and subnational level (again state, as well as private actors) that determine the pace and quality of integration. In so doing, these actors follow self–interested motives in enhancing the integrative process[12]. Particularly non–state actors that are engaged in cross–border activities turn to the supranational level and its institutions, i.e. the Commission and the Court, in order to circumvent national obstacles and improve transnational cooperation[13]. Overall, Member States have not predicted the self–dynamic character of the legal integration process, which has, at times dramatically, exceeded the original intentions of the national governments[14].

---

6 Former last name of Anne–Marie Slaughter was Burley, under which she also published literature.
7 Sandholtz & Stone Sweet, 2010, p.22
8 Stone Sweet, 2010, p.23
9 Mattli & Burley, 1993, p.53
10 formerly European Economic Community, thereafter: European Communities
11 Mattli & Burley, 1993, pp.43, 54; Sandholtz & Stone Sweet, 2010, p.5
12 Mattli & Burley, 1993, pp.43, 54; Schmitter, 2005, p.257; also: Sandholtz & Stone Sweet, 2010, pp.8 & 17
13 Sandholtz & Stone Sweet, 2010, pp.9-10
14 Bignami, 2005, p.12; Stone Sweet, 2010, p.19

One of the theory's greatest strengths is its flexibility and its ability to explain developments and changes over time as no other theoretical approach of general application has been able to[15]. It is thus not limited to only technical policies but is able to explain the central aspects of political integration[16].
The process of integration is furthered by three dynamics. First, the concept of functional spillover depicts the interconnectedness of policy sectors and results in the fact that integration in one sector will automatically necessitate closer cooperation in one or several other sectors[17]. Second, political spillover describes the adaptation of strategic behavior to changing political values, ideals and expectations. It describes a shift in the political working arena to the inclusion of external actors that want to influence sectoral integration, such as CSOs and business representatives[18]. Third, the search for a compromise that can hardly be achieved without an institutionalized mediator recognized by all the parties is termed the 'upgrading of common interests'[19]. As some of the involved parties will not want the policy project to fail or a legal dispute to remain unresolved, impartial and independent mediators have to be installed and given the power to execute final compromises and decisions. In the first situation, this role would be occupied by the Commission, while legal disputes would be settled by the ECJ.

7.1.2. Neofunctionalist approach towards European legal integration

As indicated above, neofunctionalism distinguishes itself from models originating from the realist school of thought in IR theories with regard to the key actors determining the course of inter–state collaboration. While realists and their supporters view states as black boxes and thereby neglect the influence of subnational actors, including CSOs and individuals, pay little attention to the potential role of supra– or international institutions, and attribute all power to state governments because the Heads of State and Government take the final decisions regarding the overall direction of further European integration, it is exactly those actors whose role is emphasized by neofunctionalists[20]. In other words, neofunctionalists are aware of the fact that governments are the ultimate decision–makers and that little can be achieved against the combined rejection of all Member States. However, supranational actors, here the Commission as policy initiator and the EP as the co–decider under the ordinary procedure, do have considerable powers to which Member States must adhere[21]. The ECJ has the highest judicial authority and takes final decisions with regard to the interpretation of the Treaties upon which all EU action must be based and with which legislative acts must comply.

15 Sandholtz & Stone Sweet, 2010, pp.1–2
16 Sandholtz & Stone Sweet, 2010, pp.2 & 27
17 Mattli & Burley, 1993, pp.55 & 65
18 Mattli & Burley, 1993, p.55
19 Mattli & Burley, 1993, p.56
20 Mattli & Slaughter, 1998, p.180
21 Cichowski, 2007, pp.27–28

The Court has, similar to the Commission and the EP, also encouraged greater participation of citizens in challenging breaches of EU law before national courts by making use of the preliminary reference procedure (Article 263 TFEU)[22]. Hence, the opportunities created by the ECJ for individuals and interest groups in combination with the review powers of the Court itself have furthered legal integration beyond Member State governments' area of influence[23]. In addition, national courts – and interestingly enough those at the lower end of the hierarchy – have also greatly contributed to the implementation of European principles and legislation on national level. The willingness of national judges to refer questions to the ECJ and abide by the latter's rulings when issuing their own judgments, does not only happen completely without the consent of the legislature and executive branches of government but these two institutions can even be compelled by the Court to modify their legislation[24].

Of course, the approximation of the legal systems of neighboring countries is not the primary aim of either national courts or individuals. They are not altruistic actors solely striving for the greater good but are rather motivated by their own self–interests. Each of the above–mentioned players has its own interests that, accumulated, do not contradict each other but instead result in mutual cooperation[25]. The principles of supremacy and direct effect of EU law, as well as the concept of state liability, have given incentives to the individual to challenge governmental acts or sue the state for incorrect or lacking implementation of EU legislation. It is, however, remarkable that the ECJ was careful enough to provide this avenue only for legal actions brought against Member State authorities as it ruled that neither Council nor Commission decisions could be challenged by individuals on grounds of *ultra vires*, i.e. the extension of competences. In so doing, the Court ensured that private litigants would only enhance but not stall further legal integration[26].

National courts also follow self–interested motives when making a preliminary reference to the ECJ. Those that rank at the lower end of the judicial hierarchy benefit from referrals to the ECJ as those final judgments based on a decision by the Court cannot as easily be overruled by higher national courts. As the referring court is obliged to include the findings of the ECJ into its own decision and these findings are binding upon all national courts under the territorial jurisdiction of the ECJ, the national court of appeal has only two options. Either, it must apply the decision of the ECJ equally as the lower court did and may therefore not greatly vary in its own judgment, or, if it considers the findings to be untenable, it must refer the case to the ECJ for a second opinion[27]. Thus, the overall consequence is that those courts that frequently refer to the ECJ for clarifica-

22 Mattli & Burley, 1993, pp.58–59
23 Bignami, 2005, p.13; Mattli & Slaughter, 1998, pp.180; Mattli & Burley, 1993, p.60; Sandholtz & Stone Sweet, 2010, p.12
24 Mattli & Slaughter, 1998, p.180
25 Mattli & Slaughter, 1998, pp.180–181
26 Mattli & Burley, 1993, pp.60–62; Bignami, 2005, p.13
27 cf. also chapter 11

tion of points of European law are less likely to be overruled by higher national courts and so stabilize their position within the legal system[28].

The incentives of the ECJ as well as national courts are interlinked and result in mutual empowerment. The Court is of course dependent on the cases filed by litigants and referred by national courts given that the great majority of disputes adjudicated by the ECJ follow the Article 267 TFEU procedure. The Court is obviously only able to interpret European law and create new rights and legal principles – thus expanding the scope of EU law – on the basis of a particular case. As any other judiciary, it may not do so upon its own initiative. On the other hand, national courts are also dependent upon the ECJ insofar as the latter is the final arbiter in matters of European law. The Court is accordingly a strategic actor motivated by the self–interest of extending its competences[29]. It thereby enhances its own legitimacy and judicial authority through the referrals by national courts[30].

The application of the three dynamics of neofunctionalism to European legal integration reveals the following. The supremacy of EU law serves an example for functional spillover, which would be of little benefit to individuals, if they could not rely on more advantageous Union provisions instead of national law[31]. Another example is the *ERTA doctrine*[32] that states that in matters, in which the EU has internal competence to achieve policy objectives, this automatically implies that the competence also extends to the external execution of these competences, as it may otherwise fail to attain the objective. Political spillover likewise affects the expectations of those involved in legal proceedings and their ability to adapt to changing circumstances[33]. With regard to the third dynamic, the 'upgrading of interests' that necessitates an impartial mediator, the role is not completely satisfactorily fulfilled by the ECJ. Rather, as an arbiter, it bases its opinion on the common interest of all actors involved within the European Union as set out in the preamble of the Treaty and thereby uses a teleological style of interpretation[34]. The final decisions by the Court more often than not resemble the arguments of the Commission that are perceived to represent objective and supranational interests rather than the biased positions of single Member State governments. The judges thus ensure the promotion of supranational goals and do not yield to the various, and sometimes opposing, pressures by Member States[35]. Through an incremental approach of developing new legal principles and strategic referrals to already established case–law, the ECJ stabilizes

28 Mattli & Burley, 1993, p.63
29 Cichowski, 2007, p.41; Sandholtz & Stone Sweet, 2010, p.25
30 Mattli & Burley, 1993, pp.64–65
31 Mattli & Burley, 1993, p.66
32 ECJ, Case 22/70 *Commission v Council (European Agreement on Road Transport)* [1971] ECR 263, para.19
33 Mattli & Burley, 1993, p.67
34 Mattli & Burley, 1993, p.68
35 Cichowski, 2007, p.43; also Sandholtz & Stone Sweet, 2010, p.25; Stone Sweet, 2010, p.20, pp.20-21

its role vis–à–vis national governments and uses it also for legitimacy reasons[36]. The dynamics of institutionalization, in which actors have pushed for new norms and rules to which they subsequently adapted in order to achieve further improvements, has been central to the process of European integration[37]. In other words, the more the Court has already ruled upon a specific policy area, the greater the probability that actors from the governmental or the private sector will initiate cases in order to have their interests preserved[38].

7.1.3. Criticism and Adaptation

It appears quite obvious that the interplay of self–interested actors will neither always receive reciprocal applause nor result beneficially in a deepened legal integration, let alone an approximation of laws and legal interpretation styles within the twenty–seven Member States. Private litigants will not always be content with ECJ decisions[39]. To an even lesser degree will national courts be able to strengthen their general position within the domestic legal hierarchy, simply due to the fact that they referred a case to the ECJ for clarification. Not only does this referral drastically lengthen the waiting time and increase the costs for the involved parties, it will also stall the whole procedure before the domestic court. In addition, the low rank of courts is not the only factor that determines a judge's attitude towards the application of EU law and the willingness to refer to the ECJ and abide by its decision. If it became apparent that national courts make preliminary references at a substantially decreasing rate, lawyers would recommend that litigants should follow an argumentation strategy that is no longer based on European arguments but bring forward national reasons. This development would in turn reduce the political pressure on Member State governments to pedantically adhere to the provisions of EU law[40]. Of course, this development as outlined by Karen Alter does not appear to impose a realistic and immediate threat to the EU legal system as established to date.

Another possible restriction of the extent and the pace of European legal integration is the combined action of all or at least a substantial number of Member State governments to modify the meaning and ultimate effects of ECJ judgments. This was the case with the so–called *Barber protocol* annexed to the Treaty that was to protect the inviolability of traditional and established national policies[41]. However, this is only very rarely successful. In the vast majority of the cases, Member States will neither be able to prevent litigation nor overrule decisions of the Court[42].

36 Cichowski, 2007, p.42
37 Sandholtz & Stone Sweet, 2010, p.16
38 Stone Sweet, 2010, p.27
39 Alter, 2000, p.515
40 Alter, 2000, p.512
41 Alter, 2000, p.513
42 Sandholtz & Stone Sweet, 2010, p.13

For the purpose of this dissertation project, however, the neofunctionalist assumption that supranational organizations and transnational society are decisive components for the institutionalization of EU rules in one policy area, which subsequently spill over to other policy domains and ultimately shift policy competences to the supranational level[43], will provide the theoretical foundation upon which the further research is based. The same assumptions with regard to the relations between the political institutions of the EU and civil society can thus also be applied to the relations between the latter and the European judiciary.

7.2. Jurisdiction of the Court

The general responsibility of the ECJ since its establishment in 1952 within the framework of the ECSC has not changed despite the rapid and comprehensive development of European law[44]. Its primary task to "ensure that in the interpretation and application of the Treaties the law is observed" is enshrined in Article 19(1) first subpara. second sentence TEU LT. Similarly, despite the continuous reformation of the institutional framework, the position and functions have remained untouched even though criticism of the Court's pro–integrative jurisprudence has been announced occasionally[45]. The limits of the Court's authority are defined by the principle of conferral as spelled out in Article 5(1) & (2) TEU LT, which requires the ECJ, as any other EU Institution, to "act within the limits of the powers conferred upon it by the Member States in the Treaties to attain the objectives set out therein"[46].

In order to cope with the increased caseload and to accelerate the proceedings, the Court of First Instance (now: General Court) was established in 1989[47]. Over time, their respective jurisdictions have been separated and clearly defined in the Treaties. Of interest with regard to the purpose of this study are the following areas of the ECJ's jurisdiction. The Court is authorized to hear applications filed by privileged applicants, the institutions and Member States, concerning the legality of a specific EU act (Article 263 TFEU) or the admonishment of an institution's failure to act (Article 265 TFEU). It furthermore rules upon Treaty infringements caused by any institution or one or more Member States brought to its attention either by the Commission (Article 258 TFEU) or a Member State (Article 259 TFEU). Finally, composing the great majority of all cases pending before it, the ECJ adjudicates upon questions relating to "the interpretation of the Treaties" (Article 267(1)(a) TFEU) and "the validity and interpretation of acts of the institutions, bodies, offices or agencies of the Union"(Article 267(1)(b) TFEU).

43 Cichowski, 2007, p.3
44 Tohidipur, 2008, pp.88
45 Tohidipur, 2008, p.89
46 cf. also Thiele, 2006, p.39
47 Tohidipur, 2008, p.86

Article 256 TFEU stipulates the competences of the GC, which basically hears all disputes between natural or legal persons and EU Institutions subject to appeal on points of law by the ECJ (para.2)[48]. The Treaty of Nice added a third paragraph to what is now Article 256 TFEU allowing the GC to take preliminary rulings on questions referred by national courts "in specific areas laid down by the Statute". In practice, however, the preliminary reference procedure remains exclusively in the hands of the ECJ. If the GC finds after in–depth examination that it is not responsible, it can refer the application to the ECJ. If that Court also concludes that the matter does not fall under its authority and refers the case back to the GC, the latter is then bound by the ECJ's referral[49].

Decisions by the two instances are immediately legally effective and bind the parties to the dispute. Under specific circumstances are appeals against decisions of the GC to the ECJ possible; a revision of ECJ decisions, however, is not possible. The Court is able to determine the point in time to which the decision shall take effect, if this is necessary for the fulfillment of the principle of legitimate expectations or practical reasons[50]. Finally, the Court also decides upon the division of the costs of the proceeding[51].

Both instances of the Court of the European Union are relevant in the discussion on access for environmental interest groups to European justice. The (potentially) available procedures will be outlined in greater detail in chapter 11.

Yet, as practice reveals, the effective and, most importantly, homogeneous application of European law depends on national administrative authorities and national courts. The division of competences and jurisdiction is thereby very clearly defined. While national courts, subject to their respective competences, check the constitutionality and validity of national acts implementing EU legislation and control whether national authorities adhere to Union rules, the ECJ owns the monopoly power to interpret Treaty provisions, control the validity of Union acts, and admonish infringements of the Treaty on part of an institution or one or more Member States[52]. The legal review of national law is thereby interdicted[53]. In this regard, the preliminary reference procedure under Article 267 TFEU shows the interconnectedness, cooperation and even mutual dependence between the ECJ and national courts of all instances[54]. National courts refer questions concerning the interpretation or validity of European primary or secondary law to the ECJ, whose response binds the referring court as well as all other national instances that adjudicate in the very same dispute. Yet, the decision on the merits is exclusively reserved to

48 cf. also Kwanka, 2006, p.19

49 Thiele, 2007, p.23

50 cf. ECJ, Case 81/72 *Commission v Council* [1973] ECR 575, point 2 of operative part; ECJ, Case C–21/94 *EP v Council* [1995] ECR I–1827, point 2 of operative part; ECJ, Case C–262/88 *Barber* [1990] ECR I–1889, point 5 of operative part; Oppermann, Classen & Nettesheim, 2009, pp.257–258

51 Oppermann, Classen & Nettesheim, 2009, pp.257–258

52 Thiele, 2007, pp.20, 24

53 Thiele, 2006, p.40

54 Tohidipur, 2008, pp.134–135

the Member State courts according to the national legal order and rules of procedure[55]. The fact that Article 274 TFEU does not exclude *per se* that disputes to which the EU is a party can be settled before national tribunals and courts but only "where jurisdiction is conferred on the [...] [ECJ] by the Treaties" underlines the demand in Article 5 TEU LT and clarifies that the ECJ only bears those competences that are enumerated in the Treaty[56]. However, on the basis of the principle of sincere cooperation of Article 4(3) TEU LT and effective legal protection, national courts must set aside national procedural law, if a legal position protected by EU law can otherwise not be guaranteed[57].

7.2.1. Modes of Interpretation employed by the ECJ

Intense studies have not only revealed that the types as well as the frequency of the modes of interpretation employed by the ECJ distinguish themselves from most legal interpretation traditions in the Member States, but moreover indicate that applicants may orientate their litigation strategies and their overall decision to file an application on the basis of the style of interpretation of European law by the ECJ.

There is broad consensus within academic literature that the European Court of Justice does not invent legal interpretation types completely on its own but rather reverts to the traditional modes established in the EU Member States[58] and those enumerated in the *Vienna Convention on the Law of the Treaties* of 1969[59], of which Article 31 specifically addresses the establishment of the legal force and meaning of international treaties[60].

Overall, the ECJ has been found to make use of first, referring to preceding cases, second, formal grammatical interpretation of legal norms, systematical interpretation linking norms together, teleological interpretation emphasizing the *effet utile* of EU law, and third, embedding the act in question into its historical context[61].

---

55 Kwanka, 2006, p.55; Bieber, Epiney & Haag, 2005, p.280; Oppermann, Classen & Nettesheim, 2009, pp.270 & 273; Lasok, Millet & Howard, 2004, p.181

56 cf. also Kwanka, 2006, p.8

57 Tohidipur, 2008, pp.151–152; cf. ECJ, Case C–221/89 *The Queen v Secretary of State for Transport, ex parte: Factortame Ltd and others (Factortame)* [1991] ECR I–3905, point 1 of operative part

58 Oppermann, Classen & Nettesheim, 2009, p.196; Harratsch, Koenig & Pechstein, 2009, p.199

59 Sloot, 2005, p.21

60 Vienna Convention on the Law of the Treaties. Article 31. General rule of interpretation

1. A treaty shall be interpreted in good faith in accordance with the ordinary meaning to be given to the terms of the treaty in their context and in the light of its object and purpose. 2. The context for the purpose of the interpretation of a treaty shall comprise, in addition to the text, including its preamble and annexes:

(a) any agreement relating to the treaty which was made between all the parties in connection with the conclusion of the treaty; (b) any instrument which was made by one or more parties in connection with the conclusion of the treaty and accepted by the other parties as an instrument related to the treaty. 3. There shall be taken into account, together with the context: (a) any subsequent agreement between the parties regarding the interpretation of the treaty or the application of its provisions; (b) any subsequent practice in the application of the treaty which establishes the agreement of the parties regarding its interpretation; (c) any relevant rules of international law applicable in the relations between the parties. 4. A special meaning shall be given to a term if it is established that the parties so intended.

61 cf. e.g. Harratsch, Koenig & Pechstein, 2009, p.199–200

The fact that the ECJ most often refers to preceding decisions is plausible for a number of reasons. First of all, it renders the argumentation of a case more efficient as it decreases the workload of the judges and simultaneously reduces the length of proceedings. The repetition of the Court's conclusions thereby creates precedents[62]. Continuous references either confirm and specify decisions or overrule earlier judgments and offer the opportunity to formulate new positions and to depart from earlier 'outdated' ones[63]. Although a number of judgments have been codified in the Treaties or legislation[64], the Court highlights findings of its former decisions, even where it could have cited provisions of legislative acts[65]. Most importantly, however, the reference to former judgments and affirmation of the Court's position primarily ensures legal certainty[66]. Parties to the dispute also refer to former cases to substantiate their argumentation[67]. In addition, the decision to litigate may be influenced by whether similar applications in the past have already been successful.

Grammatical interpretation is used as a starting point to determine the natural meaning of the words and the sequences of sentences not in isolation but placed into the context of the whole provision[68]. The ECJ had stated that following the *acte clair*, once the wording is determined unambiguously, there is no need to resort to the other modes of interpretation. Thus, these are usually only applied subsequently or complementary[69]. The multiplicity of working languages, however, constitutes one of the greatest challenges as all linguistic versions should contain the same meaning (cf. Article 55(1) TEU LT)[70]. Hence, the ECJ makes profitable use of a comparative analysis of concepts and notions and their respective meanings in the different languages[71].

Academic literature attaches 'outstanding' meaning to the Court's teleological interpretation[72]. A study undertaken by Dederichs confirms the importance of teleological interpretation, yet, qualifies the quantity of utilization[73]. The teleological style searches meaning, purpose and aim of a legal provision[74]; here primarily furthering European integration. Single provisions are read in light of the original will of the drafters and

62 Dederichs, 2004, p.42
63 Dederichs, 2004, p.51; Bieber, Epiney & Haag, 2005, pp.253–254
64 Dederichs, 2004, pp.47–48
65 cf. e.g. ECJ, Case C–379/97 *Pharmacia & Upjohn SA v Paranova* [1999] para.13 ECR I–6927; Dederichs, 2004, pp.47–48
66 Dederichs, 2004, p.59
67 Dederichs, 2004, pp.55, 57
68 Oppermann, Classen & Nettesheim, 2009, p.196; Sloot, 2005, p.21; Thiele, 2007, p.29; Dederichs, 2004, pp.64, 65
69 Dederichs, 2004, pp.76–79
70 Sloot, 2005, p.22; Thiele, 2007, p.29; Bieber, Epiney & Haag, 2005, p.252; Dederichs, 2004, p.71
71 Dederichs, 2004, pp.72–73
72 Oppermann, Classen & Nettesheim, 2009, p.198; Bieber, Epiney & Haag, 2005, p.253; Thiele, 2007, p.32
73 Dederichs, 2004, pp.90–91 & 94–95
74 Dederichs, 2004, p.80

the general context (also referred to as *effet utile*)[75]. Indications are usually retrieved from the preamble of a legal text, the articles declaring the general purpose and aims of the act as well as the text of the treaty as a whole, including, where necessary, its annexes[76]. The utilization of the teleological interpretation mode confirms the dynamic character of the European legal system and the pro–integrative position of the Court[77]. It awards constitutional character to the Treaties and the "*sui generis*" character of the EU legal order[78]. Through the use of teleological interpretation, the ECJ has indeed taken landmark decisions that have fostered European integration in a remarkable manner and speed[79] that Member States would not have initiated themselves but which have become a well–accepted basis of European law.

Systematic interpretation then considers the paragraph, neighboring provisions, chapter, or the whole document of the relevant provision[80]. Legislation is additionally tested against the legal basis in the Treaties[81]. Conflicting interpretations of obligations among legal norms are thereby to be avoided[82] but rather highlight the coherent meaning and aims of all provisions in relation to each other.

Finally, historical interpretation receives comparatively little attention by the ECJ[83] given that the European legal system is generally regarded as a flexible and dynamic system striving for ever closer integration whose meaning should always be placed into its contemporary context[84]. Yet, regarding legislation, the availability of sources is substantially higher and includes, *inter alia*, former legislative provisions, new draft proposals, records of working group and committee meetings, as well as plenary deliberations in the EP and external expert advice[85]. In addition, the Commission is obliged to attach the considerations of the particular act in the recitals preceding the legally binding text[86].

The modes of interpretation as employed by judges of the ECJ have been presented because it may be helpful for private litigants, including environmental CSOs, to be familiar with the Court's operation methods when deciding to use litigation as a tool to achieve their objectives. The knowledge of the style and tools utilized by the Court may be advantageous when formulating arguments and preparing the litigation strategy.

75 Sloot, 2005, p.25; Dobler, 2008, p.519; Dederichs, 2004, p.81
76 Sloot, 2005, pp.23–24
77 Sloot, 2005, p.24
78 cf. ECJ, Case 26/62 *Van Gend en Loos* [1963] ECR 1; Oppermann, Classen & Nettesheim, 2009, p.198
79 Oppermann, Classen & Nettesheim, 2009, p.198
80 Thiele, 2007, p.31; Bieber, Epiney & Haag, 2005, p.253; Dederichs, 2004, p.99
81 Oppermann, Classen & Nettesheim, 2009, p.197
82 Thiele, 2007, p.31; Dederichs, 2004, p.99
83 Bieber, Epiney & Haag, 2005, p.252; Dederichs, 2004, p.122
84 Oppermann, Classen & Nettesheim, 2009, pp.197–198; Thiele, 2007, pp.30–31
85 Dederichs, 2004, p.111
86 Dederichs, 2004, p.115

8. Private Litigants before the Court

It is remarkable that political scientists have only recently acknowledged the impact of litigation strategies employed by CSOs on the political process of decision–making[1]. In the 1960s, the landmark decision in *Van Gend en Loos*[2] and subsequent case–law of the ECJ established the principle of direct effect of Treaty provisions as well as – under specific circumstances – that of secondary legislation. Taken together with the supremacy of European over national law, the doctrine enables individuals to invoke more favorable rights arising from European law against their own state authorities before national courts[3]. Hence, by creating these direct and judicially enforceable rights, the ECJ strengthened the position of individuals, i.e. in the early days mostly economically active private individuals and undertakings, as well as the position of national courts. It thereby empowered those that should, ideally, control the 'government'; namely citizens and the judiciary[4]. Throughout the following decades, the ECJ broadened the scope of rights of individuals by complementing the vertical direct effect, i.e. rights enforceable against the state, with horizontal direct effect of specific provisions, i.e. the enforcement by individuals against other private parties and indirect effect[5].

In addition, the Court has continuously publicly announced that the right to go to court is a fundamental component of democratic governance systems that are based on the rule of law and upon which European citizens must be able to rely under any circumstances. The judges furthermore emphasized that Member State governments are under the obligation to ensure the right to challenge state (in–)actions under EU law in the same manner (equality principle) and under the same conditions (effectiveness principle) as under national law[6].

In recent years, scholars of both legal and political science paid increasing attention to the potential effects of litigation in furthering European legal integration, which in turn has implications on political integration. There is general consensus that ECJ litigation based on complaints filed by private litigants has succeeded in expanding the scope of EU law and forcing Member State governments to bring their national law in confor-

---

1 Hilson, 2002, p.238

2 ECJ, Case 26/62 *N. V. Algemene Transport– en Expeditie Onderneming van Gend & Loos v. Nederlandse administratie der belastingen* [1963] ECR 1

3 Cichowski, 2006, p.27 & p.41

4 Alter, 2000, pp.492, 493

5 interpreting national legislation in light of European law; cf. e.g. ECJ, Case C–106/89 *Marleasing* [1990] ECR I–4135

6 Costa, 2003, p.743

mity with European law[7]. Increasing calls to the ECJ resulted in a form of judicialization and have given the Court the opportunity to "constitutionalize" the Treaties and nourish European governance[8]. Particularly the preliminary reference procedure has evolved into an effective mechanism for non–state actors to hold governments accountable for breaches of EU law[9]. By introducing litigation opportunities that distinguish themselves from the traditional judicial dispute arrangements in the Member States, European law offers an alternative route to circumvent national law and to compel Member State governments and courts to abide by European law[10].

Civic rights and duties form the basis upon which all modern democratic state systems are built and which essentially govern the relations between the state and its citizens. In the context of this dissertation, political rights – and particularly those enabling participation within political processes – are of primary importance. Yet, rights of participation are of little significance, if they are not legally enforceable. This is confirmed by the structure of the Aarhus Convention as was already mentioned. Rights must be guaranteed to the person relying on them and at the same time, those persons or authorities against whom these rights could be enforced must be aware of their existence and effects. Political rights of participation are in this regard closely intertwined with the concept of accountability and the principle of checks and balances among governmental branches. If they cannot be invoked, i.e. if state actors cannot be forced to grant these rights and abide by the outcome of participation, the existence of these rights is practically ineffectual. In addition, the ability of an individual to invoke his or her civic rights may not only be of benefit to him or her but, under certain circumstances, may also aid to improve the situation of other similarly affected persons, who are not in the position to enforce their rights.

Hence, the right of participation, i.e. the right to access official documents of the government, may further enable external actors to be consulted in formal processes or to participate in expert meetings etc. The same type of right may also be extended to new actors within the policy process, which can be observed, *inter alia*, in the development of the civil society dialog that has been broadened from purely economic private actors to public groups representing a great variety of economic, social and citizen interests[11]. Summarizing the above findings, Cichowski declares that "as rights become more formalized and judicially enforceable, we would expect increased opportunities for participation through law enforcement, rights claiming and expanded protection"[12]. Furthermore, "[a]s judicial institutions with a wider scope of review powers increase in accessibility to private parties who possess the resources and expertise to litigate, the

7 Alter, 2000, pp.492, 493; Greenwood, 2007a, p.39; Stone Sweet, 2010, p.2
8 Stone Sweet, 2010, p.34; Bouwen & McCown, 2007, p.426
9 Börzel, 2006, p.134; Bouwen & McCown, 2007, p.426
10 Alter & Vargas, 2000, p.453; Stone Sweet & Brunell, 2010, p.4; Sandholtz & Stone Sweet, 2010, p.10
11 Cichowski, 2006, pp.53–54
12 Cichowski, 2006, p.55

opportunities for participation through law enforcement, rights claiming and expanded protection would increase as well"[13]. In other words, the mere existence of litigants enable the ECJ to issue decisions and their respective identities, motivations and intentions may even influence the direction of further European legal integration[14].

8.1. Benefits and Costs of Litigation Strategies employed by public interest groups

Private litigants are primarily driven by two types of motivations when initiating cases before the ECJ. First, actors that are engaged in activities across national borders have an interest in the removal of any national obstacles that might impede transnational cooperation and engagement. Second, whenever impediments occur under the domestic legal systems, litigants attempt to improve the status quo by referring to more beneficial provisions under European law[15]. Given the "prescriptive" nature of ECJ decisions and the potentially clear instructions to the legislative, litigants may be able to heavily influence form and content of subsequent policies[16]. Yet, groups that aim instead at slowing down the process of European integration would be rather ill–advised when turning to the ECJ due to its general pro–integrationist and liberal legacy[17].

Hence, pressure groups and NGOs often try to achieve changes through both political lobbying, as well as litigation strategies, and thereby take advantage of as many access opportunities as possible[18].

The decision by groups to employ a litigation strategy in order to change policies, the interpretation of legal texts, or the aspiration of newly created rights that individuals can invoke before courts, depends on a number of factors. Some of these are inherent to the legal system, while others depend on the organizational structure and objectives of the public interest groups, and finally, of course, also on the probability of success.

8.1.1. Characteristics inherent to the legal system

Those circumstances that CSOs are less able to influence are those rules that govern the national court structure and procedural aspects of litigation[19]. Although groups may pursue public and political campaigns in order to alter the rules on *locus standi*, the denial of access to national courts is usually the first and also final obstacle for a litigation strategy aimed at having European law reviewed and potentially contested. With regard

13 Cichowski, 2006, p.62
14 Mattli & Slaughter, 1998, p.186
15 Stone Sweet, 2010, pp.24–25
16 Bouwen & McCown, 2007, p.426
17 Bouwen & McCown, 2007, p.430
18 Bouwen & McCown, 2007, pp.424 & 427
19 Börzel, 2006, p.132

to the application of EU law, it is particularly under the preliminary reference procedure (Article 267 TFEU) that national rules on *locus standi* determine whether a litigant gains access to judicial adjudication. Only those litigants that have standing rights before the respective national court may be referred to the ECJ. It is therefore reasonable to assume that CSOs are comparatively active and influential in those countries that grant more liberal rules concerning standing rights for groups and collective claimants. The lack of standing rules reflect a rather weakly organized civil society also on political level as it could try to invoke pressure upon legislators to grant more favorable access to courts[20]. Given that a comparative analysis of standing rights to environmental groups is undertaken in chapter 11, it shall suffice at this point to state that these rights differ greatly among Member States[21].

CSOs have even less ability to achieve changes with regard to the attitude of national judges towards the application and interpretation of EU law, which is usually determined by the legal traditions within a society and the training of lawyers and judges including or excluding the use of precedent. This in turn will also be reflected in their willingness to refer questions to the ECJ and to stall their own proceeding until the Court has issued its judgment. After having received the decision of the ECJ, the national judge is under the obligation to abide by its content when declaring the final judgment. Research by Karen Alter has revealed that courts obtaining a lower position in the national hierarchy are more willing to make a preliminary reference because their judgment, based on the ECJ's decision, is less likely to be overruled by higher courts of appeal[22]. Other features of the national legal system include procedural requirements, as for example the method of filing complaints, the burden of proof, and available legal aid[23]. In addition, many administrative systems provide for the status quo to be maintained until a negative ruling has been issued, which can amount to a considerable time delay until the undesired policy has been modified. Even more dramatic is, of course, the loss when the court upholds the present status and verifies its validity. In these cases, the efforts of the concerned interest group have not only been a waste of time but, even more dramatically, have created high financial costs, especially if the costs of the opposing party have to be compensated as well. These are then borne by fee–paying members, donors, or state funds, i.e. taxpayers[24].

The probability of having the case decided in the CSOs' favor also depends on their own non–material resources, namely access to EU information and the level of knowledge of applicants and their legal representatives[25]. Even more important is their ability to pursue a line of argumentation that is compatible with the supranational interests pursued by the EU Institutions and the overall aim of enhanced integration within the

20 Alter & Vargas, 2000, pp.470–471

21 Cichowski, 2007, p.34

22 cf. Alter, 2001, *Establishing the Supremacy of European Law: The Making of an International Rule of Law in Europe* New York: Oxford University Press.

23 Alter & Vargas, 2000, pp.471–472; Alter, 2000, p.496

24 Hilson, 2002, pp.240–241

25 Costa, 2003, p.749

Union[26]. Hence the legal expertise available to organized interests, i.e. the number of qualified and competent lawyers, who are well trained in employing an EU litigation strategy, varies considerably between Member States and may thus be a crucial factor for the use of the Article 263 TFEU procedure[27].

Another very important factor, yet not directly linked to the legal system *per se* but rather to the political system including the constitutional premises, is the magnitude of discrepancy between an EU directive and the national implementation measure. The greater the misfit between these two pieces of legislation in terms of content or time delays in the implementation period; in other words, the greater the discrepancy between the more beneficial European legislative act as opposed to the national one, the greater the probability for those interest groups that are most burdened to turn to litigation[28].

In sum, the characteristics of traditional legal systems, the personal attitudes of national judges towards EU law, the level of knowledge by all involved in settling a dispute arising under European law, and the ability to bear the financial costs and time delays by the parties determine whether the contested matter will reach European adjudication in the first place, and second, whether it is likely to be successful.

At the European level, direct access to the Court for public interest litigation is even more difficult (cf. chapters 11–13). In addition, the time aspect may be a very crucial factor for groups not to initiate judicial proceedings. The whole procedure usually takes several years and the trend has been rather prolonging than shortening[29]. Quick results are accordingly not to be expected.

8.1.2. Type of litigants

Overall, Bouwen and McCown emphasize that the amount of resources (financial, time and specialized staff) at the disposal of the interest group is one of the factors determining whether an organization choses lobbying, litigation, or a combination of both strategies[30]. Lobbying strategies are usually less expensive and lead quicker to results and are therefore preferred where only minor changes are advocated[31]. In addition, groups may take a decision on the basis of a cost–benefit analysis on the grounds of its own organizational capacity[32], as well as on how accessible political decision–makers are to their specific interest and whether other access opportunities are given. The choice in favor of a litigation strategy may therefore be influenced by the degree of openness of political institutions and the accessibility to the legislative process for external stakeholders. Bouwen and McCown have found that exclusive litigation strategies have been

26 Costa, 2003, pp.745–746; Alter & Vargas, 2000, p.759; Alter, 2000, p.489
27 Cichowski, 2007, p.33
28 Cichowski, 2007, p.35
29 Bouwen & McCown, 2007, p.430
30 Bouwen & McCown, 2007, pp.428-429
31 Bouwen & McCown, 2007, p.431
32 Bouwen & McCown, 2007, p.431

utilized by groups in policy areas in which a "significant legislative deadlock" exists and by groups that are not able to address MEPs or Commission officials[33]. Organizations that dispose of sufficient resources may decide to combine lobbying and litigation strategies. Litigation is thereby either used as a threat, as an alternative, when other options have already been exhausted, or as an accompanying strategy at the same time as political lobbying[34].

Litigants pursuing legal action on the basis of rights enshrined in European law can be further classified into three broad categories. The first is occupied by large interest groups and companies that have sufficient resources to prevent becoming vulnerable to the typical obstacles; primarily being the great expenses in financial costs, procedural hindrances and time delays[35]. These litigants are internally well–structured and have manifested their position as transnational actors and underline their durability[36]. They strive for a change in EU policies through a modified interpretation of secondary law by the ECJ. Usually, recourse to judicial arbitration is not the sole activity of these groups, as they employ a combined strategy of litigation and lobbying methods[37]. In some instances, particularly well–funded and highly organized CSOs employ a test–case strategy by using one case with a particular problem or specific circumstances and attempt to create a precedent judgment in the best interest of the interest group in order to influence subsequent case–law and legislation[38].

Second, small and medium–sized enterprises and private interest groups have acquired a substantial level of experience in exploiting the benefits of litigation despite their restricted financial resources[39]. Primarily actors of the first but at times also those of the second category develop a 'repeat player' strategy. These groups do not exclusively aim at resolving a legal dispute before the Court in the interest of one single individual but primarily intend to expand existing EU law on a specific matter or to create new legal rights for individuals in order for other affected persons to benefit from the decision of the Court as well[40]. In addition, Alter and Vargas discovered that those groups that have a clearly limited focus and identity are more willing to accept the lengthy and expensive process of litigation[41] given that they only represent one specific type of interest and are prepared to invest comparably much in order to achieve their aims. The third category comprises private individuals as the smallest group of litigants. They usually neither possess sufficient financial and legal means nor the time to undergo the complete judicial process under EU law[42]. Only the first two categories are considered.

33 2007, p.432
34 Bouwen & McCown, 2007, p.432
35 e.g. Bouwen & McCown, 2007, p.427
36 Cichowski, 2007, p.33
37 Costa, 2003, pp.474–478; Bouwen & McCown, 2007, p.424
38 Alter, 2000, pp.497–498; Harlow, 2002, p.12
39 Costa, 2003, p.478
40 Mattli & Slaughter, 1998, p.187
41 2000, p.473; Alter, 2000, p.498; also Bouwen & McCown, 2007, p.427
42 Costa, 2003, p.478, Cichowski, 2007, p.31

8.1.3. Prospects of Success

The strategy of striving for long–term politically significant results coincides with the tendency of the ECJ to broaden the material scope and technical depth of European law through its decisions. The judges thereby use an incremental method through which they establish a new general legal principle, which, in most cases, is found not to be applicable to the given case. Through this tactic, Member State governments win the case at hand and therefore do not object to the new legal principle or extension of EU law. Thus, even though the applicant in this particular legal dispute is placed at a disadvantage, in the long term, similarly affected persons will benefit from the judgment[43].

The introduction of precedent–based adjudication, which is unknown to most continental Member States, as well as to international mechanisms of dispute settlement, into the supranational legal system has been crucial for the Court's law–making powers[44]. Even though the Treaties do not confer this power to the ECJ, it has, since its establishment, been heavily engaged in shaping the overall aims of the Union and modified the content of legislative acts[45]. The effects of precedents are fairly obvious. Not only is the ECJ itself bound to follow its line of case–law but even national courts are under an obligation to interpret national legislation as far as possible in the light of European law, including earlier judgments by the supranational court. This facilitates a homogeneous and traceable interpretation of EU law within all twenty–seven Member States. In addition, many ECJ decisions have subsequently been codified by legislation adopted by the Council and the EP, which illustrates that the opinion of the Court is respected and even acknowledged by the EU legislators. Hence, CSOs may find it beneficial to undertake litigation attempts given the realistic probability that a positive decision by the ECJ will provide the basis for future amendments to existing or the creation of new legislation[46]. Yet, another very practical advantage for CSOs that want to use adjudication in order to shift the policy outcomes to their benefit is the possibility to rely on established case–law. Taking this in combination with the principle of legal certainty, lawyers and legal advisors of public interest groups may be able to predict the potential outcome of a legal dispute and may furthermore adapt their argumentation strategy accordingly.

Sometimes, recourse to litigation is used as a threat to political bodies or is simply the last resort because other strategies to influence policy–making, including lobbying at the local or national government or complaining to the European Commission, have failed to achieve the aim sought[47]. However, increasingly, litigation has become an alternative mode of activism to achieve policy changes[48]. Taking litigation strategies as the final attempt is quite reasonable as the judicial evaluation of policies occurs at the very last stage of the policy cycle. Yet, it is also important to note that, even though,

43 Mattli & Slaughter, 1998, pp.189–190
44 McCown, 2006, p.182
45 McCown, 2006, pp.175 & 177
46 Mazey & Richardson, 2002, p.262
47 Alter, 2000, p.493
48 Bouwen & McCown, 2007, p.428

litigation may be a part of a more comprehensive political strategy, those groups that enjoy preferred access to political decision–making are less likely to embrace adjudication methods[49]. However, once political entrance routes are closed, access to courts may be the best (remaining) means to execute influence[50]. The immediate effect of an ECJ decision will, at first, only influence the final judgment of the referring court and the national legal system. In the medium– and long–term, however, the national courts of other Member States equally have to abide by the interpretation of the ECJ on a specific point of law. Respective CSOs may then try to trigger public debates on this very matter and to promote the judicial outcome. These campaigns may increase the awareness of governments of the additional expenses of non–compliance with a judgment. This would ideally result in a modification of the existing policy[51]. The negative effects on governments are even greater when the application of European legislation is concerned. Quite obviously, it is more difficult for governments to reverse or even modify the effects of judicial decisions by the ECJ than by their domestic courts because legislation must be adopted according to the majority rules in the Council on European and not simply on national level. Furthermore, Treaty revisions would demand unanimous approval by the Heads of State and Government in the European Council[52]. This ”follow–through” tactic of a ”multipronged” strategy employed by CSOs underlines again the assumption that most strategies involving the recourse to courts are not taken in isolation but are part of a greater and diverse political campaign[53].

8.2. Judicial Opportunity Structure

In conclusion, the probability to decide a case in the CSO's favor depends on the careful application of four separate but consecutive steps that have been identified by Alter and Vargas[54]. First, and most obvious, litigants must be able to invoke a specific right under European law before national courts (cf. directly effective provisions[55]), which, ideally, is more beneficial to them than those that national law provides for. It is, however, also very difficult to successfully do so in the field of environmental law (cf. chapters 11 and 12). Second, in order to solve the case to their advantage, litigants should put forward arguments based on European law and should aim at promoting the overall interest of the European Union. Yet, the success of such a strategy is also dependent on the willingness of the respective national judge to refer questions on law to the ECJ and to interpret national law in light of EU law (cf. indirect effect).

The last step is crucial with regard to the first two categories of litigants mentioned above who aim at a broader change in policy. Litigation can in these instances not be

49 Alter & Vargas, 2000, p.472
50 Alter, 2000, p.498
51 Alter, 2000, p.507
52 Alter & Vargas, 2000, p.453
53 Alter & Vargas, 2000, pp.462–463
54 2000
55 Greenwood, 2007a, p.39

used in complete isolation but must be rather accompanied by public deliberation campaigns and political strategies of lobbying in order to rely upon the ECJ precedent and increase the costs for Member State governments for not abiding by the Court's decision[56]. The more often 'repeat player'–litigants follow this strategy, the greater the political pressure on governments and EU Institutions to make a change in approach within a particular policy and the more likely becomes the final success of the litigant[57]. All of these findings can, of course, also be applied to CSOs that consider pursuing a litigation strategy at the GC and ECJ directly without the detour over national courts.

It is for the above mentioned reasons that the ECJ has become an attractive target for CSOs to pursue their interests. Its settled institutional position within the organizational structure of the EU comparable to that of a constitutional court, the relative wide discretionary powers of Treaty interpretation and legislation review and, most importantly, its willingness to grant rights to individuals and promote democratic values suggests some of the reasons why this has happened.

56 Alter, 2000, p.489; Alter & Vargas, 2000, pp.453–454
57 Alter, 2000, p.489; Costa, 2003, p.747; Bouwen & McCown, 2007, p.427

Part III.

The Aarhus Convention at the EU

Part III

9. Access to Environmental Information

As previously indicated, access to information is regarded as the decisive prerequisite for transparency and public participation in decision–making processes and deeply embedded in the overall concept of participatory democracy in modern Western democracies. The refusal to disclose information possessed by public authorities would amount to a prevention of public participation[1].

Environmental information is defined in Article 2(3) of the Aarhus Convention as comprising information on (a) the state of the elements of the environment and the respective interactions; (b) factors that affect or are likely to affect those elements referred to in subparagraph (a) as well as analyses that are employed in environmental decision–making; and finally, (c) the state of human health and safety[2]. While Article 4 is engaged in the disclosure of environmental information upon request, Article 5 of the Convention establishes rules on the general collection of information by public authorities and their dissemination. In general terms, public authorities, holding any information relating to the matters referred to in Article 2(3)AC, are obliged to release this information except for any of the exemptions listed in Articles 4(3)(a)–(c) and 4(4)(a)–(h)AC[3]. These exemptions are to be interpreted restrictively[4] and may not be misused as excuses not to disclose information[5]. Overall, the provisions on access to information can be considered to be quite "extensive and comprehensive"[6].

The parties to the Convention are obliged to ensure that public authorities release the relevant information to the applicant "as soon as possible" and in any case no later than one month after the submission of the request[7]. An extension by another month is justified, if the volume and complexity of the requested information so require and the applicant is informed about the new date and the reasons justifying the extension in due time[8]. The release of information after the expiration of the time limit or an incomplete

1 cf. Savoia & Skrylnikov, 2003, p.23; Rodenhoff, 2002, p.345; Lee & Abbott, 2003, p.88

2 Article 2(3)(a),(b),(c) of the Aarhus Convention; cf. also Rose–Ackermann & Halpaap, 2001, pp.3–4

3 Rodenhoff, 2002, p.345

4 Article 4(4) second indent of the Aarhus Convention

5 Savoia & Skrylnikov, 2003, p.25

6 Rose–Ackermann & Halpaap, 2001, p.7

7 Article 4(2) of the Aarhus Convention

8 Article 4(2) of the Aarhus Convention

disclosure of the relevant documents can be considered as failure to respond[9] and may result in administrative or judicial proceedings.

One remarkable innovation of the Aarhus Convention is the fact that individuals or NGOs applying for copies of the actual documents comprising the relevant environmental information do not have to state an interest (cf. Article 4(1)(a)AC)[10]. This is rather uncommon in principles of administrative law as in most legal systems, at least in review proceedings of administrative activities, an interest in the issue at stake must be proven by the relevant actor in order to be admitted.

9.1. Access to Environmental Information in the EU

Many EU Member States have already provided for access to information on their own initiative[11]; yet European legislation establishes a greater legal obligation as well as stricter and homogenized rules for public authorities on how to disclose such information. The EU has adopted three legislative acts in order to comply with the requirements of the Aarhus Convention. Directive 2003/4/EC addresses the national level and requires implementation and execution by the Member States. The act concerns access to environmental information held by any national public authority and stipulates the framework of obligations and requirements with which these authorities need to comply. Member States, themselves being parties to the Aarhus Convention, have, of course, also enacted laws according to the national procedures to ensure compliance with the convention[12].

Regulation 1367/2006/EC[13] for the most part specifies the general rules on access to documents possessed by the Commission, Council and European Parliament respectively that are governed by Regulation 1049/2001/EC[14]. The former regulation overcomes some of the deficiencies of Regulation 1049/2001/EC and is most elaborate with regard to the requirements under the AC's first pillar[15]. Directive 2003/4/EC[16] and Regulation 1049/2001/EC[17] have been adopted and applied after signature, yet prior to the approval of the Aarhus Convention by the then European Community. Regulation 1367/2006/EC, however, has only entered into force two years and four months after the convention had been incorporated into European law and became binding upon the institutions. The EU is still in the process of bringing its legislation and daily administrative practice into compliance with the requirements of the Aarhus Convention. Referring to

9 Savoia & Skrylnikov, 2003, p.24
10 Rose–Ackermann & Halpaap, 2001, p.4; Rodenhoff, 2002, p.345
11 Lee & Abbott, 2003, p.88
12 Hallo, 2007, p.4
13 adopted on 6 September 2006; applicable as of 28 June 2007
14 Hallo, 2006, p.7
15 Hallo, 2007, p.37
16 adopted on 28 January 2003; implementation deadline: 14 February 2005 (cf. Article 10 Dir.2003/4/EC)
17 adopted on 30 May 2001; applicable as of 3 December 2001

the discussion on the definition of 'institutions' in the European context and the applicability of the provisions of the Aarhus Convention to organs in the framework of the EU, it must be said that legislation only governs national authorities in the Member States as well as the EP, Council and Commission on EU level; thereby excluding other European bodies, offices or agencies.

Overall, the comparison[18] of the premises required by the Aarhus Convention with the above introduced legislative acts reveals a fairly satisfying result. The formal rules on access to environmental information comply with the provisions of the UNECE Convention. In some instances, EU legislation seems to be more detailed and specific than the Aarhus Convention. Several provisions even go beyond the Convention's minimum requirements, which is explicitly allowed by Article 3(5)AC. A survey undertaken by the European Environmental Bureau (EEB) in 2007 has further affirmed that, on paper, the implementation of the directive on national level has been satisfying despite some delays. In some instances, however, practice still reveals transposition problems[19].

Briefly summarized, any natural or legal persons irrespective of their nationality, citizenship or place of registered seat, or main activity[20] have the right to request access to environmental information in written and other forms[21] without having to state a reason or interest[22]. The importance of the non–discrimination principle regarding the applicant cannot be overestimated. As the discussion on the right to a healthy environment has shown, the stable and healthy state of the environment is of concern to "every person of present and future generations"[23] individually and the public in general as defined in Article 2(4)AC. Accordingly, the Convention is based on the premise that everybody is in one form or another affected by the environment and should therefore also be granted, among other things, access to environmental information without having to qualify in personal or substantive matters. Keeping in mind this emphasis, the implementation by the EU is less concise. However, the definition of 'applicant' in Article 2(5) Directive 2003/4/EC as "any natural or legal person" read in conjunction with Article 18(1) TFEU on the general prohibition of discrimination on grounds of nationality can be interpreted to allow unrestricted access to environmental information for anybody, even though it is not explicitly confirmed in the legislative act.

Access to environmental information held by any of the EU Institutions appears at first sight to be restricted. Article 2(1) Regulation 1049/2001/EC limits the beneficiaries thereof to "[a]ny citizen of the Union, and any natural or legal person residing or

18 Own comparison undertaken; cf. also European Commission, 2008, SEC(2008) 556, *Aarhus Convention Implementation Report – European Community*

19 Hallo, 2007, pp.11 & p.13

20 Non–discrimination: required by Article 3(9)AC; fulfilled by Article 2(5) Dir.2003/4/EC; Article 3 Reg.1367/2006/EC

21 required by Article 4(1)(b)AC; fulfilled by Article 3(4) Dir.2003/4/EC; Article 10 Reg.1049/2001/EC

22 required by Article 4(1)(a)AC; fulfilled by Article 3(1) Dir.2003/4/EC; Article 6(1) last sentence Reg.1049/2001/EC

23 Article 1 AC

having its registered office in a Member State". The extension of the right to access to information to "any natural or legal person not residing or not having its registered office in a Member State" lies at the discretion of the relevant institution[24]. However, the provisions of the regulation relate to any kind of information contained in documents of EU Institutions, which is not merely restricted to those that may have an effect on the environment. In the latter case, Regulation 1367/2006/EC is the first legislative act that needs to be consulted and which explicitly refers to the non–discrimination principle of the Aarhus Convention in its preamble no. 6[25] and copied the wording of the Aarhus Convention in Article 3 when declaring that:

> Regulation (EC) No 1049/2001 shall apply to *any request* by an applicant for access to environmental information held by Community [EU] institutions and bodies *without discrimination* as to citizenship, nationality or domicile and, in the case of a legal person, without discrimination as to where it has its registered seat or an effective centre of its activities. [emphasis added]

Thus, EU legislation distinguishes information relating to the state of the environment from those concerning other policy areas and enables preferential and easier access for applicants seeking the former kind of information. In addition, it is important to note that Article 2(6) of Regulation 1049/2001/EC explicitly allows for wider access to information and documents held by EU Institutions, if so provided for by "instruments of international law or acts of the institutions implementing them"[26].

Requests for environmental information must be processed "as soon as possible" but not later than one month from the submission or the receipt of the request[27] resulting in the disclosure of the information or the reasoned refusal to do so. Here, Regulation 1049/2001/EC, read on the basis of Regulation 1367/2006/EC, stipulates the even stricter time frame of fifteen working days[28] in cases where the Aarhus Convention as well as Directive 2003/4/EC for Member State authorities only require one month[29]. In the case that more time is needed to execute the request, due to the volume and complexity, an extension by the same time period[30] is allowed, if the applicant is informed about the reasons and the length of the extension in due time[31]. The effectiveness of these provisions is, however, limited insofar as no sanctions are designated in cases of non–compliance with the strict time frames[32].

---

24 Article 2(2) Reg.1049/2001; cf. also Rodenhoff, 2002, p.352

25 "As a general principle, the rights guaranteed by the three pillars of the Aarhus Convention are without discrimination as to citizenship, nationality or domicile". Cf. also Hallo, 2006, p.7

26 cf. also Hallo, 2006, p.7

27 required by Article 4(2) Aarhus Convention; fulfilled by Article 3(2)(a) Dir.2003/4/EC; Articles 7(1) & 8(1) Reg.1049/2001/EC

28 Articles 7(1) and 8(1) Reg.1049/2001

29 Article 4(2) Aarhus Convention Article 3(2)(a) Dir.2003/4/EC

30 One month: Article 4(2) Aarhus Convention; Article 3(2)(b) Dir.2003/4/EC; fifteen working days: Reg.1049/2001/EC

31 required by Article 4(2) Aarhus Convention; fulfilled by Article 3(2)(b) Dir.2003/4/EC; Articles 7(3) & 8(1) Reg.1049/2001/EC

32 Hallo, 2006, p.9

The Aarhus Convention lists eleven grounds upon which the disclosure of environmental information in the possession of public authorities may be refused, provided that a restrictive interpretation is employed and weighed against the public interest in each individual case[33]. Overall, the application of the exceptions is very similar, yet the list in Directive 2003/4/EC for national authorities in the Member States is more concrete and names a number of specific examples that are not listed in the Aarhus Convention[34]. Most of these exceptions concern matters relating to state sovereignty, as well as confidential and personal information, or those relating to ongoing investigations or proceedings[35]. The latter two incidents listed in Article 4(2) second and third indent of Regulation 1049/2001/EC have become subject to heavy criticism. On the basis of these provisions, the Commission regularly inhibits access to information relating to a pending infringement proceeding before the ECJ. In line with the same reasoning, Article 5 of Regulation 1049/2001/EC then exacerbates potential access to documents held by national authorities in the Member States relating to court proceedings. It is, however, at least questioned whether this exception is lawful under Article 4(4) AC as long as it does not affect (a) the confidentiality of proceedings or (c) the right to a fair trial[36]. The regulation furthermore allows Member States in its Article 4(5) to veto the disclosure of any information originating from it. Although opposing the general aim of the Aarhus Convention, Regulation 1367/2006/EC does not modify this exception and may therefore result in a breach of the obligations under the convention[37].

A refusal to disclose the requested information must be accompanied by the reasons and information about the remedies available to the applicant in order to challenge an authority's decision[38]. A refusal can also be only partial. Public authorities are called upon to separate those information that fall under any of the exceptions from those that do not and to deliver the latter to the applicant[39]. Hence, public authorities fall under a duty to place applicants in the position to be able to collect as much relevant information as the applicant desires. This is in line with the obligation on part of the authority to which a request has been made but does not possess the requested information. It must then aid the applicant by referring the claim to the responsible authority. It is interesting to note that Regulation 1049/2001/EC on access to non–specified documents of the

---

33 For a detailed list of the reasons and the provisions of the respective legal acts, see table 1. below; allowed by Article 4(3)(a)–(c) & 4(4)(a)–(h) Aarhus Convention; taken over by Article 4(1)(a)–(e) & 4(2)(a)–(h) Dir.2003/4/EC; Article 4(1)–(4) & 6(2) Reg.1049/2001 in conjunction with Article 6 Reg.1367/2006/EC

34 e.g. Article 4(2)(d) Dir.2003/4/EC: "[...] to protect a legitimate economic interest, including the public interest in maintaining statistical confidentiality and tax secrecy"

35 Directive 2003/4/EC

36 Jans, 2003, pp.62–63

37 Hallo, 2007, pp.37–38

38 required by Article 4(7) Aarhus Convention; fulfilled by Article 4(5) Dir.2003/4/EC; Articles 7(1) & 8(1) Reg.1049/2001/EC

39 required by Article 4(6) Aarhus Convention; fulfilled by Article 4(4) Dir.2003/4/EC; Article 4(6) Reg.1049/2001/EC

Commission, Council and Parliament does not consider the fact that a request could be lodged for information that are not at their disposal. Rather, it is stipulated in Article 2(3) that the provisions of the regulation only govern those documents that were "drawn up or received by it [the EU Institution] and in its possession". There is no indication in the text that assistance to the applicant is neither welcomed nor required. The regulation implies that the applicant applies to the correct institution. However, Regulation 1367/2006/EC is aware of this shortcoming and, again, introduces a provision in order to comply with the Aarhus Convention. Article 7 of the aforementioned legislative act obliges authorities that receive a request about information that they do not hold to inform the applicant "as promptly as possible, but within 15 working days at the latest [...] of the authority to which [...] [they believe] it is possible to apply for the information requested or transfer the request to the relevant" authority.

Yet, provided that requests for information are "manifestly unreasonable", public authorities may refuse to release any information on the basis of Article 4(3)(b) AC. While Directive 2003/4/EC provides for that exception with regard to national authorities holding environmental information, neither Regulation 1049/2001/EC on access to documents held by EU Institutions, nor Regulation 1367/2006/EC introduced a similar provision for environmental information on EU level. The Aarhus Convention furthermore grants discretion to authorities in the release of information, if the request was formulated in "too general a manner" by the applicant so that it could not be executed by the authority[40]. However, both legislative acts for Member State authorities as well as Union Institutions impose a duty upon the authority to which the demand for environmental information was made, to assist the applicant in the clarification and specification of the request "by providing information on the use of the public registers". Directive 2003/4/EC still concedes the possibility to refuse the request to public authorities, while legislation governing the EU Institutions remains silent on this matter[41].

As a preliminary conclusion, the EU satisfactorily complies with the requirements of the Aarhus Convention on access to environmental information. It is remarkable that the legislation explicitly distinguishes between applicants that seek information relating to the environment and those that concern other policy areas. As a negative point, however, these rules only govern access to documents on the environment held by the 'EU Institutions', whereas agencies and other bodies that may also be heavily concerned with the destruction or protection of the environment are not bound by the legislative acts under study. With regard to institutions, access to environmental information is more easily offered to anybody on the basis of non–discrimination without any further conditions and with greater assistance in finding the relevant information. The question resulting from this preferential access to environmental information is accordingly, how this privileged treatment could also be introduced for access to justice in environmental disputes.

40 Article 4(3)(b) Aarhus Convention

41 Article 4(1)(c) in conjunction with Article 3(3) Dir.2003/4/EC; Article 6(2) Reg.1049/2001/EC

Table 1: Comparison of the Aarhus Convention and EU legislation
implementing access to environmental information in the Member States (MS) and EU

Keyword	*Aarhus Convention*	*Directive 2003/4/EC*	*Regulation 1049/2001/EC*	*Regulation 1367/2006/EC*
Definitions 'public authority' 'environmental info.' 'public'	**Article 2** **2(2)(a)–(d)** **2(3)(a)–(c)** **2(4)**	**Article 2** **2(2)(a)–(c)** 2(1)(a)–(f) **2(6)**	**Article 3** – – – – **3(a)** (documents) – – – –	**Article 2** **2(1)(c)** EU Institutions **2(1)(d)(i)–(vi)** **2(1)(b)**
No discrimination as to citizenship, nationality, domicile, registered seat	**3(9)**	**18 TFEU+2(5)**: def. applicant= *any* natural/legal person; discretio–nary	**18 TFEU + 2(1)** discriminatory BUT: **2(2)**	**Preamble (6)+ Art.3**: non–dis–criminatory appli–cation of Reg. 1049/2001/EC
Request interest need not to be stated	**4(1)(a)**	**3(1)**	**6(1)** last sent.: No reasons to be stated	→
– as soon as possible or within 1 month – ext. to 2 months poss. + inform applicant & reasons	**4(2)** (submission) **4(2)**	**3(2)(a)** receipt **3(2)(b)**	**7(1)** & **8(1)**: promptly; 15 working days **7(3)** & **8(2)**: ext. by 15 working days	→
Refusal + state–ment of reasons Inform about available remedies	**4(7)**	**4(5)** last sentence	**7(1)** & **8(1)**	→
Information not held by authority & duty to inform about available remedies	**4(5)**	**4(1)(a)**	Indirectly presumed	**7**: promptly inform applicant within 15 working days
If not all info. can be disclosed, separate, if poss., & release parts of the document	**4(6)**	**4(4)**	**4(6)**	
Form of information	**4(1)(b)**	**3(4)** first subpara.	**10**	→
Inexpensive charge & schedule	**4(8)**	**5(1)**: free–of–charge **5(2)&(3)**: schedules	**10(1)** 2nd & 3rd sentences; free: 4th sent; no schedule	
Exceptions	**Article 4**	**Article 4**	**Article 4**	**Article 6**
Authority does not hold info.	**4(3)(a)**	**4(1)(a)**	**2(3)**: indirectly presumed	**7**: inform applicant w/in 15 days
Request is mani–festly unreasonable	**4(3)(b)**	**4(1)(b)**	– – – –	
Request formulated in too general a manner	**4(3)(b)**	**4(1)(c)** + **3(3)**: assistance	**6(2)**: not suffi–ciently precise + assistance	
In course of completion	**4(3)(b)**	**4(1)(d)**	– – – –	
Internal commu–nication	**4(3)(c)**	**4(1)(e)**	**4(3)** unless public interest	→
Confidentiality of public proceedings	**4(4)(a)**	**4(2)(a)**	4(2) 2nd & 3rd dash	→
IR, nat. defense, public security	**4(4)(b)**	**4(2)(b)**	**4(1)(a)** first three dashes	→
Justice: fair trial, enquiry orginating	**4(4)(c)**	**4(2)(c)**	**4(2)** 2nd & 3rd dash+ legal advice	→
Confidential commer–cial & industrial info.; except emissions	**4(4)(d)**	**4(2)(d)**	**4(1)(a)** 4th dash + financial, monetary & econ. policy of MS	→

Keyword	*Aarhus Convention*	*Directive 2003/4/EC*	*Regulation 1049/2001/EC*	*Regulation 1367/2006/EC*
Intellectual property rights	**4(4)(e)**	**4(2)(e)**	**4(2)** 1st dash	→
Confidential personal data of natural persons, who did not consent to disclosure	**4(4)(f)**	**4(2)(f)**	**4(1)(b)**	→
3rd party that supp–lied the info. volun–tarily & did not consent to release	**4(4)(g)**	**4(2)(g)**	**4(4)** + obligation to consult 3rd party	→
Environmental site e.g. rare species	**4(4)(h)**	**4(2)(h)**		**6(2)**
MS request not to disclose info.	----	----	**4(5)** (probably ltd. by Dir.2003/4	→

10. Public Participation in Environmental Decision–Making

10.1. Public Participation in Environmental Decision–Making under the Aarhus Convention

The Aarhus Convention is not the first environmental agreement to provide for public participation in environmental decision–making. However, it certainly is more far–reaching and detailed than preceding international attempts[1]. Participation of the interested public has been recognized as "[o]ne of the fundamental prerequisites for the achievement of sustainable development"[2] in Agenda 21 at the 1992 UN Conference on Environment and Development[3].

As mentioned above, effective participation by non–state actors may only be possible, if the relevant information is accessible free of charge and capable of being understood by the respective participants because the use of technical language and terminology is avoided[4]. Equally important, however, is the condition that participation by laypersons should not only be a formal requirement but an actual practice that is incorporated into the general decision–making process[5]. It is generally agreed that the opinion by all participants should be taken into account by decision–makers in order to benefit from external expertise and innovative suggestions[6]. The Convention provides for public participation in environmental decision–making in three instances[7]. Article 6 of the Aarhus Convention most elaborately describes the procedure to allow for the public to exert strong influence in decision–making concerning specific activities that may have an impact on the environmental status quo[8]. The article lists in detail under which circumstances and relating to which activities[9] comprehensive participation opportunities

1 Rodenhoff, 2002, p.347

2 UN Department of Economic and Social Affairs, 1992, *Agenda 21*, Section III - Strengthening the role of major groups, Chapter 23, Preamble 23.2, Website.

3 Rodenhoff, 2002, p.346

4 Kravchenko, Skrylnikov & Bonine, 2003, p.30

5 Kravchenko, Skrylnikov & Bonine, 2003, p.29

6 Kravchenko, Skrylnikov & Bonine, 2003, p.31

7 Articles 6 on public participation in decisions on specific activities, 7 on public participation concerning plans, programmes and policies relating to the environment and 8 on public participation during the preparation of executive regulations and/or generally applicable legally binding normative instruments of the Aarhus Convention respectively

8 Lee & Abbott, 2003, p.99

9 cf. Annex I of the Aarhus Convention

shall be provided by the parties to the convention to the public concerned. Amongst others, it establishes strict time frames and minimal requirements for public authorities to provide the public with opportunities to be heard and their opinion to be taken into consideration as early in the decision–making process as possible[10]. To control whether due account has been taken of suggestions by external participants, the convention demands all final decisions to be published and well–reasoned. The reasons explaining the outcome of a decision may furthermore provide the basis for judicial review of a decision[11].

The provisions in Article 7 on participation regarding plans, programs and policies are less comprehensive than those relating to specific activities, although that article refers to some provisions of Article 6 for the involvement of the public in the formulation of plans and programs[12]. Generally, the parties to the convention "shall make appropriate practical and/or other provisions for the public to participate during the preparation of plans and programmes relating to the environment, within a transparent and fair framework"[13]. The reluctant wording in the formulation of the duties of governments to "endeavour to provide opportunities for public participation" in the development of environmental policies only "[t]o the extent appropriate"[14] reflects a rather vague commitment to the aim of the Aarhus Convention[15]. This language is often used in soft law, i.e. recommending rather than legally binding texts[16]. An augmentation in vagueness and corresponding diminution in commitment is to be found in Article 8 AC on the preparation of executive regulations or generally applicable legally binding normative instruments. Although the article even stipulates that (a) time frames should be adhered to, (b) draft rules should be made publicly accessible, and (c) the "public should be given the opportunity to comment, directly or through representative consultative bodies", much of the strong rules are taken away by the formulation that "[e]ach party shall strive to promote effective public participation at an appropriate stage [...]". In addition, public opinion shall not merely be taken into consideration but rather "taken into account as far as possible"[17].

10.2. Access to Participation in EU Decision–Making

10.2.1. EU Legislation applying to the Member States

In its report on the state of the implementation of the Aarhus Convention in the EU[18], the Commission declared that the adoption of decisions relating to activities listed in Annex I of the Aarhus Convention continues to be reserved to the competence of the

10 Rodenhoff, 2002, p.347; Lee & Abbott, 2003, p.97
11 Lee & Abbott, 2003, p.97; cf. Articles 6(8) & (9) of the Aarhus Convention
12 Rose–Ackermann & Halpaap, 2001, p.5
13 Article 7, first sentence of the Aarhus Convention
14 Article 7, last sentence of the Aarhus Convention
15 Rodenhoff, 2002, p.347
16 Lee & Abbott, 2003, p.101
17 Article 8 of the Aarhus Convention; Rose–Ackermann & Halpaap, 2001, p.5
18 European Commission, 2008

Member States. The transposition of the requirements laid out in Article 6 AC is therefore executed by national governments on the basis of former EC directives[19], whose implementation is in turn weaker than that relating to environmental information[20].

In particular, Directive 2003/35/EC[21] has been adopted for the purpose of amending existing legislation in order to bring it into conformity with the requirements of the Aarhus Convention[22]. This directive establishes general rules of public participation which Member States shall adhere to when taking decisions in areas falling under the list of Annex I of the Aarhus Convention and in particular with regard to projects requiring environmental impact assessments as governed by Directive 85/337/EC (EIA Directive), as well as the integrated pollution prevention and control tools of Directive 96/61/EC (IPPC Directive). While the substantive parts of the two last–mentioned legislative acts have remained unaltered, Directive 2003/35/EC has considerably refined the provisions on public participation. While the article on public participation of the EIA Directive has been amended only in some regards in order to meet the requirements of Article 6 AC, it was necessary to insert a complete new Article 15(1) and Annex V to the IPPC Directive on the details of the procedure to include public participation opportunities.

Yet, overall and in similar terms as the requirements concerning environmental information, one can conclude that the European Union has met its obligations under the Aarhus Convention; at least on paper. It is, however, important to remember that, although the EU offers broad public participation opportunities in environmental matters not only since the implementation of the Aarhus requirements but since the 1990s and particularly the Commission's White Paper on Governance, at least the Commission has initiated broad consultation schemes for the interested public.

The definitions of 'the public' and 'the public concerned' have been added to the two substantive legislative acts[23] by Directive 2003/35/EC and mirror the wording of the Aarhus Convention[24]. The areas of activity are always specified in the relevant piece of legislation of which several categories fall within the list in Annex I, which are then to be handled strictly (cf. Article 6(1)(a) AC), while others fall under the more lenient regulations of Article 6(1)(b) AC. After amendment, all pieces of legislation provide for public

19 European Commission, 2008, p.16

20 Hallo, 2007, p.11

21 adopted on 26 May 2003; applicable as of 25 June 2005; three months after the EU's approval of the Aarhus Convention

22 Cf. Article 1 Objective: "The objective of this Directive is to contribute to the implementation of the obligations arising under the Århus Convention, in particular by: (a) providing for public participation in respect of the drawing up of certain plans and programmes relating to the environment; (b) improving the public participation and providing for provisions on access to justice within Council Directives 85/337/ EEC and 96/61/EC".

23 Articles 2(1) & 3(1) first subpara.; 3(1) second subpara.; Dir.2003/35/EC; 1(2) first and second subparas. Dir.85/337/EEC; 2(13) & (14) Dir.96/61/EC

24 Articles 2(4) and (5) of the Aarhus Convention respectively

participation early in decision–making in a timely, adequate and effective manner[25]. It is further prescribed that the public shall be informed by public notice or, as the EU legislation adds, any other appropriate, preferably digital, means[26] of the proposed activity[27] and the nature of the possible decision[28]. In addition, it shall be guaranteed that the public is informed about the public authority that is responsible to take the relevant decision[29], the authority from which information can be retrieved[30], and the one to which comments and opinions can be delivered[31]. The former should also receive information about the envisaged procedure[32], including the possibilities for public participation[33]. Furthermore, Article 6(6) AC demands the disclosure of information relating to the nature, coverage, location and, if applicable, the duration of the proposed activity[34]. In addition, the impact on the environment must be assessed[35], the respective measures introduced[36], and a non–technical summary be provided to the lay public[37].

While the above–requested information is also covered by Article 5 of the EIA Directive, the legislation makes no mentioning of public access to the main alternatives studied by the applicant[38] or the main reports and advice given externally to the public authority at the relevant time[39]. However, indirectly, one can assume that these requirements are also covered by the information that the public concerned may receive upon request.

In addition, throughout the whole decision–making process, parties to the Convention are under the obligation to ensure that the public receives the relevant information in due time and is granted by the relevant public authority "reasonable time–frames [...] to prepare and participate effectively" in the deliberation of environmental activities and

25 Article 6(2) AC; Article 2(2) Dir.2003/35/EC; Article 6(2) & (4) Dir.85/337/EEC; Article 15(1) in conjunction with Annex V, 1 Dir.96/61/EC

26 Article 6(2)AC; Article 2(2)(a) Dir.2003/35/EC; Article 6(2) Dir.85/337/EEC; Article 15(1) in conjunction with Annex V, 1 Dir.96/61/EC

27 Article 6(2)(a) AC; Article 6(2)(b) Dir.85/337/EEC

28 Article 6(2)(b) AC; Article 6(2)(d) Dir.85/337/EEC; Article 15(1) in conjunction with Annex V, 1(d) Dir.96/61/EC

29 Article 6(2) AC; Article 2(2)(a) Dir.2003/35/EC; Article 6(2) Dir.85/337/EEC; Article 15(1) in conjunction with Annex V, 1(c) Dir.96/61/EC

30 Article 6(2)(d)(iv) AC; Article 6(2)(f) Dir.85/337/EEC; Article 15(1) in conjunction with Annex V, 1(c) & (f) Dir.96/61/EC

31 Article 6(2)(d)(v) AC; Article 2(2)(a) Dir.2003/35/EC; Article 6(2)(c) Dir.85/337/EEC; Article 15(1) in conjunction with Annex V, 1(c) Dir.96/61/EC

32 Article 6(2)(d) Dir.2003/35/EC; Article 2(2)(a) Dir.2003/35/EC; Article 6(2)(a) Dir.85/337/EEC; 15(1) in conjunction with Annex V,1(f) Dir.96/61/EC

33 Article 6(2)(d)(ii) & (iii) AC; Article 6(2)(f) & 6(3)(c) (referral to Dir.2003/4/EC) Dir.85/337/EEC; Article 15(1) in conjunction with Annex V,1(g) referral to point 5 Dir.96/61/EC

34 Article 6(6)(a) AC; Article 5 first indent Dir.85/337/EEC

35 Article 6(6)(b) AC; Article 5, third indent Dir.85/337/EEC

36 Article 6(6)(c) AC; Article 5 second indent Dir.85/337/EEC

37 Article 6(6)(d) AC; Article 5 fourth indent Dir.85/337/EEC

38 Article 6(6)(e) AC

39 Article 6(6)(f) AC

projects[40]. Both legislative acts place, after amendment, the same requirement upon the EU Member States[41]. After having prepared itself, the public should be given the opportunity to submit "any comments, information, analyses or opinions that it considers relevant to the proposed activity" in any form, otherwise, effective participation would not be possible[42].

The effectiveness of public participation also depends upon the final outcome of the decision–making process for which the Aarhus Convention demands that "due account" shall be taken of the opinions delivered by the public[43]. While the new Annex V, 4 of the IPPC Directive, inserted by Directive 2003/35/EC, corresponds to the wording of the Aarhus Convention, Article 8 of the EIA Directive merely states that "information gathered [...] must be taken into consideration". Of course, it remains a matter of interpretation what exactly is to be understood by 'due account'; yet, the unaltered formulation in Directive 85/337/EEC appears to be substantially weaker than what is required by the Aarhus Convention. Yet, the requirement that the public must be informed about the fact that the decision has been taken, its nature, and the reasons and considerations upon which it is built is again complied with efficiently in EU law[44]. Finally, the convention as well as European legislation, require that, when an activity is reconsidered or updated by a public authority, the procedure and requirements outlined in the above–discussed Article 6 must be applied *mutatis mutandis*[45].

Table 2: Comparison of the Aarhus Convention and EU legislation
implementing Article 6 AC in the Member States

Keyword	*Aarhus Convention*	*Dir.85/337/EEC (EIA)* as amended by *Dir.2003/35/EC*	*Dir.96/61/EC (IPPC)* as amended by *Dir.2003/35/EC*
Definitions			
'the public'	**2(4)**	= **1(2)** 1st subpara. [cf.3(1) Dir.2003/35]	**2(13)** [added by 4(1)(b) Dir.2003/35]
'public concerned'	**2(5)**	= **1(2)** 2nd subpara. [cf.3(1) Dir.2003/35]	**2(14)** [added by] 4(1)(b) Dir.2003/35]
Provide particip. opportunities for decisions relating to specific activities	**6(1)(a)**; **(b)** other activities= wider discretion **6(1)(c)**: activities on nat. defence purposes = even wider discretion **Annex I**, p.20:	**Annexes I & II** EIA projects replacing **1(4)**: non–cover of nat. defence **with**: MS may decide, on case–by–case basis not to apply this Dir. to nat.	**Annex I** [amendments by Dir.2003/35]

40 Article 6(3) AC
41 Article 6(6) Dir.85/337/EEC; Article 15(1) in conjunction with Annex V, 5 second sentence
42 Article 6(7) AC; Article 6(4) & (5)Dir.85/337/EEC; Article 15(1) in conjunction with Annex V, 3 & 5 Dir.96/61/EC
43 Article 6(8) AC
44 Article 6(9) AC; Article 9(1) first and second indent Dir.85/337/EEC; Article 15(1) & (5)(a) & (b) Dir.96/61/EC
45 Article 6(10) AC; Article 4(1) & (2) in conjunction with Annex I, 22 & II, 13 first indent Dir.85/337/EEC; Article 15(1) third indent Dir.96/61/EC

Keyword	*Aarhus Convention* EIA projects	*Dir.85/337/EEC (EIA)* defence purposes, if they deem adverse effects [cf. 3(2) Dir.2003/35]	*Dir.96/61/EC (IPPC)*
		as amended by *Dir.2003/35/EC*	as amended by *Dir.2003/35/EC*
Inform the public concerned about activities early in decision–making procedure adequate timely & effective	**6(2)**	**6(2)** & **6(4)** [cf.3(4) Dir.2003/35]	**15(1)** in conj. with **Annex V, 1**
Provide for early public particip. when all options are open	**6(4)**	**6(4)** [cf.3(4) Dir.2003/35]	
Inform public individually	**6(2)**	**6(2)** [cf.3(4) Dir. 2003/35]: or other appropriate means	**15(1)** in conj. with **Annex V, I**; or other appropriate means
Inform: proposed activity & application on which a decision will be taken	**6(2)(a)**	**6(2)(b)** [cf.3(4) Dir.2003/35]	
Inform of the nature of poss. decisions or the draft decision	**6(2)(b)**	**6(2)(d)** [cf.3(4) Dir.2003/35]	**15(1)** in conj. with **Annex V, 1(d)**
Inform of the public authority responsible for making the decision	**6(2)**	**6(2)** [cf.3(4) Dir.2003/35]	**15(1)** in conj. with **Annex V, I(c)**
Inform of the envisaged procedure incl. as & when this information can be provided	**6(2)(d)**	**6(2)(a)** subject to EIA [cf.3(4)(a) Dir.2003/35/EC]	**15(1)** in conj. with **Annex I,1(f)**: time & place of info.
Inform of the commencement of the procedure	**6(2)(d)(i)**		
Opportunities for the public to participate	**6(2)(d)(ii)**	**6(2)(f)** [cf.3(4)(f) Dir.2003/35/EC]	**15(1)** in conj. with **Annex V,1(g)**
Time & venue of any envisaged public hearing	**6(2)(d)(iii)**	**6(3)(c)** (referral to Dir. 2003/4/EC [cf.3(4)(3)(c) Dir.2003/35/EC]	**15(1)** in conj. with **Annex V,1(g)**, point 5
Indicate public authority from which relevant info. can be obtained & where it has been deposited	**6(2)(d)(iv)**	**6(2)(f)** [cf.3(4)(f) Dir.2003/35/EC]	**15(1)** in conj. with **Annex V,1(c)**; **15(1)** in conj. with **Annex V, 1(f)**: time & place of available info.
Indicate relevant public authority to which com- ments or questions can be submitted & of the time schedule for this	**6(2)(d)(v)**	**6(2)(c)** [cf. 3(4)(c) Dir.2003/35/EC]	**15(1)** in conj. with **Annex V,1(c)**
Indicate what environm. info. relevant to the proposed activity is available	**6(2)(d)(vi)**	**6(2)(e)** [cf.3(4)(e) Dir.2003/35/EC]	
Activity is subject to a national or transboundary EIA procedure	**6(2)(e)**	**1(1)**	
Identify the public concerned; enter into discussions & provide info. regarding the objectives of their application before applying for a permit	**6(5)**		
Reasonable time–frames for the public to prepare	**6(3)**	**6(6)** [cf. 3(6) Dir. 2003/35/EC]	**15(1)** in conj. with **Annex V, 5** 2nd sent.
Access for the public con– cerned to examination (upon request), free of charge & as soon as it is available – no prejudice to the	**6(6)** 1st subpara.	**6(6)**: MS shall ensure that, w/in reasonable time, the following is made available to the public concerned [cf.3(4)	

Keyword right of parties to refuse to disclose certain info.	*Aarhus Convention*	*Dir.85/337/EEC (EIA)* Dir.2003/35/EC]	*Dir.96/61/EC (IPPC)*
		as amended by *Dir.2003/35/EC*	as amended by *Dir.2003/35/EC*
Release: Description of the site & physical & technical characteristics of the proposed activity, incl. an estimate of the expected residues & emissions	**6(6)(a)**	**5** 1st indent site, design & size of the project	
Description of the signifi–cant effects of the pro–posed activity on the environment	**6(6)(b)**	**5** third indent including data	
Description of the measures envisaged to prevent & /or reduce the effects incl. emissions	**6(6)(c)**	**5** 2nd indent	
Non–technical summary of the above	**6(6)(d)**	**5** 4th indent	
Outline of the main alternatives studied by the applicant	**6(6)(e)**		
Main reports & advice issued to the public authority at the time when the public concerned shall be informed	**6(6)(f)**		**15(3)**
Inform other MS, if they are likely to be affected by an activity		**7(1)** [cf.3(5) Dir.2003/35/EC]	
Description of the project, together with any available info. on its possible transboundary impact		**7(1)(a)** [cf.3(5) Dir.2003/35/EC]	
Nature of the decision		**7(1)(b)** [cf.3(5) Dir.2003/35/EC]	
Allow the public to submit comments, info., analyses or opinions that it considers relevant	**6(7)**	**6(4) & (5)** [cf.3(4) Dir.2003/35/EC]	**15(1)** in conj. with
Ensure that due account is taken of the outcome of the public participation	**6(8)**	**8** (info. gathered) must be taken into consideration	**15(1)** in conj. with **Annex V,3 & 5**
Inform public promptly about the decision taken	**6(9)**	**9(1)** [cf.3(6)(a) Dir.2003/35]	**15(1)** 2nd subpara. & **(5)** [added by 4(3)(b) Dir.2003/35/EC]
Publish the decision & the reasons & conside–rations upon which the decision is based	**6(9)**	**9(1)** 1st indent & 2nd indent subsequent updates	**15(1)**2nd subpara., **15(5)(a)** [added by 4(3)(b) Dir.2003/35] any **15(5)(b)** info. about public particip. process
Description of the main measure to avoid, reduce and, if poss., offset the major adverse effects		**9(1)** 3rd indent	
When reconsidering or up–dating the operating con–ditions, provisions are applied *mutatis mutandis*	**6(10)**	**4(1) & (2)** in conj. with **Annex I,22** & **Annex II,13** 1st indent	**15(1)** 3rd indent [cf. 4(3)(a) Dir.2003/35]
Where feasible & appro–priate, apply provisions to decisions on release of GMOs into the environm.	**6(11)**		

Table 3: Comparison of the Aarhus Convention and EU legislation
implementing Article 7 AC in the Member States and in the EU

Keyword	*Aarhus Convention*	*Directive 2003/35/EC* (Member States)	*Reg.1367/2006* (EU Institutions)
Definitions 'the public' 'Plans & Programs' (P&P)	 **2(4)**	 =**2(1)** & **3(1)** 1st subpara. **Annex I**; referral to other pieces of legislation	 =**2(1)(b)** **Title I, Art.2(1)(e) (i)–(iv)**
Make appropriate practical & or other provisions for the public to participate [...] within a transparent and fair framework	**7** 1st sent.	**2(2)** **2(2)(b)** the public is entitled to express comments & opinions when all options are open; before the P & P decisions are made	**Title III, Art.9(3)(c) (ii)** & **(4)**: indirectly implied that the public is entitled to express comments etc.
Provide the necessary info. to the public	**7** 1st sent.	**2(2)(a)**: Public notice or appropriate means about any proposals: – any relevant info. about proposals incl. right to participate in dec–making; – competent authority from which info. can be obtained – competent authority to which comments or questions may be submited	**Title III, Art.9(3)** – **Title III, Art.9(3)(a)**; draft proposal, where available; **Title III, Art.9(3)(b)**: relevant env. info. or assessment, where available – **Title III,Art.9(3)(c)(i)** – **Title III,Art.9(3)(c)(ii)**
Give public early & effective opportunities to participate in the preparation & modification or review of the P&P required	**7** in conj. with **6(4)**	**2(2)** (Annex I) **2(3)** 2nd subpara.: detailed arrangements for public particip. [...] determined by the MS to enable the public to & prepare to participate effectively	**Title III,Art.9(1)** + in particular where the Commission prepares a proposal for such a P or P which is submitted to other EU Institutions or bodies for decisions, it shall provide for public participation at that preparatory stage
Identify the public that is entitled to participate by the relevant public authority, taking into account the objectives of the AC	**7** 3rd sent.	**2(3)** 1st subpara.: identify the public concerned entitled to participate incl. NGOs [...]	**Title III,Art.9(2)**: identify the public affected or likely to be affected by, or having an interest in, a plan or program
Reasonable time–frames allowing sufficient time for each of the diff. stages of public participation	**7** in conj. with **6(3)**	**2(3)** 3rd subpara.	**Title III,Art.9(3)(c)(iii)** **9(4)**: time limit of 8 weeks; prior to meetings = 4 weeks; shorten time limits in urgent cases
Take due account of the results of the public participation	**7** in conj. with **6(8)**	**2(2)(c)**	Title III, Art.(5) 1st sentence
Inform public about the decision taken, incl. text reasons & considerations on which the decision is based		**2(2)(d)**: competent authority *makes reasonable efforts* to inform the public [...]	**Title III, Art.9(5)** 2nd sentence incl. info. on public participation
To the extent appropr. [...] public participation in the preparation of env. policies	**7** last sent.	– – –	– – –

10.2.2. EU Legislation on plans, programs and policies applying to the European Institutions and the Member States

Whereas the focus of the implementation of Article 6 AC has been placed upon national authorities, the working procedures of EU Institutions are likewise affected concerning the public participation requirement for plans and programs that potentially affect the state of the environment as demanded in Article 7 AC. Thus, the EU has adopted two legislative acts that repeat the necessity to effectively involve the interested public into the decision–making process concerning environmental plans and programs. Yet, the EU has, so far, not provided legal guidelines for participation opportunities in the development of environmental policies as suggested by the last sentence of Article 7, which discretely asks that "to the extent appropriate, each Party shall to provide opportunities for public participation in the preparation of policies relating to the environment"[46].

The requirements stipulated in Article 7 AC are not only fewer in number but also less detailed and concrete. This gives national governments and EU Institutions considerable leeway in the implementation of the provisions. In line of the same reasoning, Directive 2003/35/EC leaves it up to the Member States to determine "the detailed arrangements for public participation under this Article [...] so as to enable the public to prepare and participate effectively"[47]. All provisions[48] require effective participation by the public when drawing up environmental plans and programs[49].

The wording in the Aarhus Convention is formulated in vague and broad terms and hence leaves much room for interpretation. Even though the EU acts prescribe somewhat more specific the requirements for national authorities and EU Institutions, the provisions still greatly lag behind the specifications of Article 6, as well as the provisions regarding access to environmental information. Yet, where the Convention broadly presupposes for the "necessary information" to be provided to the public[50], both the directive and the regulation on the institutions require that any proposals for environmental plans or programs must be communicated to the public through any appropriate means. This public notice must include information about the right to participation in decision–making[51]. In addition, EU Institutions have to release the draft proposal and, where available, the relevant data, statistics on environmental information, or assessments[52]. The public must be informed about the competent authorities from which additional information can be obtained[53] and with which authority opinions can be lodged[54].

46 cf. Hallo, 2007, p.39
47 Article 2(3) second subpara. Dir.2003/35/EC
48 Article 7 AC, Article 2 Directive 2003/35/EC and Title III, Article 9 Regulation 1367/2006/EC
49 Article 2(4) AC; Article 2(1) & 3(1) Dir.2003/35/EC; Article 2(1)(b) & Title III, Article 9 Reg.1367/2006/EC
50 Article 7, first sentence
51 Article 2(2)(a) Dir.2003/35/EC; Title III, Article 9(3) Reg.1367/2006/EC
52 Title III, Article 9(3)(a) & (b) Reg.1367/2006/EC
53 Article 2(2)(a) Dir.2003/35/EC; Title III, Article 9(3)(c)(i) Reg.1367/2006/EC
54 Article 2(2)(a) Dir.2003/35/EC; Title III, Article 9(3)(c)(ii) Reg.1367/2006/EC

In the following, the Aarhus Convention merely demands from its parties that they offer a transparent and fair framework for public participation in the early stages of the preparation or review of plans and programs relating to the environment[55]. The European Union implemented this request by entitling the public to submit comments and opinions to accessible draft proposals[56]. The Commission is particularly called upon to provide for public participation at the preparatory stage of plans and programs that are forwarded to other EU Institutions for adoption[57]. However, no specific criteria that need to be fulfilled were indicated.

In order for public participation to be effective, all legal texts require that the public concerned and potentially affected by the proposed plans and programs must be identified and invited to participate in the decision–making process. Furthermore, the directive explicitly mentions NGOs under the public that is entitled to participate[58]. Similar to the procedure on decision–making for environmental activities, the necessity to provide for reasonable time frames for the preparation of those that desire to participate[59] and to take due account of the outcome of public participation in the decision are acknowledged[60]. Finally, although not required by the Aarhus Convention, EU Institutions are obliged to inform the public about the final decision, its content, and the reasons and considerations upon which it is based, and the relevant participation by the public, while national authorities are merely called upon to make "reasonable efforts" to do so[61].

In sum, participation opportunities are fairly well developed within the EU. Legislation implementing the legal obligations created by the Aarhus Convention is sufficiently complementary to the latter's provisions. Previous chapters have examined the various access channels that EU Institutions provide to CSOs in general, thus including environmental interest groups. Diverging from the findings on access to environmental information, it appears that those aiming to participate in environmental decision–making processes are not placed in a privileged position compared to other policy procedures. It has been shown that interest groups in general enjoy fairly well–established channels of influence. Environmental CSOs are thereby not disadvantaged and the requirements of the Aarhus Convention are being adequately complied with.

55 Article 7 in conjunction with 6(4) AC; Article 2(3) Dir.2003/35/EC

56 Article 2(2)(b) Dir.2003/35/EC; Title III, Article 9(3)(c)(ii) & (4) Reg.1367/2006/EC: indirectly implied

57 Title III, Article 9(1) Reg.1367/2006/EC

58 Article 7 third sentence AC; Article 2(3) first subpara. Dir.2003/35/EC; Title III, Article 9(2) Reg.1367/2006/EC

59 Article 7 in conjunction with 6(3) AC; Article 2(3) third subpara. Dir.2003/35/EC; Title III, Article 9(3)(c)(iii) & (4) Reg.1367/2006/EC

60 Article 7 in conjunction with 6(8) AC; Article 2(2)(c) Dir.2003/35/EC; Title III, Article 9(5) first sentence Reg.1367/2006/EC

61 Title III, Article 9(5) second sentence Reg.1367/2006/EC; Article 2(2)(d) Dir.2003/35/EC

11. Access to Justice in Environmental Matters

11.1. Access to Justice in Environmental Matters in the Aarhus Convention

As discussed above, the primary goal of the Aarhus Convention is to ensure an environment adequate to the health and well–being of present and future generations of the parties' citizens. It is, accordingly, indispensable for the enjoyment of this right and the enforcement of the rights concerning access to information and public participation to be granted access to the judiciary[1]. Preamble paragraph 18 reflects this approach as it depicts the concern of the parties to the convention "that effective judicial mechanisms should be accessible to the public, including organizations, so that its legitimate interests are protected and the law is enforced". Access to Justice concerning environmental matters is covered in the Aarhus Convention by Article 9 concerning three areas. Paragraph 1 thereof provides for administrative and judicial review procedures relating to the request to release environmental information according to Article 4 AC. Paragraph 2 enables natural and legal persons, including NGOs promoting environmental protection, subject to the respective regulations on *locus standi*, to have the procedural and substantive legality of decisions reviewed[2]. Paragraph 3, again limited by the rules on standing in each legal system, allows the challenge of "acts and omissions by private persons and public authorities which contravene provisions of its national law relating to the environment"[3].

The provisions on *locus standi* are one of the most controversial and innovative ones within the convention. It is quite a novelty that not only individuals but also NGOs promoting environmental protection gain facilitated access to judicial review. The Aarhus Convention permits two standing requirements in its Article 9(2)(a) & (b), namely to be in the possession of an interest or "[m]aintaining impairment of a right", depending on the respective traditions in a given legal system. These requirements are rather common; however, it is remarkable that the convention further asserts in Article 9(2) subparagraph 2 that "the interest of any non–governmental organization fulfilling the requirements referred to in article 2, paragraph 5, shall be deemed sufficient for the

1 Crossen & Niessen, 2007, p.332
2 Crossen & Niessen, 2007, pp.333–334
3 Crossen & Niessen, 2007, pp.333–334

purpose of subparagraph (a). Such organizations shall also be deemed to have rights capable of being impaired for the purpose of subparagraph (b) above". Hence, NGOs promoting environmental protection should be admitted to lodge complaints to courts more easily on the basis of the convention. It is thus not possible to prevent environmental CSOs from challenging acts, omissions or decisions taken by public authorities. On the other hand, Article 9 AC refers to national regulations on numerous occasions and thereby practically weakens the intention to grant greater access to potential claimants in a broader range of environmental matters[4].

Non–procedural Obstacles

However, one aspect has been criticized as constituting great practical obstacles to access to justice in environmental matters. These are primarily financial expenses, including court fees, attorney and expert costs, and possible payments for interim relief that may easily exceed an individual's or NGO's budget. The Aarhus Convention only obligates its parties to "ensure that such a person [the claimant] also has access to an expeditious procedure established by law that is free of charge or inexpensive"[5] but it neither considers the additional costs nor suggests or requires the introduction of one–sided fee shifting[6] instead of two–sided fee shifting as is generally applied in European courts. One–sided fee shifting determines that the attorney fees of victorious citizen plaintiffs are to be paid by the losing defendant; while the losing citizen plaintiff must not cover the winning defendant's costs[7]. However, subject to interpretation, the demand to all parties of the convention in Article 9(5) to "consider the establishment of appropriate assistance mechanisms to remove or reduce financial and other barriers to access to justice" may give rise to confidence despite the soft law language employed.

Remedies

The importance of "adequate and effective remedies, including injunctive relief as appropriate", is emphasized by Article 9(4) first subparagraph AC. In some legal systems, these appropriate and effective remedies may include moral damages, which the court can impose upon the convict for the non–material harm caused to the victim. Due to the non–material nature of the harm suffered, the determination of the amount lies primarily within the judges' discretion. These payments may execute an educating effect on authorities to more strictly adhere to existing environmental regulations[8].

Another remedy, possibly the most crucial, in environmental disputes are interim measures even though their importance does not seem to be reflected in the Aarhus Conven-

4 Rose–Ackermann & Halpaap, 2001, pp.10 & 11
5 Article 9(1) second subparagraph of the Aarhus Convention
6 also called 'loser–pays principle'
7 Rose–Ackermann & Halpaap, 2001, p.11
8 Rohan & Jacobstein, 2003, p.54

tion given the fact that they should only be initiated "as appropriate"[9]. This vague and undefined formulation may give rise to great differences in the interpretation as to under which circumstances such action is considered to be 'appropriate'. Injunctive relief is granted during a court proceeding whenever the realization of the proposed or the continuance of the commenced activity at dispute would cause irrecoverable damages, in this context, to the environment. In other words, the status quo will be guaranteed from the initiation of the legal proceeding to the court's final decision and possibly further onwards. Financial payments would be insufficient to compensate harm that occurred.

Final injunctions are included in the judgment of the court and may prohibit the overall implementation of an activity. However, the judge may already decide to issue a temporary injunction, which prohibits the execution of the challenged activity for the duration of the judicial proceedings. If the final decision of the court concludes that the activity remains illegal, no further harm would have been done, the final costs would have been reduced, and no moral damages would have been levied. In the opposite case, however, these expenses may increase overall costs and might result in defendants suing the losing applicant for losses caused by the unnecessary injunctive relief. The potential scale of these damage payments may be tremendous and in any case exceed the budget of private individuals and smaller NGOs. A financial security reserve may already be asked as soon as the temporary injunctive relief is initiated. These 'bond payments' will be returned, if the necessity of the interim measure is confirmed by the court's final decision. If the judgment opposes the initial measure, the money is paid to compensate for the defendant's losses that have been incurred by the injunctive relief.

Despite the critical assessment of the practical execution of judicial remedies in administrative law disputes, it would give the wrong impression not to emphasize that the drafters of the Aarhus Convention indeed aimed at a consistent and effective set of remedies available for environmental law cases.

Preliminary proceedings

The Aarhus Convention recognizes as well the importance and practicality of non–judicial dispute settlement procedures[10]. Article 9(1) second subparagraph of the Aarhus Convention declares that a party "shall ensure that such a person also has access to an expeditious procedure established by law that is free of charge or inexpensive for reconsideration by a public authority or review by an independent and impartial body other than a court of law". Further, Article 9(2) subparagraph 3 AC acknowledges "the possibility of a preliminary review procedure before an administrative authority" prior to appealing to a court, if national legal systems so require or at least offer them an alternative dispute settlement mechanism. Indeed, most European systems already require the exhaustion of such a preliminary proceeding as a general principle of administrative law (e.g. German Code of Administrative Procedure)[11]. The advantages for claimants

9 Article 9(4) first sent. Aarhus Convention

10 Savoia, 2003, p.39

11 Savoia, 2003, p.39

include the rapidity and charge–free nature of proceedings before that administrative authority against whom an appeal was lodged. The preliminary procedure furthermore reduces the workload of administrative or specialized courts given that a substantial percentage of disputes can be resolved at this stage. Nonetheless, the appeal to courts or comparable bodies established by law is always possible[12].

Decisions by the EU Institutions regarding the disclosure of environmental information must be assessed anew by the same institution, if the applicant so desires. The deadline for reconsideration for the EP, the Council and the Commission is 15 days from the day of the respective request. This time frame is considered to be an example of good practice given that most states have deadlines of one month[13].

Several countries, as well as the EU, have established an Office of the Ombudsman to which citizens and representative associations may complain about maladministration regarding environmental policy. The ombudsman is usually competent to hear complaints concerning decisions, acts or omissions by administrative authorities with the primary goal to protect citizens against the violations of their rights or other misconduct on side of the public authority, including *ultra vires* actions, abuse of powers, or negligence. It, secondly, aids to improve the authority's public legitimacy and accountability through good practices[14]. The institution of an ombudsman may be enclosed in national constitutions or established by legislation and usually parliaments elect the ombudsman or his or her appointment is approved by the head of state or government. Ombudsmen are empowered to initiate objective investigations, either upon complaint by a representative of the public or on their initiative.

If one interprets the office of an ombudsman as an "independent and impartial body established by law" other than a court, he or she could be considered to fall under the definition of a review body in Article 9(1) Aarhus Convention. NGOs and individuals may possibly prefer to lodge complaints to ombudsmen given that proceedings may be shorter and less costly but as effective as judicial review procedures. However, there are serious objections regarding ombudsmen as an alternative to administrative or judicial review proceedings[15]. This is primarily due to the fact that, in most instances, the ombudsman is neither empowered to deliver decisions that legally bind the accused public authority to comply with his or her recommendations nor to provide injunctive relief to the injured party. Hence, the ombudsman merely issues recommendations or advisory opinions that only dispose of moral authority and must rely on the institution's good will to comply[16]. It therefore remains subject to interpretation, whether or not the ombudsman can be considered to cover the requirements of Article 9 of the Aarhus Convention.

12 Savoia, 2003, p.39
13 Savoia & Skrylnikov, 2003, p.24
14 Savoia, 2003, p.40
15 Savoia, 2003, p.40
16 Rodenhoff, 2002, p.349; Savoia, 2003, p.40

11.1.1. Indirect Access via EU offices

The EU remedial system provides environmental CSOs, as any other legal or natural person, with pre–judicial mechanisms that may be employed instead of or prior to judicial proceedings. These two procedures described below are intended to be alternatives to court trials and, in some instances, provide the sole means of reviewing administrative irregularities or other Treaty infringements. Even though these procedures are not prerequisites for judicial proceedings, it may also be useful for the applicant to bring the demand before the court. Time limits for administrative proceedings or appeals before court remain unaffected by lodging a complaint to the European Ombudsman[17].

Both proceedings resemble each other insofar as authorities of the European Union attempt to resolve complaints lodged by private persons regarding infringements of European law. However, the addressees of such complaints are crucially different. The Commission investigates indications for violations of Treaty obligations by the Member States, i.e. national authorities, whereas the European Ombudsman is only empowered to examine the accuracy in administrative practice by the EU Institutions and bodies. The 'jurisdictions' of the two complaint arbitrators are therefore strictly defined and clearly separated. It is, however, possible for an individual to complain to the European Ombudsman about the Commission, if he or she considers that his or her complaint about a Member State's non–compliance with EU law has not been handled correctly according to the own rules of the Commission[18].

The following sections outline those procedures before administrative arbitrators or judicial bodies that are currently available to private litigants, including environmental CSOs, within the European legal system. The description comprises the respective purpose of each proceeding, its subject–matter and formal procedure. Finally, the legal and practical effects of the authority's decision are delineated.

11.1.2. Complaints to the European Ombudsman

Purpose

The office of the European Ombudsman serves as a pre–judicial and administrative–like means of investigating possible maladministration within the institutions and bodies[19] (as well as against offices and agencies under Article 228(1) TFEU) of the European Union. His or her independence from any other occupation[20] and the impartiality of the performance of his or her duties must be guaranteed and unquestionable[21]. He or she

17 Article 2(6) *Decision of the European Parliament on the regulations and general conditions governing the performance of the Ombudsman's duties* [1994]

18 European Commission, 2002, COM 2002/141/final, *Communication on relations with the complainant in respect of infringements of Community law*, Article 14

19 Article 228(1) EC

20 Article 228(3) TFEU; Article 10(1) Decision of the EP [1994]

21 Article 228(3) TFEU; Article 9 Decision of the EP [1994]

is solely subject to the general interest of the EU and its citizens[22]. The Ombudsman is elected by the European Parliament for five years corresponding to the parliamentary term of office and is eligible for reappointment[23]. Prior to the entry into force of the Lisbon Treaty, the EP *appointed* the Ombudsman under the same conditions. The desired outcome is a rapid and mutually satisfactory settlement of conflicts[24].

Subject–Matter of the Complaint

European citizens[25] as well as businesses, associations etc. that have registered office in one of the Member States may file a complaint to the Ombudsman about administrative malpractices, including, e.g. irregularities, abuse of power, failure to reply, refusal of information, and unnecessary delay on part of any EU authority. Excluded from his or her competences are the activities of the ECJ and the GC acting in their judicial capacities[26] as well as national authorities, including government, judicial bodies and national ombudsmen. Complaints about misbehavior by private individuals; i.e. natural as well as legal persons are also inadmissible.

Procedure

Applicants may file their complaints in writing either via the online form posted on the Ombudsman's website or by mail, fax or email within two years of becoming aware of the alleged misconduct and only after having exhausted the relevant preliminary administrative proceedings of the office concerned[27]. The Ombudsman then considers whether he or she is able to start investigations, i.e. whether the complaint is addressed against an EU authority and whether it concerns administrative malpractice. However, he or she may not investigate "where the alleged facts are or have been the subject of legal proceedings"[28].

In the affirmative case, the Ombudsman carries out his or her investigation and informs the concerned institution thereabout[29]. The institution in question is obliged to hand over any requested information including those originating from a Member State except

22 Article 9(1) Decision of the EP [1994]

23 Article 228(1) & (2) TFEU

24 Article 228(1) & (2)TFEU; Article 6(1) Decision of the EP [1994]; cf. Article 6(2) Decision of the EP [1994]: "The Ombudsman shall be chosen from among persons who are Union citizens, have full civil and political rights, offer every guarantee of independence, and meet the conditions required for the exercise of the highest judicial office in their country or have the acknowledged competence and experience to undertake the duties of Ombudsman".

25 Article 20(2)(d), second option TFEU and Article 20, last sentence TFEU; Article 24, third sentence TFEU

26 Article 228(1) TFEU

27 Article 2(4) Decision of the EP [1994]

28 Article 228(1) second subpara. TFEU; cf. Article 1(3) Decision of the European Parliament on the regulations and general conditions governing the performance of the Ombudsman's duties

29 Article 3(1) Decision of the EP [1994]

those falling under the rules of secrecy and confidentiality[30]. In addition, if demanded, Member States must also release information held in their possession, if relevant for the inquiry and not covered by any security exceptions[31]. The Ombudsman may not divulge any such received information[32]. Should the institution not process his or her request for access to information satisfactorily, the Ombudsman may contact the EP in search for support[33]. He or she is under a duty to inform the complainant in due time about any action he or she has taken[34].

The Ombudsman may act as a mediator and help the two parties to reach a satisfactory compromise[35]. If this conciliation remains without effective results, he or she may propose own draft recommendations for the solution of the conflict to which the relevant institution must respond with a detailed opinion within three months[36]. His or her conclusions on either the existence of a violation of the principles of good administrative practice or the statement that the authority has operated within the general rules and standards are communicated to the accused institution as well as reported to the EP. The report may contain recommendations as well. Finally, the original complainant receives detailed information about the findings of the inquiry, the opinion of the institution, and potential recommendations suggested by the Ombudsman[37]. Of less relevance to the individual is the annual report of the Ombudsman about the outcome of his or her inquiries[38]; however, this is crucial for the overall control of good administrative practice within the EU.

Effects of the Decision

The European Ombudsman has no law–enforcing authority. His or her recommendations do not have legally binding force upon the parties to the dispute and therefore do not contain any penalty consequences in case of non–compliance. His or her decisions, however, develop binding force insofar as a persisting conflict creates unnecessary and additional workload and would entail negative publicity for the relevant institution, which in turn decreases the population's support.

Practical case example

An example for a successful appeal to the European Ombudsman in the area of environmental protection is *Friends of the Earth v Commission.* Friends of the Earth, an environmental interest group, requested DG–Environment of the Commission to release

30 Article 3(2) Decision of the EP [1994]
31 Article 3(3) Decision of the EP [1994]
32 Article 4(1) Decision of the EP [1994]
33 Article 3(4) Decision of the EP [1994]
34 Article 2(9) Decision of the EP [1994]
35 Articles 3(5) & (6) Decision of the EP [1994]
36 Article 2(1) Decision of the EP [1994]; Article 3(6) Decision of the EP [1994]
37 Article 3(7) Decision of the EP [1994]
38 Article 3(8) Decision of the EP [1994]

copies of two studies concerning the implementation record of the habitat and waste directives by the UK. The copies were provided but were incomplete because many lines were blacked out for reasons of public interest. Friends of the Earth lodged an appeal to the Secretary General of the Commission, who confirmed the DG's undertaking. The environmental interest group then complained to the European Ombudsman about the two negative decisions. The ombudsman, after closely examining the case, concluded that the exemption on grounds of public interest reasons must be interpreted restrictively, for instance in cases where the information relate to an infringement proceeding pending before the Court of Justice, which had not happened in this case. Thus, the Commission was found guilty of maladministration and acting in breach of the Aarhus Convention when refusing to disclose full copies of the studies[39].

11.1.3. Complaints to the European Commission

Purpose

The complaint procedure serves the purpose of aiding the Commission with its function as 'guardian of the Treaties'. The Commission monitors the implementation of European law and Member States' compliance with Treaty obligations. Individuals and associations can, through this procedure, bring malpractice, late or incomplete implementation of European secondary law etc. to the attention of the Commission. The latter may, after investigation, start infringement proceedings against the respective Member State(s) that could end before the ECJ on the basis of Article 258 TFEU. Civil society is an important ally of the Commission with regard to the national implementation of EU law in general and in particular concerning environmental laws and regulations.

It is also possible for citizens and associations to petition their concerns and complaints to the European Parliament under Article 227 TFEU. The Petitions Committee as well as single MEPs, who have been approached, will also turn to the Commission for the initiation of an official infringement procedure[40], given that solely the Commission (Article 258 TFEU) or other Member States Article (259 TFEU) are in a position to bring Treaty infringements before the Court of Justice.

Subject–Matter of the Complaint

Any individual can complain to the Commission about breaches of EU primary as well as secondary law caused by national authorities in one or more Member States[41].

Procedure

The Commission has arranged a formal complaint handling procedure to enable individuals to bring infringements of EU law by Member States free of charge to the attention

39 Savoia & Skrylnikov, 2003, p.25 & pp.40–41
40 European Commission, *Infringements of EU law*, Website
41 cf. European Commission, *Exercise your rights*, Website

of the European executive[42]. The Commission's *Communication to the European Parliament and the European ombudsman on relations with the complainant in respect of infringements of community law* [43] offers guidance on the principles and guarantees governing the complainant procedure.

Complainants must file their request in writing, whether via mail, fax or email, in one of the Union's official languages[44] with the Secretariat–General or an office of the Commission in a Member State[45]. It is also possible, though not obligatory, to use an online complaint form provided for on the Commission's website[46]. The admissibility of a complaint solely depends on the fact that a Member State, i.e. state authority, is accused of violating Treaty obligations through any legal act or administrative practice[47]. It is not, contrary to direct actions in front of the Court, required for the individual to be able to prove an interest or an individual concern relating to the infringement[48].

Furthermore, the complainant must ensure that his or her information is complete and accurate. Acknowledgment of the receipt of the papers must be issued by the Secretariat–General within fifteen working days to the applicant[49]. In case of uncertainty, the secretariat consults the responsible department(s) within fifteen working days[50]. At the latest, one month after the initial acknowledgment of the correspondence, the Secretariat–General must have decided whether to classify the request as a formal complaint or not[51] and, in the affirmative case, it is registered with the secretariat. Each Directorate–General is responsible for the processing of the content of the complaints relating to its specific policy area[52].

It lies within the discretion of the Commission to decide whether or not to start infringement proceedings against a Member State. Complainants neither have a guarantee nor a right to oblige the Commission to do so[53]. Yet, provided that the correspondence has been classified as a complaint, the relevant DG starts to collect additional information from the accused national authorities in the respective Member States and, if necessary, by contacting the applicant anew in order to be able to assess its further actions[54].

42 Article 2 first sentence, COM 2002/141/final
43 COM 2002/141/final
44 Article 5 first and second sentences, COM 2002/141/final
45 Article 5 sixth sentence, COM 2002/141/final
46 Article 5 third and fifth sentences, COM 2002/141/final
47 Article 2 first sentence, COM 2002/141/final
48 Article 2 second sentence, COM 2002/141/final; cf. European Commission, *Exercise your rights*, Website
49 Article 4 first sentence, COM 2002/141/final
50 Article 3 last sentence, COM 2002/141/final
51 Article 4 second sentence, COM 2002/141/final
52 Article 3 first sentence, COM 2002/141/final; cf. also European Commission, *1. Methods of submitting a complaint*, Website
53 "The Commission may decide whether or not further action should be taken on a complaint". Article 2 third sentence and Article 9 second sentence, COM 2002/141/final
54 European Commission, *2.1 Information gathering*, Website

If the gathered information indicates a potential infringement of EU law, the College of Commissioners sends a letter of formal notice to the respective Member State[55], which should respond with its own observations regarding the arguments that form the basis of the accusation on infringements of the Treaty. As a response to the opinion of the Member State or its lack, the Commission may issue a reasoned opinion, in which it identifies the infringement and specifically lists the facts and arguments upon which it is based. The Commission further stipulates a period of time, usually eight weeks, in which the Member State should take action in order to comply with the requirements under EU law. The Commission may of course also conclude that it will not continue with the investigation of the infringement, for instance, if the Member State has initiated modifications of national rules in order to undo the infringement of European law[56].

The vast majority of the cases can be settled prior to the Commission's reasoned opinion[57]. However, in case of non–compliance with the requirements of the Commission, the latter may decide to refer the case to the ECJ. Legal proceedings usually take roughly two years until a formal decision is made by the Court. The judgment may state that the Member State has failed to fulfill its obligations under the Treaties. The Court can, however, not define how to remove the infringement or award damage payments to individuals in this proceeding. This competency remains with national courts; as does the power to annul decisions issued by a national authority. Thus, it is considered reasonable, either alternatively or in combination, to complain to national administrative and judicial authorities[58]. Yet, if the infringement persists over a certain period of time, the Commission may again call upon the ECJ on the basis of Article 260 TFEU, which has at its disposal the possibility to impose either a lump sum or a periodic penalty payment upon the Member State until it complies with EU law[59].

Throughout the whole process of the infringement proceeding, the responsible Commission department informs the complainant in writing about any action and decision taken regarding his or her complaint; including the decision to close proceedings or refer the case to the ECJ[60]. In the case that no further action is intended, the complainant will be informed and given the opportunity to submit remarks within four weeks prior to the final closure[61], which may motivate the Commission to proceed with its investigation[62]. As a general rule, and particularly regarding the communication between the Commission and the Member State concerned, the identity of the applicant is concealed by the Com-

55 Article 9 first sentence, COM 2002/141/final

56 European Commission, *2.2. Opening of an infringement procedure: formal contacts between the Commission and the Member State concerned*, Website

57 European Commission, 2002b, *Communication: Better monitoring of the application of Community law*, COM(2002)725 final/4, p.13

58 European Commission, *3. National means of redress*, Website

59 European Commission, *2.3. Referral to the European Court of Justice*, Website

60 Article 7 first sentence and Article 9 third sentence, COM 2002/141/final

61 Article 10 first sentence, COM 2002/141/final; Closure of irrelevant or groundless complaints will be handled under the simplified closing procedure of Article 11

62 Article 10 fourth sentence, COM 2002/141/final

mission, unless the person has given permission to disclose it[63]. Fixed time frames are not guaranteed; however, the Commission strives to have taken a decision on whether or not to initiate infringement proceedings within one year of the complaint's registration at the Secretariat–General[64]. Otherwise, the responsible Commission service informs the applicant in writing about the delay[65]. Applications for access to documents relating to infringement proceedings are regulated by Regulation 1049/2001/EC[66]. The decisions taken by the Commission are made publicly available on the website of the Secretariat–General within one week of their adoption[67]. Those relating to a reasoned opinion or a referral to the Court of Justice are, in general, published through press releases[68].

New problem solving pilot scheme The European Commission has – with a view to an improved, more efficient and rapid processing of complaints concerning infringements by Member States – created a pilot scheme[69] that started in April 2008 and included 15[70] of the 27 Member States. Complaints are still registered at the Commission but also forwarded to the Member State concerned. National authorities are given a short period of time (usually ten weeks)[71] within which they need to submit the relevant information, observations and potential solutions directly to the citizen or association that originally complained about the infringement without having to involve the Commission. The Commission, of course, remains to be informed as well. Member States are further expected to provide remedies before a stipulated deadline. Otherwise the Commission may initiate ordinary infringement proceedings against the country "in accordance with existing practice"[72].

It is desired that infringements would, under this pilot scheme, be resolved more rapidly and closer to the interests of the original complainant given that a solution could be reached within the national legal and institutional system[73]. Communication is facil-

---

63 Article 6, COM 2002/141/final; European Commission, *2.1 Information gathering*; *4(b) Administrative guarantees*; *5. Protection of the complainant and personal data*, Websites; cf. particularly Regulation 45/2001/EC *on the protection of individuals with regard to the processing of personal data by the Community institutions and bodies and on the free movement of such data* and Regulation 1049/2001/EC *regarding public access to European Parliament, Council and Commission documents.*

64 Article 8 first sentence, COM 2002/141/final; European Commission, *4 (c) Administrative guarantees*, Website

65 8 second sentence, COM 2002/141/final; European Commission, *4(d) Administrative guarantees*, Website

66 Article 13, COM 2002/141/final

67 Article 12 first sentence, COM 2002/141/final

68 Article 12 second sentence, COM 2002/141/final

69 European Commission, 2007a, COM(2007) 502 final, *Communication: A Europe of Results – Applying Community Law*

70 Austria, Czech Republic, Denmark, Germany, Finland, Hungary, Ireland, Italy, Lithuania, the Netherlands, Portugal, Slovenia, Sweden, Spain and the United Kingdom

71 European Commission, *Better monitoring. New! EU Pilot*, Website

72 European Commission, 2007a, p.8

73 European Commission, 2007a, p.8

itated between the Commission and the accused Member State by a contact point. The results of the cases are still recorded with the Commission and include "the volume, nature and seriousness of problems remaining unresolved, indicating, if additional specific problem–solving mechanisms or more tailored sector initiatives are needed"[74]. The new system primarily reduces the time span and workload of the Commission in the first phases of the infringement procedure, namely the information gathering and categorization of the complaint. Indeed, it may also have the potential to shorten the periods of time throughout all stages of the formal infringement proceeding.

Effects of the Decision

Given that the Commission enjoys wide discretion in its investigations and actions relating to infringement proceedings, its decisions are final. As stated before, individuals may complain to the European Ombudsman, if they find that the Commission has made procedural mistakes while processing their complaints[75]. Yet, an appeal on the substance of the decision is not possible. Thus, a decision by the Commission to start, proceed with, or close infringement proceedings against a Member State is irreversible by another EU Institution. Similarly, the decision to involve the Court of Justice in the infringement proceeding can only be withdrawn by the Commission itself[76]. Decisions by the Commission must always state the grounds upon which they are based and usually stipulate a period of time until which the Member State should have removed the infringement.

Judgments by the ECJ are, as already indicated, mostly declaratory and state that the respective Member State has indeed violated its Treaty obligations and mention a specified period of time within which the Member State has to remediate the infringement. These decisions bind the two parties, i.e. the Commission and the Member States, involved and cannot be appealed. If, however, Member States fail to comply with the Court's judgment, the Commission may start a new round of infringement proceedings, including the pre–litigation stages, such as the letter of formal notice and the reasoned opinion. In cases where the ECJ is referred to anew, the Commission's application contains a proposal for a penalty payment to be levied either as a lump sum or periodic payment[77].

---

74 European Commission, 2007a, p.9

75 European Commission, *Complaint to the European Ombudsman*, Website

76 European Commission, *Infringements of EU law* (last paragraph), Website

77 Rules on the application of Article 228 EC are stipulated in European Commission, 2005, Communication SEC(2005) 1658 – *Application of Article 228 of the EC Treaty [now: Article 260 TFEU]* and European Commission, *Action under Article 260 TFEU*, Website

11.2. Judicial proceedings available to associations in the EU legal system

Private Parties, i.e. natural and legal persons, individuals and associations, are provided with a number of opportunities to receive remedy for administrative malpractice within the European legal system. Theoretically, three types of proceedings are offered to environmental CSOs in order to sue EU Institutions or national authorities whose (in–) actions breach European law. This chapter outlines the purpose of the individual proceedings, their subject–matter and procedures, including the specific arrangements on how to gain access and finally, the effects of the court's decision. Only the specificities for non–privileged actors are considered here; the rules for EU Institutions and Member States as applicants are not discussed.

Direct Access European law provides for two direct actions without the detour over national legal mechanisms[78]. Non–state applicants only gain direct access to the General Court[79]. The ECJ takes the role of an appeal court and can be called upon by the applicant, if the lower instance denies *locus standi*. It is, of course, also possible to appeal to the final instance of the EU judiciary in order to have a decision by the General Court affirming *locus standi* of the applicant or the merits of a case overruled.

11.2.1. Action for annulment (Article 263(4) TFEU)

Purpose

The action for annulment is the sole legal remedy available to individuals, in which they can defend their interests against actions undertaken by EU Institutions directly before the ECJ[80]. The desired outcome of an action for annulment for private applicants is the withdrawal of a legally binding act (most commonly a decision) that had previously directly and individually affected the individual in a negative manner[81]. This is indispensable for the primary importance of granting legal protection to individuals within the European legal system[82]. The second objective of this kind of legal action is to control the EU Institutions' compliance with their obligations under the Treaty; i.e. the legality of the institutions' actions is constantly controlled[83].

---

78 Thiele, 2006, p.46

79 Thiele, 2006, p.52; Harratsch, Koenig & Pechstein, 2009, p.214

80 Thiele, 2006, p.58; Thiele, 2007, p.83

81 Bieber, Epiney & Haag, 2005, p.263

82 Thiele, 2006, p.45; Harratsch, Koenig & Pechstein, 2009, p.213

83 cf. Thiele, 2006, p.42; Bieber, Epiney & Haag, 2005, p.263; Oppermann, Classen & Nettesheim, 2009, p.262; Harratsch, Koenig & Pechstein, 2009, p.213

Subject–matter of the Lawsuit

The first prerequisite for the subject matter of an action for annulment is the necessity that the producer of the contested act must be an EU authority[84]. The form or nature of the act is irrelevant as long as the act is intended to produce legal effects vis–à–vis third parties. Decisions taken by national authorities, even if taken on the basis of obligations arising under EU law, must be tried before national courts[85].

As mentioned above, Article 263(1)TFEU furthermore requires the act to "produce legal effects vis–à–vis third parties" and accordingly explicitly excludes recommendations and opinions from the list of potential subject matters of an action. The 'label' given to the act is, however, irrelevant. It does not need to be a legal act in the sense of Article 288 TFEU[86]. Of importance is rather, whether or not the applicant is directly and individually concerned by it[87]. The so–called *Plaumann* doctrine, formulated by the ECJ in 1963, has been strictly applied by the Court ever since in order to establish an applicant's individual concern regarding a decision addressed to another person:

> Persons other than those to whom a decision is addressed may only claim to be individually concerned if that decision affects them by reason of certain attributes which are peculiar to them or by reason of circumstances in which they are differentiated from all other persons and by virtue of these factors distinguishes them individually just as in the case of the person addressed[88].

The two criteria of direct and individual concern for the admissibility of a case constitute the greatest hurdle for private parties to gain access to the EU judiciary and have been subjected to widespread criticism in the academic literature. In this section, the requirements will be described and a thorough examination of the discussion will follow in Part IV on the "critical assessment of the status quo".

Summarized, Article 263(4) TFEU allows three types of acts to be challenged by private individuals before the Court. The relevant provision of the Treaty explicitly lists decisions addressed to the litigant and a decision that, despite being "in the form of a regulation or decision addressed to another person, is of direct and individual concern to the" applicant. The Lisbon Treaty not only extended the range of the producers of an act (the European Council [89] as well as the EU bodies, offices or agencies) but also added the possibility to challenge regulatory acts that do not entail implementing measures and are of direct concern to the litigant[90].

---

84 Under Article 230(1) EC only acts adopted jointly by the EP and the Council, acts of the Council, Commission or ECB could be challenged, whereas Article 263(1) TFEU adds those acts adopted by bodies, offices and agencies

85 Lasok, Millet & Howard, 2004, pp.44–45

86 cf. ECJ, Case C–316/91 *EP v. Council* [1994] ECR I–625, para.8; cf. also: Oppermann, Classen & Nettesheim, 2009, p.262

87 ECJ, Case 60/81 *IBM v Commission* [1981] ECR 2639, para.9; cf. also Thiele, 2007, p.89

88 ECJ, Case 25/62 *Plaumann & Co. v Commission* [1963] ECR 95, para.I–8

89 Article 263(1) TFEU

90 Article 263(4) TFEU; cf. also Dougan, 2008, p.676

Legally binding decisions distinguish themselves from other legal acts insofar as the circle of addressees is determined beforehand[91]. There is, thus, no need for applicants challenging a decision that is addressed to them to prove a direct and individual concern in the subject matter of the case[92]. The demonstration of a litigant's individual and direct concern with regard to a decision that has been addressed to a third person is more problematic. The ECJ has confirmed in its *Plaumann* decision that the rescission by non–privileged applicants is not restricted to decisions addressed to other private persons but can also be directed against decisions applying to Member States[93].

Certain regulations that are substantially material decisions, given that the range of addressees is specified beforehand and can neither be changed nor extended afterwards, may become subject to an action for annulment by non–privileged applicants[94]. The act thereby does not lose its general character as a regulation; rather the number of affected persons can be identified[95]. According to the Court's most recent decisions, the former assumption of the fact that 'real' regulations cannot be challenged is overruled and admissible provided that the individual is able to prove his or her individual and direct concern[96].

A similar situation reveals the Court's attitude with regard to directives even though Article 263(4) TFEU makes no mentioning of them. By now, both, the GC and ECJ have acknowledged that 'pretended directives' can be challenged; again of course under the condition that the litigant is directly and individually concerned. Regarding 'real' directives, the GC seems to accept them as subject matters of a case under the above–mentioned conditions regarding the applicant's concerns[97], while the ECJ acts on the assumption that directives cannot be rescinded[98]. There is thus no established case–law in this regard[99].

Procedure

Article 263(4) TFEU does not restrict the identity of applicants to those natural persons possessing EU citizenship or natural and legal persons living or having registered office in one of the Member States. Rather, "any natural or legal person" may initiate an action for annulment provided that the other conditions discussed above are fulfilled[100].

---

91 Article 288 fourth subpara. TFEU

92 Thiele, 2006, p.117

93 Thiele, 2006, p.118; Lasok, Millet & Howard, 2004, p.50

94 Thiele, 2007, pp.90–91; Harratsch, Koenig & Pechstein, 2009, p.215; Lasok, Millet & Howard, 2004, pp.50–51; cf. e.g. ECJ, Joined Cases 41–44/70 *International Fruit Co NV v Commission* [1971] ECR 411

95 Lasok, Millet & Howard, 2004, p.51

96 Thiele, 2006, pp.149–150 & 167; Thiele 2007, pp.92–93; ECJ, Case C–309/89 *Codorníu v Council* [1994] ECR I–1853 and CFI, Joined Cases T–481/93 & T–484/93 *Vereniging von Exporteurs in Levende Varkens et. al. v Commission* [1995] ECR II–2941

97 CFI, Case T–135/96 *UEAPME v Council* [1997] ECR II–373

98 ECJ, Case C–298/89 *Government of Gibraltar v Council* [1993] ECR I–3605

99 Thiele, 2006, pp.161 & 167; Thiele, 2007, pp.94–95

100 Bieber, Epiney & Haag, 2005, p.263; Thiele, 2006, p.49

The application for an action for annulment must be filed with the chancellor of the Court[101] within two months[102]. After expiration of the deadline, which is handled strictly by the Court for reasons of legal certainty[103], it is not allowed to lodge an action for annulment under Article 263(4)EC or to seek remedy via the preliminary reference procedure[104] (cf. below). The determinant of the two–month time period is the date on which the act, depending on its nature, is published in the Official Journal or notice has been given to the addressees[105].

The General Court first checks the admissibility of the action and thereby thoroughly examines the prerequisites of direct and individual concern. If – and many cases are already dismissed at this stage – the complaint is declared admissible, the judges proceed with the merits of the case.

In general, the Court accepts those grounds with which an annulment of an EU act can be justified as enumerated in Article 263(2) TFEU. These relate without exception to acts that have been adopted in infringement of Treaty obligations and dispose of a "lack of competence[106], infringement of an essential procedural requirement [107] (such as the failure to state reasons)[108], infringement of the Treaties, or of any rule of law relating to their application (including general principles, as for instance proportionality[109], legal certainty[110] and legitimate expectations[111]) or misuse of powers"[112]. The judges then proceed to examine the applicant's concern with regard to the contested legal act. Direct concern is to be established, if there exists a causal link between the legal act in question and the effects that the litigant wishes to avoid.

---

101 Article 21, Statute of the Court of Justice of the European Union, Articles 37ff, Rules of Procedure of the European Court of Justice

102 Article 263(6) TFEU; cf. also Thiele, 2006, p.47; Oppermann, Classen & Nettesheim, 2009, p.264

103 Lasok, Millet & Howard, 2004, p.55

104 ECJ, Case C–188/92 *TWD v Germany* [1994] ECR I–833; Oppermann, Classen & Nettesheim, 2009, p.264

105 Lasok, Millet & Howard, 2004, p.55

106 i.e. the lack of the power to adopt a legal act, cf. e.g. ECJ, Case 66/63 *Netherlands v High Authority* [1964] ECR 533; wrongful delegation of competence cf. ECJ, Case 9/56 *Meroni & Co, Industrie Metallurgiche, SpA v High Authority* [1958] ECR 133; Lasok, Millet & Howard, 2004, p.57

107 ECJ, Case 119/86 *Spain v Council and Commission* [1987] ECR 4121

108 ECJ, Case 24/62 *Germany v Commission* [1963] ECR 63

109 ECJ, Case 8/55 *Fédération Charbonnière de Belgique v High Authority* [1956] ECR 245

110 ECJ, Joined Cases 42 & 49/59 *Société Nouvelle des Usines de Pontlieue–Aciéries du Temple v High Authority* [1961] ECR 53

111 ECJ, Case 223/85 *Rijn–Schelde–Verolme (RSV) Maschinefabrieken en Scheepwerven v Commission* [1987] ECR 4617

112 ECJ, Case 6/54 *Netherlands v High Authority* [1955] ECR 103; cf. also Article 263(2) TFEU; cf. also: Oppermann, Classen & Nettesheim, 2009, p.263; Lasok, Millet & Howard, 2004, pp.56–61

Effects of the Decision

The disputed act retains its legal force until the Court has publicized its judgment[113]. Decisions by the General Court can be appealed before the European Court of Justice. The latter's judgments are, however, final and incontestable.

If the Court confirms the position of the applicant, the challenged act is *ex tunc* deprived completely of its legal force and is then considered not to have existed at all[114]. The decision not only binds the two parties to the dispute but unfolds *erga omnes*[115] and retroactive effects[116]. It is also possible for the Court to stipulate that solely certain parts of the act are to be annulled, while other parts remain intact and legally binding[117]. In addition, the ECJ may, if it deems adequate, stipulate payments to compensate the litigant for potential damages suffered.

However, the Court is not empowered to grant the act as desired by the litigant[118]. Article 266(1) TFEU rather obliges "[t]he institution or institutions whose act has been declared void or whose failure to act has been declared contrary to this Treaty [...] to take the necessary measures to comply with the judgment of the Court of Justice"[119]. This usually necessitates the adoption of a new act by the respective authority within a reasonable period of time. If the act has been annulled on procedural grounds, the institution is not prevented from re–installing the content of the former act as long as procedural guarantees are complied with[120]. Finally, the Treaties do not prescribe any particular sanction in cases where institutions fail to comply with the decision of the ECJ[121]. The applicant may, however, initiate new proceedings once more.

11.2.2. Action for failure to act (Article 265 TFEU)

Purpose

The aim of the procedure laid out in Article 265 TFEU is to compel an EU Institution to undertake an action to which it is obligated under EU law but which it has, up to that moment, failed to carry out[122]. The action for failure to act is thereby the necessary complement of the action for annulment in light of effective legal protection under Eu-

113 Thiele, 2006, p.47

114 Thiele, 2006, pp.46–47; Oppermann, Classen & Nettesheim, 2009, p.212; Harratsch, Koenig & Pechstein, 2009, p.223

115 Thiele, 2006, p.58; Oppermann, Classen & Nettesheim, 2009, p.212; Harratsch, Koenig & Pechstein, 2009, p.223; Lasok, Millet & Howard, 2004, p.62

116 Lasok, Millet & Howard, 2004, p.62

117 ECJ, Case 6/54 *Netherlands v High Authority* [1955] ECR 103; Harratsch, Koenig & Pechstein, 2009, p.223; Lasok, Millet & Howard, 2004, p.62; Thiele, 2006, p.47

118 Lasok, Millet & Howard, 2004, p.62

119 Oppermann, Classen & Nettesheim, 2009, p.212; Lasok, Millet & Howard, 2004, pp.62–63

120 Lasok, Millet & Howard, 2004, p.63

121 Lasok, Millet & Howard, 2004, p.64

122 Oppermann, Classen & Nettesheim, 2009, p.265; Harratsch, Koenig & Pechstein, 2009, p.225

ropean law[123]. While an action for annulment can only be directed against an 'action' of an EU Institution, i.e. a decision, an act etc., that is of direct and individual concern to the applicant, the action under Article 265 TFEU closes the gap in judicial remedies for such situations of inactions.

The procedure serves first and foremost as the legal protection of the individual's interest that his or her application for action does not remain unanswered. Secondly, however, the procedure also allows for a control of the objective legality of the actions by the institutions. If an institution remains inactive despite the fact that a Treaty provision obliges it to become active in such circumstances, this results in an infringement of the Treaty[124]. In this regard, one important remark needs to be made. The Lisbon Treaty goes beyond the definition of a formerly potential 'Community' defendant and adds in Article 265(3) TFEU next to the institutions also bodies, offices and agencies against whom such an action may be taken under equal conditions. With regard to the legal protection for the individual, this exceeds even the amendment under Article 263(5) TFEU, where the availability of an action for annulment will be regulated by the acts of the Council setting up a body, office or agency. Actions for failure to act can, if an activity is required by the Treaties, always be initiated against any of these official EU authorities. This amendment should also be welcomed from a political science point of view because those offices and agencies compose of delegated executive competences and are, at the moment, difficult to be held accountable for their actions and inactions. Such agencies and offices have been heavily criticized for a lack of democratic transparency and accountability.

Subject–matter of the Lawsuit

The action can exclusively be directed against an illegal inactivity on part of an EU Institution or body as well as offices and agencies. An indispensable requirement is that the institution in question has remained inactive; a denial of action would constitute a decision not to act addressed to the person[125] and would therefore have to be attacked under Article 263(4) TFEU[126]. A mere indication that a pending application is processed, on the other hand, is insufficient[127].

Natural and legal persons may begin judicial proceedings against institutions that have failed to address a legally binding act to them. Article 265(3) TFEU thereby explicitly excludes "recommendations or opinions"[128]. It also follows from the formulation in that

123 Thiele, 2006, p.73; Thiele, 2007, pp.117; Bieber, Epiney & Haag, 2005, p.271
124 Harratsch, Koenig & Pechstein, 2009, p.225; Thiele, 2006, p.73
125 Oppermann, Classen & Nettesheim, 2009, p.265; Thiele, 2006, p.73
126 ECJ, Case 8/71 *Komponistenverband e.V. v Commission* [1971] ECR 705, para.3; Thiele, 2007, p.130
127 Oppermann, Classen & Nettesheim, 2009, p.265
128 Bieber, Epiney & Haag, 2005, p.272; Harratsch, Koenig & Pechstein, 2009, p.226; Lasok, Millet & Howard, 2004, p.65

article[129] that the applicant must be the potential addressee of the alleged action by the respective EU Institution. Acts of a generally applicable nature (e.g. regulations or directives[130] that address the general public or the Member States[131]) cannot be rescinded through the Court[132]. Decisions that should have been directed to the applicant are admissible without problem. It is not yet clarified whether decisions that should have been addressed to a third person but would also have been of direct and individual interest to the applicant can be challenged by the latter before the Court. Thiele, drawing from the relevant provision of the former EC Treaty and case–law in the action for annulment procedure, assumes that such an application would be admissible before the General Court. Only then could full legal protection be guaranteed to the individual[133], while others deny this possibility relying on the case *Lord Bethell*[134].

Procedure

Access to the General Court is dependent on a pre–judicial proceeding. Applicants file their request for action with the respective institution "within a reasonable time from the moment at which the intention of the institution not to act has become evident"[135]. Administrative law of many Member States contains such a preliminary proceeding that enables the administrative authority to correct its misconduct itself and to solve the dispute by mutual consent[136]. Administrative proceedings are usually quicker and substantially less costly than recourse to courts. With regard to the EU, the preliminary proceeding also intends to reduce the caseload of the judiciary. It furthermore identifies matter and parties in the dispute and distinguishes the action from one seeking annulment of an action[137]. For these reasons, Article 265(2) TFEU requires the applicant to "call upon" the respective institution and grants a two–month period in order to undertake the required action. If, after the elapse of the time period, the institution remains inactive, the applicant may within another two months file the case with the General Court[138].

---

129 "Any natural or legal person may, under the conditions laid down in the preceding paragraphs, complain to the Court that an institution, body, office or agency of the Union has failed to address to that person any act other than a recommendation or an opinion.". Article 265(3) TFEU

130 ECJ, Case 134/73 *Holtz & Willemsen GmbH v Council* [1974] ECR 1, para.5

131 Thiele, 2007, p.125

132 Thiele, 2006, pp.74–75; Thiele, 2007, p.123; Lasok, Millet & Howard, 2004, pp.65–66; cf. e.g. ECJ, Case 134/73 *Holtz & Willemsen GmbH v Council* [1974] ECR 1

133 Thiele, 2006, pp.76–77, Thiele, 2007, pp.122–123; indirectly confirmed by: Harratsch, Koenig & Pechstein, 2009, p.228

134 ECJ, Case 246/81 *Lord Bethell v Commission* [1982] ECR 2277; cf. Lasok, Millet & Howard, 2004, p.66

135 Lasok, Millet & Howard, 2004, p.68; cf. e.g. ECJ, Case 59/70 *Netherlands v Commission* [1971] ECR 639

136 Harratsch, Koenig & Pechstein, 2009, p.225; Thiele, 2007, p.125; Lasok, Millet & Howard, 2004, p.66

137 Thiele, 2007, p.125

138 Harratsch, Koenig & Pechstein, 2009, p.225; Thiele, 2007, pp.126, 129; Lasok, Millet & Howard, 2004, pp.66 & 68

If the application is admitted, the ECJ then proceeds to examine the merits of the case. If the institution remained inactive despite obligations under EU primary or secondary law to become active, this would amount to a Treaty infringement[139]. However, it is crucial to assess whether the relevant authority was granted a scope of discretion. Yet, on the other hand, it is irrelevant whether the institution encountered practical problems in the execution of such obligations[140]. An exception may, however, be granted for justified reasons[141]. An objective inactivity is considered to be sufficient to admit the case[142]. Any additional proof for legal protection is not necessary. Problems can, however, occur, when the relevant institution becomes active after the expiration of the two–month time limit. If it undertakes the desired action before the application is filed with the Court, neither an action for failure to act nor for annulment is admissible. If the institution refuses to take the requested action, the applicant can no longer sue for failure to act but would have to consider an action for annulment of this decision. Finally, if the institution becomes active after the initiation of judicial proceedings but prior to the declaration of the Court's decision, there is also no further need for a challenge on failure to act. The Court will then use its discretion in allocating the costs of the proceeding[143].

Effects of the Decision

The decision taken by the ECJ is of declaratory nature[144]. The Court states that, by failing to act, the accused institution infringed its obligations under the Treaty[145]. As with the action for annulment, Article 266(1)TFEU requires the authority concerned to take the relevant measures arising out of the obligations of the Court's decision. The General Court thereby demands these "necessary measures" to be taken within a "reasonable period of time as assessed by the court"[146]. If the applicant is of the opinion that the fixed period of time has elapsed, he or she may initiate judicial proceedings for the failure to act anew[147]. The Court is not able to compel the institution in question to execute the action that is desired by the applicant but must rely upon the cooperation of the institution. The judges are not allowed to undertake the relevant action themselves. The decision is solely declaratory and may therefore not exceed the limits of judicial control or touch upon law–making[148].

139 Harratsch, Koenig & Pechstein, 2009, p.228; Bieber, Epiney & Haag, 2005, pp.271, 273

140 Bieber, Epiney & Haag, 2005, pp.271, 273; Thiele, 2007, pp.130–131

141 Thiele, 2007, p.131

142 Bieber, Epiney & Haag, 2005, p.273; Thiele, 2007, p.118

143 Thiele, 2007, pp.129–130; Lasok, Millet & Howard, 2004, p.68

144 Harratsch, Koenig & Pechstein, 2009, p.229

145 ECJ, Case 13/83 *EP v Council* [1985] ECR 1513, para.69

146 Thiele, 2007, p.131; Bieber, Epiney & Haag, 2005, p.273; Harratsch, Koenig & Pechstein, 2009, p.229; Lasok, Millet & Howard, 2004, pp.68–69

147 Thiele, 2007, p.131

148 Thiele, 2006, p.77; Thiele, 2007, p.131; Harratsch, Koenig & Pechstein, 2009, p.229; Lasok, Millet & Howard, 2004, pp.68–69

11.3. Indirect Access via the Member States – Preliminary Reference Procedure under Article 267 TFEU

11.3.1. Purpose

Great significance is attributed to the uniform application of EU law within all Member States by the responsible national authorities. The preliminary reference procedure provides an optimal tool to eliminate disparities in the application of Union law among Member States' authorities and to clarify the interpretation of the Treaties[149]. Given that national administrative authorities and courts primarily implement and apply EU law, the importance of the ECJ's authority to ensure a uniform application and interpretation thereof cannot be underestimated[150]. The case *Simmenthal II*[151] may be quoted as an example, in which the ECJ declared that national law must be set aside when standing in conflict with Community [now: EU] law[152]. In other words, preliminary rulings may increase the compatibility between the two legal systems[153]. Given that especially lower national courts have increasingly referred to the ECJ, the latter was given the opportunity to develop an extensive and elaborate jurisprudence on European law in a predominantly pro–integrative manner[154]. The preliminary reference procedure thereby facilitates the interlinkage of Union with national law and enables open communication between the respective judiciary of the two legal systems[155]. A third purpose that cannot be emphasized enough is the closing of the gaps in the legal protection of the individual within the EU legal system. Under certain circumstances, individuals are offered the opportunity to attack the legality of Union acts. This applies particularly where national rules are more beneficial and the seeking of direct actions before the GC is subject to the strict rules on *locus standi*[156].

11.3.2. Subject–matter of the Lawsuit

Article 267 TFEU actions originate from legal disputes before national courts and concern the interpretation or application of European law, including international agreements to which the Union is a party[157], in the relevant national context. In other words, whenever questions concerning the meaning, applicability or validity of European law arise in front of courts in the Member States, national judges seek answers from the Eu-

149 Kwanka, 2006, p.57; Bieber, Epiney & Haag, 2005, p.280; Lasok, Millet & Howard, 2004, p.164
150 Thiele, 2007, pp.134–135; Bieber, Epiney & Haag, 2005, p.280
151 ECJ, Case 106/77 *Simmenthal II (Amministrazione delle Finanze dello Stato v Simmenthal SpA.)* [1978] ECR 629, para.24
152 Kwanka, 2006, p.57
153 Lasok, Millet & Howard, 2004, p.166
154 Oppermann, Classen & Nettesheim, 2009, pp.269–270; Thiele, 2007, p.135
155 Oppermann, Classen & Nettesheim, 2009, p.270; Bieber, Epiney & Haag, 2005, p.281
156 Lasok, Millet & Howard, 2004, pp.165 & 166
157 Lasok, Millet & Howard, 2004, p.169

ropean Court of Justice. Article 267(1) TFEU therefore stipulates that the clarification of questions concerning

(a) the interpretation of the Treaties [TFEU and TEU];

(b) the validity and interpretation of acts of the institutions, bodies, offices or agencies of the Union

is reserved exclusively to the ECJ[158]. This is quite reasonable in light of the above–mentioned aim concerning the uniformity of EU law. Under no circumstances can questions relating to national law be the subject of a preliminary reference[159]. Hence, roughly summarized, national judges may call upon the ECJ, whenever they are uncertain, how a specific provision of EU primary or secondary law is to be interpreted or whenever they doubt the legality of a Union legal act[160].

11.3.3. Procedure

A referral for a preliminary ruling is free of charge and usually held orally[161]. The form is irrelevant as long as the ECJ is provided with the relevant material and legal facts relating to the dispute as well as the matter of EU law in question[162]. A general deadline is not prescribed for initiating judicial proceedings before national courts in the course of which questions for a preliminary ruling may be referred to the ECJ. However, problems occur, if the matter–in–dispute could also have been challenged via the direct action for annulment under Article 263 TFEU. Litigants may choose whether to challenge a given act under either kind of procedure. They may thereby attempt to circumvent the strict rules on *locus standi* under Article 263(4)TFEU provided that the national legal system provides for more lenient rules on access to courts for private applicants. However, they must do so within the two–months time span as specified in Article 263(5) TFEU. This will avoid applicants, who have missed the deadline for bringing an action for annulment, from taking the Article 267 TFEU route. Applications after the expiration of this deadline are inadmissible[163]. In general, however, national rules determine the procedure for the referral of preliminary questions and vary among Member States[164].

The Treaty distinguishes between a right and a duty to call upon the ECJ for a preliminary ruling. Article 267(2) TFEU leaves courts and tribunals discretion on whether or

158 After amendment of the EC Treaty, a new paragraph 3 was added to Article 225 EC, which confers upon the General Court the competence "to hear and determine questions referred for a preliminary ruling under Article 234, in specific areas laid down by the Statute". GC decisions are then subject to appeal in front of the ECJ. However, this opportunity has not yet been taken in practice. Cf. Oppermann, Classen & Nettesheim, 2009, p.269; Bieber, Epiney & Haag, 2005, p.281; Harratsch, Koenig & Pechstein, 2009, p.236; Lasok, Millet & Howard, 2004, p.157

159 Thiele, 2007, p.141

160 Thiele, 2007, p.143; Bieber, Epiney & Haag, 2005, pp.283–284; Lasok, Millet & Howard, 2004, p.156

161 Oppermann, Classen & Nettesheim, 2009, p.273

162 Lasok, Millet & Howard, 2004, p.175

163 Thiele, 2007, p.166; Harratsch, Koenig & Pechstein, 2009, p.240; cf. also: e.g. ECJ, Case C–188/92 *TWD v Germany* [1994] ECR I–833; Thiele, 2006, pp.65–66; Lasok, Millet & Howard, 2004, p.165

164 Lasok, Millet & Howard, 2004, p.176

not to make a request for a preliminary ruling. Paragraph 3 of the Article, however, obliges "a court or tribunal of a Member State against whose decisions there is no judicial remedy under national law" to refer any questions listed in paragraph 1(a) and (b) to the ECJ[165]. However, established case–law of the Court of Justice lists three exemptions for courts of last instance from the obligation to refer. First, "when the question raised is materially identical with a question which has already been the subject of a preliminary ruling in a similar case"[166]. Second, if there already exists settled European case–law on the basis of which the questions at hand can be correctly answered[167]. Third, the ECJ has established the so–called *acte clair*, which states that the obligation to submit questions for a preliminary ruling is exempted where the correct application of EU law is so obvious as to leave no scope for any reasonable doubt[168].

Other than these three exceptions, national courts determine whether a referral is necessary in the given case. The ECJ has explicitly confirmed this in its case–law and has declared that it refrains from assessing the necessity of the national judge to refer or not refer[169]. Sole exemptions are referrals of a hypothetical nature[170], thus, "if it is quite obvious that the interpretation of Community [EU] law or the examination of the validity of a rule of Community [EU] law sought by that Court bears no relation to the actual nature of the case or to the subject–matter of the main action"[171], in order to prevent misuse of referrals[172].

The sovereignty of the legal rules and regulations within the Member States remains untouched and determines which court is competent to hear the dispute as long as the rights of the individual arising out of EU law are sufficiently protected[173]. Given that it is generally left to the national legal systems to provide individuals with sufficient

---

165 e.g. Harratsch, Koenig & Pechstein, 2009, p.238; Lasok, Millet & Howard, 2004, p.165

166 ECJ, Joined Cases 28–30/62 *Da Costa (Da Costa en Schaake NV, Jacob Meijer NV, Hoechst–Holland NV v Netherlands Inland Revenue Administration)* [1963] ECR 31; Thiele 2007, p.155; Harratsch, Koenig & Pechstein, 2009, p.239; Lasok, Millet & Howard, 2004, p.178

167 ECJ, Case 283/81 *CILFIT (Srl CILFIT and Lanificio di Gavardo SpA v Ministry of Health)* [1982] ECR 3415, para.16; Thiele 2007, p.156; Harratsch, Koenig & Pechstein, 2009, p.239; Lasok, Millet & Howard, 2004, p.178

168 cf. *CILFIT* case; cf. also Harratsch, Koenig & Pechstein, 2009, p.239; Thiele 2007, p.156; Oppermann, Classen & Nettesheim, 2009, p.272

169 Bieber, Epiney & Haag, 2005, p.285; ECJ, Case 35/85 *Procureur de la République v Tissier* [1986] ECR 1207; cf. Lasok, Millet & Howard, 2004, p.179

170 ECJ, Case 104/79 *Foglia v Novella I* [1980] ECR 745 ; Thiele, 2007, pp.146–147

171 ECJ, Case 126/80 *Maria Salonia v Giorgio Poidomani and Franca Baglieri, née Giglio* [1981] ECR 1563, para.6; also: ECJ, Case C–415/93 *Bosman* [1995] ECR I–4921, para.59, cf. Thiele, 2007, pp.146–147; Lasok, Millet & Howard, 2004, p.178

172 Thiele, 2007, p.148

173 ECJ, Case 179/84 *Piercarlo Bozzetti v Invernizzi SpA and Ministero del Tesoro* [1985] ECR 2301, para.17 "[...] it is for the legal system of each Member State to determine which court has jurisdiction to hear disputes involving individual rights derived from Community law, but at the same time the Member States are responsible for ensuring that those rights are effectively protected in each case. Subject to that reservation, it is not for the Court to intervene in order to resolve any questions of jurisdiction which may arise, within the national judicial system, as regards the definition of certain legal situations based on Community [EU] law".

legal protection guaranteed by a system of remedies and procedures[174], it is not yet resolved, whether the right of lower courts to refer preliminary questions to the ECJ at their own discretion may be changed into a general duty by national procedural law. In light of the legal protection of the individual, this would be affirmed[175]. On the other hand, however, this would obviously dramatically increase the caseload of the ECJ and automatically prolong the duration of proceedings and may be disputable under the subsidiarity principle.

The long average duration of ECJ proceedings may endanger to violate an individual's rights protected by law. The Court has formulated cumulative conditions, under which national courts are exceptionally allowed to suspend the "enforcement of national measures adopted in implementation of a Community [EU] regulation" in *Zuckerfabrik Suederdithmarschen*[176]:

> (i) if that court entertains serious doubts as to the validity of the Community [EU] measure and, should the question of the validity of the contested measure not already have been brought before the Court, itself refers that question to the Court;
> (ii) if there is urgency and a threat of serious and irreparable damage to the applicant;
> (iii) and if the national court takes due account of the Community's [EU's] interests.

Further, in *Atlanta II*[177], the ECJ has clarified that a national court may only grant interim relief "with respect to a national administrative measure adopted in implementation of a Community [EU] regulation" in addition to the above–cited conditions where

> the interim relief is necessary to avoid serious damage being caused to the party seeking the relief; [...] [and] the court in its assessment of all those conditions [...] respects any decisions of the Court of Justice or the [...] [General Court] ruling on the lawfulness of the regulation or on an application for interim measures seeking similar interim relief at EU level.

Courts[178] ranking lower in the national hierarchy and against whose decisions a remedy is available enjoy relative discretion on whether or not to refer questions to the ECJ[179]. The exceptions in this regard concern those situations, in which even a court of lower instance is obliged by EU law to request the ECJ to rule preliminarily on one or more of the above–listed questions. In *Foto–Frost*[180], the ECJ declared that all courts must call upon the ECJ, if they challenge the legality of Union acts and consider not applying

---

174 ECJ, Case C–50/00P *Union de Pequenos Agricultores v Council* (*UPA*) [2002] ECR I–6677

175 Thiele, 2007, pp.148–149

176 ECJ, Joined Cases C–143/88 and C–92/89 *Zuckerfabrik Suederdithmarschen and Zuckerfabrik Soest* [1991] ECR I–415, para.33

177 ECJ, Case C–465/93 *Atlanta II, Atlanta Fruchthandelsgesellschaft mbH and others v Bundesamt für Ernährung und Forstwirtschaft* [1995] ECR I–3761, para.51; cf. also Thiele, 2007, p.152

178 The referring institution must be an independent judicial body, i.e. a tribunal or a court established by law, which has the authority to adjudicate disputes under national law and take legally binding decisions; cf. Thiele, 2007, p.137

179 ECJ, Case C–407/98 *Katarina Abrahamsson & Leif Anderson v Elisabet Fogelqvist* [2000] ECR I–5539; cf. Oppermann, Classen & Nettesheim, 2009, pp.269–272; Thiele, 2007, p.148

180 ECJ, Case 314/85 *Foto–Frost v Hauptzollamt Lübeck–Ost* [1987] ECR 4199, para.11

them[181]. The same applies to situations, in which national rules are considered to be annulled, if they were adopted on the basis of EU law requirements[182]. The ECJ is the sole institution that is authorized to annul acts adopted under EU law. National courts therefore have to refer a question in which they doubt the legality of the respective act and await the ECJ's response. It would obviously contradict the aim of ensuring a uniform application of EU law, if single national courts were able to set aside Union law. Another scenario that would impose a duty to refer upon any tribunal or court is where the court considers annulling, not applying, or suspending the application of a Union act under the framework of interim measures for the judicial protection of one party to the dispute.

If a court does not refer the case to the ECJ although it is obliged to do so, the inaction results in an infringement of the Treaty and the Commission may initiate proceedings according to Article 258 TFEU against the relevant Member State. In how far liability claims can be proclaimed is not yet clarified and must be assessed on a case–by–case basis[183]. Union law does not prescribe specific consequences within the national legal system. Hence, sanctions vary among Member States and include a lack of any consequences in some countries[184].

Once a tribunal or court has, voluntarily or as required, referred questions to the ECJ for a preliminary ruling, the national trial is suspended until the ECJ has delivered its decision[185]. Admissible questions relate to either the interpretation or the doubted legality of EU law and must be attributable to those categories listed in Article 267(1)(a)–(b) TFEU mentioned above. One remark needs to be made with respect to legality questions. Whenever, in a national trial, the legality of EU acts is contested, the relevant national court must call upon the ECJ to review the act's validity. The same arguments can be put forward as in an action for annulment; yet the decisive distinguishing factor is that a person does not have to prove his or her individual and direct concern because this would be contrary to the wording in and the aim of Article 267 TFEU[186]. Under certain circumstances, therefore, the detour around Member State judiciaries may be more appealing to individuals than a direct action for annulment before the ECJ would be. Inadmissible are, however, questions concerning national law[187], as well as those about the interpretation or validity of international agreements[188]. Those that have been

---

181 Thiele, 2007, p.151; Oppermann, Classen & Nettesheim, 2009, p.273; Harratsch, Koenig & Pechstein, 2009, p.238; Bieber, Epiney & Haag, 2005, p.283

182 Bieber, Epiney & Haag, 2005, p.283; cf. ECJ, Case C–6/99 *Greenpeace v Ministère de l'Agriculture et de la Pêche* [2000] ECR I–1651

183 Harratsch, Koenig & Pechstein, 2009, p.239; Oppermann, Classen & Nettesheim, 2009, p.273; Thiele, 2007, pp.157, 158

184 Thiele, 2007, p.159

185 Article 23(1), ECJ, Protocol on the Statute of the Court of Justice; cf. Lasok, Millet & Howard, 2004, p.177

186 Thiele, 2007, p.144

187 Thiele, 2007, p.141

188 Harratsch, Koenig & Pechstein, 2009, pp.236–237; Thiele, 2007, p.139–140

concluded as mixed agreements are problematic given that the ECJ could touch upon Member State competences when examining EU actions that were based on the international agreement[189]. Only on very rare occasions, i.e. the EEA Agreement between the then EC and the EFTA countries[190], have parties to the agreement consented to the referral of the jurisdiction to the ECJ under the conditions that are stipulated in the agreement. Disputes over the interpretation of e.g. the Aarhus Convention would therefore have to be settled according to the dispute settlement provisions of Article 16 of the Convention, which envisages negotiation, the referral to the ICJ, or arbitration as laid out in Annex II.

Questions that are formulated wrongly or incompletely according to the ECJ are either sent back for reformulation[191] or, if possible, rephrased by the Court itself and answered accordingly[192]. Those relating to the interpretation of EU law are examined according to the modes of interpretation as outlined in chapter 7, whereas those concerning the validity are tested against higher ranking legal norms of European law[193] (cf. chapter 1). Unfortunately, and to some extent owing to the great and ever–increasing number of referrals, the average duration of preliminary reference proceedings is more than two years[194].

11.3.4. Effects of the Decision

The decision of the European Court of Justice does not settle the dispute in question. It is, as the term already indicates, a preliminary ruling that only answers the afore–defined questions on EU law. It is for the national court to apply the decision by the ECJ to the concrete case and to interpret national law in light of the Court's judgment and to assess its compatibility[195]. This authority has been explicitly excluded from the jurisdiction of the ECJ[196].

Although the Treaty remains silent regarding the legal effects of the judgment[197], some findings have emerged over time. It follows from the principle of sincere cooperation in Article 4(3) TFEU in a likewise manner that the referral to the EU judiciary

189 Thiele, 2007, p.141

190 Agreement on the European Economic Area, Part VII, Chapter 3, section 3, Article 111.3

191 Article 104(5), ECJ, Rules of Procedure of the Court of Justice; cf. Lasok, Millet & Howard, 2004, p.180

192 ECJ, Case 4/79 *Société coopérative "Providence agricole de la Champagne" v Office national interprofessionnel des céréales* [1980] ECR 2823; cf. Oppermann, Classen & Nettesheim, 2009, pp.269–272

193 Thiele, 2007, pp.166–167

194 Bieber, Epiney & Haag, 2005, p.281; cf. also Court of the European Communities, 2008a, *Annual Report*, p.94 (point 12)

195 Kwanka, 2006, p.55; Bieber, Epiney & Haag, 2005, p.280; Oppermann, Classen & Nettesheim, 2009, p.273; Lasok, Millet & Howard, 2004, p.181

196 Oppermann, Classen & Nettesheim, 2009, p.270

197 Harratsch, Koenig & Pechstein, 2009, p.241; Thiele, 2007, p.167; Bieber, Epiney & Haag, 2005, p.288

stalls the national trial and the final decision by the ECJ binds the referring court[198] as well as all instances that adjudicate that very same dispute[199]. If the same court or one of appeal is of another opinion, the judges may not simply overrule those aspects of a judgment that relate to the preliminary reference but are rather obliged to call upon the ECJ themselves and request a reconsideration of its previous decision or formulate their own questions[200]. National courts usually carefully abide to the rulings of the European Court of Justice[201].

Decisions on the interpretation of Treaty articles or legislative acts require, in light of the uniform application of EU law, that the interpretation does not only apply to the concrete case but generally serves as a precedent for following cases[202]. National executive authorities are therefore bound to ECJ judgments regulating the interpretation of specific provisions and are obliged to inform themselves about the current state of case–law. This is necessary given that the 'new' interpretation may result in the requirement to repeal national administrative decisions in order to comply with EU law[203].

Decisions on the legality of Union acts are settled either by the confirmation of the legality or their annulment. These decisions apply *erga omnes*, i.e. in relation to everyone and generally *ex tunc*, i.e. as of the moment, of its declaration[204]. Decisions on the interpretation of provisions also generally have an *ex tunc* effect[205]. However, the Court may stipulate in its judgment the point of time at which the effects of its decision will go into effect. It is thereby able to negate a retrospective effect in order to, for instance, prevent a flood of claims of damages against Member States[206].

198 e.g. ECJ, Case C–320/88 *Staatssecretaris van Financiën v Shipping and Forwarding Enterprise Safe* [1990] ECR I–285; Lasok, Millet & Howard, 2004, p.182; Harratsch, Koenig & Pechstein, 2009, p.241; Thiele, 2007, p.167; ECJ, Case 69/85 *Wünsche Handelsgesellschaft v Germany* [1986] ECR 947; cf. Bieber, Epiney & Haag, 2005, p.288

199 Thiele, 2007, p.167; Bieber, Epiney & Haag, 2005, p.288

200 Harratsch, Koenig & Pechstein, 2009, p.241; Lasok, Millet & Howard, 2004, p.182; cf. e.g. ECJ, Case 69/85 *Wünsche v Germany* [1986] ECR 947; ECJ, Case C–206/94 *Brennet AG v Paletta* [1996] ECR I–2357; ECJ, Case 112/76 *Manzoni v Fonds National de Retraite des Ouvriers Mineurs* [1977] ECR 1647; cf. Harratsch, Koenig & Pechstein, 2009, p.241

201 Lasok, Millet & Howard, 2004, p.183

202 Bieber, Epiney & Haag, 2005, p.288

203 ECJ, Case C–453/00 *Kühne & Heitz NV v Productschap voor Pluimvee en Eieren* [2004]; cf. also Thiele, 2007, p.169

204 Thiele, 2007, p.173; cf. ECJ, Case 112/83 *Produits de mais v Adm. des douances et droits indirects* [1985] ECR 719; Bieber, Epiney & Haag, 2005, p.288

205 Thiele, 2007, p.171

206 Harratsch, Koenig & Pechstein, 2009, pp.241–242; ECJ, Joined Cases C–453/02 and C–462/02 *Finanzamt Gladbeck v Edith Linneweber and Finanzamt Herne–Westcontre Savvas Akriditis* [2005] para.42; cf. Thiele, 2007, p.171; ECJ, Case C–262/88 *Barber v Guardian Royal Exchange Assurance* [1990] ECR II–1889; cf. Bieber, Epiney & Haag, 2005, p.289

11.3.5. Access to the preliminary reference procedure: Environmental Locus Standi within the Member States

The chapter has so far illustrated the general rules governing access to the European Court of Justice and its General Court for *all* non–privileged applicants. This subsection now discusses the findings of a study undertaken by Milieu Ltd. as mandated by the Commission on the rules on *locus standi* for *environmental* CSOs that have been in force within twenty–five of the EU Member States in 2007[207]. Given that the opportunities of gaining access to the ECJ are under study, the respective systems of legal and non–judicial remedies will not be considered. Simply the rules governing access to national courts will be assessed as judicial bodies are the sole institutions (excluding administrative authorities or ombudsmen) that may call upon the ECJ for a preliminary ruling. The conclusions of the comparative study are presented in general terms, while allowing for the discussion of distinctive national measures as examples.

Locus Standi for Environmental CSOs before national courts

Overall, the rules on *locus standi* for individuals in general and, where special conditions are enforced, for associations in particular, reveal a very heterogeneous landscape among the EU Member States. For instance, some national systems enact special procedures towards associations and other non–governmental entities, while others have not done so. These organizations must generally fulfill certain criteria in order to be eligible for the preferential rules on standing. However, this privilege does not extend to all proceedings before national courts. Most Member States have explicitly restricted the scope to specific types, as for instance litigation relating to EIA (Environmental Impact Assessment) and IPPC (Integrated Pollution Prevention and Control) disputes.

Actio Popularis Public interest lies at the core of an *actio popularis*. The decisive factor is not whether the subjective rights of an individual have been violated but rather whether the public interest has been affected. This objective control can be initiated by any litigant without the need of having to demonstrate additional conditions. *Actiones popularis* in their narrow sense originate from Ancient Rome and have widely disappeared within national legal systems[208]. Yet, the Milieu study interpreted the concept in such wide terms as to include those regulations on *locus standi* that impose hardly any requirements on legal claimants.

Portugal clearly stands out in this context as it remains the sole country with a general *actio popularis*. Article 52(3)(a) the third item of the Constitution explicitly grants "[e]veryone [...] the right of *actio popularis*, including the right to apply for the appropriate compensation for an aggrieved party or parties, in such cases and under such terms as the law may determine, either personally or via associations that purport to

207 Unfortunately, Bulgaria and Romania have not been included

208 Neugärtner, 2002, pp.4–5

defend the interests in question" in order to "[p]romote the prevention, cessation or judicial prosecution of offenses against [...] the quality of life or the preservation of the environment"[209]. This right is further specified by the Participating Procedures Law[210] allowing citizens, municipalities as well as associations and foundations, to participate in administrative procedures. It is irrelevant whether it involves Portuguese nationals or associations[211]. While citizens do not have to demonstrate a specific interest in the claim, municipalities must act in the protection of the interests of their residents[212].

Despite the ruling of the Supreme Court that declares

> that the effectiveness of the right to an adequate environment included in Article 45 of the Constitution does not necessarily require the recognition of an *actio popularis* [and that] [i]t is enough that these rights can be protected in the ordinary Courts through the standing recognised to associations, groups and citizens affected by the act/omission in defence of this diffuse interest[213],

Spain has also introduced the possibility of *actiones popularis* in specific cases. For instance, anybody is allowed to challenge acts and omissions relating to land–use planning, coastal water and nature protection[214]. In addition, criminal law foresees three offenses, in which a claim before a court may be raised by anyone against the misuse of power by public authorities in environmental matters[215]. The Law of 27/2006, which implements Article 9 AC, was found to grant recognized NGOs that fulfill the conditions stipulated in its Article 23 an *actio popularis* before administrative courts when challenging administrative decisions "which contravene the rules relating to the environment"[216]. Moreover, at the sub–national level, a number of "Communidades Autónomas" recognize *actio popularis* when challenging administrative decisions relating to specific matters, as for instance EIA, IPPC, industrial pollution, nature protection, waste, wetlands, air or even open *locus standi* for all general aspects of environmental protection[217].

In Estonia, the exception to the rule of a generally restrictive *locus standi* exclusively concerns land–use planning, where the interpretation of the Aarhus Convention by Estonian courts in combination with Article 26(1) of the Planning Act empowers "[e]very person [...] to contest the decision in court". The Supreme Court confirmed this practice

209 Tribunal constitucional, 2005, *Constitution of the Portuguese Republic* cf. also Framework Law on the Environment: Law 11/87 (DR 81/87, 07.04); as cited by: Milieu Ltd., 2007, Portugal, p.8
210 Law 83/95 from 31.08 (DR 201/95, 31.08); as cited by: Milieu Ltd., 2007, Portugal, p.9
211 Milieu, 2007, p.6
212 Milieu, 2007, Portugal, p.9
213 as cited by: Milieu, 2007, Spain, p.32
214 Milieu, 2007, Spain, pp.7; Milieu, 2007, pp.6–7
215 Milieu, 2007, Spain, pp.7, 10, 15
216 1. their statutes must proclaim the active protection of the environment or of one of its elements as; 2. they have to have legally existed and been active for at least two years; 3. geographic proximity; Milieu, 2007, Spain, pp.7, 20 & 29
217 Milieu, 2007, Spain, p.14

in a decision in 2004[218]. Similarly, Slovenia does not provide for *actiones popularis* in general. However, recognized NGOs "acting in the public interest" may be included in administrative processes as participants and would, accordingly, have sufficient interest in subsequent judicial proceedings[219]. In addition, any person, individually or in association, is confronted with few impediments in civil law suits on the basis of the Environmental Protection Law[220].

Finally, the researchers of Milieu Ltd. classified the very broad application of "sufficient interest" by the common law judges in the UK as practically constituting *actio popularis* conditions[221]. Contrary to the three last mentioned countries, these wide rules on *locus standi* do not only apply in particular situations or to specific types of litigants but rather pertain to the general conditions. Yet, it remains to be stated that the judges decide each case individually and in combination with its merits[222].

Impairment of a Right or Interest at Stake

Broad Interpretation A number of national systems employ a rather broad application of the above–mentioned standing criteria. For instance, Lithuania, Italy, The Netherlands and Spain all accept the representation of collective and diffuse interests before the court. The latter three furthermore allow ad–hoc groups access to courts; thus no specified number of years of existence is required as in other Member States. However, these associations still need to prove that their interests have been affected. They need not be individually distinguishable interests but nevertheless "legitimate" ones[223], which are, *inter alia*, geographic proximity to the territory that is affected by the disputed administrative decision[224], or the action falls under the scope of the group's environmental activity[225]. Another example originating from The Netherlands stipulates that groups should support the concerns of the members of the organization[226]. Criteria can also be required in combination; for instance, the neighboring condition and the declared scope of the organization's activities[227]. In Denmark, a link must be visible between the law applying to the dispute at hand and the declared aims of an association as stipulated in its statute[228].

---

218 Milieu, 2007, Estonia, p.9
219 Milieu, 2007, Slovenia, p.5
220 Milieu, 2007, p.7
221 Milieu, 2007, p.xiii
222 Milieu, 2007, UK, p.21
223 e.g. Spain: Milieu, 2007, Spain, p.30
224 e.g. Italy: Milieu, 2007, p.8 & Milieu, 2007, Italy, p.22
225 e.g. Poland: Milieu, 2007, p.8 & Milieu, 2007, Poland, p.19
226 Milieu, 2007, p.8 & Milieu, 2007, The Netherlands, p.18
227 cf. Milieu, 2007, p.8; e.g. Cyprus: Milieu, 2007, Cyprus, pp.6 & 20; France: Milieu, 2007, France, pp.6, 19 & 20–21; Greece: Milieu, 2007, Greece, pp.22 & 23; Hungary: Milieu, 2007, Hungary, p.10
228 Milieu, 2007, pp.8–9 & Milieu, 2007, Denmark, pp.15 & 17

Milieu identified the present situation in Lithuania as unsatisfactory. Lithuanian courts do not have a uniform interpretation of the concept 'interest'; some interpret it broadly, while others apply strict rules. The system is therefore deprived of legal certainty[229].

Strict Interpretation Among the countries with the strictest rules for *locus standi*, Austria and Germany rank highest. In order to be granted standing before courts, it is generally required that a "subjective right" of the claimant has been affected by the administrative act. Individuals, organizations or other members of the public may merely informally persuade public authorities to reconsider their decisions[230]. Exceptions are listed in legislation[231]. In Austrian criminal proceedings, anyone may report to the prosecutor, however, is excluded from participating in judicial procedures[232]. In constitutional proceedings, concerned citizens and NGOs may claim on their own and NGOs may litigate on behalf of concerned citizens[233].
The Belgian high courts grant limited *locus standi* to neighbors and individuals and only grant CSOs standing, if their territory of activity concurs with the area covered by the challenged administrative decision. "If the statutory purpose of the association is formulated in too general terms, it will be considered as tantamount to the general interest and therefore inadmissible as a basis for action"[234].

A prerequisite for associations to be granted legal standing is their possession of a legal personality. In the vast majority of the Member States, this is the case for NGOs; yet Malta does not (at the time of the study) grant them legal personality and thereby deprives them of gaining access to courts[235]. In Ireland, only ad hoc groups seem to be excluded from standing on this basis[236].

Other countries have enumerated specific types of administrative decisions that are not challengeable before courts. The Dutch "negative list" even prevents litigants whose interests have been impaired from going to court[237], while Poland merely excludes any claimant but direct addressees[238].

Overall, the Milieu study found access to courts to be impeded in Austria, Belgium, Germany and Malta (whereas the last–mentioned country may change its position with the draft legislation granting legal personality to NGOs). Furthermore, a very restrictive

---

229 Milieu, 2007, p.8 & Milieu, 2007, Lithuania, pp.5, 22, 23 & 24

230 Milieu, 2007, p.7; Austria: Milieu, 2007, Austria, p.9.; Germany: Milieu, 2007, Germany, pp.9–10 & 13

231 e.g. EIA and IPPC; cf. Austria: Milieu, 2007, Austria, pp.10 & 13; "Verbandsklage" established in the German *Länder* in the 1980s; cf. Milieu, 2007, Germany, p.13

232 Milieu, 2007, Austria, p.11

233 Milieu, 2007, Austria, p.12

234 Milieu, 2007, Belgium, p.14

235 At the time of the study, only a draft legislative act granted legal personality to NGOs; yet it had not been adopted, nor implemented. Milieu, 2007, p.9 & Milieu, 2007, Malta, pp.5, 10 & 17

236 Milieu, 2007, Ireland, pp.11 & 14

237 Milieu, 2007, p.7 & Milieu, 2007, The Netherlands, pp.9, 12 & 23

238 Milieu, 2007, p.7 & Milieu, 2007, Poland, p.16

conception of 'participant' has been identified in the Czech Republic as well as Hungary and Slovakia. Similarly, Sweden and Slovenia strictly hamper access to preferential access routes[239].

Specific Regimes for NGOs A number of Member States grants standing to interest groups and non–profit associations before courts, provided that they had previously made use of the right to participate in the decision–making process of the administration. Thus, the conditions for legal standing are dependent upon the procedural rights in public authorities at the administrative stage. These participation opportunities in turn are available for NGOs that fulfill predetermined criteria. Amongst these are a specified duration of existence[240] and the aim of promoting environmental protection[241] regarding its content, as well as the territory it operates in. For instance, NGOs in Germany may only be registered for participation[242] upon the condition that their activities cover several *Bundesländer*; at least more than one *Land* only[243]. Also other countries require the geographic criterion[244]; however, in Poland, for example, it is sufficient for NGOs to state that, potentially, their activities may cover the entire territory of the country. Comprehensibly, most Polish environmental CSOs include such a clause[245]. In addition, these associations should be classified as non–profit[246] and have open and voluntary membership[247]. Most countries, however, limit these procedural rights to specific areas of environmental protection, mostly for decisions concerning EIA[248], IPPC[249], nature protection[250] and waste management[251].

Other countries have institutionalized special regimes to allow for privileged access to the judiciary for recognized environmental CSOs. Similar to the arrangements concern-

239 Milieu, 2007, p.11

240 mostly three years of existence; Milieu, 2007, p.9; Austria: Milieu, 2007, Austria, p.10; Germany: Milieu, 2007, Germany, p.14

241 Milieu, 2007, p.9; e.g. Austria: Milieu, 2007, Austria, p.10; Finland: Milieu, 2007, Finland, pp.11 & 12; Germany: Milieu, 2007, Germany, p.14; Poland: Milieu, 2007, Poland, pp.14, 15 & 16

242 Milieu, 2007, p.9; Germany: Milieu, 2007, Germany, p.14; prior registration is also required in Finland: Milieu, 2007, Finland, pp.11 & 12

243 Milieu, 2007, Germany, p.14

244 e.g. Finland: Milieu, 2007, Finland, pp.11 & 12

245 Milieu, 2007, p.9 & Milieu, 2007, Poland, pp.14, 15 & 16

246 Austria: Milieu, 2007, p.9 & Milieu, 2007, Austria, p.10

247 Germany: Milieu, 2007, p.9 & Milieu, 2007, Germany, p.14

248 Milieu, 2007, p.9; e.g. Austria: Milieu, 2007, Austria, p.11; Czech Republic, p.15, The Netherlands and Poland, pp.10 & 28

249 Milieu, 2007, p.9; e.g. Austria: Milieu, 2007, Austria, pp.10, 11, Czech Republic, p.15, The Netherlands and Poland, p.10

250 e.g. Czech Republic: Milieu, 2007, Czech Republic, p.11, Finland: Milieu, 2007, Finland, pp.11 & 12 and Germany: Milieu, 2007, Germany, p.13

251 Milieu, 2007, p.9; e.g. Austria; Milieu, 2007, Austria, pp.9, 10, 11 & 13 and Finland: Milieu, 2007, Finland, pp.11 & 12

ing procedural rights, such associations need to meet certain criteria before being granted preferred standing rules; for instance, not being required to prove an interest in the disputed decision in France, Greece, Italy and Spain[252]. Obviously, as these rules relate to environmental disputes, all countries require groups to work actively for environmental protection[253]. Again, the conditions that an organization must have been established for a certain amount of time[254] and should be continuously active in several regions of a country[255] or have other geographical connections are most often mentioned. Greece furthermore requires these organizations to be independent, not–for–profit and dedicated to the general interest[256]. Democratic internal structures are additionally required for Italian CSOs[257].

Luxembourg has installed special legal standing regulations in specific areas of environmental law[258] for registered environmental CSOs that have been established for at least three years, have been engaged in environmental protection activities, and possess official statutes[259]. Environmental CSOs that have been active in Sweden for a minimum of three years and constitute of considerable size, i.e. at least two thousand members, may challenge decisions relating to the issuance of permits, as well as supervisory decisions concerning contaminated land. Still, in practice, only a small number of NGO claims have been admitted so far[260].

Finally, the Slovenian rules on *locus standi* for environmental CSOs distinguish between administrative and civil jurisprudence. In the former type of court proceedings, NGOs are only treated preferentially in cases concerning nature conservation. In civil law disputes, the Environment Protection Law grants individuals and CSOs meeting certain criteria privileged standing. Most of these conditions resemble those mentioned before in the context of other Member States. However, it should be emphasized that the geographical criterion is neither restricted to the territory affected nor the territory of the country but the preferential treatment also extends to foreign environmental organizations that are active in at least five EU Member States[261].

Further Obstacles – Fees The Milieu study identified as a general rule that fees that need to be paid in order to initiate cases before courts do not constitute an appreciable obstacle for access to courts within the EU Member States, although there exists great

252 Milieu, 2007, p.10
253 Milieu, 2007, p.10
254 Milieu, 2007, p.10; France: Milieu, 2007, France, pp.6, 20–21; Spain: Milieu, 2007, p.10 & Milieu, 2007, Spain, p.7
255 Italy: Milieu, 2007, Italy, pp.5, 21 & 28
256 Milieu 2007, p.10 & Milieu, 2007, Greece, p.21
257 Milieu, 2007, Italy, pp.5, 21 & 28
258 These areas cover classified facilities, air pollution, water protection & waste management; cf. Milieu, 2009, p.10
259 Milieu, 2007, p.10 & Milieu, 2007, Luxembourg, pp.6, 8–9, 19 & 20
260 Milieu, 2007, pp.10–11
261 Milieu, 2007, p.11 & Milieu, 2007, Slovenia, pp.12–13

variation. Court fees range from none in France[262], Luxembourg[263] and Sweden [264], to minimal payments on average not exceeding 50 Euros in, for instance, Estonia[265], Greece[266], Hungary[267], Latvia[268], Lithuania[269], Poland[270], and Slovenia[271], to well over one hundred Euros up to 7.700 Euros in some Member States depending on the type of court[272] and the value of the dispute[273]. In the vast majority of the Member States, court fees increase at each instance[274] with the exception of Poland[275] and Latvia[276]. Several Member States, in particular, Portugal[277], Slovakia[278] and Spain[279], provide for extensive regulations that exempt specific litigants, e.g. NGOs and similar associations, from the payment of court fees.

While court fees constitute a relatively small amount of the overall expenses of initiating court proceedings, the costs for legal representation and experts easily create a significant obstacle for access to justice. The representation of the litigant by a lawyer in judicial proceedings is required in all Member States at higher instances[280]; some already do so at first instance. The costs to cover the remuneration of lawyers and experts differ considerably among the countries but often greatly exceed citizens' income or NGOs' budgets[281].

---

262 Milieu, 2007, p.13 & Milieu, 2007, France, p.22

263 Milieu, 2007, p.13 & Milieu, 2007, Luxembourg, pp.6 & 21

264 Milieu, 2007, p.13 & Milieu, 2007, Sweden, pp.9 & 12

265 Milieu, 2007, p.xviii & Milieu, 2007, Estonia, pp.6 & 18

266 A Stamp duty and deposit payment of 15 Euros respectively, although the deposit is usually reimbursed; cf. Milieu, 2007, p.xviii & Milieu, 2007, Greece, pp.25–26

267 Fees range from 28 to 66 Euros; cf. Milieu, 2007 p.xix & Milieu, 2007, Hungary, p.14

268 Fees range from 7,11 to 14,23 Euros; cf. Milieu, 2007, p.xix & Milieu, 2007, Latvia, p.15

269 Stamp duty: 29 (+ 14,50); cf. Milieu, 2007, p.xix & Milieu, 2007, Lithuania, p.19

270 Fees do not exceed 50 Euros; cf. Milieu, 2007, p.xx & Milieu, 2007, Poland, p.20

271 Fee for initiating judicial review is 6,40 Euros and the fee for the judgment is 7,93 Euros and for appeal, it is 15,86 Euros; cf. Milieu, 2007, Slovenia, p.14

272 Type of court: The Netherlands, cf. Milieu, 2007, p.xix; Slovenia, cf. Milieu, 2007, p.xx

273 Value of the dispute: Austria (civil courts), cf. Milieu, 2007, p.xvii; Germany (set by the court up until 4.200 or 7.700 Euros), cf. Milieu, 2007, p.xviii; The Netherlands (percentage of the value of the dispute), cf. Milieu, 2007, p.xix

274 Milieu, 2007, p.13

275 The court fee at first instance constitutes 50 Euros, while every other instance only costs 25 Euros; cf. Milieu, 2007, p.xx & Milieu, 2007, Poland, pp.20–21

276 The Constitutional Court is free of charge; cf. Milieu, 2007, p.xix & Milieu, 2007, Latvia, p.19

277 Legislation exempts, *inter alia*, NGOs from the payment of fees, even if they lose the case or to which they assisted the prosecutor; cf. Milieu, 2007, p.14; Milieu, 2007, Portugal, pp.18–19

278 NGOs are not obliged to pay court fees; cf. Milieu, 2007, p.xx & Milieu, 2007, Slovakia, p.20

279 Milieu, 2007, p.xxi & Milieu, 2007, Spain, p.35

280 Exceptions are, for instance, Estonia where legal representation is not obligatory at the Administrative Supreme Court. Cf. Milieu, 2007, p.14 & Milieu, 2007; or Latvia where legal representation is not required before the Constitutional Court; Milieu, 2007, Latvia, p.19

281 Milieu, 2007, p.14

Further Obstacles – Loser–Pays Principle The system of punitive damages of the USA, in which claimants are financially rewarded for having initiated a proceeding and thereby avoid potential damage, is not applied in any European country[282]. Rather to the contrary, all Member States with the exception of Belgium[283] and Sweden[284] oblige, as a general rule, the defeated party of the case to bear all costs relating to the proceeding of itself as well as the other party[285]. In Ireland, NGOs may be requested to deposit a specified amount at the beginning of the proceeding, which would be reimbursed in case of victory but given to the opponent, if the NGO loses the case[286].

In all countries but Austria, it usually remains within the discretion of the court to decide whether or not to apply the loser–pays principle in a given case[287]. Criteria may include the weighing of private as opposed to public interests, the importance of the case for the general public, as well as the merits of the case[288]. The Portuguese legal system can be attributed to the one end of the spectrum, which only obligates individuals to compensate for the other party's expenses. NGOs are exempted from this principle in all court proceedings[289]. At the other end, the UK can be found, where judges release associations from that duty only on very rare occasions. In addition, the request for a 'Protected Cost Order', which may prescribe the claimant's liability to a specific amount, is subject to strict conditions that are difficult to meet[290].

Other exceptions exist in many countries, yet vary in their application. For instance, in Spain, associations that lost the case must only also cover the other party's costs when they acted "manifestly *mola fides*"[291], whereas the defeated administration needs to reimburse the other litigant's expenses. Similarly, Finland and The Netherlands only oblige NGOs to bear the additional costs, if their claim is "manifestly unfounded" or the right to enact proceedings had obviously been misused[292]. In Germany, a 'cap' amount has been specified for the payment of court and lawyers' fees at each judicial level. Any expenses that exceed this threshold, as well as the costs for expert opinions in general, have to be borne by each party itself[293]. Administrative authorities always bear their own costs in the Czech Republic, even in cases of legal defeat. As this is most often the case in cases involving environmental CSOs, they do not have to pay for the authority's expenses[294].

---

282 Milieu, 2007, p.21
283 A lump sum of 243 Euros needs to be paid by the losing party in Belgium; cf. Milieu, 2007, p.14
284 Sweden does not apply the principle in administrative but in civil court proceedings; cf. Milieu, 2007, pp.12 & xxii; Milieu, 2007, Sweden, pp.9 & 12
285 Milieu, 2007, p.21
286 Milieu, 2007, Ireland, p.15
287 Milieu, 2007, p.15
288 e.g. in Ireland; cf. Milieu, 2007, p.xix
289 Milieu, 2007, p.xx & Milieu, 2007, Portugal, p.19
290 Milieu, 2007, p.xxii & Milieu, 2007, UK, pp.6 & 15
291 Milieu, 2007, pp. 14 & xxi & Milieu, 2007, Spain pp.8 & 30–31
292 Finland: Milieu, 2007, pp.14–15 & Milieu, 2007, Finland, p.12; The Netherlands: Milieu, 2007, pp.14 & xx & Milieu, 2007, The Netherlands, pp.13–14
293 Threshold: 700 – 3.000 Euros; cf. Milieu, 2007, p.xviii & Milieu, 2007, Germany, p.16
294 Milieu, 2007, p.xvii & Milieu, 2007, Czech Republic, p.14

Further Obstacles – Miscellaneous The fact, whether or not the enforcement of the contested administrative decision is suspended while the case is pending, constitutes an additional – and indeed crucial – aspect of unrestricted access to courts. If the disputed action is carried out despite the initiation of judicial proceedings, there is a realistic risk that the final judgment may be delivered after a non–reversible harm has been committed. While several countries[295] put the execution of an administrative decision on hold during the administrative appeal procedure and suspension in court must be requested, four EU Member States[296] and, in some countries, in combination with a reasonably well founded *prima facie* case (*fumus boni iuris*)[297], provide for automatic suspension in both administrative and judicial proceedings. In the remaining states, injunctive relief is granted by the judges only upon request. The Milieu study identified that, in general, the requirement of *periculum in mora* (the execution of the administrative decision would cause irrecoverable damage and render the final judgment irrelevant) is applied[298]. In addition, some states stipulate in their legislation which supplementary or alternative means of interim relief may be adopted by the administrative authority or the court[299]. The researchers concluded that interim relief is easiest available in Estonia, Lithuania and Portugal, whereas courts in Belgium, Cyprus, Czech Republic, Spain, and the UK only exceptionally grant injunction[300]. A qualification needs to be made concerning Belgium as disputes over environmental protection diverge from the general principle and a specific injunctive relief procedure for non–profit environmental protection associations has been instituted[301]. Some legal systems even require the payment of a lump sum accompanying the request for an interim measure. If the party applying for the suspension of the action wins, the money will be reimbursed. If, however, the final judgment of the court confirms the original decision, the sum will be disbursed to the party that suffered disadvantages effectuated by the injunctive relief. The amount is

---

295 Austria: Milieu, 2007, p.xiv & Milieu, 2007, Austria, p.10; Denmark: Milieu 2007, p.xiv & Milieu, 2007, Denmark, p.16; Hungary: Milieu, 2007, p.xv & Milieu, 2007, Hungary, pp.15–16, 26 & 30; Luxembourg: Milieu, 2007, p.xv & Milieu, 2007, Luxembourg, pp.5, 6, 14, 16, 20, 22 & 23; Poland: Milieu, 2007, p.xvi & Milieu, 2007, Poland, pp.6, 22, 26 & 28 and Slovakia: Milieu, 2007, p.xvi & Milieu, 2007, Slovakia, pp.12, 15 & 16

296 Milieu, 2007, pp.11–12; Finland: Milieu, 2007, p.xiv & Milieu, 2007, Finland, p.12; Germany: Milieu, 2007, p.xv & Milieu, 2007, Germany, pp.9, 12 & 17; Greece: Milieu, 2007, p.xv & Milieu, 2007, Greece, pp.17 & 25; Sweden: Milieu, 2007, p.xvi & Milieu, 2007, Sweden, p.**x**

297 Milieu, 2007, p.12; Czech Republic: Milieu, 2007, p.xiv; Estonia: Milieu, 2007, p.xiv; Hungary: Milieu, 2007, p.xv; Ireland: Milieu, 2007, p.xv; Latvia: Milieu, 2007, p.xv; Poland: Milieu, 2007, p.xvi; Slovakia: Milieu, 2007, p.xvi; Slovenia: Milieu, 2007, p.xvi

298 Milieu, 2007, p.12; Belgium: Milieu, 2007, p.xiv; France: Milieu, 2007, p.xiv; Italy: Milieu, 2007, p.xv; Luxembourg: Milieu, 2007, p.xv; Portugal: Milieu, 2007, p.xvi; Spain: Milieu, 2007, p.xvi

299 This is the case in France. Luxembourg, The Netherlands, Ireland, Italy, Poland and Spain; cf. Milieu, 2007, p.12

300 Milieu, 2007, p.13

301 Milieu, 2007, pp.12–13 & Milieu, 2007, Belgium, pp.8, 10–13, 15, 16, 18 & 19. Criteria are: existence of three years, adherence to administrative formalities as prescribed by law, aiming at environmental protection, which is laid down in their statutes as well as geographical proximity and the demonstration of effective activity in environmental protection.

inconsiderable in Belgium and the Czech Republic, while judges in Spain and the UK may specify large sums[302].

Legal Aid The rationale of legal aid mechanisms is to enable litigants with scarce financial resources to be able to afford judicial proceedings. This is particularly important in light of the above–discussed loser–pays principle, which otherwise constitutes a considerable obstacle to access to justice[303]. Hence, most European countries offer, though under very different and either strictly or laxly applied conditions, legal aid mechanisms for specified categories of litigants. The vast majority of legal aid systems covers litigation expenses, including court fees and, though not always, remuneration of lawyers[304]. The costs for expert reports will usually not be reimbursed. Three Member States, however, do not provide for any financial support irrespective of the claimant[305]. In some states, legislation has installed such mechanisms, yet, restricted its entitlement to natural persons upon the condition that they only dispose of an "insufficient income"[306]. NGOs are in some countries excluded from the range of potential beneficiaries[307]. In Malta, the deprival of legal personality of NGOs renders *locus standi* impossible and consequently legal aid becomes unattainable but also unnecessary[308]. Others theoretically grant non–governmental associations the opportunity to apply for financial support in judicial proceedings; yet, in practice, strict criteria prevent judges from allowing it more often than on an exceptional basis[309]. In the remaining EU Member States, NGOs are generally eligible for legal aid when acting in the general interest of the public[310]. In Spain and Slovenia[311], NGOs, whose status has been recognized, receive free legal aid and environmental associations are placed in a particularly beneficial position. In addition, a substantial number of law firms in some countries offer *pro bono* legal services

302 Milieu, 2007, p.15

303 According to the Milieu study, this is the case in Cyprus, Estonia, France, Germany, Greece, Hungary, Ireland, Italy, Luxembourg, Netherlands, Portugal (for individuals), Slovakia (for individuals) and the UK; cf. Milieu, 2007, p.16

304 Milieu, 2007, p.16

305 Cyprus: Milieu, 2007, p.xvii & Milieu, 2007, Cyprus, pp.22 & 24 ; Greece: Milieu, 2007, p.xviii & Milieu, 2007, Greece, pp.17 & 26; Ireland: Milieu, 2007, p.xix & Milieu, 2007, Ireland, p.16

306 e.g. Belgium: Milieu, 2007, p.16

307 cf. Finland: Milieu, 2007, p.xviii & Milieu, 2007, Finland, p.12; Latvia: Milieu, 2007, p.xix & Milieu, 2007, Latvia, p.15; Lithuania: Milieu, 2007, p.xix & Milieu, 2007, Lithuania, p.19; Luxembourg: Milieu, 2007, p.xx & Milieu, 2007, Luxembourg, pp.6 & 21; The Netherlands: Milieu, 2007, p.14 and the UK: Milieu, 2007, p.17

308 Milieu, 2007, p.xx; Milieu, 2007, Malta, p.11

309 Austria: Milieu, 2007, p.xvii & Milieu, 2007, Austria, p.11; Belgium: Milieu, 2007, p.xvii & Milieu, 2007, Belgium, pp.15–16; Estonia: conditions are, *inter alia*, bankruptcy or insolvency, cf. Milieu, 2007, p.xviii & Milieu, 2007, Estonia, pp.6 & 12; France: Milieu, 2007, France, pp.5 & 23; Italy: Milieu, 2007, p.xix & Milieu, 2007, Italy, pp.25 & 28; Germany: Milieu, 2007, Germany, p.16

310 Denmark: Milieu, 2007 pp.xvii & xviii & Milieu, 2007, Denmark, pp.5 & 19; Poland: Milieu, 2007, p.xx & Milieu, 2007, Poland, p.20; Slovenia: Milieu, 2007, p.xxi & Milieu, 2007, Slovenia, p.17; Hungary: Milieu, 2007, p.xix & Milieu, 2007, Hungary, p.14

311 cf. e.g. Milieu, 2007, Slovenia, p.17

to not–for–profit organizations[312]. Portugal deserves to be distinguished again as well. Recalling that NGOs are already, as a general rule, exempted from court fees, they are also automatically granted aid to cover for the costs of legal representation[313].

Evaluating access opportunities from a comparative perspective

Milieu Ltd. concluded its findings on the access opportunities available to individuals and particularly non–governmental organizations with a classification of the EU Member States into four different categories. Only Denmark was considered to perform "well"[314] in the sum of the categories[315]. The majority of the countries had been attributed to the middle categories with nine countries[316] being classified as "satisfactory" while access opportunities "could be better" in ten other Member States[317]. However, the juridical systems in Austria, Germany, Hungary, Malta and the UK have been marked as "ineffective", i.e. at least one major deficiency was not sufficiently addressed.

Yet, considering the criterion of "*locus standi*" in isolation offers a diverse picture. Worst classified are again Austria, Germany and Malta, which coincides with the overall assessment. However, Hungary and the UK, both having an overall classification of an "ineffective" legal system, are both graded "good" concerning their rules on *locus standi*. This group furthermore contains Estonia, France, Ireland, Italy, Latvia, Portugal and Spain and accordingly comprises most members as compared with the other three categories. Again, the remaining Member States are distributed between the two middle categories[318].

At first sight, this conclusion appears positive, given that one–third of the EU Member States provides for "good" standing rules in environmental legal disputes. Yet, this still means that two–thirds remain under this standard. Overall, the Milieu researchers seem to suggest implicitly that reform and improvement of the rules governing access to justice in environmental matters are advisable in each European country.

Despite the fact that twenty–five countries had been grouped according to four categories, it should be pointed out that they still reveal great heterogeneity and the reasons for the classification vary considerably. Hence, the legal systems and their respective shortcomings are as individual and challenging as are their solutions.

---

312 Milieu, 2007, p.16; France: Milieu, 2007, France, p.25; Hungary: Milieu, 2007, Hungary, p.25; Italy: Milieu, 2007, Italy, p.25; Spain: Milieu, 2007, p.xxi & Milieu, 2007, Spain, pp.8, 14 & 36 and the UK: Milieu, 2007, p.xxi & Milieu, 2007, UK, p.21

313 Milieu, 2007, p.xx & Milieu, 2007, Portugal, pp.18 & 21

314 category was labeled: "good"

315 Legal Standing, Effective Remedies, Costs and Length of the Procedure (incl. legal aid) and Transparency and others; cf. Milieu, 2007, p.18

316 Estonia, France, Greece, Italy, Lithuania, Luxembourg, Portugal, Slovakia, Slovenia; cf. Milieu, 2007, pp.17–18

317 Belgium, Cyprus, Czech Republic, Finland, Ireland, Latvia, The Netherlands, Poland, Spain, Sweden; cf. Milieu, 2007, pp.17–18

318 "could be better": Cyprus, Czech Republic, Finland, The Netherlands, Poland & Sweden and "satisfactory"

11.3.6. The failed Directive

To address the different regimes on *locus standi*, the Commission submitted in 2003 a proposal for a directive *on access to justice in environmental matters* within the Member States, which, however, failed to be adopted by the European Parliament and the Council. The directive proposal acknowledged that the restrictive rules on *locus standi* are one of the factors that hamper an efficient enforcement of environmental law within the European Union. The proposal explicitly suggested that access to environmental review procedures should be granted to "representative associations seeking to protect the environment" in order to "enhance the implementation"[319] and *"general application* of environmental law"[320]. Thus, it was recognized that the effectiveness of European environmental law and consequently the state of environmental protection crucially depend on the ability of the public to gain access to courts and have the law judicially reviewed[321]. As a result of this improved enforcement of environmental law, the Commission prognosticated that public expenditure arising out of reparation and compensation demands would decrease[322].

The Commission was aware of the fact that European law still needed to be "align[ed] [...] to the requirements of the [Aarhus] Convention"[323]. The necessity to provide "citizens and non–governmental organisations [...] [with] the required access to justice as far as Community [now: European] law is concerned" was pointed out[324]. This "required access" included that "[p]roceedings should be fair and should not be excessively long or expensive" as well as that opportunity to receive interim relief should be given[325].

It was hoped that all Member States would apply a "common minimum framework"[326] in order to account for the "transboundary dimension of environmental problems" and ensure "uniform application" of legislative responds to these problems[327]. Of course, Member States may install rules on standing in environmental disputes that exceed those required by the common minimum framework of the directive[328].

With regard to the content of the directive and its compatibility with the requirements of Article 9 of the Aarhus Convention on access to justice, the definition of "members of the public" coincide[329]. Those would be granted access to administrative acts and omissions

319 European Commission, COM(2003) 624 final – *Proposal for a Directive of the European Parliament and of the Council on access to justice in environmental matters*, p.3
320 European Commission, COM(2003) 624 final, p.4
321 European Commission, COM(2003) 624 final, p.4 & preamble (1), p.15
322 European Commission, COM(2003) 624 final, p.8
323 European Commission, COM(2003) 624 final, preamble (2), p.15
324 European Commission, COM(2003) 624 final, p.4
325 European Commission, COM(2003) 624 final, preamble (5), p.15
326 European Commission, COM(2003) 624 final, p.4
327 European Commission, COM(2003) 624 final, p.5
328 European Commission, COM(2003) 624 final, preamble (13), p.17
329 cf. Article 2(1)(b), COM(2003) 624 final and Article 2(4) AC

provided that they either "have a sufficient interest, or"[330] "maintain the impairment of a right [...]"[331]. It remained within Member State authority to decide what is to be understood under these two conditions[332]. The intentional exclusion of an *actio popularis* in environmental matters is clearly in line with Article 9(2) of the Aarhus Convention and would otherwise have been incompatible with the principle of subsidiarity[333].

Preferential treatment was offered to "qualified entities"[334], which correspond to the "public concerned" of the Aarhus Convention[335] provided that they meet certain criteria specified in Article 8 and recognized according to Article 9 of the proposed directive. These criteria referred to any "international, national, regional or local association, organisation or group" that

> (a) [...] must be an independent and non–profit-making legal person, which has the objective to protect the environment;
> (b) [...] must have an organisational structure which enables it to ensure the adequate pursuit of its statutory objectives;
> (c) [...] must have been legally constituted and worked actively for environmental protection, in conformity with its statutes, for a period to be fixed by the Member State in which is constituted, but not exceeding three years;
> (d) [...] must have its annual statement of accounts certified by a registered auditor for a period to be fixed by each Member State, in accordance with provisions set out by virtue of paragraph 1 (c)[336].

Those 'qualified entities' must not prove a "sufficient interest" or "[maintain] the impairment of a right" in order to be granted standing but must rather show that their action "brought is covered specifically by [...] [their] statutory activities" as well as their "geographical area of activities"[337]. "[A] request for internal review" can be filed under the same conditions in any other Member State[338]. These provisions clearly go beyond the requirements of the Aarhus Convention and would have greatly facilitated transboundary litigation[339].

Unfortunately, this legislative proposal was not adopted. To date, the Commission has failed to initiate a successive proposal for a directive on access to justice in environmental matters. Thus, there does not exist a common framework of rules on *locus standi* in environmental disputes within the EU and the differences as shown above remain in existence.

---

330 Article 4(1)(a), COM(2003) 624 final
331 European Commission, COM(2003) 624 final, Article 4(1)(b)
332 European Commission, COM(2003) 624 final, Article 4(2)
333 European Commission, COM(2003) 624 final, p.12
334 European Commission, COM(2003) 624 final, Article 2(1)(c)
335 Article 2(5) of the Aarhus Convention
336 European Commission, COM(2003) 624 final, Article 8
337 European Commission, COM(2003) 624 final, Article 5(1)
338 European Commission, COM(2003) 624 final, Article 5(2)
339 European Commission, COM(2003) 624 final, p.13

However, two crucial points need to be raised regarding this directive proposal. First of all, the Milieu study has shown that, although differences and disparities exist between the various national systems, nevertheless, several Member States have installed quite satisfactory systems on *locus standi* that exceed the requirements demanded by the Aarhus Convention as well as those listed in the Commission's proposal. Secondly, the minimum common framework would only be addressed to the Member States[340]. Hence, only those proceedings before the European Court of Justice would be affected that had been initiated on the basis of Article 267 TFEU. Standing concerning direct actions before the General Court challenging the legality of acts or omissions of any of the EU Institutions, bodies, offices or agencies would have remained unchanged.

It is nevertheless a step backwards in the often declared commitment of the European Union to comply with its obligations under the Aarhus Convention that no common minimum framework could have been agreed upon.

340 European Commission, COM(2003) 624 final, Article 14

Part IV.

Critical Assessment of the Status Quo

12. Examination of the Standing Requirements

With few exceptions, the literature reveals great consensus in the criticism of the current interpretation and application of the standing rules by the European Court of Justice. There have been consistent calls for a relaxation of the requirements; particularly with regard to the condition of individual concern.

12.1. The Evidence of Concern

As already indicated in the description of the action for annulment in the previous chapter, individuals, i.e. natural and legal persons including environmental civil society organizations, need to prove their concern with regard to the disputed legislation or action. No problem occurs regarding the proof of concern of decisions that "intended to produce legal effects vis–á–vis" the applicant[1]. In cases, where the applicant is not the addressee of the disputed act[2], however, he or she must be able to prove his or her "direct and individual concern"[3] thereof.

The purpose of the strict application of the two tests – and in particular that of individual concern – is to inhibit popular actions and prevent the ECJ from being flooded by an unsurmountable mass of cases[4]. The underlying rationale concerns the fact that adopted legislation is usually a sensitive compromise achieved through diplomatic bargaining within the Council and several readings in the EP before the vote. Moreover, the Commission's task as 'guardian of the Treaties' is found to suffice to ensure the objective control. Too many judicial challenges by individuals would then undermine the formal procedures at EU level[5].

12.1.1. Direct Concern

The test of direct concern stipulates that applicants may only instigate annulment proceedings against those legal acts that *directly* affect their position. Hence, there must exist a causal link between the act and the affected interest[6]. The ECJ has declared in

1 Article 263(1) TFEU
2 Article 263(4) first option TFEU
3 Article 263(4) second and third option TFEU
4 Busse–Muskala, 2007, pp.98 & 102; Thiele, 2006, p.204 & p.249
5 Thiele, 2006, pp.204–205
6 Thiele, 2007, p.101

its case–law that legal acts originating from the EU are of direct concern to the litigant where no implementation measures are adopted or where there is practically no discretion granted to the addressee[7].

The direct concern of decisions and regulations, which do not require any implementing measures is accordingly comparatively easy to prove. Yet, directives, which by definition of Article 288(3)TFEU "leave to the national authorities the choice of form and methods", are only capable of transferring direct concern to individuals, where the scope of discretion to Member State governments is only theoretical[8].

The test of direct concern is not disputed; neither in judicial practice nor in the literature. Indeed, the fact that a violation of a subjective right is not necessary but a mere effect on the litigant's interest is deemed sufficient to reveal a comparatively manageable requirement[9]. It has also been suggested that the jurisprudence of the Court concerning the conditions of direct effect is "less rigid and more consistent"[10].

Direct concern needs to be established in each case individually[11]. Indeed, the ECJ begins its examination of admissibility in many cases with assessing whether the applicant is directly concerned by the contested legal act. If the Court decides negatively, it dismisses the action for annulment "without the necessity of broaching the question whether the applicant is individually concerned by the contested decision"[12].

12.1.2. Individual Concern

Whereas the test of direct concern addresses the question on *what* legal act can be challenged, the test of individual concern identifies those, *who* may do so. Crucial is therefore not the relation between the contested act but rather the position of the claimant in relation towards other persons.

In 1963, the ECJ formulated the 'closed class test', also called *Plaumann formula.* According to this regularly cited judgment,

> [p]ersons other than those to whom a decision is addressed may only claim to be individually concerned if that decision affects them by reason of certain attributes which are peculiar to them or by reason of circumstances in which they are differentiated from all other persons and by virtue of these factors distinguishes them individually just as in the case of the person addressed[13].

---

7 cf. e.g. ECJ, Joined Cases 106 & 107/63 *Toepfer v Commission* [1965] ECR 405; ECJ, Joined Cases 41–44/70 *International Fruit Company v Commission* [1971] ECR 411 and ECJ, Case 92/78 *Simmenthal v Commission* [1979] ECR 777; ECJ, Case 62/70 *Bock v Commission* [1971] ECR 897, ECJ, and Case 11/82 *Piraiki–Patraiki* [1985] ECR 207; cf. Albors–Llorens, 2003, p.75; Thiele, 2006, p.233; Oppermann, Classen & Nettesheim, 2009, p.266

8 Thiele, 2007, p.102

9 Thiele, 2007, pp.98–99

10 Albors–Llorens, 2003, p.75

11 Thiele, 2007, p.103

12 cf. e.g. CFI, Case T–137/04 *Mayer and Others v Commission* [2006] para.67

13 ECJ, Case 25/62 *Plaumann v Commission* [1963] ECR 95, para.I–8

The Court has furthermore accepted that individuals may be considered to be individually concerned by regulations, although they, by definition, have general applicability, if they are nevertheless able to prove "by reason of certain attributes which are peculiar to them or by reason of circumstances [...] [that] they are differentiated from all other persons"[14]. Yet, the jurisprudence of the two instances of the Court of Justice of the European Union does not reveal consistency in this regard[15].

Associational Standing

As this work is concerned with participation and access opportunities of environmental civil society organizations, the specific circumstances under which standing before the ECJ is granted to associations deserves separate mention, as the test of individual concern constitutes a particularly severe obstacle[16]. In *Federolio v Commission*, the then Court of First Instance summarized the "three types of situations" under which "actions brought by associations [...] have been held to be admissible"[17]: First, "where a legal provision expressly grants [...] associations a series of procedural rights"[18]; in other words, if associations have participated in previous proceedings. It is not required that such participation is formally prescribed. The actual participation, even upon voluntary invitation by the respective EU Institution, in most cases the Commission, suffices[19]. The same applies to cases, in which the applicant was not able to execute his or her participation right through no fault of his or her own[20]. However, the condition is not fulfilled, if the claimant interfered into existing procedures upon his or her own initiative[21] (cf. chapter 13, discussion on the *Greenpeace* case).

Second, an action by an association is admitted by the ECJ "where the association represents the interests of undertakings which would be entitled to bring proceedings in their own right"[22]. Hence, associations may file a suit on behalf of its members for whom a direct and individual concern can be identified[23]. If the association itself, as a legal person, fulfills the criteria for direct and individual concern, it may obviously

14 ECJ, Case C–309/89 *Codorníu SA v Council* [1994] ECR I–1853, paras.20–22

15 Tridimas & Poli, 2008, p.88

16 Albors–Llorens, 2003, pp.77–78

17 CFI, Case T–122/96 [1997] ECR II–1559, para.60

18 CFI, Case T–122/96 *Federolio v Commission* [1997] ECR II–1559, para.60(a); cf. e.g. ECJ, Case 191/82 *Fediol v Commission* [1983] ECR 2913, paras. 28 to 30

19 Thiele, 2006, p.254; Thiele, 2007, pp.105–106; Busse–Muskala, 2007, p.121

20 Thiele, 2006, p.255 & Thiele, 2007, pp.105–106

21 Thiele, 2006, p.255

22 CFI, Case T–122/96 *Federolio v Commission* [1997] ECR II–1559, para.60(b); cf. e.g. CFI, Joined Cases T–447/93, T–448/93 and T–449/93 *AITEC and Others v Commission* [1995] ECR II–1971, para.62

23 Albors–Llorens, 2003, p.78; Harratsch, Koenig & Pechstein, 2009, p.221; Busse–Muskala, 2007, pp.121–122; Thiele, 2006, p.274

lodge a complaint as well[24]. Yet, it does not suffice that merely the *general interests* of an association are affected[25].

Finally, the third situation, in which associations are granted *locus standi* is "where the association is differentiated because its own interests as an association are affected, and especially where its position as negotiator is affected by the measure which it seeks to have annulled"[26].

12.2. General Criticism

Obviously, the requirement for a claimant to be individually concerned creates great difficulties in gaining access to the ECJ. It is also understandable that this area of European law has been "one of the most difficult and controversial issues"[27] being perceived as "anomalous and deeply unsatisfactory"[28]; particularly because the ECJ has applied these tests in a narrow interpretation. Criticism has especially been raised on the basis of the fact that the concepts of direct and individual concern are not defined anywhere in the Treaties and the approach taken by the Court in *Plaumann*[29] is not the only option[30]. Support of this view has been given by the Court itself in exactly the aforementioned case. The provision of today's Article 263(4) TFEU according to the ECJ

> neither defines nor limits the scope of these words. The words and the natural meaning of this provision justify the broadest interpretation. Moreover provisions of the Treaty regarding the right of interested parties to bring an action must not be interpreted restrictively. Therefore, the Treaty being silent on the Point, a limitation in this respect may not be presumed[31].

It seems counterproductive to the general pro–integrative stance of the Court that substantially improved legal rights of EU citizens via its case–law to uphold the restrictive reading of individual concern given that, in most instances, applicants fail to fulfill the test[32]. It is particularly unintelligible to dismiss an applicant's claim on the basis that it

24 ECJ, Joined Cases 67/85, 68/85 & 70/85 *Van der Kooy* [1988] ECR 219; cf. Harratsch, Koenig & Pechstein, 2009, p.221

25 e.g. ECJ, Joined Cases 16/62 & 17/62 *CNPFL et al v Council* [1962] ECR 471; cf. Busse–Muskala, 2007, p.121; Thiele, 2006, p.275

26 CFI, Case T–122/96 *Federolio v Commission* [1997] ECR II–1559, para.60(c); cf. e.g. ECJ, Joined Cases 67/85, 68/85 and 70/85 *Van der Kooy and Others v Commission* [1988] ECR 219, paras. 21 to 24 and CFI, Case C–313/90 *CIRFS and Others v Commission* [1993] ECR I–1125, paras.28 to 30

27 Albors–Llorens, 1999, p.33

28 Albors–Llorens, 2003, p.81

29 ECJ, Case 26/62 *Plaumann & Co. v Commission* [1963] ECR 95

30 Albors–Llorens, 2003, p.74

31 ECJ, Case 26/62 *Plaumann & Co. v Commission* [1963] ECR 95, para.I–2; cf. also Gérard, 1996, p.156

32 Albors–Llorens, 2003, p.81

cannot be excluded that other persons may be affected by the contested measure as well in the future in the same manner [33].

The Court's Position

Many scholars have noted, not without slight sarcastic astonishment, that the conditions governing the admissibility of direct actions by private applicants are uncommon when compared with the overall progressive stance of its jurisprudence. Not only is the Court "uncharacteristical[ly] reluctant" in relaxing standing requirements[34], but it also persistently, with the exception in *Plaumann*, confirms this position. One can furthermore not be convinced that the refusal by the ECJ to change its interpretation of the second admissibility test stems from the Court's perception of its own role in the institutional framework of the EU and the need to abide by prior case–law but rather from a self–imposed censorship. There have indeed been instances, in which the Court has departed from previous interpretations of provisions of the Treaty and doctrines of law[35].

It is furthermore questionable whether a regularly repeated concern about a dramatic cumulation of claims resulting in unmanageable caseload for the ECJ provides a strong argument against a reformulation of the individual concern test. Doubts as to the validity of such argumentation have not only arisen in the literature but Advocate–General Jacobs has even dismissed this concern in his *UPA*[36] Opinion[37].

As has been discussed in chapter 7, the ECJ relies primarily on earlier case–law in its decisions and indeed employs a teleological method of "*in dubio pro communitate*"[38], when interpreting provisions of the Treaties and secondary law[39]. The Court thereby strives to achieve the balance of filling the legal 'gaps' through its dynamic and evolutionary interpretation on the one hand, and abiding by the fundamental principles of *subsidiarity* and *conferral* on the other hand, in order to avoid *ultra vires* actions[40]. The Court has created the very fundamental principles of supremacy and direct effect of European law without any explicit – and also doubtfully implicit – mentioning in the Treaties. These principles were born out of practical reasoning rather than a legitimate written basis in the Treaties. It is therefore incomprehensible why the ECJ refuses to depart from its rigid course in the area of *locus standi* requirements[41].

Not only academic scholars promote a relaxed notion of individual concern, but also the two instances of the ECJ have shown different positions regarding the determination

33 Tridimas & Poli, 2008, p.78
34 Tridimas & Poli, 2008, p.78
35 Albors–Llorens, 2003, p.89
36 ECJ, Case C–50/00P *Unión de Pequeños Agricultores v Council* [2002] ECR I–6677
37 Albors–Llorens, 2003, pp.89–90
38 Weber, 2008, pp.417–418
39 cf. Part III, Chapter 7
40 Weber, 2008, pp.417–418; Dobler, 2008, pp.523, 527, 534 & 536
41 Albors–Llorens, 2003, p.90

of the admissibility of claims. While the ECJ has resisted any invitation to facilitate access to it, the former CFI has been more willing to consider a broader perception of *locus standi*[42]. It should, however, be remembered that the ECJ does not oppose a broadening of standing requirements *per se* but rather perceives the current position of political decision–makers regarding reforms as evidence for the preservation of the *Plaumann formula* and has inflicted this uncharacteristic relative idleness upon itself[43].

Responsibility of the Member States The ECJ admitted in its *UPA*[44] judgment, possibly influenced by the progressive Opinion of the Advocate–General, that "a system of judicial review of the legality of Community [Union] measures of general application different from that established by the founding Treaty and never amended as to its principles"[45] could be installed. Yet, the Court averred that only Member States could initiate a reform in accordance with the amendment procedure in Article 48 TEU LT[46].

Moreover, in its jurisprudence, the ECJ has repeatedly confirmed that "the Treaty established a complete system of legal remedies and procedures designed to permit the Court of Justice to review the legality of measures adopted by the Institutions"[47]. The Court, however, denied the responsibility to amend the notion of individual concern and the requirements for admissible claims altogether for itself and instead referred it to the Member States. The judges declared for instance in the 1976 *Rewe*[48] decision that, based on the principle of sincere cooperation[49], national courts are obliged to provide the necessary legal remedies to citizens under European law[50]. The conditions governing access to courts shall be determined by each Member State provided that they are not "less favourable than those relating to similar actions of a domestic nature"[51]. In addition to this non–discrimination principle, Member States must ensure that the procedural rules regulating respites and prosecution of judicial proceedings do not render access to national courts under EU law practically impossible[52].

---

42 cf. CFI decision in *Jégo Quéré*; cf. below

43 de Bùrca, 2003, p.68; cf. also Albors–Llorens, 2003, p.91

44 ECJ, Case C–50/00P *Unión de Pequeños Agricultores v Council (UPA)* [2002] ECR I–6677, para.67

45 ECJ, Case C–50/00P *Unión de Pequeños Agricultores v Council (UPA)* [2002] ECR I–6677, para.45

46 ECJ, Case C–50/00P *Unión de Pequeños Agricultores v Council (UPA)* [2002] ECR I–6677, para.41; cf. also de Bùrca, 2003, p.65; Harratsch, Koenig & Pechstein, 2009, p.219; Busse–Muskala, 2007, pp.133–134

47 ECJ, Case 294/83 *Parti écologiste "Les Verts" v European Parliament* [1986] ECR 1339, para.23

48 ECJ, Case 33/76 *Rewe–Zentralfinanz eG et Rewe–Zentral AG v Landwirtschaftskammer für das Saarland* [1976] ECR 1989

49 formerly: Article 5 EC and now replaced by Article 4(3) TEU LT

50 ECJ, Case 33/76 *Rewe–Zentralfinanz eG et Rewe–Zentral AG v Landwirtschaftskammer für das Saarland* [1976] ECR 1989, para.5, second sentence; cf. also Tohidipur, 2008, p.152

51 ECJ, Case 33/76 *Rewe–Zentralfinanz eG et Rewe–Zentral AG v Landwirtschaftskammer für das Saarland* [1976] ECR 1989, para.5, third sentences

52 ECJ, Case 33/76 *Rewe–Zentralfinanz eG et Rewe–Zentral AG v Landwirtschaftskammer für das Saarland* [1976] ECR 1989, para.5 fifth, sixth and seventh sentences cf. also Kwanka, 2006, p.95

However, in its memorandum to the summit in 1995, the Court departed from its position and raised concerns about the effectiveness of the current system of judicial protection. The Court questioned

> whether the right to bring an action for annulment under Article 173 of the EC Treaty [now Article 263 TFEU] ... which individuals can enjoy only in regard to acts of direct and individual concern to them, is sufficient to guarantee for them effective judicial protection against possible infringements of their fundamental rights arising from the legislative activity of the institutions[53].

It may well be for the reason that neither at this summit nor any following treaty revisions the provision that is now Article 263(4) TFEU has been amended by the Member States, that the Court feels confirmed in its assumption that national governments are not open to such modifications[54].

Yet, the above–mentioned case–law has been codified by the Lisbon Treaty in Article 19(1) second subparagraph TEU LT, which reads that "Member States shall provide remedies sufficient to ensure effective legal protection in the fields covered by Union law". This fact provides a strong argument for those, who are of the view that national legal systems should be the preferred route and modifications of the conditions of admissibility of claims before the ECJ (or CFI respectively) should be undertaken by Member State governments rather than supranational judges[55].

Critics, for instance Tridimas and Polis, proponents of Advocate–General Jacobs, accuse the ECJ of indeed being aware of the fragility of the principle of judicial protection on European level, yet pass over the responsibility for enhancement to the Member States in order to "preserv[e] the presumed integrity of the letter of the Treaty"[56]. It must be admitted, however, that the provision, introduced by the Constitutional Treaty and effectively set into force by Article 19(1) second subparagraph TEU LT, on the duty of the Member States to "provide remedies sufficient to ensure effective legal protection in the fields covered by Union law" rather supports the position of the ECJ.

Right to effective judicial protection

The primary intention of the principle of effective judicial protection is to provide private persons with legal remedies against political decision–makers. It thereby fulfills two functions. The first is the *objective* control of legality of the actions of governing actors; i.e. the preservation that ruling decision–makers act within the powers attributed by the respective constitutional document (here: the Treaties) and prosecute *ultra vires* actions. The second aim is to grant opportunities for the governed to receive compensation for

53 as cited from "Report of the Court of Justice on certain aspects of the application of the Treaty on European Union", May 1995, p.13 by: Tohidipur, 2008, p.159 & Baumeister, 2005, p.3; cf. also de Bùrca, 1996, p.349

54 Albors–Llorens, 2003, pp.91-92

55 cf. also comments by Tohidipur on the same provision in the Constitutional Treaty in: Tohidipur, 2008, p.165

56 Tridimas & Poli, 2008, pp.90–91

damages caused by actions or measures carried out by political decision–makers. The *subjective* interest of the claimant is thereby placed in the focus.

Initially, some of the founding Member States voiced serious concerns about offering remedies on supranational level to challenge actions executed and measures adopted by national governments and supranational institutions to individuals, who were adversely affected by those actions and measures[57]. In 1975, however, the *Tindemans report*, prepared by the then Belgian Prime Minister Leo Tindemans, emphasized, *inter alia*, the importance of the legal protection of the rights of the citizens of the EU; particularly in areas out of the reach of national legal systems[58].

Since the Court's famous ruling in *Internationale Handelsgesellschaft*[59] in 1970, it is settled case–law that "respect for fundamental rights forms an integral part of the general principles protected by the Court of Justice [...] [whose protection] must be ensured within the framework of the structures and objectives of the Community"[60].
The ECJ had further declared in its *Johnston*[61] judgment in 1986 that "[t]he requirement of judicial control [...] reflects a general principle of law which underlies the constitutional traditions common to the Member States"[62]. The Court also referred to the incorporation of the principle in the ECHR[63]. It is now settled case–law that it constitutes a *comprehensive* right to effective remedies[64].

With regard to objective judicial control, the ECJ clearly "emphasized in this regard that the [then] European Economic Community is a community based on the rule of law, inasmuch as neither its Member States, nor its Institutions can avoid a review of the question whether the measures adopted by them are in conformity with the basic constitutional charter, the Treaty" in its 1986 decision in *Les Verts*[65].

By now, effective judicial protection, as a principle, is endorsed within European legal systems, including the supranational one. Criticism of the ECJ's restrictive reading of the *Plaumann* formula has, therefore, particularly concentrated on the preservation of this fundamental right as enshrined in, for instance, Article 8 of the Universal Declaration of Human Rights[66]; Article 13 of the European Convention of Human Rights; Article 47

57 Tohidipur, 2008, pp.29–31

58 Bauer, 2008, pp.21–22; cf. also, european navigator, *The Tindemans report*, Website

59 ECJ, Case 11/70 *Internationale Handelsgesellschaft mbH v Einfuhr– und Vorratsstelle für Getreide und Futtermittel* [1970] ECR 1125

60 ECJ, Case 11/70 *Internationale Handelsgesellschaft mbH v Einfuhr– und Vorratsstelle für Getreide und Futtermittel* [1970] ECR 1125, para.4

61 ECJ, Case 222/84 *Marguerite Johnston v Chief Constable of the Royal Ulster Constabulary* [1986] ECR 1651

62 ECJ, Case 222/84 *Marguerite Johnston v Chief Constable of the Royal Ulster Constabulary* [1986] ECR 1651, para.18

63 cf. also Baumeister, 2005, p.9; Oppermann, Classen & Nettesheim, 2009, p.250; Tohidipur, 2008, p.152

64 Kwanka, 2006, p.110

65 ECJ, Case 294/83 *Parti écologiste "Les Verts" v European Parliament* [1986] ECR 1339; cf. also Baumeister, 2005, pp.8–9; Oppermann, Classen & Nettesheim, 2009, p.250

66 United Nations, 1949, *The Universal Declaration of Human Rights*

of the Charter of Fundamental Rights of the European Union[67], which was attributed the "same legal value as the Treaties" by Article 6 TEU LT[68]. Interestingly enough, however, Graínne de Bùrca found that, while the former CFI and Adovcates–General of the Court have already referred to the EU Charter in a number of decisions and opinions respectively, the ECJ itself has remained silent from its adoption onwards[69]. Indeed, concern about insufficient judicial protection of EU citizens has been the primary intention underlying both reformulations by Advocate–General Jacobs and the CFI of the conditions to determine whether a person is individually concerned (cf. below)[70].

Furthermore, the ECJ concurs in its decision in *UPA*[71] with the Opinion of its Advocate–General in the same case[72] insofar as the Court acknowledges the necessity of interpreting the notion of individual concern "in light of the principle of effective judicial protection by taking account of the various circumstances that may distinguish an applicant individually"[73]. However, the significance attributed to this principle was manifestly smaller and may merely aid in determining the circumstances under which a person can be held to be individually concerned; yet, it may not overrule the condition as enshrined in the Treaty[74].

Nevertheless, the insufficient application of the principle of effective judicial protection at EU level has been the greatest point of criticism in the *Greenpeace* decision of the ECJ (cf. chapter 13). Opponents of this judgment emphasize that the restrictive interpretation of individual concern excludes claims of individuals and associations, who are also deterred from gaining access to other judicial proceedings[75].

In its 2007 communication[76] on the changes brought about by the Reform Treaty, the Commission stated that a new focus will be shed "on the rights of individuals as citizens in the Union"[77]. Yet, despite the incorporation of the EU Charter of Fundamental Rights and the improvement of various social rights, the issue of effective judicial protection was formulated rather vaguely and noncommittally given that "[t]he gaps in judicial

---

67 European Parliament, 2000, *Charter of Fundamental Rights of the European Union*; cf. also de Bùrca, 2003, pp.67–68

68 Opinion of Advocate–General Jacobs in Case C–50/00P *Unión de Pequeños Agricultores v Council (UPA)* [2002] ECR I–6677, para.39 as well as CFI in Case T–177/01 *Jégo–Quéré v Commission* [2002] ECR II–2365, para.47

69 de Bùrca, G., 2003, p.68

70 cf. e.g. Albors–Llorens, 2003, p.83

71 ECJ, Case C–50/00P *Unión de Pequeños Agricultores v Council (UPA)* [2002] ECR I–6677

72 Opinion of Advocate–General Jacobs in Case C–50/00P *Unión de Pequeños Agricultores v Council (UPA)* [2002] ECR I–6677

73 Opinion of Advocate–General Jacobs in Case C–50/00P *Unión de Pequeños Agricultores v Council (UPA)* [2002] ECR I–6677, para.44; cf. also Albors–Llorens, 2003, pp.88–89

74 Craig, 2008, pp.62–63

75 Sands, 2008, p.120

76 European Commission, 2007b, COM(2007) 412 final – *Communication from the Commission to the Council. Reforming Europe for the 21st Century*

77 European Commission, 2007b, p.6

protection ensured by the European Court of Justice will be filled [...] to improve the individuals' rights of recourse to the Court"[78].

The ECJ recognized in *UPA* the principle of effective judicial protection, yet once more assured that this right was not in need of improvement via a modification of the standing conditions to gain access to the Court[79]. The CFI had in the same case at first instance[80] declared

> that the principle of equality for all persons subject to Community law in respect of the conditions for access to the Community judicature by means of the action for annulment requires that those conditions do not depend on the particular circumstances of the judicial system of each Member State. In this regard it should also be observed that, in accordance with the principle of sincere cooperation laid down in [now: Article 4(3) TEU LT], the Member States are required to implement the complete system of legal remedies and procedures [...].

The Court then refused to acknowledge the argument about the time length of alternative proceedings as a valid ground "for departing from the system of remedies"[81] and declared that "[i]n no case can such an argument enable an action for annulment [...] to be declared admissible"[82].

12.3. Reformulations of the individual concern test

Apart from repeated calls for a special treatment of claims relating to environmental protection resulting in the relaxation of the standing requirements, a few proposals have been advanced in order to modify the general interpretation of individual concern. The application of these suggestions is not restricted to particular policy areas or classes of claimants but are rather of general application.

12.3.1. Criticism by A–G Jacobs of the current system

The proposed reformulation of the individual concern test followed a long list of criticism of the current system. Advocate–General Jacobs found it "unacceptable" when individuals are not able to "challenge directly a measure [of general application] which" has adverse effects on them. He emphasized that the conditions of admissibility "must be interpreted in such a way as to comply with the principle of effective judicial pro-

78 European Commission, 2007b, p.7; cf. also Tohidipur, 2008, p.131

79 ECJ, Case C–50/00P *Unión de Pequeños Agricultores v Council* (*UPA*) [2002] ECR I–6677, paras. 33 & 38–39; cf. also Craig, 2008, p.62

80 CFI, Case T–173/98 *Unión de Pequeños Agricultores v Council* [1999] ECR II–3357, para.62

81 ECJ, Case C–50/00P *Unión de Pequeños Agricultores v Council* (*UPA*) [2002] ECR I–6677, para.63

82 ECJ, Case C–50/00P *Unión de Pequeños Agricultores v Council* (*UPA*) [2002] ECR I–6677, para.64

tection"[83]. Recourse to national courts does not, in many instances, offer an alternative remedy. Moreover, judicial proceedings before national courts resulting in preliminary references to the ECJ are less appropriate to decide upon the validity of European law while at the same time, they may increase legal uncertainty[84] rather than ensuring that an "individual who considers himself wronged by a measure which deprives him of a right or advantage under Community law [...] [gains] access to a remedy against that measure and [...] [is] able to obtain complete judicial protection"[85]. He pointed to the limited competence of national courts to merely apply and interpret European law, which, however, excludes the authority to decide upon its validity[86].

The preliminary reference procedure furthermore bears considerable insecurities and disadvantages. In addition to the tremendous time delay that occurs when applicants have to get through several levels before a court is willing – or, as the last instance, obliged – to refer to the ECJ, the questions formulated by the referring national court might invalidate the applicant's complaint on the validity of the contested measure[87]. In addition, Union law that does not need consecutive national measures for implementation can, in principle, not be challenged by individuals before national courts. The sole possibility left to persons, in the view of the Advocate–General, is to purposely violate a measure and insist on its invalidity. Yet, he concluded that "[i]ndividuals clearly cannot be required to breach the law in order to gain access to justice"[88].

In addition to the aforementioned time delay, the initiation of possibly a number of parallel proceedings in different Member States, in order to be granted interim measures according to the specific rules within each legal system, demands supplementary efforts in time, finances and legal staff on part of the applicants. This scenario would furthermore entail the threat of a heterogeneous application of European law by the different national courts, which is clearly one of the primary objectives of the EU to prevent[89]. In paragraph 46 of his Opinion, Advocate–General Jacobs summarized the reasons for a preference of direct actions over preliminary rulings as follows.

> The procedure is more appropriate because the institution which adopted the impugned measure is a party to the proceedings from beginning to end and because a direct action involves a full exchange of pleadings, as opposed to a single round

83 Opinion of Advocate–General Jacobs in Case C–50/00P *Unión de Pequeños Agricultores v Council (UPA)* [2002] ECR I–6677, para.37

84 Opinion of Advocate–General Jacobs in Case C–50/00P *Unión de Pequeños Agricultores v Council (UPA)* [2002] ECR I–6677 & para.40

85 Opinion of Advocate–General Jacobs in Case C–50/00P *Unión de Pequeños Agricultores v Council (UPA)* [2002] ECR I–6677, para.38

86 Opinion of Advocate–General Jacobs in Case C–50/00P *Unión de Pequeños Agricultores v Council (UPA)* [2002] ECR I–6677, para.41

87 Opinion of Advocate–General Jacobs in Case C–50/00P *Unión de Pequeños Agricultores v Council (UPA)* [2002] ECR I–6677, para.42

88 Opinion of Advocate–General Jacobs in Case C–50/00P *Unión de Pequeños Agricultores v Council (UPA)* [2002] ECR I–6677, para.43

89 Opinion of Advocate–General Jacobs in Case C–50/00P *Unión de Pequeños Agricultores v Council (UPA)* [2002] ECR I–6677, para.44

> of observations followed by oral observations before the Court. The availability of interim relief under Articles 242 and 243 EC [now Articles 278 & 279 TFEU], effective in all Member States, is also a major advantage for individual applicants and for the uniformity of Community law.

Further, intervention by individuals as third parties in direct actions[90] is possible, given that the latter have to be published in the Official Journal to which persons have unrestricted access. Yet, intervention is only possible in preliminary reference proceedings, if the respective person has already done so in the original national proceeding. Individuals may not be able to intervene sufficiently early based on lack of information, if, for instance, the national proceeding originates from a Member State other than their own[91]. The final argument supporting direct actions over preliminary reference proceedings forwarded by the Advocate–General is based, *inter alia*, on legal certainty, and concerns the prompt examination of a measure's validity immediately after its execution. The narrow time–limit listed in paragraph six of Article 263 TFEU ensures this[92]. Advocate–General Jacobs argued that the adherence to the *Plaumann formula* by the ECJ stands in "anomalous" contrast to its "case–law on other aspects of judicial review and recent developments in the administrative laws of the Member States"[93].

Proposal of Advocate–General Jacobs in UPA

In the appeal case before the ECJ by *UPA*[94], Advocate–General Francis Jacobs criticized the status quo and proposed an innovative test to determine whether an applicant can be considered to be individually concerned within the meaning of an unamended then Article 230(4)EC [now: Article 263(4)TFEU]. The Advocate–Generals are installed at the ECJ in order to assist the Court "with complete impartiality and independence"[95] in settling legal disputes by examining in detail the legal and practical facts of the case and by applying and re–evaluating previous judgments, i.e. the case–law of the Court[96]. The Opinion is not binding upon the judges and may merely offer guidance and assistance. Yet, the Court is free to depart from those suggestions[97].

The facts of the case concerned an application of UPA, a Spanish association possessing legal personality and representing the interests of agricultural businesses to the Court, to annul a regulation that reformed the common market of oils and fat. The Court

---

90 cf. Article 37, Statute of the Court of Justice

91 Opinion of Advocate–General Jacobs in Case C–50/00P *Unión de Pequeños Agricultores v Council (UPA)* [2002] ECR I–6677, para.47

92 Opinion of Advocate–General Jacobs in Case C–50/00P *Unión de Pequeños Agricultores v Council (UPA)* [2002] ECR I–6677, para.48

93 Opinion of Advocate–General Jacobs in Case C–50/00P *Unión de Pequeños Agricultores v Council (UPA)* [2002] ECR I–6677, para.37

94 ECJ, Case C–50/00P *Unión de Pequeños Agricultores v Council* (*UPA*) [2002] ECR I–6677

95 Article 252 second para. TFEU

96 Tridimas & Poli, 2008, p.77

97 There is only an obligation to hear the Advocate–General before the judgment is delivered; cf. Article 63 ECJ Rules of Procedure

of First Instance denied standing to UPA based on the lack of individual concern, or alternatively, the three exceptional circumstances for associations.

UPA itself suggested that in situations, in which no alternative judicial proceeding was available to the applicants, their action for annulment should always be declared admissible before the ECJ, as they would otherwise be denied their right to effective judicial remedy[98]. On the grounds to be discussed below in detail, Advocate–General Jacobs rejected UPA's position, yet was also discontent with the current reading and thus proposed a new test of individual concern which would circumvent this dilemma.

By his definition, "a person is to be regarded as individually concerned by a Community [now: EU] measure where, by reason of *his particular circumstances*, the measure has, or is liable to have, a *substantial adverse effect* on his interests" [emphasis added][99].

Among his greatest concerns is the endeavor not to exclude individuals from the possibility to file an action under the fourth paragraph of what is now Article 263 TFEU solely because the "measure adversely affects a large number of individuals, causing wide–spread rather than limited harm"[100].

Advantages The advantages of his reformulation of the test of individual concern are proclaimed by Advocate–General to be numerous. First, and most importantly, the approach advanced by him would circumvent a *déni de justice*; a situation in which the individual whose interests have been affected by an EU measure could neither turn to the national courts with the aspiration for a preliminary reference nor to the General Court for a direct action[101]. This was also one of the arguments put forward by the applicants in the *Greenpeace* appeal[102]. The availability of the Article 263 TFEU [then Article 234 EC] procedure depends on first, the formal rules on standing and admissibility within the respective legal systems of the Member States, and second, on the willingness of national judges to refer questions to the ECJ for a preliminary ruling. Those proceedings furthermore are prone to cause greater costs, financially and in time[103].

The new test would end criticism about the "complexity and lack of coherence" of the Court's stance on *locus standi* and would thereby increase legal certainty and accordingly render the current practice of filing parallel suits in national courts and the GC (as

98 ECJ, Case C–50/00P *Unión de Pequeños Agricultores v Council* [2002] ECR I–6677 para.12; cf. also Albors–Llorens, 2003, p.83

99 Opinion of Advocate–General Jacobs in Case C–50/00P *Unión de Pequeños Agricultores v Council (UPA)* [2002] ECR I–6677, para.60

100 Opinion of Advocate–General Jacobs in Case C–50/00P *Unión de Pequeños Agricultores v Council (UPA)* [2002] ECR I–6677, para.59

101 Opinion of Advocate–General Jacobs in Case C–50/00P *Unión de Pequeños Agricultores v Council (UPA)* [2002] ECR I–6677, para.62; cf. also Albors–Llorens, 2003, p.82

102 ECJ, Case 321/95P *Greenpeace and Others v Commission* [1998] ECR I–1651

103 Albors–Llorens, 2003, p.82

was also the case in *Greenpeace*, cf. chapter 13) unnecessary[104]. The "anomalies" in the ECJ's case–law would finally be removed[105].

Jacobs furthermore emphasized that direct actions should be preferred as "the procedure which is best suited to resolving" questions as to the validity of measures having general application because the possibility of interim relief is given[106]. Among the advantages of direct actions as opposed to preliminary reference procedures are not only arguments concerning the delay of court proceedings but also the enhancement of the uniform application of EU law and an increase in legal certainty[107], which, as a principle, is highly valued within the EU legal system. The application of the new test of individual concern would, in addition, "shift the emphasis of judicial review from questions of admissibility to questions of substance"[108]. This may allow for "the application of substantive standards of judicial review" of EU legislation. Hence, while maintaining the institutions' "margin of discretion", the merits of a case would no longer be "blindly exclud[ed]" on grounds of the applicant's lack of standing[109].

ECJ Decision The ECJ did not follow the progressive proposal of its Advocate–General in its judgment[110]. The judges acknowledged that effective judicial protection is a component of a person's fundamental rights which the EU values as a legal system based on the rule of law. Yet, while they regard it "admittedly, possible to envisage a system of judicial review of the legality of Community measures of general application different from that established by the founding Treaty and never amended as to its principles", they nevertheless regard it as the duty of Member States' governments "to reform the system currently in force"[111]. Contrary to Advocate–General Jacobs, the judges did not grasp the opportunity to change the interpretation of the notion of individual concern without changing the meaning of the provision in the Treaty, as they considered it an action *ultra vires*[112].

---

104 ECJ, Case 321/95P *Greenpeace and Others v Commission* [1998] ECR I–1651, para.64; cf. also Albors–Llorens, 2003, pp.82 & 85

105 Opinion of Advocate–General Jacobs in Case C–50/00P *Unión de Pequeños Agricultores v Council (UPA)* [2002] ECR I–6677, para.67

106 Opinion of Advocate–General Jacobs in Case C–50/00P *Unión de Pequeños Agricultores v Council (UPA)* [2002] ECR I–6677, para.63

107 Opinion of Advocate–General Jacobs in Case C–50/00P *Unión de Pequeños Agricultores v Council (UPA)* [2002] ECR I–6677, para.65

108 Opinion of Advocate–General Jacobs in Case C–50/00P *Unión de Pequeños Agricultores v Council (UPA)* [2002] ECR I–6677, para.66

109 Opinion of Advocate–General Jacobs in Case C–50/00P *Unión de Pequeños Agricultores v Council (UPA)* [2002] ECR I–6677, para.66; cf. also Albors–Llorens, 2003, p.82

110 ECJ, Case C–50/00P *Unión de Pequeños Agricultores v Council (UPA)* [2002] ECR I–6677; cf. also Tridimas & Poli, 2008, p.99

111 ECJ, Case C–50/00P *Unión de Pequeños Agricultores v Council (UPA)* [2002] ECR I–6677, para.45

112 ECJ, Case C–50/00P *Unión de Pequeños Agricultores v Council (UPA)* [2002] ECR I–6677, paras.44–45; cf. also de Bùrca, 2003, p.65; Harratsch, Koenig & Pechstein, 2009, p.219; Busse–Muskala, 2007, pp.133–134

Proposal of the CFI in Jégo–Quéré

Two months after Advocate–General Jacobs had delivered his Opinion in UPA[113], the then Court of First Instance issued a judgment[114] that shared the opinion of the Advocate–General regarding the obligation to ensure effective judicial protection[115], as well as the possibility to change the interpretation of individual concern, without having to amend the Treaty text[116].

The case concerned a measure of general application that was not in need of further implementation[117]. After having excluded any potential alternative remedies (e.g. actions of annulment [now: Article 263 TFEU], action for failure to act [Article 265 TFEU], preliminary reference proceedings [Article 267 TFEU], or compensation for damages [Article 268 TFEU]) as insufficient, the CFI found that "the strict interpretation, applied until now, of the notion of a person individually concerned according to the fourth paragraph of Article 230 EC [Article 263 TFEU], must be reconsidered"[118].

The reformulation reads as follows:

> [...] in order to ensure effective judicial protection for individuals, a natural or legal person is to be regarded as individually concerned by a Community measure of general application that concerns him directly if the measure in question affects his legal position, in a manner which is both definite and immediate, by restricting his rights or by imposing obligations on him[119].

The Court thereby eliminated the restrictive 'closed class' test and declared that "[t]he number and position of other persons who are likewise affected by the measure, or who may be so, are of no relevance in that regard"[120].

The CFI based its suggestion on the wording of Article 47 of the Charter of Fundamental Rights of the European Union, which also guarantees "effective remedy" to persons "whose rights and freedoms [...] are *violated*" [emphasis added][121]. The Charter does not further specify the nature or quality of such violations.

Decision of the ECJ While the CFI negated the applicant's individual concern under the original *Plaumann formula*, the application of the new test in combination with the

113 Case C–50/00P *Unión de Pequeños Agricultores v Council (UPA)* [2002] ECR I–6677
114 CFI, Case T–177/01 *Jégo–Quéré v Commission* [2002] ECR II–2365
115 CFI, Case T–177/01 *Jégo–Quéré v Commission* [2002] ECR II–2365, paras.45, 47 & 51; cf. also Tridimas & Poli, 2008, p.86; Albors–Llorens, 2003, p.83
116 CFI, Case T–177/01 *Jégo–Quéré v Commission* [2002] ECR II–2365, para.49
117 cf. e.g. Harratsch, Koenig & Pechstein, 2009, p.218
118 CFI, Case T–177/01 *Jégo–Quéré v Commission* [2002] ECR II–2365, para.50; cf. also Tridimas & Poli, 2008, pp.86–87; Busse–Muskala, 2007, p.131
119 CFI, Case T–177/01 *Jégo–Quéré v Commission* [2002] ECR II–2365, para.51
120 CFI, Case T–177/01 *Jégo–Quéré v Commission* [2002] ECR II–2365, para.51
121 cf. Tridimas & Poli, 2008, p.87

fulfilled criteria for direct concern rendered the claim admissible[122]. Yet, the ECJ[123] overruled the judgment of the CFI and declared the claim of the applicants inadmissible due to a lack of individual concern, determined on the basis of the *Plaumann formula.* The Court once more referred to the Member States to provide sufficient remedies for its citizens[124].

Given that the ECJ had ignored both, the CFI's proposal and Advocate–General Jacobs' reformulation of individual concern, Advocate–General Jacobs again criticized the traditional interpretation of the *Plaumann formula*, nevertheless applied it to the applicants in *Jégo–Quéré*. Thus, criticism arose against the Court's unwillingness to interpret standing conditions more liberally. Particularly criticized is the fact that the ECJ insists that the *Plaumann forumla* is the sole interpretation of what is now Article 263(4) TFEU, while opponents in literature, as well as Advocate–General Jacobs in *UPA* and the judges of the CFI in *Jégo–Quéré*, declare that "nothing in the Treaty [...] dictates" such a restrictive reading[125].

Comparison of the two tests

The successive reformulations of the test of individual concern have not only been issued within a short time span but share similar motivations. It has been pointed out that both, Advocate–General Jacobs, as well as the CFI, have been concerned with the threat that the current system of remedies may not provide effective judicial protection to the individual, contrary to what was often proclaimed by the ECJ before. In other words, applicants would be confronted with a de facto *déni de justice*. Both questioned the reliance of the ECJ on the judicial proceedings of the Member States to ensure full legal protection where direct actions before the Court are declined[126]. This is particularly the case where access to Member State courts is impeded and individuals affected by a legal measure find themselves without any remedy to challenge its validity[127]. Moreover, they refused the assumption of a causal and subordinated relation of the latter as towards the availability of legal procedures before national courts. Rather to the contrary, direct actions should be preferred over the route of preliminary references or damage claims[128]. Neither the Court nor Advocate–General accepted that the narrow application of the *Plaumann* formula is irrevocably determined by the wording of the fourth paragraph of Article 230 EC [now: Article 263 TFEU][129]. Accordingly, the decisive criterion was demanded by both to no longer be the definite identification of as few individuals as possible, thereby rendering the number of affected persons irrelevant[130].

---

122 Tridimas & Poli, 2008, p.87; Albors–Llorens, 2003, p.84
123 ECJ, Case C–263/02P *Commission v Jégo–Quéré* [2004]
124 cf. Tridimas & Poli, 2008, p.89, Thiele, 2006, pp.201–203
125 cf. e.g. Tridimas & Poli, 2008, pp.90 & 99
126 Albors–Llorens, 2003, pp.83, 84
127 Baumeister, 2005, p.8
128 Tridimas & Poli, 2008, p.88
129 Albors–Llorens, 2003, p.84; Tridimas & Poli, 2008, p.87
130 Tridimas & Poli, 2008, p.88; Thiele, 2006, pp.208–209

Despite the same origin, namely the concern about a potential *déni de justice* to individuals within the EU legal system, the two tests of individual concern not only reveal similarities. The greatest distinction is to be drawn in the substantive requirements for establishing the type and the extent of their concern.

Commentators agree that the criterion formulated by Advocate–General Jacobs bears greater potential for the relaxation of the rules on *locus standi* than the one employed by the CFI. The judges demand the applicant to be able to show a "definite and immediate effect" on his "legal position"[131]. Advocate–General Jacobs, however, merely employs a "substantial adverse effect" test. He regards it as sufficient, if the person's interests are substantially adversely affected[132]. According to Albors–Llorens, the test based on the examination of the damage caused by the disputed measure is closer to economic reality[133].

Although the CFI judgment does not utilize the word *actual*, it seems as if the fact that a measure may *potentially* affect the applicant's legal position would not qualify as individual concern[134]. It can, however, be assumed that the test proposed in *UPA* would also be applicable in situations, in which measures possess the potential of affecting the applicant's interest in the future[135].

The CFI furthermore explicitly referred to the general application of measures for which individual concern would be determined[136]. In addition, the Court emphasized the fact that "no acts of implementation capable of forming the basis of an action before national courts" existed in the case at hand[137]. The direct effect of a measure is thereby accentuated and becomes an inseparable prerequisite of individual concern[138]. It is therefore unsettled, whether the reformulated test is exclusively reserved to regulations, or whether it could also be applied to decisions[139] and measures requiring further implementation measures. Advocate–General Jacobs remains silent with regard to any restrictions of his test to specific types of legal acts or policy areas and therefore indicates general applicability[140].

---

131 CFI, Case T–177/01 *Jégo–Quéré v Commission* [2002] ECR II–2365, para.51

132 Opinion of Advocate–General Jacobs in *UPA*, para.60; cf. also Albors–Llorens, 2003, pp.84–85; Busse–Muskala, 2007, p.131

133 2003, p.85

134 Tridimas & Poli, 2008, p.88; Albors–Llorens, 2003, p.85

135 Albors–Llorens, 2003, p.85; Tridimas & Poli, 2008, pp.88–89

136 CFI, Case T–177/01 *Jégo–Quéré v Commission* [2002] ECR II–2365, para.51; cf. also Busse–Muskala, 2007, p.132

137 CFI, Case T–177/01 *Jégo–Quéré v Commission* [2002] ECR II–2365, para.45

138 "[...] a natural or legal person is to be regarded as *individually concerned* by a Community *measure of general application* that *concerns him directly* if the measure in question affects his legal position, in a manner which is both definite and immediate, by restricting his rights or by imposing obligations on him. The number and position of other persons who are likewise affected by the measure, or who may be so, are of no relevance in that regard". CFI, Case T–177/01 *Jégo–Quéré v Commission* [2002] ECR II–2365, para.51

139 Albors–Llorens, 2003, p.85; Tridimas & Poli, 2008, pp.88–89

140 Albors–Llorens, 2003, p.85

Overall, the test as formulated by the CFI would change the current regulations on *locus standi* to a lesser degree than the proposal of Advocate–General Jacobs. The former would rather offer an additional exception to the general rule, where the *Plaumann* formula would still remain applicable, and thereby in line with previous exceptions as provided by the ECJ in its *Codorníu* and *Extramet* rulings (cf. below). On the contrary, the definition of individual concern by Advocate–General Jacobs would completely replace the *Plaumann* formula in any circumstances and, thus, would render the maintenance of additional exceptions, as for instance *Codorníu*, dispensable[141].

Tridimas and Poli suggest that, while under the *UPA*–test of Advocate–General Jacobs, there could be a possibility for claims of applicants constituting of similar circumstances as those in, for instance, *Plaumann*[142] or *Greenpeace*[143] to be declared admissible, the CFI's test in *Jégo–Quéré* would not provide as broad standing[144]. Overall, it would, however, be highly optimistic to expect that environmental associations could easily fulfill the conditions for admissibility of either reformulated test[145].

Learning from other policy areas The literature repeatedly points towards exceptions to the rule provided in several policy areas, including anti–dumping cases[146] and primarily competition[147], as well as most often–quoted cases concerning state aids[148]. In 1986, the Court admitted in *Cofaz* a complaint by an undertaking on grounds of having participated in the investigation stage of an proceeding examining potential violations of European law and their market position having been affected by the aid[149].

The *Codorníu* case[150] is most often cited to illustrate the extension of the applicability of individual concern to other legally binding texts, which are, in their form, not decisions but acts of general application, i.e. regulations. The applicant was considered to be sufficiently distinct from other persons insofar as the prohibition of the use of the term "cremant" would deprive her from using her well–known trade mark and cause serious damages to her[151].

---

141 cf. e.g. Tridimas & Poli, 2008, pp.88–89

142 ECJ, Case 25/62 *Plaumann & Co. v Commission* [1963] ECR 95

143 ECJ, Case C–321/95P *Greenpeace and Others v Commission* [1998] ECR I–1651

144 Tridimas & Poli, 2008, p.89

145 Albors–Llorens, 2003, pp.85–86

146 ECJ, Case 264/82 *Timex v Council* [1985] ECR 849; ECJ, Joined Cases 239 and 275/82 *Allied Corporation v Commission* [1984] ECR 1005; ECJ, Case C–358/89 *Extramet v Council* [1991] ECR I–2501

147 ECJ, Case 26/76 *Metro v Commission* [1977] ECR 1875

148 ECJ, Case 169/84 *Cofaz v Commission* [1986] ECR 391;
cases cited from: Albors–Llorens, 1999, pp.35–36 & Albors-Llorens, 2003, pp.73–74;
cf. also Krämer, 1996, pp.11 & 12 & Baumeister, 2005, p.10

149 ECJ, Case 169/84 *Cofaz v Commission* [1986] ECR 391, paras.23 & 24; cf. also Gérard, 1996, pp.153–154

150 ECJ, Case C–309/89 *Codorníu v Council* [1994] ECR I–1853

151 Albors–Llorens, 2003, p.80; Busse–Muskala, 2007, pp.66–67

Generous reading of specific excerpts of the ECJ's case–law indicates that the Court has indeed been willing to depart from the restrictive interpretation of individual concern. Particularly in cases where the merits of the application seem specifically promising, the Court has been found to apply a relaxed interpretation of individual concern[152].

12.3.2. Argument against a relaxation of *locus standi*

One powerful argument that supports the position of the ECJ, confirmed by settled case–law, is the fact that it is the obligation of the Member States to provide for effective remedies in their respective legal systems and not for the Court to autonomously change the interpretation of individual concern. This is confirmed by Article 19(2) TEU as introduced by the Lisbon Treaty. This Treaty, drafted in the second half of the last decade, signed in 2007, and finally ratified and entered into force in December 2009, has been formulated in the time following the proposals suggested by Advocate–General Jacobs and the CFI and the respective response by the ECJ.

12.3.3. Amendment of the Treaty

The peak of the academic debate about and the two judicial reformulations of the test of individual concern came at the time the Convention drafted the failed *Treaty establishing a Constitution for Europe*. The provision equivalent to what was Article 230(4) EC governing the Court's jurisdiction on actions of annulment was amended to no longer require the evidence of a person's individual concern, as long as the contested measure was "a regulatory act which is of direct concern to" the applicants "and does not entail implementing measures". Article 263(4) TFEU maintains the same wording.

At the time of writing, it is still too early to fully appreciate the implications of the amendment. It certainly bears great potential to silence much, yet not all, criticism. The added option seems to have codified the exceptions declared by ECJ decisions in *Extramet*[153] and *Codorníu*[154]. At first sight, the additional option might be capable of filling the gap in the system of effective judicial protection that was pointed out by Advocate–General Jacobs in *UPA*[155]. EU regulations, which need not be transposed into national law, cannot be challenged as to their legality before national courts so that a refusal of admissibility would inevitably result in a *déni de justice*. If the proof of individual concern is no longer required in these situations, direct actions will become far more easy to undertake. A closer examination, however, reveals that the amendment might actually only slightly improve access to justice under very specific circumstances and may accordingly remain merely a "minimalist solution"[156].

152 e.g. ECJ, Case C–309/89 *Codorníu v Council* [1994] ECR I–1853; Tridimas & Poli, 2008, p.80

153 ECJ, Case C–358/89, *Extramet* [1991] ECR I–2501

154 ECJ, Case C–309/89, *Codorniu* [1994] ECR I–1853

155 Opinion of the Advocate–General in Case C–50/00P *Unión de Pequeños Agricultores v Council* (*UPA*) [2002] ECR I–6677

156 Dougan, 2008, p.677

The main reason for the uncertainty of the effects of this amendment is the fact that 'regulatory acts' are not defined in the Treaty. The term 'regulatory' seems to indicate a resemblance to regulations, the piece of legislation defined in Article 288(2) TFEU as being directly applicable and effective in its entirety. This assumption is even furthered by a great number of versions in other official languages of the Treaty, all of which must be equivalent to each other. The Romanic languages[157] with the exception of Romanian, as well as those of Eastern Baltic origin[158], Maltese as a semitic language[159] and, as an exception among the Germanic languages, German[160] utilize similar terms for the measure which a non–privileged person may challenge according to Article 263(4) second alternative TFEU and the aforementioned legislative act. However, undoubted clarity cannot be retrieved from the linguistic comparison. The Treaty versions of another, in number not to be underestimated, group of languages comprising Romanian[161], as the exception among the Romanic languages, several Germanic languages[162] and one of Slavic origin[163] linguistically clearly distinguishes the two measures from each other.

It would be more obvious, if the newly introduced option in paragraph 4 of Article 263 TFEU concerned "measures of general application" or bluntly referred to "regulations" as the latter's definition is given in Article 288(2) of the Treaty. Another argument opposing the equalization of the "regulatory act which is of direct concern to [...] [applicants]" with 'regulations' is the fact that, if equation was intended, the condition of no further "implementing measures" would not have to be mentioned explicitly. This requirement would have already arisen out of the definition of regulations as being, *inter alia*, "directly applicable in all Member States"[164].

As explained above, the wording was taken over from the Constitutional Treaty, which distinguished between legislative and non–legislative acts and renamed the single measures. The Lisbon Treaty does not make such a categorization. In the context of the Constitutional Treaty, however, 'regulatory acts' seem to have been intended to apply only to non–legislative measures. By inference, legislative acts, even those that are self–executive, i.e. regulations, would still be excluded and evidence of the applicant's individual concern would still be required. The Treaty amendment would, according to

157 French: "actes réglementaires" & "règlement";
Italian: "atti regolamentari" & "regolamento";
Spanish: "actos reglamentarios" & "reglamento";
Portuguese: "actos regulamentares" & "regulamento"

158 Latvian: "reglamentejou aktu" & "regulas";
Lithuanian: "reglamentuojančio" & "reglamentas"

159 Maltese: "regolatorju" & "regolament"

160 German: "Rechtsakte mit Verordnungscharakter" & "Verordnung"

161 Romanian: "actelor normative" & "regulamentul"

162 Dutch (West Germanic): "regelgevingshandelingen" & "verordening";
Danish (Northern Germanic): "regelfaststtende retsakter" & "forordning";
Swedish (Northern Germanic): "regleringsakt" & "förordning"

163 Slovakian: "regulačným aktom" & "nariadenie"

164 Article 288(2) TFEU

this interpretation, not aid applicants in a situation comparable to that in *UPA* to gain access to the ECJ[165].

Thus, the interpretation of the ECJ needs to be awaited for certainty about the nature of the measures and their authors. Referring to the latter, the availability of remedies against any acts, including such "self–regulatory" ones[166], adopted by EU agencies, offices, or bodies depends on the arrangements spelled out in their respective establishment acts. At worst, this will have to be determined every time for each case individually.

The limited interpretation was intended by the Constitutional Convention to prevent making it too easy to challenge EU legislation by non–privileged applicants. Yet, this assumption is erroneous for a number of reasons. First, the restrictive reading of the term merely hinders direct actions of annulment. Yet challenge of Union legislative acts is still possible via preliminary references by national courts. As has been indicated above, the Court has already preferred the indirect route. Second, the restrictive approach may have been influenced by the legal traditions of the Member States. Judicial review of administrative acts is in most countries more easily accessible as compared with national legislation or even provisions of the respective constitutions. In the national context, an additional political argument based on democratic accountability can be put forward. The rationale is that acts of democratically elected representatives of the people should be less vulnerable to challenges than those adopted by non–legitimatized civil servants. This argument, however, does not hold as substantially at EU level for the reasons discussed in the section on the Union's democratic deficit (Chapter 5). In addition, as is also settled case–law of the ECJ, the label given to a measure adopted at EU level does not always correspond to its nature. Decision–making procedures and legal effects vis–á–vis third parties should accordingly be more decisive than its name[167].

Dougan therefore suggests that a too optimistic approach should not be expected from the ECJ. A "realistic" expectation could merely be that the Court applies a broad interpretation of the concept of 'regulatory acts' and no longer requires an applicant's individual concern when challenging any "self–executing Union measures of general application"; whether they are of a legislative nature or not[168]. In addition, the Court should reinforce its own demand that is codified in Article 19(1) second subparagraph TFEU that Member States are under the duty "to ensure effective legal protection in the fields covered by Union law". The ECJ may do so by urging national courts to admit *bona fide* applications by private persons for preliminary references, if direct actions before the General Court are denied[169].

165 Dougan, 2008, p.677
166 Dougan, 2008, p.677
167 Dougan, 2008, pp.677–679
168 Dougan, 2008, p.679
169 Dougan, 2008, p.679

The change brought about by the Lisbon Treaty as compared to the system prior to its entry into force on December 1, 2009 is therefore not expected to have resolved the predominant majority of the criticisms elaborated in previous sections on the interpretation of individual concern as a hindrance to access to European justice. The accessibility of the EU judiciary is still not easy and particularly with regard to legal disputes concerning environmental protection, access needs to be facilitated.

13. The Paradox of Individual Concern in Disputes concerning Environmental Protection

13.1. Environmental Cases before the ECJ

An overview of environmental cases covering the period of 1985 to 2009 adjudicated by the ECJ provides further evidence for the problems and obstacles which private litigants face in disputes concerning environmental matters. The data was retrieved from the case–law collection that is ordered thematically as published by the European Court of Justice[1]. The classification of the Court was used and all cases labeled as relating to the environment have been considered. The cases have then been ordered according to the type of the proceeding; i.e. infringement proceedings, preliminary references, and direct actions for annulment by private litigants. They have furthermore been attributed to the Member State from which they originated as well as the year in which they had been filed with the ECJ.

The Nature of Environmental Cases

The selection of the ECJ classified in total 296 cases as touching upon environmental matters. The categorization taken by the ECJ is, unfortunately, not very transparent. For instance, the famous Greenpeace cases that are examples for access of private persons and are discussed in detail below are not listed under the section of the environment but only under "recours en annulation". For these cases, the author has here departed from the ECJ's classification and added them in the area of environmental disputes for reasons that will become self–explanatory in the next section. Ludwig Krämer, however, even lists 455 environmental cases in the period from 1985 to 2006[2]. The difference of roughly 160 cases and may be the result of the employment of different indicators. Krämer also considered actions initiated on the basis of ex–Articles 228 (failure to comply with an ECJ ruling), 243 (interim measures), 225 (competence of the GC), 235 (compensation for damages) and 300(6) (conclusion of international treaties) EC [now Articles 260, 256 and 218 TFEU], which are small in number and can be omitted for the purpose of this work. It is, however, not irrelevant to stress that no actions for failure to

1 Court of the European Union, 2009, *Tables alphabétique de matières (Volumes 1985 —2009)*
2 Krämer, 2006, p.408

act [now Article 265 TFEU] relating to environmental protection have been referred to the ECJ so far.

The first numbers next to the slices of the pie in figure 11 show the actual number of cases, whereas the second numbers indicate the percentage share of the total number reviewed.

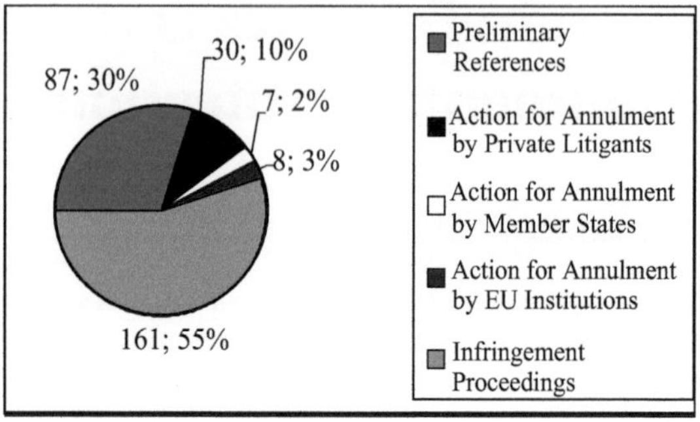

Figure 11: Environmental Cases (1985 – 2009)

Infringement proceedings constitute more than half of all the cases filed and thus, outnumber preliminary references followed by actions for annulment. The share of private applicants in actions for annulment is thereby twice as large as those initiated by Member States and EU Institutions combined. This is understandable, given that the latter actors have been formally involved in the preparation and adoption of legislation and similar actions and most claims were based on the accusation of having employed a wrong legal basis.

Comparison over Time

Figure 12 illustrates the evolution of the three main procedures before the Court that are initiated in environmental legal disputes; first, the infringement proceeding that has exclusively been initiated by the Commission on the basis of what is now Article 258 TFEU, second, preliminary references by national courts under regime that is now stipulated in Article 267 TFEU, and third, actions for annulment brought by private applicants under the current Article 263 TFEU. Be reminded that the dates that have been used in this statistics are those years in which the case was filed with the ECJ; not the date on which the Court delivered its judgment or opinion.

The graph again illustrates that infringement procedures significantly exceed the two other proceedings in actual numbers. Overall, there is also a similar development visible among the three proceedings. However, in 1985, even before the Single European Act, which introduced a chapter on a common environmental policy, five infringement proceedings had been initiated against five Member States, whereas the other two proceedings were practically not utilized during the first six years of the time under study.

Throughout the 1990s, there is no clear trend visible in the preliminary references by national courts. The mid–nineties, however, showed a small increase which was reversed again at the beginning of the new millennium. Starting from 1993, the curve of the infringement proceedings, omitting some minor turbulences, shows a steady increase until the peak in 2003 and 2004, where nineteen and seventeen cases were brought before the ECJ respectively. A sharp decline then followed, dropping to levels comparable to those of the late 1980s and mid–1990s.

Interestingly, over the most recent four years, preliminary references and direct actions of annulment experienced a similar development. As of 2004, the number of both proceedings increased and in the years 2004 to 2006, actions for annulment by private litigants even exceeded references from national courts for the first – and so far only – time. In 2007, both proceedings experienced the largest total number of cases embedded in two neighboring years with fewer applications. In 2009 then, preliminary references again rose; all three having been referred from Dutch courts, while actions for annulment stalled. Whereas eight of the twelve actions for annulment in 2007 originated from Poland and concerned the emission trading scheme, five of the thirteen preliminary references of the same year were sent from French courts and the rest was distributed among other national courts.

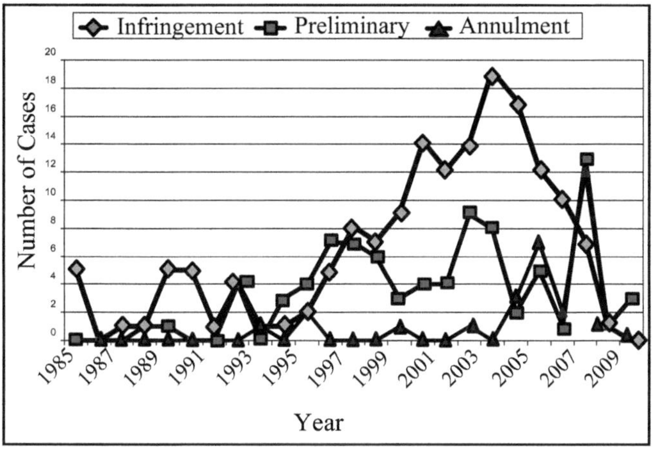

Figure 12: Comparison of Environmental Proceedings over Time

Overall, the trend seems to suggest that the Commission initiates fewer infringement proceedings; may this be based on the fact that momentarily no new environmental legislation has been implemented or that all Member States are performing well, but national courts still refer cases to the ECJ for clarification and private applicants are increasingly prepared to initiate direct actions before the Court.

Comparison according to Member State origin

Figure 13 provides a comparative overview over the actual number of cases originating from particular Member States. Thus, not only are Member States compared among one another, but the different types of procedures are also contrasted. The conclusions that can be drawn from the graphs are only indicative and are not statistically valid. A large number of infringement proceedings initiated against a Member State can therefore either point towards a country's poor record in EU law implementation or an active civil society that carefully monitors implementation. Phrased differently, one should not, based on the fact that no or only few infringement proceedings had been initiated, prematurely conclude that a Member State performs well in the transposition of EU law into national legislation. This may well be the case but it might also point towards a weakly organized civil society because the Commission is unable to monitor the implementation of all EU obligations.

One may furthermore hypothesize that a great number of preliminary references originating from one country indicate comparatively easy access to national courts (e.g. The Netherlands, France, Italy and Germany), whereas a low number of those referrals indicate either the absence of any disputes or that *locus standi* is more difficult to gain (e.g. Ireland, Luxembourg, Malta or Greece). Similarly, the existence of many direct actions before the General Court might point to difficult standing rules in the litigant's home country. Important to remember is, however, that the matter of the dispute refers in preliminary references to EU questions arising out of national disputes, and direct actions are exclusively concerned with actions of any EU Institution, body, or agency.

Finally, a correlation of a large number of referrals by national courts and a high record of infringement proceedings might indicate national problems or irregularities within environmental protection policy. If, at the same time, actions of annulment do not originate from this respective Member State, one could conclude that potential litigants are much more concerned about the deficiencies and problems on national level than challenging acts or decisions that have been adopted by the EU. Countries in which this could be the case are first and foremost Italy followed by France and Spain.

From the findings of the Milieu study (cf. chapter 11), one might have expected that most preliminary references concerning legal disputes in environmental policy originate from Denmark, Portugal, Spain and France, amongst others, given that access conditions for private persons are easier there than in other Member States. However, it needs to be kept in mind that the conclusions of the Milieu study indicate the status quo at a specific point in time; yet, the data covers a period of 24 years and therefore these findings cannot be directly compared. In addition, Milieu Ltd. examined exclusively the standing rules for environmental organizations but the cases filed with national courts and subsequently with the ECJ could have been initiated by any applicant. Of the current twenty–seven EU Member States, eighteen are listed in at least one case dealing with environmental protection; of which seven countries[3] include all three proceedings.

3 Austria, Belgium, Finland, Germany, Italy, The Netherlands and the UK

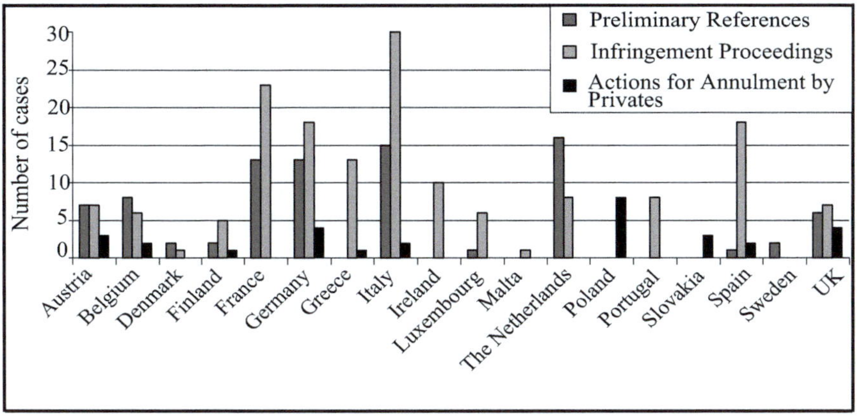

Figure 13: Comparison of Environmental Cases

In twelve Member States, national courts have referred preliminary questions to the ECJ[4]. No infringement proceedings have been initiated against three of those listed[5] – and logically – the remaining nine Member States[6] that are not listed in the graphic. Finally, applicants originating from ten Member States have tried at least one action for annulment before the GC. The positions of Poland and Slovakia need to be emphasized not only because they are among the top three countries and because they made that many referrals within a period of only five years[7], but also because only those direct actions are listed on the countries' record and the actions sought by Polish applicants were all submitted in 2007 concerning the emission trading scheme.

A regular pattern of possible positive or negative connections between the different types of proceedings cannot be identified. National courts in The Netherlands, Italy, France and Germany have referred most questions to the ECJ for a preliminary ruling. Italy, France and Germany also belong to the top group of countries against which the Commission has brought infringement proceedings before the Court. Spain needs to be added and ranks at third position in this group. In many Member States, the number of infringement proceedings clearly outnumbers preliminary references. As exceptions, The Netherlands and, to a lesser extent, Belgium may be pointed out; here national courts have made more referrals to the ECJ than the Commission brought infringement proceedings to the Court.

In addition, it might be necessary to recall the time aspect once again. Actions of annulment have to be initiated within two months of the action's execution or publication of a piece of legislation or another form of notification. Bearing this condition in mind, it is also understandable that Poland and Slovakia have, within their first five years of

4 excluding from those listed in the graphic: Greece, Ireland, Malta, Poland, Portugal and Slovakia
5 Poland, Slovakia and Sweden
6 Bulgaria, Czech Republic, Cyprus, Estonia, Hungary, Latvia, Lithuania, Romania and Slovenia
7 Both countries acceded to the EU in 2004; thus, before an action before the ECJ was impossible and it is remarkable that individuals sought direct actions that early after accession.

EU membership, only initiated direct actions before the ECJ. Infringement proceedings usually finally get to the Court after several pre–stages have been completed and a considerable amount of time after the Member State's failure to comply with its obligations under the Treaties. Similarly, significant time has passed until preliminary referrals can be made to the ECJ. A condition is that questions on European matters arise within a national legal dispute; EU law therefore has to be fully transposed into national law or create direct effect. In addition, it is not the first but the final instance of a national judiciary that is obliged to call upon the ECJ; although, as Karen Alter has shown, it is indeed the lower courts that regularly do so[8].

Actions for Annulment by Private Applicants

As shown in figure 11, ten percent of the environmental cases listed by the ECJ have been actions for annulment by private applicants. The pie chart above illustrates the rate of success of those applications. None of the cases has succeeded insofar as the claim of the applicant was confirmed by the judges. Overall, twenty–six cases have been dismissed by the former CFI and the ECJ. In fifteen of these cases, the Court found the applicants not to be directly concerned by the measure involved and therefore the Court did not need to assess whether the condition of individual concern was fulfilled. In turn, five court decisions negated the applicants' individual concern and no further examination of the direct concern test was taken. Three cases were admitted, but rejected on the merits of the case and the ECJ confirmed an appellant's position on the legal issues and referred the substantive part of the case back to the GC.

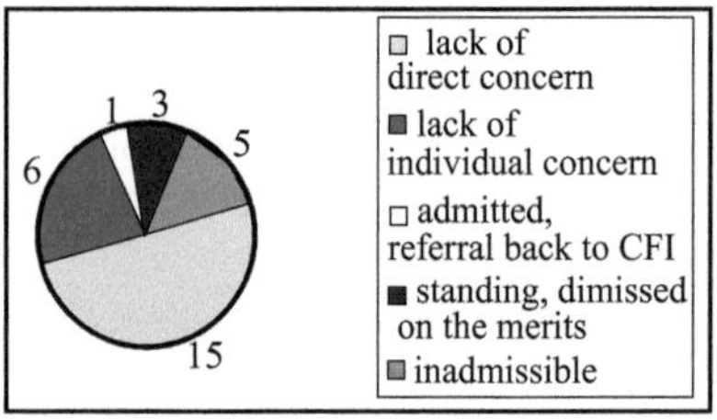

Figure 14: Actions for Annulment by Private Litigants – Court Decisions

The probability of success for private litigants in environmental legal disputes is therefore practically non–existent. As stated above, none of the applicants achieved their aim and almost ninety percent of the cases were dismissed on grounds of lack of standing. Given that only one of the tests was examined, and no prescribed order exists, it is even less encouraging that cases have been declared inadmissible on grounds of the direct concern test, which should, in general be easier to fulfill.

8 cf. Alter, 2001, *Establishing the Supremacy of European Law: The Making of an International Rule of Law in Europe* New York: Oxford University Press

13.1.1. Results

The above outlined overview on environmental cases does not aim at offering explanations for the motivations of initiating proceedings before the ECJ by any kind of litigant, i.e. an EU Institution, a Member State, or natural and legal persons. It does intend to shed light on past and current European litigation in environmental disputes and to point out the current shortcomings.

A few results can nevertheless be put on the record. First, the total number of cases reveals that the Commission is the most active litigant before the ECJ in environmental disputes. There is no data available on how the Commission becomes aware of a Member State's failure to fulfill its obligations under the Treaties; for instance, whether individuals, e.g. environmental CSOs, complained beforehand. Yet, it is still alarming that 55% of all cases in environmental protection concern Member States' violations of European law, particularly because they arrive at the Court only after a thorough administrative pre–procedure. These circumstances indicate that there are indeed cases of non–conformity with environmental standards and agreements but they are settled only after a substantial number of years of administrative and judicial procedure.

Second, in the past, infringement proceedings clearly dominated environmental litigations and where private applicants initiated proceedings, they utilized the indirect route via the preliminary reference procedure as preferred by the ECJ more often than not. Figure 12, however, shows that in recent years, they are increasingly prepared to attempt to succeed by initiating direct actions themselves. This is quite remarkable in light of the high dismissal rate of private litigants on grounds of lacking *locus standi* as shown in figure 14.

Third, a regular pattern or a direct relationship between the different types of proceedings within one particular Member State cannot indisputably be identified. Italy, France and Germany have already been identified as the countries with the highest record of infringement proceedings and preliminary references. It is, however, important to be reminded that those three countries are among the founding Member States and are, therefore, considerably longer able to violate EU law or create questions as to its interpretation as compared with those that acceded in the mid–1990s or even 2004. The position of Poland and Slovakia with regard to direct actions has also already been discussed in detail. Ireland, Portugal and Spain may, however, be named as well given that their national records only reveal a comparatively high number of infringement proceedings and none (one in Spain) preliminary reference. Finally, The Netherlands and Belgium are the only Member States, in which more preliminary references have been made by national courts to the ECJ than infringement proceedings initiated by the Commission.

Fourth, the case selection has shown that in only four of the thirty applications, the ECJ admitted the private litigant seeking to annul a decision taken or act executed by an EU Institution. In one case, the ECJ referred the case back to the CFI, which was supposed to decide on the merits and in the other three cases, standing was granted, but the applicants lost the case on the merits. Statistically speaking, only every tenth applicant is granted *locus standi* by the two instances of the Court. It is therefore even more remarkable that more private persons attempted to go directly to the CFI since 2004, despite the limited prospect of success.

The high number of infringement proceedings obviously reveals that there are still legal problems and disputes about the protection of the environment. However, these grievances are primarily challenged by the Commission as the most active litigant. Private applicants, probably for any or a number of the structural and financial reasons mentioned before, are less able to gain access to national courts, as well as the CFI and ECJ. In recent years, private applicants have begun to attempt to challenge acts and decisions directly at EU level more and no longer wait until the problem has reached the national legal system. This development supports a demand for facilitated access to the ECJ. Legal disputes regarding environmental protection do certainly exist and natural and legal individuals are willing to have them adjudicated and settled. They are simply denied the opportunity to do so by the restrictive rules on standing.

13.2. The Greenpeace cases

Environmental civil society organizations face particular obstacles when seeking access to the GC and the ECJ. As has been repeatedly claimed, this is primarily owing to the restrictive interpretation of the test on individual concern. The case most often cited in this context is *Stichting Greenpeace Council (Greenpeace International) and Others v Commission*[9] (short: *Greenpeace*) which was adjudicated by the Court of First Instance and its appeal case before the ECJ[10]. The facts of the case, arguments of the applicants and the findings of the respective instances of the Court are summarized below. The discussion of the case in the literature is placed into the greater context of the rules on *locus standi* in the area of environmental protection.

13.2.1. CFI, Case T–585/93

In this case, the applicants, *Stichting Greenpeace Council* and sixteen natural persons living and two local environmental protection associations established on Gran Canaria and Tenerife, sought annulment of a Commission's decision to disburse to the Spanish government a sum amounting to approximately ECU 12 000 000 from the European Regional Development Fund for the construction of power stations on the two Canary Islands[11].

---

9 CFI, Case T–585/93 [1995] ECR II–2205

10 ECJ, Case C–321/95P *Stichting Greenpeace Council (Greenpeace International) and Others v Commission* [1998]

11 CFI, Case T–585/93 *Greenpeace and Others v Commission* [1995] ECR II–2205, para.17

Prior to initiating judicial proceedings, several applicants informed the Commission by letter about the illegality of the construction on the basis of missing or incorrectly executed environmental impact assessments. In addition to the challenge of the authorization of an undertaking generating electricity to build these stations issued by the Canary Island Regional Ministry of Industry, Commerce and Consumption before a Spanish court, Greenpeace requested the Commission in several letters to confirm the disbursement of the money, to inform it of the envisaged timetable, and to disclose all relevant information. The demand was declined by a letter of the DG's XVI Director–General stating that he was "unable to supply this information since it concerns the internal decision making procedures of the Commission ... but [...][he could] assure [Greenpeace][...] that the Commission's decision was taken only after full consultation between the various services of the concerned"[12]. Moreover, two months prior to the initiation of the court proceeding before the CFI, a meeting was held in Brussels between DG XVI and Greenpeace at the Commission's premises in Brussels[13].

In response to the applicants' request to the CFI to "adopt a liberal approach" towards the admissibility of this case based on the fact that the existing case–law had been primarily concerned with purely economic interests and particularly originates from the area of state aid[14], the CFI confirmed in paragraph 50 of its order

> that whilst the above mentioned line of authority comprises judgments given mostly in cases concerning, in principle, economic interests, it is none the less true that the essential criterion applied in those judgments in substance, a combination of circumstances sufficient for the third–party applicant to be able to claim that he is affected by the contested decision in a manner which differentiates him from all other persons remains applicable whatever the nature, economic or otherwise, of those of the applicants' interests which are affected.

The private applicants put forward arguments as inhabitants claiming that they "have suffered or potentially will suffer detriment or loss as a result of a Community measure which affects the environment"[15]. They pointed to the likely adverse effects that the power stations would cause on their professions in, *inter alia*, fisheries, public health, public education, local flora and fauna and tourism[16]. The Court disagreed "since such harm may affect, generally and in the abstract, a large number of persons who cannot be determined in advance in a way which distinguishes them individually"[17]. The ECJ concluded that "[t]he applicants thus cannot be affected by the contested decision other than in the same manner as any other local resident, fisherman, farmer or tourist who is, or might be in the future, in the same situation"[18]. Hence, they were denied standing.

---

12 CFI, Case T–585/93 *Greenpeace and Others v Commission* [1995] ECR II–2205, para.11

13 CFI, Case T–585/93 *Greenpeace and Others v Commission* [1995] ECR II–2205, paras. 3 to 13

14 CFI, Case T–585/93 *Greenpeace and Others v Commission* [1995] ECR II–2205, paras.31–32

15 CFI, Case T–585/93 *Greenpeace and Others v Commission* [1995] ECR II–2205, para.30

16 CFI, Case T–585/93 *Greenpeace and Others v Commission* [1995] ECR II–2205, paras.35 & 36

17 CFI, Case T–585/93 *Greenpeace and Others v Commission* [1995] ECR II–2205, para.51

18 CFI, Case T–585/93 *Greenpeace and Others v Commission* [1995] ECR II–2205, para.55

With regard to the *locus standi* of Greenpeace and the two local environmental protection associations, the CFI held that, according to settled case–law,

> an association formed for the protection of the collective interests of a category of persons cannot be considered to be directly and individually concerned for the purposes of the fourth paragraph of Article 173 of the Treaty by a measure affecting the general interests of that category, and is therefore not entitled to bring an action for annulment where its members may not do so individually[19].

The CFI refused standing to the three environmental organizations on grounds of the fact that they could not "demonstrate the individual interest of their members as opposed to any other person residing in those areas"[20]. Moreover, the written correspondence and personal meeting between Greenpeace and Commission officials did not qualify as participation in preliminary proceedings from which any procedural rights could be retrieved given that these were on a mere information basis as the Commission neither consulted Greenpeace nor was the latter interlocutor during the adoption of the contested decision[21]. The applicant could therefore not rely on the special circumstances provided to associations of collective interests offered by the *Van der Koy* case[22].

The CFI was criticized for strictly adhering to the *Plaumann formula.* It was argued that "environmental interests [are], by nature, [...] collective" and the restrictive interpretation of individual concern is "fundamentally antithetical"[23]. The commitment of the Commission's Fifth Environmental Action Program to provide access to justice for environmental associations appeared in this context "naive or even ingenuous"[24]. Another point of criticism was of course the lack of available interim measures. While the applicants filed their appeal with the ECJ, the construction of the power stations and its funding went on undisturbed[25].
The fact that the Commission denied disclosure of all relevant information to the Greenpeace organization deserves mentioning. Although the decision in the first Greenpeace case was released six years before the Commission published its *White Paper on European Governance* and initiated its *Transparency Initiative* or before the Aarhus Convention went into force, the reasons for the refusal are not traceable. Even less acceptable

---

19 cf. ECJ, Joined Cases 19 to 22/62 *Fédération Nationale de la Boucherie en Gros et du Commerce en Gros des Viandes and Others v Council* [1962] ECR 491; ECJ, Case 72/74 *Union Syndicale v Council* [1975] ECR 401; ECJ, Case 60/79 *Producteurs de Vins de Table et Vins de Pays v Commission* [1979] ECR 2429; ECJ, Case 282/85 *DEFI v Commission* [1986] ECR 2469; ECJ, Case 117/86 *UFADE v Council and Commission* [1986] ECR 2483, para.12; and CFI, Joined Cases T–447/93, T–448/93 and T–449/93 *AITEC and Others v Commission* [1995] ECR II–1971

20 CFI, Case T–585/93 *Greenpeace and Others v Commission* [1995] ECR II–2205, para.60

21 CFI, Case T–585/93 *Greenpeace and Others v Commission* [1995] ECR II–2205, paras.62–63

22 ECJ, Joined Cases 67/85, 68/85 and 70/85 *Van der Kooy and Others v Commission* [1988] ECR 219, paras. 21 to 24

23 Gérard, 1996, p.152

24 Gérard, 1996, p.153

25 Gérard, 1996, p.155

is the assurance of the Director General that the contested decision was reached "only after full consultation between the various services"[26]. According to Gérard, the Court of Auditors stated that, in many instances, important decisions concerning the application of activities financed by structural funds are taken at local and regional level without informing the relevant Commission departments in detail[27].

13.2.2. ECJ, Case C–321/95P

In their appeal before the ECJ, the applicants argued

> that the approach adopted by the Court of First Instance creates a legal vacuum in ensuring compliance with Community environmental legislation, since in this area the interests are, by their very nature, common and shared, and the rights relating to those interests are liable to be held by a potentially large number of individuals so that there could never be a closed class of applicants satisfying the criteria adopted by the Court of First Instance[28]

and that this "legal vacuum [cannot] be filled by the possibility of bringing proceedings before the national courts"[29]. Amongst other arguments, the appellants emphasized again that their action is undertaken in the general interest and therefore to be distinguished from existing jurisprudence on standing requirements in the context of purely economic interests. They claimed that

> Article 173 [now: Article 263 TFEU] must not be interpreted restrictively; its wording does not expressly require an approach based on the idea of a 'closed class', as affirmed in the case–law of the Court of Justice and the Court of First Instance[30]. Rather, it should be interpreted in such a way as to safeguard fundamental environmental interests and protect individual environmental rights effectively[31].

The ECJ declared that the interpretation of the fourth paragraph of Article 173 EC [now: Article 263 TFEU] as applied by the CFI was "consonant with the settled case–law"[32].

26 CFI, Case T–585/93 *Greenpeace and Others v Commission* [1995] ECR II–2205, para.11

27 Gérard, 1996, p.157

28 ECJ, Case C–321/95P *Greenpeace and Others v Commission* [1998] ECR I–1651, para.18

29 ECJ, Case C–321/95P *Greenpeace and Others v Commission* [1998] ECR I–1651, para.19

30 ECJ, Case C–321/95P *Greenpeace and Others v Commission* [1998] ECR I–1651, para.26; judgments referred to are: ECJ, Case 11/82 *Piraiki–Patraiki and Others v Commission* [1985] ECR 207; ECJ, Case C–358/89 *Extramet Industrie v Council* [1991] ECR I–2501; ECJ, Case C–309/89 *Codorniu v Council* [1994] ECR I–1853; and CFI, Joined Cases T–480/93 and T–483/93 *Antillean Rice Mills and Others v Commission* [1995] ECR II–2305

31 ECJ, Case C–321/95P *Greenpeace and Others v Commission* [1998] ECR I–1651; cf. judgments in ECJ, Case 240/83 *Procureur de la République v Association de Défense des Brûleurs d'Huiles Usagées* [1985] ECR 531, para.13; ECJ, Case 222/84 *Johnston v Chief Constable of the Royal Ulster Constabulary* [1986] ECR 1651, paras.13 to 21; and ECJ, Case 222/86 *UNECTEF v Heylens and Others* [1987] ECR 4097, para.14

32 ECJ, Case C–321/95P *Greenpeace and Others v Commission* [1998] ECR I–1651, para.27

The Court held that the Commission's decision can "affect [the] rights [of the appellants] only indirectly"[33]. Hence, a direct concern could not be established, given that the appellants attacked a decision taken by the Commission under Directive 85/337/EC but practically wanted to prohibit the construction of the power stations. Yet, the Court refused to establish a direct link between the aforementioned decision and the plant's construction. The applicants were accordingly held not to be directly concerned by the decision[34].

Moreover, "in the circumstances of the present case those rights are fully protected by the national courts" for which it was possible to refer to the Court questions for a preliminary ruling[35]. Accordingly, the ECJ confirmed the decision of the CFI and dismissed the appeal as inadmissible on grounds of lack of concern[36] after having once more recommended to the applicants to challenge the national measure before national courts[37].

Again the hopes of those supporting greater *locus standi* in environmental disputes were disappointed. The ECJ, in their view, had not only missed the opportunity to issue a precedent on an environmental dispute, in which infringements of former Community law were alleged on a national as well as a supranational level[38]. Even more, the decision had the "consequence [...], in effect, to exclude environmental citizens' suits before the ECJ"[39]. This in turn makes it hardly possible for the Court to subject actions of Union Institutions to judicial control given that neither Commission nor Member States are very likely to lodge such complaints with the Court[40].

It was furthermore questioned, whether the rights offered to the public by Directive 85/337/EC, which was also one basis of the dispute, could not also sufficiently individualize the complainants, even though their number was not necessarily small. This was particularly the case as neither applicant was able to, as falsely suggested by the ECJ, obtain national legal remedies in order to challenge the decision of the Commission to provide funding in this case[41].

13.3. Proposals concerning standing in environmental disputes

The two proposals outlined in the previous chapter have addressed the general deficit in the system, which should provide comprehensive and effective judicial protection to

33 ECJ, Case C–321/95P *Greenpeace and Others v Commission* [1998] ECR I–1651, para.31
34 Sands, 2008, p.120; Gérard, 1998, p.342
35 ECJ, Case C–321/95P *Greenpeace and Others v Commission* [1998] ECR I–1651, para.33
36 ECJ, Case C–321/95P *Greenpeace and Others v Commission* [1998] ECR I–1651, paras.34 & 35
37 cf. also Albors–Llorens, 1999, p.35
38 Gérard, 1998, p.338
39 Sands, 2008, p.120
40 Sands, 2008, p.120
41 Bieber, Epiney & Haag, 2005, p.268

those that are affected by European law. The following proposals have been formulated with particular focus on the peculiarity of environmental policy and legal disputes arising in this area.

Appellants in Greenpeace The appellants in the above introduced *Greenpeace* case[42] also suggested a specific approach towards determining individual concern with regard to acts relating to the Union's obligations in the area of environmental protection that differs from the current interpretation of the *Plaumann* formula. Aiming at circumventing a "legal vacuum"[43], an applicant must, in order to be regarded as individually concerned, in their view, be able to fulfill the cumulative conditions that:

> (a) he has personally suffered (or is likely personally to suffer) some actual or threatened detriment as a result of the allegedly illegal conduct of the Community [EU] institution concerned, such as a violation of his environmental rights or interference with his environmental interests;
> (b) the detriment can be traced to the act challenged; and
> (c) the detriment is capable of being redressed by a favourable judgment[44].

Advocate–General Cosmas in Greenpeace In the appeal case of *Greenpeace*[45] before the ECJ, Advocate–General Cosmas issued an Opinion, in which he elaborately examined the potential "existence of an 'environmental legal interest'" and its possible effects on *locus standi* for environmental civil society groups[46].

The Advocate–General confirmed that environmental protection is indeed "one of the fundamental objectives"[47] and general and public interest of the then Community and today's Union[48] resulting in the duty of "observ[ing] legality" in this regard[49]. Cosmas, however, proceeded that this obligation "does not automatically confer on a natural or legal person a right or legal interest enforceable by an action under the fourth paragraph of Article 173 of the Treaty [today Article 263(4) TFEU]. He further explicitly ruled out the possibility of granting *actio popularis* in disputes concerning environmental protection on EU level. The fact that some violations of EU law by the Commission may not "with certainty be remedied if the task of submitting them for judicial review is entrusted exclusively to the Member States and the Community institutions, do not in practice have an interest in that regard" does not justify the general introduction of

42 ECJ, Case C–321/95P *Greenpeace and Others v Commission* [1998] ECR I–1651
43 ECJ, Case C–321/95P *Greenpeace and Others v Commission* [1998] ECR I–1651, paras.18 & 19
44 ECJ, Case C–321/95P *Greenpeace and Others v Commission* [1998] ECR I–1651, para.23
45 ECJ, Case C–321/95P *Greenpeace and Others v Commission* [1998] ECR I–1651
46 Opinion of the Advocate–General in Case C–321/95P *Greenpeace and Others v Commission* [1998] ECR I–1651, para.50
47 Opinion of the Advocate–General in Case C–321/95P *Greenpeace and Others v Commission* [1998] ECR I–1651, para.51
48 ECJ, Case C–321/95P *Greenpeace and Others v Commission* [1998] ECR I–1651, paras.51 & 52
49 Opinion of the Advocate–General in Case C–321/95P *Greenpeace and Others v Commission* [1998] ECR I–1651, para.53

locus standi for private persons[50]. Yet, the rejection of *per se* standing for environmental complaints by natural and legal persons in turn does not exclude the admissibility of such claims on grounds of rights derived from directly effective secondary law[51]. In other words, specific provisions enshrined in a series of legislative acts are capable of providing individuals with access to justice concerning "a general objective" of the EU[52].

Thus, while the Advocate–General acknowledged the peculiarity of environmental interests as "theoretically [being] shared by all natural persons"[53], he declared that granting standing to "every person whose interest in conservation of the environment is affected by an act of a Community institution would be tantamount to acceptance of an *actio popularis* in all cases having an environmental dimension"[54], which he denied. He also refused to introduce specific conditions on standing in such cases and affirmed that the interpretation of individual concern as "the starting–point for appraisal of *locus standi* cannot but be the same in all cases, irrespective of the subject–matter of the dispute"[55].

Based on the foregoing observations, Advocate–General Cosmas suggested that the determination of a 'closed class' fulfilling the conditions of individual concern should be based upon the geographic proximity of the respective persons to the "intervention in the environment[56] in combination with the "nature of the consequences"[57] and its "gravity"[58] of interference in, *inter alia*, the applicant's quality of life[59].

Environmental Organizations: 'Greening the Treaty' Six of today's *G–10* environmental civil society organizations[60] published a paper on "Greening the Treaty II:

50 Opinion of the Advocate–General in Case C–321/95P *Greenpeace and Others v Commission* [1998] ECR I–1651, para.53

51 Opinion of the Advocate–General in Case C–321/95P *Greenpeace and Others v Commission* [1998] ECR I–1651, para.54

52 Opinion of the Advocate–General in Case C–321/95P *Greenpeace and Others v Commission* [1998] ECR I–1651, para.56

53 Opinion of the Advocate–General in Case C–321/95P *Greenpeace and Others v Commission* [1998] ECR I–1651, para.102

54 Opinion of the Advocate–General in Case C–321/95P *Greenpeace and Others v Commission* [1998] ECR I–1651, para.103

55 Opinion of the Advocate–General in Case C–321/95P *Greenpeace and Others v Commission* [1998] ECR I–1651, para.103

56 Opinion of the Advocate–General in Case C–321/95P *Greenpeace and Others v Commission* [1998] ECR I–1651, para.104

57 Opinion of the Advocate–General in Case C–321/95P *Greenpeace and Others v Commission* [1998] ECR I–1651, para.105

58 Opinion of the Advocate–General in Case C–321/95P *Greenpeace and Others v Commission* [1998] ECR I–1651, para.106

59 Opinion of the Advocate–General in Case C–321/95P *Greenpeace and Others v Commission* [1998] ECR I–1651, para.109

60 Climate Action Network Europe, European Environmental Bureau, European Federation for Transport and Environment, Friends of the Earth Europe, Greenpeace Europe, World Wildlife Fund

Sustainable development in a Democratic Union" in 1995 proposing to the Intergovernmental Conference amendments to the TEU. The groups demanded the inclusion of a new provision, which should recognize "the right to a clean and healthy environment [...] as part of a general right to human development" by granting the three procedural rights that are now enshrined in the Aarhus Convention. The Convention was signed in Aarhus three years after this request by the environmental associations. With regard to access to justice, the groups proposed wide–reaching modifications to the regulations on admissibility. Amongst other things, they declared that access should be extended to natural and legal persons, who would be considered as sufficiently concerned, if they had previously filed a complaint with the Commission on the very matter. They furthermore demanded the possibility for natural and legal persons to directly institute infringement proceedings against Member State governments that had failed to implement correctly, completely, or timely European law on an equal footing with the Commission[61] or other Member States[62]. The final request called for "any natural or legal person" to be able to initiate actions of annulment or actions for failure to act without any further conditions, including the deletion of direct and individual concern[63].

Proposal on Infringement Proceedings A further proposal, inspired by procedural rights for persons granted under U.S. law, suggests that, after having informed the Commission about violations of European law by one or more Member States, and the former remaining inactive within a predetermined period of time, persons may start infringement proceedings themselves against the accused national government. The proposal suggests restricting the circle of potential applicants to public interest groups fulfilling certain criteria to be defined in concert by the Parliament and the Council. The provisions governing infringement proceedings[64] would accordingly have to be modified to read:

1. The Commission is obliged to start proceedings [...], where it considers that a Member State failed to fulfill an obligation, and to issue a reasoned opinion.
2. The letter of formal notice and the reasoned opinion shall be published.
3. Where a group, acting in the public interest, has asked the Commission to bring a matter, for which a reasoned opinion has been issued, before the Court of Justice and the Commission has failed to do so within ninety days after receipt of that request, that group shall be entitled to bring that matter before the Court.
4. The European Parliament and the Council shall determine the details of the procedure and in particular the conditions, with which a group shall comply in order to be considered to act in the public interest[65].

---

61 today Article 258 TFEU
62 today Article 259 TFEU
63 Krämer, 1996, pp.12–13
64 at that time: Article 169 EC for the Commission and Article 179 EC for Member States
65 Krämer, 1996, pp.13–14

13.3.1. Discussion of the Proposals

The four proposals briefly introduced above attempt to take account of the specific nature of (legal) interests in environmental protection. Most of these proposals envisage a causal link between an as 'illegal' alleged action by an EU Institution and the harm suffered by the applicant as a precondition for *locus standi*. In other words, the obligation to prove one's direct concern remains intact and is not subject to modifications[66].

The appellants in the *Greenpeace* case before the ECJ[67] proposed that admissibility should depend upon the likelihood of the Court's judgment to be able to grant compensation for occurred damages. This would mean that the merits of the case, including a potential decision, would already be examined when assessing whether the applicant is awarded standing or not[68]. This is not advisable.

The greatest problems, however, are affected by the first condition suggested by the claimants[69]. The undefined time period of the detriment in question is unreservedly acceptable given that harm, which occurred in the past should be capable of being recovered. In a similar vain, it is highly desirable that damages that will most likely affect a person in the near future should be prevented at the soonest possible moment.

Yet, the following requirement as to the nature of the harm suffered might be formulated too vaguely. Again "actual detriment" is fairly obvious and unobjectionable. However, the mere threat of such damages is not sufficiently identifiable and triggers a number of questions. How *actual* is this "threat"? Does the threat refer to the time component, meaning an impending detriment that will occur in the future with almost absolute certainty, although its extent might still be incalculable? Or, alternatively, does the term merely refer to a potential incident for which a certain percentage of likelihood can be determined, yet its actual existence cannot be foreseen?

These questions, if such a test was applied on EU level, should be answered by the Court in a very restrictive manner. In the area of the free movement of goods, the ECJ created such a test, in which "all trading rules enacted by Member States which are capable of hindering, directly or indirectly, actually or *potentially*, intra–Community trade [...] [were] considered as measures having an effect equivalent to quantitative restrictions [emphasis added]"[70]. Hence, the integration of the various national markets into one common market was so much desired that the introduction of a national measure, which only *hypothetically* restricted the number of imports or exports, was found to violate ex–Community law and needed to be abolished. Still, a similar approach in the area of environmental protection, although being listed in Article 3(3) TEU LT as one of the Union's fundamental objectives, cannot be assumed.

Finally, although attempted by Advocate–General Cosmas in his Opinion on this

---

66 e.g. point (b) of the proposal of the appellants in the *Greenpeace* case

67 ECJ, Case C–321/95P *Greenpeace and Others v Commission* [1998] ECR I–1651

68 point (c) of the proposal

69 point (a) of the proposal

70 ECJ, Case 8/74 *Procureur du Roi v Benoît and Gustave Dassonville* [1974] ECR 837, para.5

case, 'environmental rights' or 'environmental interests' have, according to the author's knowledge, not yet been defined. The term 'environmental *right*' obviously refers to a condition that is guaranteed by primary or secondary law which is legally enforceable before courts. 'Environmental interests' however seem to indicate a much broader applicability exceeding the definitions of 'right' or 'concern' to a substantial degree. In addition, the proposal refers to an "interference with [...][an applicant's] environmental interests", which renders the concept even less precise.

Overall, the test as proposed by the applicants in *Greenpeace*[71] is formulated in too a vague and broad manner as to be acceptable. The criteria would no longer serve a filtering function but rather enable an infinite number of claims to be adjudicated by the Court; even if the threat of a detriment caused by an interference of the applicant's environmental interests on part of EU Institutions is incalculable.

Advocate–General Cosmas was primarily concerned in his suggestion with the protection of health and the quality of life of *natural* persons. The combination of geographic proximity to and the severity of environmental damage seems reasonable and appropriate to achieve this aim. He stated that his interpretation, although possibly "not constitut[ing] a linear continuation of [...] [the] case–law"[72], succeeds in defining a "sufficiently closed" class of persons[73] and therefore remains within "the formulation and spirit" of then Article 173(4) EC; today's Article 263(4) TFEU[74].

Cosmas, however, opposed a relaxation of *locus standi* for associations and warns about potential abuse, which might cause unforeseeable repercussions on the legal system. A special treatment of environmental interest organizations may lead to an unfettered creation of groups by natural persons, who all do not meet the condition of being individually concerned, in order to take advantage of the exception. The number of potential applicants would remain irresponsibly high, if not infinite, even if it was required for the association to have been established prior to the adoption of the disputed act[75]. He therefore strongly opposed a relaxation of standing requirements for environmental associations as this would "run counter to the letter of the law, in this case of Article 173 of the Treaty [today: Article 263 TFEU]". Such practice would be *contra legem* given that the Treaty *intentionally* distinguishes between privileged applicants, who do not have to show a specific interest or concern and non–privileged ones, who have to[76].

Other than the first two proposals, the six environmental associations did not suggest

71 ECJ, Case C–321/95P *Greenpeace and Others v Commission* [1998] ECR I–1651

72 Opinion of the Advocate–General in Case C–321/95P *Greenpeace and Others v Commission* [1998] ECR I–1651, para.107

73 Opinion of the Advocate–General in Case C–321/95P *Greenpeace and Others v Commission* [1998] ECR I–1651, para.108

74 Opinion of the Advocate–General in Case C–321/95P *Greenpeace and Others v Commission* [1998] ECR I–1651, para.107

75 Opinion of Advocate–General Cosmas in Case C–321/95P *Greenpeace and Others v Commission* [1998] ECR I–1651, para.117

76 Opinion of the Advocate–General in Case C–321/95P *Greenpeace and Others v Commission* [1998] ECR I–1651, para.118

a re–interpretation of the individual concern test by the Court, but demanded a reformulation of the relevant provision in the Treaty based on the argument that it "provides a severely restricted right to natural or legal persons to challenge the legality of acts"[77]. Also distinguishing it from the other proposals, the newly written provision would not only be restricted to legal disputes concerning environmental matters but, quite to the contrary, would be of general application irrespective of the nature of the claim or the policy area concerned.

Locus standi for private applicants, i.e. any natural or legal persons, without any further conditions and on equal footing with the privileged applicants (Community Institutions and Member States) is not advisable for any of the proceedings under the ECJ's jurisdiction. This would be tantamount to allowing *actio popularis* at EU level and would substantially exceed the current regulations on standing within the Union and its Member States[78]. In addition, due to the deletion of the requirement for an applicant to prove his or her direct and individual concern, a majority of the claims may be arbitrary and unfounded.

Overall, such broad admissibility of actions for annulment, failure to act, or regarding infringements of European law is not desirable as this would indeed open the floodgates to a tremendous number of applications, thereby increasing the workload of the GC and ECJ and greatly delay proceedings, possibly over years in addition to the current average of two to three years. This proposal dispenses with any legal foundation and is to be rejected in its entirety.

The last proposal also does not specifically address environmental concerns, but is limited to infringements of 'public interest' obligations arising under the Treaty. However, direct actions by natural or legal persons in this proposal do not concern applications for annulment or measures or prosecution of illegal inactivity on part of the EU Institutions but rather infringements executed by the Member States. As stated above, the proposal foresees the possibility of limiting the number of potential applicants to public interest groups that meet the criteria mutually agreed upon by the EP and the Council.

The proposal maintains the formal procedure of an infringement proceeding and attributes the chief role to the Commission. However, it may go beyond what is necessary to ensure compliance by Member States, if private persons are granted *locus standi* within ninety days to bring the case before the Court themselves. In the author's opinion, the reformed infringement proceeding introduced before, which allows private persons to become directly involved via communication with the respective Member States deserves time to be installed and establish itself.

All of these proposals, including those formulated by Advocate–General Jacobs and the former Court of First Instance that were discussed in the previous chapter, have in common the identification of gaps within the EU system of legal protection and participation by private actors and suggest possible corrections. It has been pointed out that the first

77 as cited by: Krämer, 1996, p.13
78 Krämer, 1996, p.13

and particularly the third proposal suggest too far–reaching reforms, which should not only be rejected for practical reasons, i.e. increase in workload and time delays of proceedings. The latter would also significantly reduce legal certainty, which is also one of the arguments *for* a relaxation of standing. A rejection must also be declared on the basis of formal objections. It is the essential function of a judiciary to safeguard the rights of the subordinates within a governmental system, to control the political institutions in order to prevent *ultra vires* actions; simply: to ensure that the rule of law is obeyed. Judges cannot, however, take rulings upon their own initiative but solely when called upon by legitimate applicants, who must be affected by contested measures or actions in some form or another. This very basic condition would in the first and third suggestion not be fulfilled.

Advocate Cosmas' proposal to assess a natural person's individual concern on the basis of geographic proximity to and the severity of environmental damages on interests is helpful. Yet, it does not promise to radically reform *locus standi* for natural persons in environmental disputes and particularly is of no advantage to environmental associations which, as legal persons, cannot claim such interferences in the interests of their organizations.

The last proposal did not aim at reforming access to the ECJ for actions under Articles 263(4) or 265(3) TFEU but rather enabling direct actions for infringements of Treaty obligations of the Member States. Currently, individuals may either turn to the Commission or challenge the failures of national institutions before national courts. The new problem solving scheme provides a valuable alternative to the reform proposal; yet, the latter should not be rejected completely. Particularly the preferential treatment of environmental associations conditioned on certain criteria is worth consideration. It should be specifically welcomed that Parliament and Council conjointly determine these characteristics. Hence, some elements of this proposal may be used for a further alternative proposed in Part VI below.

13.4. Shedding Light on the Paradox

The following section provides a discussion on those arguments supporting a modification of the regulations on access to the Court for environmental CSOs. Account will be taken of the specificities of environmental policy as well as the nature of the legal rights that can be retrieved therefrom. Evidence is provided for the following arguments for the necessity of facilitating access to the ECJ. First, environmental protection is distinctive from other EU policy areas and has been valued by the Court in its jurisprudence. Second, the current rules on standing greatly lag behind the objectives of the Union; particularly in light of the prioritization of environmental protection on political agendas and the international obligations to which the EU has committed itself. Third, the paradox of the application of the current interpretation of an applicant's individual concern is discussed. Fourth, it is stated that the admissibility of private applicants is necessary to ensure objective judicial control because the privileged applicants will hardly submit complaints to the Court. Fifth, the implementation and enforcement of European environmental law would be greatly facilitated through the inclusion of environmental CSOs. Sixth, the necessity of greater participation opportunities is emphasized and clears the way for the author's subsequent proposal that is introduced and discussed in part six.

13.4.1. The specific nature of environmental protection

One of the arguments most strongly put forward by proponents of privileged access opportunities to the GC and ECJ in disputes concerning environmental matters is the fact that the Court has appreciated the necessity to protect the environment at an earlier time and to a greater extent than the Treaties.

It has already been pointed out that the Court declared in its *ADBHU*[79] decision the protection of the environment as one of the then Community's essential "objectives"[80], before environmental concerns were integrated into the Single European Act. This is quite remarkable, given that the Court did not cite any other legal basis originating, for instance, from the constitutional traditions of the Member States, international agreements, or customary law. Jacobs assumed that the judges considered "environmental protection [...] so fundamental to the public interest that no explicit justification was required"[81]. The author is not aware of any other policy area, in which the Court applied a comparable approach without any "conceptual basis"[82].

Building upon its decision in *ADBHU*[83], the Court found in *Danish bottles*[84] that, under certain circumstances, the interest of protecting the environment constitutes a mandatory requirement, which allows for the preservation of measures that restrict the free trade of goods[85]. This motion was impressive as it needs to be recalled that the ex-Community's prime objective was to abolish all barriers to trade, succeed in the establishment of, first, a customs union, a common market, and finally, an economic and monetary union. Obviously, economic interests were the key determinants of European integration, at least in the first decades. Still, the Court found that concerns about the state of the environment could justify constraints on economic objectives[86].

13.4.2. Political prioritization and international legal commitment

From the foregoing chapters and the summary above, it is reasonable to conclude that environmental protection indeed enjoys a high rank on the priority list of both political and

79 ECJ, Case 240/83 *Procureur de la République v Association de défense des brûleurs d'huiles usagées* (*ADBHU*) [1985] ECR 531

80 ECJ, Case 240/83 *Procureur de la République v Association de défense des brûleurs d'huiles usagées* (*ADBHU*) [1985] ECR 531, para.13

81 Jacobs, 2006, p.187

82 Jacobs, 2006, p.194

83 ECJ, Case 240/83 *Procureur de la République v Association de défense des brûleurs d'huiles usagées* (*ADBHU*) [1985] ECR 531

84 ECJ, Case 302/86 *Commission v Denmark* [1988] ECR 4607, para.1 of summary

85 Jacobs, 2006, p.188; Cichowski, 1998, p.389; Gérard, 1996, pp.154–155

86 Jacobs, 2006, p.194

judicial perceptions of Union objectives. The EU has committed itself to international obligations. The Aarhus Convention has already been discussed in depth. It foresaw facilitated access to courts for the public concerned, at least with regard to procedural rights arising out of the rights to information and to participate in decision–making procedures. It remains to be said that these, although voluntary commitments, are still to be complied with.

Overall, however, the current interpretation of the *Plaumann* formula impedes an effective enforcement of European environmental policy and thereby the EU legal system substantially lags behind the ambitious commitments and declarations of the EU's environmental goals[87].

13.4.3. The Paradox

As has been indicated, applicants in legal disputes concerning environmental protection particularly suffer from the problematic causality of the greater number of persons affected by a measure, the less likely their action will be declared admissible before the General Court[88]. This obvious paradoxical concept is described by Gérard as being "antithetical to the environment"[89]. In addition, and as has been illustrated above, academic scholars and practitioners alike agree, as Advocate–General Cosmas stated in his Opinion on the *Greenpeace* appeal case[90], that environmental protection "has a communal dimension"[91], i.e. enjoys a specific status among the Union's objectives. Hence, the argument that is constantly brought forward in order to justify the narrow interpretation of individual concern is precisely the argument that holds the least in environmental disputes for the basic reason that environmental interests – and rights – are collective and concern everyone everywhere[92]. The individualization of such rights is therefore practically impossible[93].

Advocate–General Cosmas stated in his Opinion in the *Greenpeace* appeal case that

> [i]n light of the particular nature of the issue of environmental protection, I consider that the Community judicature, in particular in cases where that protection is likely to have been undermined by a non–legislative act of a Community body, must not rest content with the self–evident finding that the likely harm to the environment by its very nature affects categories of persons in a general, objective and abstract manner, and must not, on that ground alone, dismiss the action brought. That is particularly so when the Community body was under a specific and clear obligation

87 Gérard, 1996, pp.149–150
88 cf. e.g. Tridimas & Poli, 2008, pp.83–84; Sands, 2008, p.119
89 Gérard, 1996, pp.152–153
90 ECJ, Case C–321/95P *Greenpeace and Others v Commission* [1998] ECR I–1651
91 ECJ, Case C–321/95P *Greenpeace and Others v Commission* [1998] ECR I–1651, para.102
92 cf. e.g. Sands, 2008, p.118; Gérard, 1996, p.153
93 Busse–Muskala, 2007, p.122

> to take account, on adoption of the contested decision, of the factor of conservation of the environment.[94]

Most critics seem to concur that the restrictive application of the test on individual concern should be relaxed in cases, where actions are filed in the general interest of protecting the environment. It is incomprehensible that the ECJ has, again without explicit legal bases in the Treaties, issued such far–reaching decisions with regard to the rights of market participants and citizens, particularly in the area of the free movement of goods and free movement of persons and establishment, but is highly reluctant to modify its interpretation of individual concern[95] or at least add another exception in the area of environmental protection.

Given that further Treaty amendments are unlikely in the near future, the ECJ is requested to remind itself of its former pro–integrationist position and acknowledge once more the Union–dimension of the interest in environmental protection and apply a more flexible interpretation of individual concern to applicants involved in disputes concerning environmental matters[96]. Moreover, the EU Charter on Fundamental Freedoms, including its Article 47 on the right to effective legal remedies in combination with the prioritization of environmental policy on the political agenda, provides an official legal basis for this suggestion.

13.4.4. No other Claimant

While the refusal of Lord Wilberforce to accept *locus standi* for associations given that "[a]n aggregate of individuals each of whom has no sufficient interest cannot itself have a sufficient interest"[97] seems reasonable, British law nevertheless offers opportunities for such organizations to be heard in court. Greenpeace, for instance, was granted standing without difficulty on grounds of possessing a valuable reputation in the area of environmental protection and a legal interest in pursuing this public aim[98].

The underlying rationale is best illustrated by a quotation of Lord Diplock, who admitted that "[i]t would be a grave lacuna in our system of public law if a pressure group or even a single public spirited citizen were prevented by outdated technical rules of locus standi from bringing the matter to the attention of the court to vindicate the rule of law and get the unlawful conduct stopped". He strongly doubted that the ability to challenge actions of the government should not be exclusively reserved to the Attorney General given that "in practice he never [...] [initiates prerogative orders] against government departments"[99].

---

94 Opinion of Advocate–General Jacobs in Case C–321/95P *Greenpeace and Others v Commission* [1998] ECR I–1651, para.104

95 cf. e.g. Tohidipur, 2008, pp.163–165

96 Gérard, 1996, p.157

97 Lord Wilberforce, 633D; as cited by: Geddes, 1992, p.33

98 *R v Secretary of State for Trade and Industry, ex parte Greenpeace Ltd Maurice Kay J*, QBD, 5 November 1999 as cited by: Sands, 2008, p.118

99 Lord Diplock, 644E; as cited by: Geddes, 1992, p.33

The same observation was made at EU level regarding environmental protection by Professor Sands, who was attorney at the *Greenpeace* cases. He anticipated that the narrow interpretation of the admissibility conditions effectively results in a denial of citizen suits in environmental protection disputes, which in turn renders the task of the Court to objectively control the legality of the other institutions' actions almost impossible, given that neither Commission nor Member States will initiate such proceedings[100].

The thereof resulting logic is as simple as intelligible.
Governmental actors do not have any desire to challenge their own decisions. The argument put forward in the context of refusing a relaxation of *locus standi* rules for private applicants for the reason that decisions taken at EU level are most often than not the result of long enduring intergovernmental bargaining in the Council and compromises found in debates within committee and plenary meetings of the EP. Even those Member States that were outvoted on this very issue might be reluctant to challenge the decision before the Court in order to avoid the possibility that decisions in which their will has dominated might await a similar fate. In addition, in environmental policy, national governments are free to apply more far–reaching standards of protection than those agreed upon at EU level. Of course, the limitation that the effectiveness of a state's strict environmental laws may be weakened by reckless regulations of an adjacent country[101].

It may be assumed as well that, as the Parliament's position in the decision–making process becomes more influential through various Treaty amendments, the likelihood of the filing of complaints with the ECJ decreases. This assumption can be undermined by the fact that many actions of annulment lodged by the Parliament in the past were based on the argument that the Council had utilized the wrong legal basis of the Treaty in order to circumvent greater influence by the EP[102]. As co–decision has now become the ordinary legislative procedure, the Parliament is as much responsible for the outcome as the Council. It will therefore execute its power during the legislative process rather than seek judicial redress from the Court.

The Commission, though not holding the monopoly on policy initiation anymore, still has great powers in this area and will also hardly ever turn to the Court in this regard. In addition, the Commission's function as 'guardian of the Treaties' may furthermore be adversely affected by the constant political interactions among the EU Institutions[103]. With regard to non–legislative measures, decisions adopted by the Commission concerning the environment are not likely to trigger much opposition by the other institu-

100 Sands, 2008, p.120; cf. also Gérard, 1998, p.338

101 cf. e.g. Sands, 2008, p.121

102 These information can be retrieved from the ECJ case selection discussed in the first section of this chapter, as indeed most actions for annulment that were initiated by EU Institutions were grounded upon claims on wrong legal bases.

103 cf. Krämer, 1996, pp.9–10

tions[104]. In fact, the peak of criticism of the Commission in particular, is the very issue of the lack of democratic accountability[105]. Thus, a tremendous number of direct actions by governmental bodies of the EU are not to be expected.

If private applicants are deprived of *locus standi*, an objective control of political institutions and the legality of their (in–)actions by the Court, which is essential to the system of checks and balances, cannot be guaranteed under these circumstances[106].

13.4.5. Improve enforcement via associational standing

A further consequence of the unlikelihood of privileged applicants to submit complaints about illegal measures, unlawful inactivity, procedural errors, or infringements of Union law are problems in the enforcement of European environmental law. Obviously, most of these violations are caused by the Member States through delayed or incomplete implementation of environmental legislation[107]. The third and fourth proposal for a modification of access to courts discussed in the previous section offer solutions to this dilemma. However, only the fourth proposal on granting certain environmental associations standing to initiate infringement proceedings against Member States themselves may be worth consideration in this context.

Associational standing is generally rejected. Most EU Member States only grant representatives of collective interests under very specific conditions standing before national courts (cf. chapter 11). However, the area of environmental protection should constitute an exception to this rule. Such claims could aid in achieving an improved balance between economic and environmental interests, both highly appreciated within the EU, and may avoid a bias towards the economic end. They would further enhance the general application of the integration principle of Article 11 TFEU, which requires the consideration of environmental concerns "into the definition and implementation of the Union policies and activities". In addition, the enforcement of environmental law would be significantly improved given that environmental CSOs would scrutinize the compliance of national authorities of European laws, regulations and standards and would, as the final resort, have direct recourse to the ECJ at their disposal[108].

As stated in previous chapters, environmental CSOs are particularly suited to fulfill this task as they are organized at the grassroots level, yet their internal structures have been institutionalized and professionalized. Such environmental associations, obviously, would have to fulfill certain criteria in order to ensure their specific expertise and the concrete nature of their interests.

104 cf. Krämer, 1996, pp.9–10
105 Gérard, 1998, p.345
106 cf. also Sands, 2008, p.120
107 Gérard, 1998, pp.345–346
108 Thiele, 2006, p.274

Part V.

Complementing Participation

The work has so far delivered arguments, obtained from political theories as well as from practical considerations, in favor of a greater inclusion of non–governmental actors throughout the policy cycle in general, as well as the policy area of environmental protection as an example. If participation by environmental CSOs is appreciated and encouraged during policy initiation, formulation and implementation, it should also be ensured that there is an effective legal remedy against decisions taken – or not taken – at any of the preceding stages. It has furthermore been acknowledged that the first four stages of this cycle (policy initiation, formulation, decision–making and implementation), overall, already provide environmental CSOs with comparatively satisfactory participation opportunities. At the legal evaluation stage, however, great need for improvement has been identified and substantiated in detail.

The current state of affairs has been mainly criticized for the narrow interpretation of an applicant's individual concern, which practically impedes *locus standi* to associations defending the public interest in a clean environment. Shortcomings have been identified, possible solutions proposed, yet, a modification of the *Plaumann formula* does not seem very likely. This is due not only to formal and legal reasons, i.e. the need for an amendment of the relevant Treaty provision, but also for various practical concerns, all of which have been discussed in the previous chapters. Attempts to relax the standing conditions in general or limited to litigants involved in legal disputes on environmental matters have faded away.

Participation is accordingly the decisive concept around which the author's proposal is constructed. Participation is thereby not limited to administrative consultation processes either in the formulation or monitoring of the implementation of policies. Rather, its actual contribution may also be extended to judicial proceedings before courts.

This part introduces the practice of *amicus curiae* briefs, a concept originating from Ancient Rome. With the exception of common law systems, where it has been applied for centuries, it has just recently been re–discovered and is increasingly utilized in the context of international legal arbitration modes. The concept's origin and purpose as well as existing rules and regulations are outlined and the likelihood of success is assessed as far as possible. The applicability of the concept to the European legal system depends upon the assessment of its general benefits and costs to courts, parties to the dispute, and *amici* themselves but also on the specificities of the *sui generis* character of the EU judiciary. Those aspects will be examined in chapter fifteen.

It will be assessed under which conditions environmental civil society organizations may become 'friends' of the European Court of Justice.

14. Amici Curiae – "Friends of the Court"

Most of the information and data available concern U.S. Supreme Court litigation, as well as the WTO dispute settlement mechanism. Hence, only these two sources of information, from which generalizable conclusions can be drawn, are relevant for the purpose of this work.

14.1. Exploring the Concept

Amici curiae submit their own observations in a brief to the court concerning a pending case in which they are not involved as a party to the dispute. As will be seen below, these submissions may be filed either upon one's own initiative, or, more rarely, upon invitation by the court.

The concept of the *amicus curiae* can be defined from two perspectives. The first takes the view of the "bystander"[1], who, although not possessing an immediate legal interest in the case, provides factual or legal information to the judge "of his own knowledge"[2]. Here, the initiative appears to originate from the *amicus* himself. A second definition focuses on the position of the judge, who might feel that the parties to the dispute did not provide the information necessary to deliver a valid judgment. He or she may then turn to the supplementary information offered by an *amicus*. The same applies to circumstances, in which "a judge is doubtful or mistaken in matter of law"[3].

The decisive criterion here is the *amicus*' 'interest' in the dispute at hand. The English term might give rise to misinterpretations given that *amici curiae* certainly are *interested* in the matter of the case and personally prefer a specific outcome[4]; however, they are not able to establish a *legal interest* as ordinarily required to be a party to a dispute or an intervenor. The distinction between an intervening third party to a case and an *amicus curiae* is, in theory, simple, yet very crucial. An intervenor has more rights than an *amicus curiae* within the proceedings and must therefore prove a legal interest in the given dispute between two or more other parties. His or her submissions must be considered by the court. In turn, however, the intervening person is as much bound by the final

1 cf. definition provided by *Abbott's Dictionary of Terms and Phrases* as cited by Krislov, 1963, p.694

2 Krislov, 1963, p.694

3 cf. definition provided by *Holthouse's Law Dictionary* as cited by Krislov, 1963, p.695

4 cf. e.g. Hedman, 1991, p.188 & Angell, 1967, p.1043

judgment as the original parties. An *amicus* to the contrary, does not have to fulfill the strict conditions for standing, which makes it attractive for entities representing general concerns in the 'public interest'. Yet, the court is also not obliged to either admit or consider the briefs filed by such *amici*. From the foregoing, it is obvious that the *amicus*, given that he or she is not as much involved in the proceeding, is furthermore not legally bound to the final decision of the court[5]. Thus, as summarized by U.S. Supreme Court Justice Posner, a brief submitted by an *amicus* should be refused admission, where the former "has too much of an interest, or to the contrary, not enough of one"[6].

The concept finds its origins in ancient Rome, where *amici* were essential in order to ensure that the court was able to make an informed decision. The information related to both factual and legal matters at stake in a given case and could have been provided even by non–lawyers. In particular, those "bystanders" reminded the court of rules or precedent cases, which had previously been neglected[7].

Today, the concept is rather linked to common law systems; most notably the U.S. American legal system. The vast majority of civil law systems, which interestingly are built upon principles of Roman law, do not know a concept equivalent to *amicus curiae*[8]. Merely a broad interpretation of intervention rights comes closest to the concept[9]. Knowledge about the utility of the concept in the United States and particularly at the country's Supreme Court has been collected since the early 19th century[10]. The frequency of *amicus curiae* brief submissions heightened so that the Supreme Court was forced to formulate rules and criteria for the submission of *amicus curiae* briefs already in 1905. These procedural rules were subsequently modified in irregular time periods in order to account for the change in number of *amicus* briefs[11]. Particularly, the 1960s and 70s witnessed a drastic increase in *amicus* submissions[12]; especially in cases concerning non–commercial disputes[13].

In recent years, international arbitration has discovered *amicus curiae* briefs as an alternative mode aiding the dispute settlement process among, primarily, states. An overview is provided below.

14.1.1. Purpose

Not only has the frequency and type of use of this concept undergone considerable change since its early Roman days, but so has its function and primary purpose. Orig-

5 Umbricht, 2001, p.780
6 Munford, 1999, p.280
7 cf. Hollis, 2002, p.239; Bilder, 1989, p.471; Ala'i, 2000, pp.84–85 & Umbricht, 2001, p.778
8 Umbricht, 2001, p.780
9 as for instance in France for environmental and Human Rights organizations; cf. Hollis, 2002, p.239
10 Krislov, 1963, p.699
11 cf. Ala'i, 2000, pp.86–87; O'Connor & Epstein, 1983, pp.35 & 37
12 Shelton, 1994, pp.618–619; O'Connor & Epstein, 1983, p.39
13 Caldeira & Wright, 1990, p.783

inally, the *amicus curiae* was to be interpreted literally as "friend of the court". The primary aim was to aid the judges in reaching a valid and prudent decision in the context of all relevant information, legal as well as factual evidence, available[14]. *Amicus curiae* briefs may offer new factual information and legal arguments that were previously unknown to the court because the parties to the dispute were either unable or unwilling to provide them. Alternatively, they may support one or more arguments given by a party with supplementary evidence[15]. The U.S. Supreme Court, however, considers "[a]n *amicus curiae* brief that brings to the attention of the Court relevant matter not already brought to its attention by the parties [...] [to] be of considerable help to the Court", whereas a "brief that does not serve this purpose burdens the Court, and its filing is not favored"[16]. However, as early as the 1940s, the role of the 'neutral informant' slowly turned into one pursuing advocacy in his or her own interest and more often than not supporting one of the parties to the dispute [17]. Hence, the statement of the Supreme Court of 1946 that amici actually serve "two masters, the court and the client" illustrates the shift "from neutrality to partisanship, from friendship to advocacy"[18].

The evolution of the role of the *amicus* correlates with the development of the type of 'friend' that sought – and gained – access to, in this case the U.S. Supreme Court. While in ancient Rome naturally 'anybody', who could provide the court with supplementary information, was admitted[19], today, three main groups of *amici* are active at the U.S. Supreme Court. Representatives of a state or the federal government have been particularly active in the early years of the *amicus curiae* practice. Private associations representing business or organizational interests, including single firms and umbrella associations, file briefs most regularly. These are followed by a large number of other private organizations of different types and organizational structures, including NGOs. The latter two form up to forty percent of *amicus* briefs submitted to the Supreme Court in the 1982 term[20].

Thus, while historically, most briefs concerned questions of legal matters[21] that were primarily submitted by governmental representatives, the admission of briefs submitted either directly or sponsored[22] by various private entities resulted in the delivery of supplementary factual information and eventually in the shift to advocacy.

---

14 cf. e.g. Munford, 1999, p.282
15 Shelton, 1994, pp.618 & 640; similarly: Krislov, 1963, p.711 & Umbricht, 2001, p.779
16 Rule 37(1) Rules of the Supreme Court of the United States
17 cf. Ala'i, 2000, p.87; Collins, 2004, p.808; O'Connor & Epstein, 1983, p.36 & Umbricht, 2001, p.778
18 Ala'i, 2000, p.87
19 Ala'i, 2000, pp.84–85
20 Angell, 1967, p.1019; Caldeira & Wright, 1990, pp.794–795 & 803
21 Ala'i, 2000, p.85
22 Sponsoring of briefs by associations "was quite commonplace" by the 1930s; cf. Krislov, 1963, p.703; also: O'Connor & Epstein, 1983, p.36

Samuel Krislov[23], who is often cited, argued in 1963 that the specificities of the U.S. legal system and the complex federal structure of the country necessitated the inclusion of *amici curiae* in order to safeguard the various state, the federal interests, as well as to countervail the numerous, otherwise unrepresented, public interests[24]. In addition, Professor Krislov further identified the creation of regulatory and executive agencies as a factor increasing the need for, and use of, *amicus* briefs. The policies enforced and administrative practices established by these agencies increasingly affected a variety of, at times conflicting, interests. In response, many agencies offered participation in hearings to persons whose interests had been affected by their undertakings. According to Krislov, it was merely the consecutive and logical next step for individuals and organizations to attempt to support preferred policies at both the administrative and judicial levels[25]. This conclusion is particularly reasonable as those groups found to be one of the first to be engaged as *amici curiae* at the U.S. Supreme Court were those whose interests were primarily at stake at a specific point of time. Examples include, for instance, racial and minority organizations during the civil rights movement and groups advocating liquor interests in the prohibition period[26].

Thus, the function of the *amicus curiae* has changed from a neutral informant to a lobbying device. Actors appearing as *amici* have developed from any person able to provide supplementary information to the judge to governmental bodies, as well as private entities, collective or individual, and from the validation of the person's contribution to the need for legal representation. Hence, the submission of *amicus curiae* briefs has evolved into a tactical consideration for interest groups either complementing or substituting for litigation strategies[27].

14.1.2. Procedure: Existence, Rules and Regulations

The practice of non–parties to a dispute to submit their own observations or opinions is no longer restricted to pure common law systems at national level but has appeared in different forms and modifications, as well at intergovernmental and international systems of arbitration and adjudication. Several frameworks, including their attitude towards and the problems experienced by *amici curiae*, are briefly outlined below as examples.

Despite the differences that exist among these systems, a crucial distinction is made regarding the acceptance of unsolicited briefs filed by *amici*, i.e. at their own initiative and those that are submitted upon explicit invitation by the court[28]. Another crucial point that has yet only slightly been touched upon is the court's discretion in accepting and considering or refusing briefs submitted by *amici curiae*.

---

23 Professor of Political Science and Law

24 Krislov, 1963, p.697

25 Krislov, 1963, p.706

26 Krislov, 1963, p.707

27 Hedman, 1991, p.188 & O'Connor & Epstein, 1983, p.36

28 Krislov, 1963, p.717

Ala'i summarized it at its best: "[t]he permission to participate as an amicus curiae has always been a privilege or 'grace' and has never been a 'right'"[29].

International Courts and Tribunals

Various systems at the international level that include an institution designed for arbitration and adjudication with different degrees of legal enforcement have allowed the introduction of *amicus curiae*[30]. The degree of openness, however, depends on the structure of the institution and particularly its thematic jurisdiction[31].

The underlying rationale relates to the fact that most of these courts and tribunals, with the exception of human rights bodies, primarily only settle disputes between states and governmental institutions, thereby excluding any direct action initiated by private parties[32]. The concept bears the advantage of granting NGOs and other private actors an opportunity of being heard without having to attribute them with rights equivalent to state actors[33]. The limited rights offered to persons and organizations as *amici curiae* is consistent with the overall participation opportunities provided for private parties in the development and enforcement of international law in general[34].

Although many international arbitrating institutions have become more receptive to participation opportunities by non–state actors, the vague concept has been implemented in various manners. Differences become already visible in the wording of the provisions in the courts' or tribunals' statutes or rules of procedure that indicate the possibility for external actors to become involved.

The International Court of Justice (ICJ) can be called upon only by states for the settlement of their disputes. It seems that the rules of the Court strictly limit participants to state actors in contentious cases[35]. Here, only "public international organizations" defined as "international organizations of States"[36] may deliver opinions and information upon request or on their own initiative. This, however, excludes any non–state actor, including, obviously, NGOs. The situation is less clear for requests for advisory opinions to which "international organizations" may submit their own statements, where they are "likely to be able to furnish information on the question" that the Court considers[37]. The term 'public' has been erased and uncertainty remains about whether this may include non–governmental organizations as well. The prevalent opinion in the literature, however, regretfully denies such an inclusion[38].

29 2000, p.85
30 cf. Hollis, 2002, pp.237–238 & Marceau & Stilwell, 2001, p.164
31 Marceau & Stilwell, 2001, p.164
32 Hollis, 2002, pp.237–238
33 Hollis, 2002, p.255
34 Hollis, 2002, p.243
35 Hollis, 2002, p.242
36 Article 34(2), ICJ Statute of the Court; Article 69, ICJ Rules of Court
37 Article 66(2), ICJ Statute of the Court
38 Shelton, 1994, p.620; Marceau & Stilwell, 2001, p.165

Other examples include, for instance, the Convention on the Law of the Sea[39], which merely provides in Article 289 for the selection of scientific and technical experts, who "sit with the court or tribunal but without the right to vote"[40].

The International Criminal Court (ICC), in accordance with Rule 103 of its Rules of Procedure and Evidence, explicitly invites or grants leave to "any observation on any issue that the Chamber deems appropriate" submitted by "a State, organization or person" either "in writing or orally"[41]. Rule 74 of the respective Rules of Procedure and Evidence of the International Criminal Tribunals for the former Yugoslavia (ICTY)[42] and Rwanda (ICTR)[43] utilizes a similar wording[44].

With regard to IOs dedicated to global economic relations, the World Bank Inspection Panel provides for comparatively broad rights of participation for non–state actors, including individuals and NGOs, whereas the doors of the International Center for the Settlement of Investment Disputes (ICSID) are literally shut for private actors[45]. Organizations regulating trade on a regional level offer different degrees of participation. The Mercosur (Mercado Común del Sur) dispute settlement procedure remains silent on the matter of intervening private parties or *amicus* submissions. It is rather preferred under this system that complaints be addressed to the relevant "National Section of the Common Market Group', which may decide to hear the case in full[46].

The ASEAN (Association of Southeast Asian Nations) agreement takes over the practice of the WTO under Article 13 DSU (cf. below) and grants panels discretion "to seek information and technical advice from any individual or body which it deems appropriate"[47]. The NAFTA (North American Free Trade Area) proceeds in a similar manner in general disputes, although further participation opportunities have been set up in the area of investment disputes and instances, in which single citizens or organizations can complain to the Commission on Environmental Cooperation about a State party's failure to implement environmental laws, which might lead to the establishment of arbitration panels that are allowed to "seek information and advice from any person or body that it deems appropriate, provided that the disputing Parties so agree and subject to such terms and conditions as such Parties may agree"[48].

---

39 International Tribunal for the Law of the Sea (ITLOS)

40 cf. Marceau & Stilwell, 2001, pp.167–168

41 Rule 103, sub–rule 1, ICC Rules of Procedure and Evidence; cf. also Hollis, 2002, p.242 & Marceau & Stilwell, 2001, p.168

42 ICTY, Rules of Procedure and Evidence

43 ICTR, Rules of Procedure and Evidence

44 cf. also Marceau & Stilwell, 2001, p.168

45 Marceau & Stilwell, 2001, pp.173–175

46 Marceau & Stilwell, 2001, pp.172–173

47 Art.6(3) Protocol; cf. Marceau & Stilwell, 2001, p.171

48 Article 30, North American Agreement on Environmental Cooperation; cf. Marceau & Stilwell, 2001, pp.171–172

Overall, tribunals entrusted with the protection of human rights and consequently the conviction of violations thereof and the European Court of Justice grant the most far–reaching access for private applicants in the international judicial arena.

This is quite reasonable, given that human rights by their very nature affect humans, i.e. citizens of a specific country. The Inter–American Court of Human Rights (IACHR) is particularly praised for its positive attitude towards *amici*. Judges have regularly accepted and considered such briefs even without explicitly referring to a provision of either the Convention, Statute or Rules of Procedure[49]. The comparatively young African Court on Human and Peoples' Rights (ACHPR) has an even more positive stance towards private actors. NGOs having an observer status – and thus fulfilling specific criteria[50] – are furthermore allowed to initiate proceedings according to Article 5(3) of the Protocol and Rule 33(1)(f) of the ACHPR Interim Rules of Court[51]. Recognition of *amicus* briefs should be covered by Rule 45 on the measures of taking evidence. It is, however, not completely clear, whether the wording includes unsolicited briefs as well, or rather relates exclusively to those requested by the Court, any of the parties, or the Commission. At the European Court of Human Rights (ECtHR), individuals, groups or NGOs whose rights protected under the ECHR have been violated may initiate proceedings against the relevant state on the basis of Article 34 of the Convention. Furthermore, since the entry into force of Protocol 11 in 1998, *inter alia*, "any person concerned who is not the applicant" may be invited by the Court's President "to submit written comments or take part in hearings" according to Article 36(2) ECHR[52]. Again, however, the required "invitation" appears to exclude the submission of unsolicited *amicus* briefs. On the other hand, the formulation indicates that the provision instead concerns intervention given that the applicants need to prove their 'concern' and because the title explicitly addresses 'third party intervention'.

The fact that the ECJ provides for some form of standing to non–governmental actors is also understandable on grounds of its broad thematic jurisdiction and the multitude of policy areas in which individuals are indeed directly affected by its decisions. However, when compared with other international tribunals, the ECJ appears to be rather a hybrid–form between an international tribunal and the court of highest instance of countries with a federal structure. The introduction of *amicus curiae* briefs may therefore be helpful; but its applicability will be assessed in the next chapter.

---

49 Umbricht, 2001, p.791; Marceau & Stilwell, 2001, p.170; Shelton, 1994, p.639; Howse, 2003, p.503

50 Article 56, African Charter on Human and Peoples' Rights

51 African Commission on Human and Peoples' Rights, *Protocol to the African Charter on Human and Peoples' Rights on the establishment of an African Court on Human and Peoples' Rights*; African Court on Human and Peoples' Rights, *Interim Rules of Court*; cf. Marceau & Stilwell, 2001, pp.169–170

52 Council of Europe, ECHR; cf. also Marceau & Stilwell, 2001, pp.170–171

The WTO Dispute Settlement Procedure

Under the former GATT–system, unsolicited statements submitted by non–members were not admitted. Disputes were considered to emerge between states and should thus be settled only with their participation. The WTO dispute settlement procedure has not followed its predecessor[53] and panels and the Appellate Body have accepted *amicus* briefs. The fact that both bodies have admitted written observations by non–member private actors provoked a heated debate and strong resistance by many states.

The Dispute Settlement Understanding (DSU) provides the legal basis for the establishment, composition of, and procedure under which panels and the Appellate Body work. Panels have relied on a broad interpretation of Article 13 DSU, which grants them "the right to seek information and technical advice from any individual or body which it deems appropriate"[54] and furthermore enables them to "seek information from any relevant source and [...] [to] consult experts to obtain their opinion on certain aspects of the matter" or request advisory reports in technical matters "from an expert review group"[55] and to consider the admission of *amicus curiae* briefs. With regard to the competence of the Appellate Body to receive such briefs, its members declared in, for instance, *US – British Steel* that, based on the ability to draw up its own working procedures in combination with rule 16.1 thereof, the body would not have a "legal duty" but "the legal authority to decide whether or not to accept and consider any information that [...] [the members of the body] believe is pertinent and useful in an appeal". In other words, while neither the consideration of such submissions is explicitly allowed nor NGOs have a legal right of being heard, it is also do not explicitly prohibited[56].

As indicated above, the opposition among WTO members against unsolicited *amicus* briefs was strong and fierce[57]. Arguments put forward ranged from the insecurity about which – if any – criteria to be applied to the content of the briefs and their authors, to the so far unrestricted time frame in which such briefs could be filed throughout the dispute settlement proceeding. This would lead to a wide discretion of the arbiters in deciding whether or not to consider such submissions and hence be untraceable for the parties, as well as for the authors of the briefs. The greatest concern, however, is that the recognition of unsolicited briefs would open the "floodgates" encouraging ever more non–WTO members to disturb ongoing proceedings. In addition, countries from the southern hemisphere feared that this could bias the results of an arbitration to the advantage of industrial countries given that firms and organizations originating from the latter are better equipped to submit *amicus* briefs than their southern counterparts[58]. This would, drastically phrased, lead to "a form of judicial lobbying"[59].

53 Ala'i, 2000, pp.67 & 68
54 Article 13(1) Understanding on rules and procedures governing the settlement of disputes (DSU)
55 paragraph 2
56 cf. Hollis, 2002, p.240; Ala'i, 2000, p.80; Charnovitz, 2000, p.7 & Howse, 2003, p.499
57 cf. e.g. Howse, 2003, p.497 or Charnovitz, 2000, p.8
58 e.g. Marceau & Stilwell, 2001, pp.163–164
59 as feared by India, Thailand and Pakistan; cf. Ala'i, 2000, p.72

For a long time, the then European Communities represented by the European Commission rejected an inclusion of *amici curiae* in the dispute settlement process of the WTO. Amongst other arguments, the EC particularly insisted on a restrictive reading of Article 13 DSU, which only allows panelists and members of the Appellate Body to actively "*seek*" information and not randomly accept or refuse information offered to them. Furthermore, the Commission pointed towards the inequality of treatment which arises from the comparison of such broad rights for 'unconcerned' *amici curiae* with those limited ones of parties to the dispute and intervening third parties[60]. The EU seems to have changed its attitude towards *amici curiae* at the WTO, given that representatives proposed new rules and guidelines for the admission and consideration of such briefs at the Doha round of the DSU reform, which, interestingly, given its former opposition, resemble the special procedure explained below[61].

In order to, at least partly, address the criticism, the Appellate Body published in the *EC–Asbestos* case a 'special' or 'additional procedure' on the basis of which *amici* needed to apply for leave to file their briefs according to a strict time schedule[62]. These rules were accessible via the website of the Appellate Body's Secretariat[63] and thereby contributed to the transparency of the procedure[64]. The primary intention was to offer a structure of the *amicus curiae* submissions that would be both reliable for potential *amici* and transparent for the parties insofar as it would reduce the body's random discretion[65]. A standardized regulation of the formal setting of such briefs would furthermore bear the potential to reduce the workload of the administrative staff, as well as members of the panels and the Appellate Body.

The formal requirements included the necessity to be typed–written and to not exceed a maximum of three pages. Applicants had to identify themselves by disclosing their membership, the general objectives sought, and activities executed, as well as their legal status and sources of funding. In order to prove some form of connectedness to the dispute at hand, applicants furthermore had to, first of all, define the nature of their interests, specify those matters of law and fact which the brief addressed, and declare in how far their submission would offer added value to the proceeding by avoiding mere repetition of the party's submissions. Finally, to prove the *amici*'s independence of all – or at least reveal their connection to one of the – parties (including third parties), applicants had to disclose any "direct or indirect" relation to one of the aforementioned, including whether they received assistance of any nature for the preparation of this brief[66].

However, although the Appellate Body explicitly stated in the 'additional procedure' that "[t]he grant of leave to file a brief by the Appellate Body does not imply that the

60 Howse, 2003, pp.499–500
61 Howse, 2003, p.506
62 Howse, 2003, p.504
63 Umbricht, 2001, p.776
64 Howse, 2003, p.504
65 cf. Howse, 2003, p.504
66 WTO, Article 3(g) Additional Procedure; cf. Ala'i, 2000, p.81; also: Howse, 2003, p.504

Appellate Body will address, in its Report, the legal arguments made in such a brief"[67], to many private organizations, the installation of a "formal screening process" appeared very promising[68], while many WTO member countries reacted with clear detestation. A Special Session was convened, in which the members, with the exception of the United States, agreed that the admission of *amicus curiae* briefs was a substantive and not a procedural matter and therefore not for the Appellate Body to decide but exclusively reserved to the members themselves[69]. Hence, the Appellate Body rejected all of the thirteen applications submitted by seventeen groups and one individual in the *EC–Asbestos* case "for failure to comply sufficiently with all the requirements" without further explanation. Thus, overall, the incident, while having aimed at clarifying the handling of *amicus curiae* briefs within the WTO dispute settlement procedure, resulted in feelings of offense on part of WTO members on the one hand, and shock on part of private actors on the other hand[70].

The 'special procedure' was not applied again after the *EC–Asbestos* case and the matter is thus still unresolved within the WTO dispute settlement procedure[71]. The remaining possibility for non–members to submit their opinion supporting one of the parties is to annex the brief to the submission of the respective party so that the panel and Appellate Body consider it as an "integral part" thereof[72]. This, however, obviously renders impossible the submission of opinions that provide complete new insights into and information for an existing dispute and which would not be accepted by either party as an attachment to their own submission.

The U.S. Supreme Court

As described above, the United States have used *amici curiae* the longest and the concept has been studied in depth within this system. The purpose of including "non–interested" actors into an existing legal dispute in the example of the USA has also already been explained; this paragraph is therefore dedicated only to the rules regulating the sub– and admission. Over the years, the Supreme Court has developed elaborate rules with which briefs of *amici* must comply in order to be granted leave. Such rules primarily aim at structuring the submission of *amcius curiae* briefs by offering guidance to those, who want to file their observations with the Court and providing transparency to the parties to the dispute with regard to the criteria according to which the judges select these briefs. For practical reasons, those rules are also installed in order to reduce the workload of the judges and their staff and to discourage the filing of an insurmountable number of briefs[73].

---

67 Ala'i, 2000, p.82
68 Howse, 2003, p.505
69 Ala'i, 2000, p.64; Umbricht, 2001, p.776
70 Ala'i, 2000, pp.64 & 82–83
71 Howse, 2003, p.505
72 cf. e.g. Ala'i, 2000, p.71
73 cf. e.g. Ala'i, 2000, p.91

Rule 37 of the Rules of the Supreme Court of the United States[74] regulates the submission of *amicus curiae* briefs to the Court. The first paragraph emphasizes the necessity for an submission to offer added value to a proceeding adjudicated before the Court as they would otherwise have rather "distortive" than beneficial effects[75].

The formal regulations require the brief to "be filed only by an attorney"[76]. The admission of a brief must be either consented to by the parties to the dispute or, in case agreement is denied, the *amicus* needs to make a "motion for leave" before the Court, which decides at own discretion whether or not to accept the brief[77]. Briefs filed by legal representatives on behalf of various governmental actors constitute an exception to the rule and need not apply for a motion for leave[78]. Deadlines for the submission of *amicus curiae* briefs vary according to the type of proceeding and the position of the *amicus*, i.e. whether this brief might be attributed to the petitioner or the defendant, but range from thirty to sixty days as of the date on which the case is placed on the docket. Furthermore, a notification of the intention to submit an *amicus curiae* brief must be sent to the parties ten days prior to the brief's submission at the latest[79]. *Amicus curiae* briefs, as any other documents submitted to the Supreme Court, must comply with a detailed and strictly applied style sheet. These requirements define, *inter alia*, the booklet–format, margins and paper size, the type–writing style, font type and size, as well as the maximum number of words as nine thousand and determine the color of the cover (light green for those supporting neither party or the appellant, plaintiff, or petitioner; and dark green for those in support of appellants, defendants, or respondents), and of course the number of copies to be filed[80] in accordance with Rule 21. The content of the brief must comply with the formal requirements specified in Rule 24 with the exception that the listing of the interest of the *amicus*, a summary of his or her arguments, the presentation of the arguments and a conclusion are deemed sufficient[81]. Finally, paragraph 6 of Rule 37 requires of *amici curiae*, as has also been requested by the WTO Appellate Body in its 'additional procedure', disclosure of any assistance obtained by any person other than the signatory in the preparation of the brief. Obviously, this provision primarily intends to contribute to the transparency of *amicus* participation in court proceedings[82].

74 Supreme Court of the United States, 2010, *Rules of the Supreme Court of the United States*

75 cf. Ala'i, 2000, p.92

76 Rule 37.1 Rules of the Supreme Court of the United States

77 Rule 37.2(a) and (b) and 3(a) and (b), Rules of the Supreme Court of the United States

78 Rule 37.4, Rules of the Supreme Court of the United States: exhaustive list: briefs submitted by the Solicitor General on behalf of the US, by any agency allowed to do so, by an Attorney General on behalf of any State, Commonwealth, Territory, or Possession, or by authorized law officers on behalf of a city, county, town, or similar entity.

79 Rule 37.2(a), Rules of the Supreme Court of the United States; time frames for oral arguments are regulated by paragraph 3(a) of Rule 37, Rules of the Supreme Court of the United States

80 Rule 33.1, Rules of the Supreme Court of the United States

81 Rule 37.5, Rules of the Supreme Court of the United States

82 cf. also: Ala'i, 2000, p.92; Collins, 2004, p.809

Other than the apparently strict and detailed rules suggest, *amici curiae* are easily granted leave by the Supreme Court to file their briefs[83]. Various scholars have attempted, as far as possible, to examine the probability of admission and consideration of *amici curiae* briefs.

Likelihood of Success The decision to file *amicus curiae* briefs depends on the probability of success as estimated by the respective organization. A study undertaken by Spriggs and Wahlbeck revealed that the U.S. Supreme Court in its 1982 term mostly considered those briefs that offered both new information and reiterated arguments of one of the parties. Contrary to the conventional opinion, briefs that exclusively presented new information were not considered by the judges, while those primarily supporting findings and arguments of one party had a greater chance of being admitted[84]. Another suggestion was made by Collins, who found that "coalitional"[85] briefs prepared by a number of authors serve "as a reliable indicator to the justices as to the number of potentially affected individuals" and hence increase the probability of being considered. He accordingly claims that interest groups may improve their chance of being read and considered by common effort and the co–signature of submitted briefs[86]. This would also reduce the incurred costs that need to be borne by the individual[87].

As a rule of thumb, the optimal situation for *amicus* submissions is given, where a complex case and its potential external implications require the court to seek additional information and where, at the same time, the interests of the *amicus* are at stake[88].

Overall, however, the literature does not provide a consistent opinion with regard to the assessment of influence executed by *amicus* briefs. While some scholars attribute "significant impact"[89] to *amici curiae* and declare them to be one of the "most influential players in judicial politics"[90], others only grant a small role to them in executing "trivial" influence[91]. A conclusion is particularly problematic as 'impact' or 'influence' cannot be objectively assessed; especially when both parties to the dispute are supported by *amici*[92].

Knowledge about the effectiveness of *amicus curiae* briefs is nonetheless essential for CSOs to decide whether or not such an effort has to be made and in order to select the strategy most suitable for achieving the desired outcome[93].

83 Caldeira & Wright, 1990, pp.784 & 785
84 Spriggs & Wahlbeck, 1997, pp.375–376 & 381–382
85 Collins, 2004, p.826
86 Collins, 2004, pp.813–814
87 Collins, 2004, p.825
88 cf. Krislov, 1963, pp.703–704 & Hansford, 2004, p.221
89 Shelton, 1994, p.619
90 McGuire, 1994, p.835; also convinced about the positive impact of *amici*: Caldeira & Wright, 1990, p.788
91 Songer & Sheehan, 1993, p.350
92 Angell, 1967, pp.1043–1044
93 Hedman, 1991, pp.187–188

14.2. Gains and Losses

The section above has introduced the concept of *amicus curiae*. Its legal origins and purpose and the adaptation in common law systems, as well as in international arbitration have been outlined as much as the key actors involved have been identified. Furthermore, the controversy about potential and actual rules that regulate the submission and acceptance of *amicus* briefs as in force in the different dispute settlement systems has been touched upon.

However, it remains yet to be assessed, whether the acceptance of *amicus curiae* briefs actually offers the promised aid to the court, or whether they rather constitute an additional burden. Both proponents and opponents provide valid and reasonable arguments for and against the practicability and efficiency of such submissions.
The following subsections therefore provide an overview on the main arguments on both sides.

14.2.1. Losses

Obviously, the greatest disadvantage concerns the issue of time and delay in judicial proceedings. This argument concerns everyone. Judges and the court's staff aim at finding a correct and fair decision by considering all relevant information without being flooded with irrelevant or superfluous workload. The two or more parties to the dispute in most cases prefer a quick and satisfactory decision. The litigants of other disputes do not want to wait too long until their case is heard. And finally, the public – and in particular taxpayers – would also prefer a timely provision of evidence and final decisions, given that postponements caused by lengthy proceedings also add to the overall costs. Such unwanted additional workload[94] is caused by, for instance, briefs that only replicate the information already provided by one of the parties or another *amici*, or where the information provided is completely irrelevant to the dispute at hand.

Another concern raised by critics is the above–illustrated shift of the function of the *amicus* from neutrality to advocacy. In any legal system, judges are required to be independent from any external influence and particularly need to be impartial. Exactly this impartiality is endangered by the attempts of *amici* to convince the court to deliver a decision in a specific perspective. Indeed, the lack of clear rules and guidelines for those persons and groups whose briefs are admitted and the wide discretion of judges to consider their content or not poses a considerable problem. This is particularly serious given that judges, once appointed[95], are not accountable to any democratic measure of control and do not need to legitimatize their decisions in any form comparable to members of the legislative or executive branch (including agencies) of government.

Related concerns have been voiced in the context of the WTO dispute settlement mechanism. The argument that only well–resourced organizations from wealthier coun-

94 cf. Umbricht, 2001, p.779

95 In the U.S. Supreme Court, the Justices are appointed for life, but may resign at their own choice. The tenure of ECJ judges is limited to term of six years; cf. Article 253 first subpara. TFEU

tries may make use of this opportunity and thereby represent the interests and manifest the power of those countries relative to others[96] is not restricted to the world trade forum but can be applied to the European Union as well. However, this fear may be qualified to some extent in the EU context. Organizations that would be active at the ECJ as *amici* are most certainly already familiar with the rules and practice at the EU Institutions and would, most likely, already have a seat in Brussels or hold ties with those representatives that do. Thus, no additional costs regarding the familiarization would arise. In addition, the financial dividing line is substantially greater among members of the WTO than within the membership of the European Union. Still, groups and associations that may not be well–funded and do not receive support by their home Member State might still be eligible for funding provided by the European Commission.

Finally, one formal argument should not be omitted. As has been illustrated, the fact that the DSU of the WTO does not include a reference to *amici curiae* has triggered great resistance among the member countries and also the EU, represented by the European Commission, has objected to an admission of such "friends" for a long time. Neither are the bodies of the dispute settlement mechanism empowered to adopt a decision that allows them to admit such briefs at their own discretion[97]. In a like manner, neither the Treaties nor the Statute or Rules of Procedure of the Court explicitly mention the possibility for 'uninterested' bystanders to submit their observations to a case pending before the ECJ. The next chapter is therefore devoted to the discussion on whether the introduction of the *amicus curiae* concept is legally possible – and practically recommendable – without the need to amend the Treaties as this will not happen in the near future.

14.2.2. Costs for the Amicus

The literature does not seem to be consistent on the point of whether persons acting as *amici* are confronted with expenses or not. Estimations range from "trifling"[98] to anything *but* "trivial" with estimated $15.000 per brief[99]. However, neither the rules at the Supreme Court[100] nor the regulations at the WTO[101] demand the payment of court or any other administrative fees for the filing of *amicus* briefs[102]. Many of those who argue that the filing of *amicus* briefs is indeed a costly undertaking claim that organizations accordingly carefully monitor and select those cases to which they submit their own observations because they presume to be most influential in order not to waste their resources[103].

The sheer number of submissions and the existence of repeat players, however, indicate either that *amici* consider the financial burden to be outweighed by the benefits

96 Umbricht, 2001, p.785
97 Umbricht, 2001, p.786
98 Angell, 1967, p.1023
99 Caldeira & Wright, 1990, p.800; of similar opinion: Collins, 2004, p.825
100 Rules of the Supreme Court of the United States, *Part VII. Practice and Procedure*, Rule 37
101 e.g. the special procedure, cf. above
102 cf. also Angell, 1967, p.1023
103 cf. e.g. Caldeira & Wright, 1990, p.800; McGuire, 1994, p.823; Songer & Sheehan, 1993, p.340

or simply that the costs are actually not that tremendous. Even without data clearly stipulating the actual costs of preparing and submitting *amcius curiae* briefs, the author considers it reasonable and logical to conclude that these expenses may be considerably lower than other lobbying tactics and particularly than initiating court proceedings as a party. Given that the length of these briefs is usually limited by a maximal number of words or pages, the printing costs should not be unbearable. Furthermore, the author assumes that no additional posts within the organization's staff pool must be created for such undertakings. Rather, the technical expertise and factual knowledge should already be present given that these organizations are usually already engaged in legislative lobbying and the preparation of surveys, data analyses and like projects. Lawyers are usually also included in an organization's permanent staff given the fact that legal skills are indispensable for engaging in the drafting of legislation and obviously particularly for the required legal representation in court proceedings.

The author therefore assumes that the overall costs of filing *amicus* briefs every once in a while do not constitute an unmanageable burden since no fees for filing are requested and the information provided in the brief usually relies on the organization's general pool of knowledge. Frequent submissions obviously increase these expenses, particularly regarding employees, whose tasks might be to a great part to continuously monitor contemporary cases at the ECJ and to prepare such briefs; yet, should be regarded worthwhile by the relevant person or organization. The author would therefore also not emphasize the fact that *amici* are not eligible to receive compensation for their expenses, as parties to the dispute may be[104], given that these are not considered to be as high as for the parties.

Another, non–material, but not to be underestimated, disadvantage for persons and organizations is that *amicus curiae* briefs must be linked to an existing judicial dispute already in the course of adjudication by a court. A pending trial is accordingly *the* prerequisite for such submissions. *Amici* cannot, therefore, draw the court's attention to a specific injustice or breach of law simply by filing a brief. In these circumstances, they would have to initiate official judicial proceedings either themselves or support other litigants in doing so.

Another argument is related to the above–mentioned fact that *amici* need not prove a legal interest in the case to which they file their briefs and are thereby differentiated from the parties to the dispute. In addition to the advantages that these circumstances might bring, the exclusion from the proceedings may entail problems as well. If not granted special leave by the court, *amici* cannot put their arguments forward during the hearings.

They further do not have the right to be fully informed about all the information and documents relating to the case in the same manner as the parties are[105]. This may create an information gap and would even fall under the exceptions provided for by the Aarhus Convention in relation to the disclosure of information relating to ongoing investigations

104 Shelton, 1994, p.612
105 Shelton, 1994, p.612

and proceedings[106]. In addition, *amici* are not positioned to demand of a court either the initiation of interim relief or the issuance of compensatory payments for damages incurred.

Moreover, given that the admission of the brief depends either on the consent of the parties or leave granted by the court and the extent of consideration solely relies within the discretion of the judges, the efforts put into the preparation of the brief may be ineffective in the end without any remedy available. Hence, *amici* are in a position less well suited to have significant influence on the final decision of the court[107].

14.2.3. Gains

The mere fact that a person not directly affected – or interested – in the particular case at hand nonetheless invests at least some degree of effort in order to bring specific issues to the attention of the judges also bears benefits. *Amici* may either reinforce matters that have already been argued by one of the parties to the dispute, or, alternatively may shed light upon aspects or information which had, until then, been (un–)intentionally ignored and withheld for various reasons, including unawareness or political and tactical motivations[108]. These supplements include discussions on points of law presented from a different perspective, including the interpretation of statutes or norms, as well as factual information about the dispute's background or possible implications of the court's judgment[109]. Repetition of arguments may, contrary to the conventional opinion, further convince the judge of their importance and validity; particularly, if provided by parties and *amici* from different interest sectors[110].

In any case, such submissions by *amici* evidentially point towards the potential weight and the significance of political, social, economic, or cultural implications that this very dispute might carry. Directly put, at first sight, the impression of the public importance of a particular case increases with the number of briefs filed[111].

Explicitly rejecting any accusations of unorthodox influence of the judges, the fact that *amici* file briefs to a case that explores new areas in litigation may encourage the court to deliver innovative decisions[112]. Howse, for instance, clearly objects to fears that *amici* may have too much influence in dispute settlement procedures, in his example at the WTO, calling them "absurd" given that having influence, at least for business groups, is by a multiple easier to achieve via lobbying tactics[113].

106 cf. Article 4(4)(c) AC; Article 4(2)(c) Directive 2003/4/EC and 4(2), second & third dash Regulation 1049/2001/EC; for a discussion (cf. Chapter 9)

107 Shelton, 1994, p.612

108 Shelton, 1994, pp.618 & 640; similarly: Krislov, 1963, p.711; Umbricht, 2001, p.779

109 Spriggs & Wahlbeck, 1997, p.372

110 Spriggs & Wahlbeck, 1997, pp.368–369 & 373

111 McGuire, 1994, pp.825; Caldeira & Wright, 1990, p.803; Spriggs & Wahlbeck, 1997, p.367; Collins, 2004, pp.808 & 809–810; Hansford, 2004, p.220

112 cf. Shelton, 1994, p.618; similarly: Hansford, 2004, pp.220–221

113 Howse, 2003, p.509

Proponents of the admission of *amicus curiae* briefs greatly appreciate the flow of information and proceed according to the motto "the more, the better". Certainly, if not continuously repeated, a broad variety of information may aid the court in reaching a well–informed decision. This is particularly the case, where not only questions of legal interpretation, but factual issues in complex relations are at stake and expert opinions (that cannot be offered by governments or some private parties) may be of help[114].

An argument that might particularly be appreciated in common law systems but also by the European judiciary is that, on the basis of their engagement in, e.g. environmental policy, *amici* can provide a thorough overview of past legislative, as well as jurisprudential developments and initiatives[115]. As has been shown in chapter 7, the ECJ regularly refers to previous judgments in its decisions and parties make use of this method in their pleadings as well.

In sum, Shelton points out that national as well as international courts and tribunals are increasingly confronted with growing case applications, limited staff, financial and time resources, and possibly work with insufficiently trained or interested lawyers that do not appropriately respect matters of public concern. In order to prevent serious legal mistakes that may undermine the public's support and trust in the legal system, the introduction and regulation of *amcius curiae* briefs is increasingly being considered[116].

14.2.4. Benefits for the Amicus

The primary aim of – or benefit for – *amici* is fairly obvious and needs no further justification or explanation. By filing *amicus curiae* briefs, organizations attempt to influence the court in delivering a final decision that is mostly preferred and optimally changes policies according to their interests[117]. Such groups thereby rationally select those cases in which they are most likely to be able to reach this aim[118]. In addition, appearance as *amici curiae* has the following benefits to CSOs as compared to complete inactivity or the struggle to gain *locus standi* as an applicant or intervenor.

With regard to the court's discretion about whether or not to consider admitted *amicus* briefs, Howse makes the simple but convincing argument that even those briefs that have not officially been considered will nevertheless have made an impact upon the judges that had read them. He strongly doubts that "a judge [can] really erase [a compelling or moving] argument from his or her mind" and claims that, depending on the "persuasiveness and relevance of the brief", judges will be more receptive to the brief's content[119].

---

114 Umbricht, 2001, pp.779 & 783; Shelton, 1994, p.618; similarly: Caldeira & Wright, 1990, pp.803–804; O'Connor & Epstein, 1983, pp.41–42

115 Shelton, 1994, p.618

116 Shelton, 1994, p.616

117 Hansford, 2004, p.222; Collins, 2004, p.825

118 McGuire, 1994, p.822; Hansford, 2004, pp.219–220

119 Howse, 2003, p.510

An argument that may compensate for the disadvantage listed above for discussion that *amici* can only add to existing cases submitted for adjudication, is the non–excluded possibility for persons to build upon their knowledge prepared and the experience gained in a former case in which they acted as *amici* or to take specific issues of that former case for new litigation. Yet, concerning the case at hand, the *amicus* is not bound by the final judgment of the court[120]. No costs of implementation, monitoring, or other forms of adherence occur. This is a considerable procedural, as well as financial advantage.

With regard to providing information, it should also be noted that *amici* are not as restricted in the matters they bring to the judges' attention and the arguments underlying them as the parties may be in their pleadings [121]. It is indeed the essence of the concept that *amici* should rather explore additional areas and arguments.

Moreover, there might also be a further motivation for interest groups to file briefs that should not be omitted. Most of these organizations, all environmental protection organizations that the author is aware of, are composed of – and depend upon – individuals, who aim at achieving a specific aim. Such "membership–based interests"[122] need to prove their engagement and effectiveness in order to ensure their members' support. This is particularly the case where specific interests are represented by a multitude of rival groups that compete for support. Successful *amicus* participation might aid binding present members to the organization, attract attention of the media and thereby the public, and possibly gain new supporters[123]. This may even be the case where the *amicus* organization supported the losing party or its submission had been rejected[124].

14.2.5. Conclusion

This chapter has discussed the concept of *amicus curiae* participation in court proceedings and concludes that an introduction of this practice within the EU legal system for environmental concerns should at least be considered. The concept fits perfectly well with the claim of this work and the goals of the Aarhus Convention with regard to broader participation rights for groups in the interest of the general public, i.e. protection of the environment. The overall advantages to the court and the general public, as well as the benefits for the individual *amicus* will have to be assessed against the potential disadvantages and costs for each case individually. This overview suggests that there is a great likelihood that the examination will result more often than not in a decision to allow *amicus curiae* participation. However, experiences from non–common law systems and particularly from intergovernmental organizations suggest that such participation should only be offered under predefined rules and standards and must be properly installed.

120 Shelton, 1994, p.611
121 Shelton, 1994, p.611
122 Hansford, 2004, p.221
123 cf. Umbricht, 2001, p.790; Hansford, 2004, pp.221 & 229; Songer & Sheehan, 1993, pp.340 & 351
124 Songer & Sheehan, 1993, p.351

15. *Amici curiae* in *rei naturae* in the EU – Environmental friends of the Court of the EU

15.1. Solicited briefs

Chapter 14 has illustrated that only unsolicited briefs submitted by *amici curiae* on their own initiative have been matter for debate in various arbitration and adjudication systems[1]. Opinions provided by actors that are not parties to the respective dispute upon explicit invitation or request by a court or tribunal are without controversy and may be compared with witness reports or expert opinions.

The same applies to the European Court of Justice, given that witnesses and experts can be heard at the request of the Court on the basis of the rules laid out in Articles 25 to 32 of the Statute of the Court. Article 25 is formulated broadly in stating that "[t]he Court of Justice may at any time entrust any individual, body, authority, committee or other organisation it chooses with the task of giving an expert opinion".

It is thus indisputable that the judges have the authority to determine who provides supplementary information and to decide to what extent the opinion will influence the final court decision. In other words, it is the judges, who decide whether and which information they seek and from whom.

15.2. Arguments

The following section presents those arguments that can be put forward against an introduction of the *amicus curiae* concept in legal disputes that threaten to affect the environment and are adjudicated by the ECJ and those in favor of such an innovative approach.

15.2.1. CONTRA

The practical hindrances that *amici curiae* might face and the theoretical concerns that their participation might provoke are discussed first.

1 cf. Ala'i, 2000, pp.73–74

Top–down perspective

There are indeed several realistic and valid objections that can be put forward against an intervention into the ongoing arbitration of a case by non–affected private persons. This section presents those from the perspective of the national governments and EU Institutions that want to preserve the institutional balance and legal system as currently operated. The admission of *amicus curiae* briefs might thereby endanger this institutional equilibrium for the following reasons.

First, neither the Statute or the Rules of Procedure of the Court of Justice of the European Union nor the Treaty on European Union and the Treaty on the Functioning of the European Union in their current versions[2] provide for even an implicit indication for a comparable institution as the *amicus curiae*. Not even a broad reading of the provisions on expert opinions, witness reports, or the Court's capability of seeking other external information would offer a strong and indisputable legal basis for such an inclusion.

Second, Advocate–General Cosmas strongly opposed a relaxation of standing requirements for environmental associations in his Opinion on the *Greenpeace* case as this would, according to him, "run counter to the letter of the law, in this case of Article 173 of the Treaty [today: Article 263 TFEU]"[3]. He would classify such a practice as *contra legem* given that the Treaty intentionally distinguishes between privileged applicants, who do not have to show a specific interest or otherwise effect, and non–privileged ones, who are under the obligation to prove their concern. The admission of *amicus curiae* briefs may trigger similar criticism given that non–privileged applicants would be released from the obligation to show their individual and direct concern to the given case[4].

A third argument relates to the, so far, unwillingness of the Member States to allow the Court to employ a broader interpretation of the individual concern requirement in order to grant standing to non–privileged applicants more often. Despite the criticism raised in the literature and numerous proposals suggested also by the then CFI and Advocates–General Jacobs and Cosmas, opposition against the admission of *amici curiae* can be expected on part of the national governments. They would certainly have to fear that these *amici* would "interfere" continuously in cases, in which their are involved. In addition, the abolition of the explicit distinction between privileged and non–privileged applicants in direct actions before the ECJ is also not expected to be welcomed by the Member States.

Furthermore, the fear of judicial lobbying may arise and endanger the impartiality of judges, which is a quality expressly required by Article 2 of the Statute of the Court of Justice. The high priority attributed to the impartiality and qualification of the high legal staff of the ECJ is underlined by recent modifications to their selection by the Lisbon

---

2 August 8th 2010

3 Opinion of the Advocate–General in Case C–321/95P *Greenpeace and Others v Commission* [1998] ECR I–1651, para.118

4 Opinion of the Advocate–General in Case C–321/95P *Greenpeace and Others v Commission* [1998] ECR I–1651

Treaty. Prior to the appointment of the Judges and Advocates–General of the Court, a panel comprising seven members "of recognised competence", either coming from the ECJ, the General Court or national courts[5], shall "give an opinion on candidates' suitability"[6]. The establishment of the panel is intended to distance the selection of the high personnel of the ECJ from tactical Member State preferences and underline the independence, impartiality and objectivity of the judiciary[7]. However, it would be naive to assume that the admission of *amicus curaie* briefs would bias the impartial position of judges in favor of a more environmental–friendly judgment as opposed to economic or other interests. Judges are already, as much as any other person, confronted with demands and activities of environmental protectionists or information and calculations released and models created by research institutes on the effects on climate change and other environmental changes. The concern that environmental CSOs might only practice judicial lobbying could be easily invalidated by strict requirements with which *amicus curiae* briefs have to comply not only formally but also with regard to the suitability, reliability and validity of the arguments and information provided. *Amici*, whose briefs are mere lobbying papers, would damage their own reputation and will not be considered in another case.

The EU is interested in making the decision–making procedures of its institutions more transparent and accountable. The discretion of the judges in the decision whether or not to admit *amicus curiae* briefs might, however, lead to greater non–transparency and would, accordingly, stand in contrast to such an interest.

Yet, it could also be argued that the admission of *amicus curiae* briefs and the citation of their arguments in the ECJ's decision would contribute to the transparency of the decision–making process rather than disturbing it. This is, of course, conditional upon the adherence of the *amicus* with the rules on the disclosure of all relevant information about its internal composition and relationships. In theory, increased transparency of decision–making processes and enhanced institutional legitimacy are generally equated with growing public support[8]. Though the Court is less dependent on democratic legitimacy and public support than the political institutions, this might nevertheless be appealing.

Last but not least, the description of the argument is comparatively short, yet its effects might be far–reaching and should not be underestimated. It might be the case that the processing of these briefs could lengthen the already long duration of proceedings before the ECJ. This point of criticism could be addressed by installing strict time schedules and fixing maximum page or word limits with which *amici* need to comply (cf. proposal in section 3).

5 Article 255, second subparagraph TFEU
6 Article 255, first subparagraph TFEU
7 Harratsch, Koenig & Pechstein, 2009, p.131
8 cf. in relation to the WTO dispute settlement mechanism: Charnovitz, 2000, pp.21–22

Bottom–up perspective

Contrary to the arguments listed above, in which *amici curiae* would disturb the current legal system, the essence of the arguments presented below from the perspective of potential *amici* could be summarized that such a participation might not be sufficiently far–reaching.

One of the first and most important arguments that has already been discussed in chapter 14 is that *amici* are not able to initiate new cases on their own. An *amicus curiae* brief must always be filed with a dispute that is already submitted to the Court for adjudication. Thus, whenever environmental CSOs are of the opinion that a specific action or omission should be annulled or amended and in the latter case enforced, they would first have to appeal to those who can initiate cases, either an individually and directly concerned private party or Member States or EU Institutions. CSOs could then, for instance, complain to the European Commission under the current conditions and, provided that infringement proceedings are initiated, could then submit a brief when the case is adjudicated by the ECJ. Thus, CSOs are still very dependent upon the EU Institutions and Member States, however, would be offered an opportunity to participate in the judicial proceeding, which is currently not possible.

The second disadvantage is closely connected to the aforementioned one. The unfortunate problem with the criteria for *locus standi* would remain unresolved. The mere admission of observations by 'friends' would not bring an end to the claimed "lack of coherence" in standing requirements before the ECJ[9].

Third, *amici* cannot demand interim measures in their briefs in order to prevent the continuance of an action that might harm the environment during the proceeding. Whether such an injunction is granted, therefore depends on the national legal system from which the case originates in cases of preliminary references, or where acts and omissions of the EU Institutions, bodies, agencies and offices are challenged, on the ECJ. By the same token, other remedies, for instance, damage payments cannot be invoked either.

The fact that parties may refuse consent to the submission of *amicus curiae* briefs and the, at worst, arbitrary discretion on part of the judges to accept or decline them may also create uncertainty and confusion for potential *amici*. Their efforts may even have been worthless if, without declaring the reasons, their briefs are declined, as has been the situation in the WTO's *EC–Asbestos* case (cf. chapter 14).

15.2.2. PRO

The following section now enlists those arguments in favor of an introduction of *amicus curiae* briefs at the ECJ. Again, the advantages are classified as those relating to the legal system and governmental actors and those that might motivate potential *amici* to file briefs.

9 ECJ, Case 321/95P *Greenpeace and Others v Commission* [1998] ECR I–1651, para. 64

Top–down perspective

Given that the list of negative arguments started with the legal conditions and Member States' potential opposition, the first point raised here is not an argument of valuable content but a positive indication. For a long time, the former European Community represented by the European Commission opposed the introduction of *amici curiae* within the WTO dispute settlement mechanism. It could, accordingly, be interpreted as a positive sign that the Commission now openly supports the submission of such briefs (cf. chapter 14). One might, therefore, dare to predict a positive attitude of the Commission towards *amici curiae* in the EU context for reasons of greater civil society inclusion and primarily because of the second argument below.

Amici can offer a substantial amount of new information to the court that would otherwise not be available. As has been presented, the original intention is to offer the court new information or provide additional insights that may realistically also lead to a position that is not the same as either of the other two. However, repetition of valid arguments has also been found to underline their importance. Of course, all of this information must be valid, reliable and up–to–date. Benefits may also occur to the European Commission in infringement proceedings as it will usually be the party accusing one or several Member States of having failed to comply with Treaty obligations. The case can currently only be intervened in by other Member States that commonly support the defending Member State. The introduction of *amicus curiae* participation could give environmentalists a voice in judicial proceedings. In order to supplement the Commission's indictment, *amicus* briefs may provide additional information to represent their concerns, which may otherwise not be sufficiently considered[10].

Another argument in favor of *amicus* participation is the danger that specific interests are simply not sufficiently represented. It has already been shown that countries with a federal structure threaten to under–represent some interests. These effects may be even more dramatic within the EU's multi–level system of governance comprising complex networks and 'inside' as well as 'outside' groups. Submitting *amicus curiae* briefs may be one possibility to counteract such an exclusion.

Moreover, it has been found in common law systems that such briefs provide a helpful overview of precedents and other case–law that might be relevant for the dispute that is adjudicated at the moment (cf. chapter 14). Given that the ECJ proceeds quite similarly and heavily relies on previous judgments (cf. chapter 7), this might be an additional argument in favor of *amicus curiae* briefs.

Fifth, it should further not be underestimated that *amici curiae* might aid to place the emphasis of a case on the substantive matters rather than the procedural assessments of the right of standing. This was also an argument raised by Advocate–General Jacobs in his *UPA*–Opinion[11] in favor of a reformulation of the individual concern requirement in direct actions (cf. chapter 12).

10 cf. Umbricht, 2001, p.783

11 ECJ, Case C–50/00P *Unión de Pequeños Agricultores v Council* (*UPA*) [2002] ECR I–6677

In addition, CSOs can intervene in cases that might have negative repercussions on the environment which would otherwise be neglected and add an 'environmental protection dimension' to the merits. Flango, Bross and Corbally termed the indication of the broader political implications and significance as one of the three essential functions of *amici curiae*[12]. This would certainly strengthen the environmental integration clause enshrined in Article 11 TFEU.

Moreover, environmental protection belongs to a public concern that should be shared by all and cannot be individualized enough to fulfill the *locus standi* requirements of the ECJ; either for initiating lawsuits themselves or as intervening third parties. This deprives persons and organizations that have a non–legal interest in the preservation of the environment from the opportunity to create and enforce rights. It is, in this very policy area, specifically suitable to offer participation via the submission of *amicus curiae* briefs, in order to ensure the public interest to be at least given the opportunity to be heard in a trial and inform the decision–making process, where such an interest may be affected[13]. As Shelton argued, "[s]uch participation reinforces the concept of obligations *erga omnes* and can lead to enhancing the role of the court and the long–term development"[14] of the law whose observance it shall ensure[15].

Although the standing requirements would remain unchanged, the introduction of *amici curiae* may improve effective judicial protection insofar as it will offer an alternative approach. The environment certainly does not have any other opportunity to be defended in court. *Amicus curiae* briefs may start filling the claimed (by the applicants in the *Greenpeace* case) "legal vacuum"[16]. The transdisciplinary nature of environmental policy that has been shown to touch upon various other policy areas supports this claim.

Seventh, the argument that has been raised most often against a relaxation of the standing requirement to be *individually* concerned by a measure related to the sheer number of additional cases that would be filed with the General Court and the Court of Justice. As a consequence, this is said to lead to an unmanageable increase of the caseload. Yet, as has already been pointed out, no additional cases would be filed by these *amici*; only existing cases would be examined more closely. In order to prevent additional workload, specific rules and regulations would be installed regarding form, length and deadlines (cf. section 3). The benefits would surely outweigh the additional effort.

The main argument, on which this project is based, is the hypothesis that good environmental governance can only be achieved, if access to participation opportunities to any EU Institution is guaranteed at any stage throughout the policy cycle as a whole.

12 2006, p.182
13 Shelton, 1994, pp.611–612; cf. also Charnovitz, 2000, p.16
14 1994, p.642
15 cf. e.g. Article 19(1) TEU LT
16 ECJ, Case C–321/95P *Greenpeace and Others v Commission* [1998] ECR I–1651, para.19; cf. also chapter 13

Arguments in favor of this position have already been provided in detail and are primarily based on the presumption that participation increases the democratic legitimacy of decision–makers, improves compliance with laws and judgments, and increases citizens' political awareness and support for the European Union as a whole.

This approach towards comprehensive participation is in line with the demands of the Aarhus Convention with regard to information, decision–making and judicial proceedings. It should be emphasized once more that these participation opportunities are only procedural and not substantive rights. Participation would be an offer to those interested to become involved in the policy process but the extent of influence would neither be prescribed nor legally guaranteed, as is the case at, for instance, the respective Directorates–General in the European Commission during the agenda–setting and formulation stages of the policy cycle.

Finally, it has been correctly argued that the Treaties and the documents regulating the working of the ECJ currently do not provide for the introduction of *amici curiae*. Amendment of the TFEU would furthermore be long–lasting, cumbersome and overall improbable. Yet, this would not have to be necessary. Although the current status quo of the Court's Statute and Rules of Procedure also do not – even if employing a generous interpretation – offer a legal basis for the introduction of the *amicus curiae*, the necessary amendments would be minor and much easier and practicable to execute than an amendment of the Treaty. The Statute of the Court is drawn up by the ECJ and the Commission and put forward for adoption by the European Parliament and the Council according to the ordinary legislative procedure[17]. The Rules of Procedure are formulated by the Court and approved by the Council[18]. No ratification processes, including popular referendums, would be necessary.

Currently, Article 25 of the Court's Statute reads: "The Court of Justice may at any time entrust any individual, body, authority, committee or other organisation it chooses with the task of giving an expert opinion". The linguistic versions of this provision in English (*entrust*), German (*betrauen*), Dutch (*opdragen*), French (*confier*) and Spanish (*encomendar*) refer to an actively seeking position on part of the ECJ. Unsolicited *amicus* briefs would thus – momentarily – not be covered.
A potential reformulation of that provision in the Statute could be:

> The Court of Justice may at any time accept expert opinions given by any individual, body, authority, committee or other organisation it chooses.

The ultimate decision, whether or not to admit and consider those expert opinions would remain with the Court. This is consistent with the general concept of the *amicus curiae*, in which courts enjoy full discretion on the submission of such briefs (cf. section 15.3).

17 Article 281 second subparagraph TFEU
18 Article 253 sixth subparagraph TFEU

Bottom–up perspective

In addition to those gains for *amici curiae* discussed in the previous chapter, which would apply to the "friends" of the ECJ without exception, the following more specific EU–related benefits for environmental CSOs are identified, when becoming involved in environmental disputes.

First, it has already been discussed that the submission of such briefs provides a cost–efficient alternative to other forms of lobbying – in particular to initiating legal proceedings as a complainant. The practice of drawing up and submitting these briefs has been found not to create unbearable additional costs for the *amicus* (cf. chapter 14). In order to keep the expenses at a minimum level, it should be processed as expert opinions or witness reports insofar as no specific language or translation requirements should be attached to the submission of such *acmius* observations, i.e. any of the official EU languages should suffice. In addition, one could argue for reimbursement of incurred expenses (cf. section 3 on the proposal).

Second, as stated in chapter 14, no familiarization costs would arise for CSOs when acting as "friends" of the ECJ. One may assume that it would be the rule for organizations to already have a working knowledge of the institutional setting and working environment at EU level. Most of these organizations or associations are usually already established in Brussels and would only have to add compliance with the rules and standards specifically requested by the Court. Travel expenses would of course occur, as these organizations are established in Brussels and the Court's seat is in Luxembourg. However, these costs remain manageable.

Third, in the context of the WTO dispute settlement mechanism, less industrialized countries were concerned that only organizations originating from the wealthier member countries would submit briefs as *amici* and would thereby influence the panel's final decision to a constant bias towards the interests of the Western countries. This threat, regardless of whether it is of value within the WTO or not, is substantially lower within the European Union. Not only are the Member States much less heterogeneous in terms of democratic values, national stability and existence and support of an independent civil society as compared with the variety that is represented at the WTO. But organizations are under certain circumstances also eligible for financial support by the European Commission. It might, however, admittedly be much more problematic for interest groups originating from smaller countries with a weakly developed social network and the necessary infrastructure to meet the requirements for representativeness as demanded by the Commission (cf. chapter 3).

Fourth, organizations may feel responsible to represent clients, who otherwise could not be heard by the Court due to lack of standing but would nevertheless be affected by the Court's final decision[19]. This includes human beings, who cannot establish an *indi-*

19 cf. e.g. Flango, Bross & Corbally, 2006, p.182

vidual concern, as much as animal wildlife whose habitat is threatened or the endangered botanical diversity.

Finally, and most importantly, the limitations imposed upon private interveners would not seize against *amici curiae*. It has already been stated both on the list in favor and against the admission of such briefs that *amici* need not establish a legal interest in the given dispute. Furthermore, as "friends", they may position themselves in support of one of the parties to the dispute or rather attempt to provide "neutral" information to the court. Yet, even if they affiliate with either party, they remain unaffected by the court's final judgment, including its decision on the costs.

15.3. Proposal

The discussion of the arguments in favor of an introduction of *amici curiae* to the proceedings before the European Court of Justice have already suggested a slight re–formulation of Article 25 of the Statute of the Court. The following proposes the addition of a new provision to the Rules of Procedure of the ECJ that directly allows for environmental *amici curiae* to file their observations under clearly defined and specified rules. The proposal has taken over the requirements and, in some subparagraphs, the wording of other articles of the ECJ's Rules of Procedure, the Rules of the U.S. Supreme Court, or other legal provisions.

Rules of Procedure of the Court of Justice of the European Union

Title III

SPECIAL FORMS OF PROCEDURE

Chapter 4

ENVIRONMENTAL AMICUS CURIAE BRIEFS[20]

Article 94[21]

1. The Court may accept and consider *amicus curiae* briefs that bring to its attention information not already brought by the parties which is relevant to the protection of the environment. Such briefs shall aid to ensure "a high level of protection and improvement of the quality of the environment" within the EU as enshrined in Article 2(3) TEU[22].

20 new; subsequent chapters are re–numbered
21 new; subsequent articles are re–numbered
22 based on Rule 37(1), Rules of the Supreme Court of the United States

2. An organization may qualify as an *amicus curiae* eligible to submit a brief in accordance with paragraphs 3 and 9 of this Article provided that

(a) the organization is dedicated to the protection of the environment as proclaimed by its statute[23];

(b) it has established branches in at least three Member States[24];

(c) the geographic area of activity covers the territory of at least three Member States of the EU and correlates with the area affected by the dispute at hand[25];

(d) it is granted legal personality under the national law of the Member State, where it has its registered seat or headquarter[26];

(e) the organization has existed for at least three years[27];

(f) it is democratically organized internally[28]; and

(g) the organizations discloses its financial resources, whereby receipt of funding by the European Commission is accepted[29].

3. An application to submit an *amicus curiae* brief must be made within six weeks of the publication of the notice referred to in Article 16(6) of these Rules[30].

The application shall contain:

(a) the description of the case;

(b) the description of the parties;

(c) the name and address of the *amicus*;

(d) the *amicus*' address for service at the place where the Court has its seat;

(e) if applicable, the form of order sought, by one or more of the parties, in support of which the *amicus* is applying for leave to submit an opinion[31]; and

(f) an indication of the additional points in law and in fact provided by the *amicus*.

---

23 based on Member State regulations for *locus standi* in environmental disputes; cf. chapter 11

24 based on Commission regulations on financial support; cf. chapter 3

25 based on Member State regulations for locus standi in environmental disputes; cf. chapter 11 and Commission regulations for financial support; cf. chapter 3

26 based on Member State regulations for locus standi in environmental disputes; cf. chapter 11

27 based on Member State regulations for locus standi in environmental disputes; cf. chapter 11

28 based on Member State regulations for locus standi in environmental disputes; cf. chapter 11 and Commission regulations for financial support; cf. chapter 3

29 based on Commission regulations for financial support; cf. chapter 3 and Rule 37(6), Rules of the Supreme Court of the United States

30 cf. Article 93(1), Rules of Procedure of the Court of Justice

31 cf. Article 93(1), Rules of Procedure of the Court of Justice

4. The lawyer acting for an *amicus* must lodge at the Registry a certificate that he is authorized to practice before a court of a Member State or of another State which is a party to the EEA Agreement[32].

5. The application shall be served on the parties[33] for their consent.

When a party to the case has withheld consent, the *amicus* may file a motion for leave with the Court. The President shall, in consultation with the Judges and after hearing the Advocate–General[34], decide upon the admission of the brief[35].

6. No consent of the parties or motion for leave to file an *amicus curiae* brief is necessary[36] where a measure adopted by an EU Institution, body, office or agency is, in whole or in part, at dispute and to whose development the organization has actively contributed.

7. If the President allows the submission of the *amicus brief*, the *amicus* shall receive a copy of every document served on the parties. The President may, however, on application by one of the parties, omit secret or confidential documents[37].

8. The President shall prescribe a period within which[38] the *amicus* may submit a brief in accordance with the requirements listed in Article 37 paragraphs 1, 3, 4 and 6 of these Rules.

9. In addition, the brief shall not exceed a word limit of 6.000[39]
and shall contain:

(a) the name and address of the *amicus*;

(b) the case to which the brief relates;

(c) the pleas in law and arguments relied on by the *amicus*; and

(d) the nature of any evidence offered in support[40].

---

32 cf. Article 38(3), Rules of Procedure of the Court of Justice; Rule 37(1) & Rule 5, Rules of Procedure of the Supreme Court of the United States
33 based on Article 93(2), Rules of Procedure of the Court of Justice
34 Article 47(1), Rules of Procedure of the Court of Justice
35 based on Rule 37(2b), Rules of Procedure of the Supreme Court of the United States and Article 93(2) third subparagraph, Rules of Procedure of the Court of Justice
36 cf. Rule 37(4), Rules of the Supreme Court of the United States
37 Article 93(3), Rules of Procedure of the Court of Justice
38 cf. Article 93(5), Rules of Procedure of the Court of Justice
39 based on the regulations for *amicus curiae* briefs at the U.S. Supreme Court; cf. Rule 33(1)(g)(x), Rules of Procedure of the Supreme Court of the United States
40 based on Article 93(5), Rules of Procedure of the Court of Justice

10. After the brief has been lodged, the President shall, where necessary, prescribe a time–limit within which the parties may reply to that brief[41].

11. Consideration may be given to an application to submit *amicus curiae* briefs which is made after the expiry of the period prescribed in paragraph 3 but before the decision to open the oral procedure provided for in Article 44(3).

In that event, if the President allows the brief, the *amicus* may submit his observations during the oral procedure, if that procedure takes place[42].

12. The *amicus curiae* shall bear only his own costs and is exempted from the Court's decision on costs.

15.3.1. Comments and Explanations

The first paragraph defines the desired function of potential *amici curiae* in light of the overall political objective of the European Union to guarantee a high standard of environmental protection. To highlight this, reference is made to the relevant provision of the Treaty on European Union. The emphasis on the provision of new or supplementary information and the explicit exclusion of the possibility to merely repeat information already provided by any of the parties to the dispute was taken over from the Rules of the Supreme Court of the United States.

Paragraph 2 of the provision then accurately stipulates those features that organizations must fulfill in order to be eligible to submit a brief to a pending lawsuit. The aim of this list of criteria is to ensure that such organizations act in the public interest only and to avoid abuse. These criteria are mandatory and cumulative.

The criteria have mainly been influenced by those required by several Member States when granting preferential standing rules to organizations in specific cases. These are primarily the requirement of having the statutory dedication to environmental protection (criterion (a)), the geographic criterion (c), the condition to possess legal personality (criterion (d)), the minimum number of years of existence (criterion (e)), and democratic internal structure (criterion (f)). Another source of inspiration were the guidelines of the Commission on the basis of which it decides upon financial support to environmental interest groups. From these stem the condition of having established branches in at least three Member States (criterion (b)), the territorial activity requirement (criterion (c)), as well as the democratic condition and the disclosure of the organization's financial resources (criterion (g)). The latter is also explicitly required by the Rules of the Supreme Court of the United States in order to ensure the *amicus*' financial independence from the parties to the dispute and other relevant actors[43].

41 Article 93(6), Rules of Procedure of the Court of Justice
42 Article 93(7), Rules of Procedure of the Court of Justice
43 Rule 37(6), Rules of the Supreme Court of the United States

The underlying rationale of each criterion is outlined in the following. As paragraph 1 has already explained, a "high level of protection and improvement of the quality of the environment" will be the goal of the *amicus* briefs. It is therefore quite reasonable that organizations that file such briefs incorporate such a clause in their statutes. Second, most decisions taken at EU level, political or legal, possess a transnational character and hardly ever solely affect one Member State in isolation. The 'transnationality' criterion in establishment and activity therefore reflects the boundlessness of environmental problems and their cures. This was also a point raised in the proposal made by Advocate–General Cosmas in his *Greenpeace* Opinion (cf. chapter 13). Third, the requirement that organizations possess legal personality is necessary for several practical reasons. Most notably, in combination with the minimum number of years of existence, it will avoid the impulsive creation of ad hoc groups. Organizations possessing a legal personality, as well as a number of years of experience in the political and judicial environment, are more likely to submit briefs that are of help to the ECJ regarding the content, data, legal arguments and manner in which they are presented.

Fourth, the demand for the organizations to be internally democratically organized is primarily called for for legitimacy reasons. Most environmental CSOs are member–based and should, although usually sending representatives of umbrella associations to Brussels and Luxembourg, keep in contact with their members at local level.

Finally, the disclosure of financial resources and funding information is crucial in order to ensure the organization's material independence of the parties to the dispute. It will furthermore ensure the objectivity of the data and facts presented and underline the fact that the organization is not selfishly engaged but acts in the interest of the general public. This point is separately listed in the Rules of the U.S. Supreme Court[44].

The deadline of six weeks as of the publication of the case to submit an application for leave for an *amicus curiae* brief has been taken from Article 93(1) of the Rules of Procedure governing the time periods for those that want to intervene in a pending case. The period of six weeks seems quite reasonable and manageable. To those that, without question, need to inform themselves constantly about EU jurisprudence anyway, this time frame is short but should suffice.

The regulated content of such an application was also taken over from the rules applying to persons intervening in a case. The first points serve to identify the *amicus* and enable fast communication. Under point (e) *amici* shall state, whether their brief is submitted in support of the order sought by one of the parties to the dispute. This may facilitate the classification of the supplementary information concerning legal as well as substantive matters of the case provided by the *amicus* (cf. point (f)).

Parties of legal disputes adjudicated by the ECJ and the GC must, as prescribed by Article 38(3) of the Rules of Procedure of the Court of Justice, be represented by a lawyer who obtains the authority to practice before a court of a Member State or a country of

44 cf. Rule 37(6), Rules of the Supreme Court of the United States

the EEA Agreement. Although *amici curiae* do not qualify as a 'party' for the reasons outlined before, their brief should nevertheless be submitted by a legal advisor. This has primarily practical reasons, as the facts and legal arguments will then be presented in an adequate manner. In addition, the U.S. Supreme Court similarly, yet even more strictly, attaches conditions to legal representatives of *amici*[45].

Paragraph 5 of the Article requires that the application must be referred to the parties to the dispute and necessitates their consent accepting the *amicus* brief. This is again similar to the requirements for applications of intervening persons. It is intended that both parties agree to the submission of the *amicus*. If one of the parties does not do so, *amici* may still file a motion for leave with the ECJ. This ensures that the Court has the final say in the admission of *amicus* briefs. The President of the chamber adjudicating the dispute decides whether or not to accept the *amicus* brief. This conforms with the rules on *amcius curiae* briefs at the U.S. Supreme Court[46] and those governing applications to intervene at the ECJ[47]. It should be emphasized, however, that this decision should be taken in collaboration with the other judges as well as after the opinion of the Advocate–General has been heard. The inclusion of the Advocate–General in the decision–making correlates to the fact that he or she has an equal position in the summoning of witnesses under Article 47(1) of the Rules of Procedure of the Court of Justice.

Paragraph 6 constitutes an exception to the general rule prescribed in the paragraph before. Organizations that have actively taken part in the development of a measure adopted by any of the EU Institutions, bodies, offices or agencies may file *amicus curiae* briefs without having to obtain the consent of the parties or the Court. This approach is consistent with the demands of the Aarhus Convention as well as with the rules on *locus standi* for organizations in several Member States and before the ECJ. The basis of this preferential treatment is that the organizations have already been found to be eligible for participation in previous administrative processes, which grants them further procedural rights. At the U.S. Supreme Court, only representatives of federal or state governmental agencies or the Solicitor General are exempted from such an application[48]. Given, however, that the focus of this work lies exclusively on the possibility of enhancing the opportunity to gain access for non–governmental actors in environmental disputes, this exception has been included.

Paragraphs 7, 8 and 9 are self–explanatory and merely stipulate that *amici* must be provided with all information relating to the dispute except for matters of secrecy and confidentiality, refer to the regulations under which the brief must be submitted, and determine its content. These exceptions are conform with those listed in the Aarhus Convention. Paragraph 7 has intentionally been included in order to avoid the creation of an 'information gap' between parties and the *amicus*. This would be quite contrary

45 cf. Rule 37(1) & Rule 5, Rules of Procedure of the Supreme Court of the United States
46 Rule 37(2b), Rules of Procedure of the Supreme Court of the United States
47 Article 93(2) third subparagraph, Rules of Procedure of the Court of Justice
48 cf. Rule 37(4), Rules of Procedure of the Supreme Court of the United States

to the objectives of the Aarhus Convention, which envisaged the 'public concerned' to be placed on an equal footing with state authorities in terms of obtaining the relevant information (cf. also chapters 9 & 14). Paragraph 10 then offers the opportunity for the parties to respond to the *amicus* brief.

Amicus curiae briefs should, in general, be submitted during the written procedure of the two–staged court proceeding. Subject to the President's approval, observations of the *amicus*, which would otherwise have been delivered in a brief in writing, may also be presented during the oral procedure. Paragraph 11 thereby relies on the exception provided for intervening persons in Article 93(7) of the Rules of Procedure of the Court of Justice. The discretion of the Court's President remains at the focus.

Finally, paragraph 12 of the proposed article concerns the financial expenses of submitting an *amicus curiae* brief. First of all, given that, *amici* do not qualify as a party to the dispute, they also remain untouched by the court's decision on costs. Thus, even if the party, in whose support the brief was filed, loses the case, the *amicus* cannot be held liable to bear the costs of the dispute. He or she merely will have to cover those expenses incurred by him or her. In light of the possibility for experts and witnesses to apply for a reimbursement of the costs of traveling and potential loss of earnings or that they may receive fee–payment for their services[49], it may be worth consideration, whether the costs for the legal counsel and travel could be reimbursed. In the majority of the cases, the travel distance should be between the organization's EU–branch in Brussels and the Court's seat in Luxembourg and therefore not exceedingly high.

15.3.2. Restriction to the promotion of environmental protection

After it has been shown that the advantages of *amicus curiae* participation before the ECJ outnumber in quantity and quality the potential negative effects and the proposal offered a legal basis for its introduction, one question remains to be answered. Should the institution of *amicus curiae* be generally installed at the EU judiciary or should it rather be limited to disputes affecting environmental concerns only?

This is a rather difficult question and a definite answer will not be provided here. The Supreme Court of the United States does not distinguish between policy areas in the admission of *amicus curiae* briefs and although the international arbitration institutions introduced in chapter 14 already have a clearly defined and limited jurisdiction, neither of them specifically welcomes or refuses briefs submitted in particular thematic areas. Nevertheless, the European Court of Justice does indeed acknowledge differential treatment of policy areas and particularly of standing rules, for instance in the area of competition policy, as discussed in chapter 12. This is quite understandable as these areas fall under the exclusive competence of the Union[50] and Commission and Court

49 cf. Article 51 & Article 73(1)(a), Rules of Procedure of the Court of Justice
50 Article 3(1)(b) TFEU

enjoy far–reaching discretionary powers[51]. Still, a new legal instrument has never been introduced to the exclusive use of ensuring the achievement of one – among the many – objectives of the European Union.

Yet, while the author does not exclude the admission of *amicus curiae* briefs *per se* in any legal dispute adjudicated by the ECJ, the author is of the opinion that the suitability for each policy area should be examined separately[52]. Thus, for the following reasons, the proposal is limited to only those cases that negatively affect the state of the environment.

The author would abstain from extending the authorization to economic interests concerning, for instance, competition rules, state aid and other subsidies, etc. as well as any matter relating to the four freedoms of the common market, social policy or let alone aspects of regional security and defense. In the latter area, most documents are confidential in any case and would not have to be disclosed. The author is not an expert in any of these policy areas. Surely, a substantial number of individuals and organizations would be willing to submit their own observations to a given case at hand to the ECJ. However, in the author's opinion, the rules on *locus standi* are indeed reasonable and valid given that the establishment of *individual concern* is indeed possible and the dispute only affects those that are *legally* concerned by the merits of the case. The 'intervention' by numerous briefs would most likely be hampering rather than helpful. If the submission of *amicus curiae* briefs remains restricted to disputes involving environmental matters or at least those affecting a public interest that cannot otherwise be defended, the length of the proceedings will continue to be manageable and acceptable. If such observations are admitted without restriction, delay might increase.

While, of course, environmental protection is not the most important policy area within the context of European integration, it is, as has been shown, by its very nature, almost impossible to meet the criterion to be individually concerned (cf. chapter 13). In the doubtless important areas of, for instance, social policy, individual concern can far more easily be established and thus applicants are granted access to the ECJ.

Environmental problems are non–reversible and cross time (a generation dilemma) and space (e.g. geographic borders) as no other area of political action and also touch upon other policy areas. It would not be wise to extend the admission of *amici curiae* to any policy areas without a detailed analysis. The model proposed here explicitly addresses the gap between the restrictive rules on *locus standi* for private litigants and the need to protect and defend the public interest of protecting the environment for which an *individual* concern cannot (easily) be established. Thus, where the fulfillment of the standing criteria are manageable, the need for *amici* to compensate for a deficiency within the legal system is not given.

Support for the restriction of the *amicus curiae* concept to environmental legal disputes can also be found in the fact that several EU Member States offer preferential

51 Scharpf, 2009, pp.8–9

52 cf. Conclusion, section "Outlook – potential, further studies"

rules on standing before courts exclusively to not–for–profit organizations dedicated to environmental protection in cases affecting (specific areas of) the environment (cf. chapter 11).

The author would finally like to address the concerns that the exclusive admission of *amici curiae* briefs submitted by environmental civil society organizations might result in a one–sided bias of cases and consequently delay or hamper business expansions or economic growth and create financial costs for the industrial sectors by obliging them to utilize more environmental friendly machines. Examples might include states subsidizing renewable energy sources instead of fossil fuels, forcing companies to reduce greenhouse gas emissions, and making new "greener" equipment mandatory for manufacturers.

However, the argument can easily be reversed and then even gains in importance. Much published research has calculated, according to various scenarios and different models, that governmental inactivity concerning global warming would produce even higher costs for the economy, let alone the population, in terms of not only financial expenses but health matters or loss of property. For instance, *the Stern Review Report on the Economics of Climate Change*, published in 2006, estimated that, on the basis of formal economic models, inaction concerning climate change would lead to "overall costs and risks [...] [that] will be equivalent to losing at least 5% of global GDP each year, now and forever". A scenario that takes into consideration "a wider range of risks and impacts" predicted a percentage number of twenty or higher of GDP that would have to be paid in order to compensate for the damages; again annually. The Stern Review Report contrasted these sums with the annual costs for taking appropriate action against the worst impacts of climate change that amount to approximately 1% of global GDP[53]. Another argument in support of taking action is that it might foster technological innovation aiming at environmental friendly technology, which, over time, would also reduce overall acquisition costs and ancillary expenses and might expedite a country's technological exports.

Thus, it might be even beneficial to the long–term economic interests of the EU, economic cooperation as the main vehicle for European integration, to consider environmental concerns in policy development, as well as in jurisprudence affecting environmental matters and to offer those a voice in the whole process who are dedicated to its protection and preservation.

53 HM Treasury, 2006, *Stern Review Report on the Economics of Climate Change, summary of conclusions*, p.vi; cf. also Chapter 10 *Macroeconomic models of costs*

15.4. Recommendation

It has been shown that the benefits of *amicus curiae* participation in judicial proceedings in both perspectives, i.e. those affecting the legal system and working habits of the ECJ, as well as those for CSOs that potentially "befriend" the court, clearly outweigh the disadvantages. In addition, the – momentary – restriction of the concept to environmental disputes has further been explained and justified.

In the conclusion which follows, the author assesses the practicability and feasibility of the proposal in order to submit a recommendation affirming this innovation to admit *amicus curiae* briefs in legal disputes affecting the state of the environment that are adjudicated by the European Court of Justice and the General Court.

Conclusion

The dissertation aimed at offering a comprehensive illustration of the current institutionalized participation opportunities for environmental civil society organizations to EU decision–making bodies as well as at pointing out their structural deficiencies with a special focus on the European Court of Justice.
The research question specifically asked how environmental CSOs could be granted easier access to the Court. The assumptions presented in the introduction have been examined and validated by this work.

It was first assumed that participation by environmental CSOs would be beneficial to EU governance. This has been illustrated particularly by chapters 4 and 5. Second, evidence for the assumption that access and participation is more readily available to the political institutions of the EU has been provided by the discussion of the EU participatory policy cycle in chapter 6 and the analysis of the legislation implementing the first two pillars of the Aarhus Convention in chapters 9 and 10.

The third assumption on the problems for environmental CSOs in gaining direct access to the ECJ and the General Court has been shown by a detailed discussion on the access opportunities to judicial evaluation and the prevailing criticism of the standing requirements, as well as by the analysis of the Court's environmental jurisprudence in chapters 11 to 13. Fourth, on the basis that some premises of regulated political participation could be applied as well to the European Court of Justice, the introduction of *amicus curiae* has been proposed, assessed, and recommended (cf. chapters 14 & 15). Finally, a comparison of political rights of participation and the rights of *amici curiae* is depicted below.

Guided by these assumptions, the underlying rationale was that *good* environmental *governance* can only be achieved through an inclusion of such organizations throughout the policy process as a whole, rather than limiting participation to single stages or only political institutions. This idea found support in the demands of the Aarhus Convention with regard to access opportunities for the 'public concerned' to receive information, participate in decision–making processes, and to gain access to court proceedings.

Environmental–related Participation at the EU

The importance of 'participatory democracy' within the context of EU environmental policy has become visible throughout the research for this project. Theories on democracy dedicated to the inclusion of non–state actors into political decision–making processes have emphasized the benefits for politicians, administrative staff and the citizens.

It is assumed that civil society organizations are able to mediate between citizens and political and administrative decision–makers by being active at the grassroots level and in regular contact with their members. At the same time, these associations are professionalized and compose of an organized internal structure that enables them to become a valuable partner of, for instance, the Commission providing expert knowledge and the monitoring of Member States' performance in the implementation of EU law.

In this regard, civil society has been identified with an potential for alleviating for the EU's democratic deficit. In particular, the multi–level system of governance, in which political power and decision–making authority is distributed among several institutions, offers multiple opportunity structures for participation to citizens' functional representatives and their ability to effectively contribute to EU policies.

This was found to be particularly helpful in the area of environmental protection, given that this public interest ranks high on the political prioritization of national, supranational and international agenda. In addition, the Union shares legislative competence, as well as the ability to enter into international agreements with third parties with its Member States. There is broad consensus that political action must be taken. Yet, also among EU Member States, there still prevails a very heterogeneous level of environmental protection. Hence, participation of transnational actors whose interests extend beyond national borders is particularly suitable in an area, in which potential damage is at least regional, if not global.

Thus, it has been shown that political action is needed to ensure a minimum level of protection of the environment and to prevent further damage. In addition, sufficient evidence exists that politicians and administrative staff are in need of external expertise for the provision of scientific data and its interpretation.

Participation Opportunities at the EU Institutions

This work has provided evidence for a correlation of the rights granted to the 'public concerned' in the three pillars of the Aarhus Convention and the five stages of the policy cycle, namely agenda–setting, policy formulation, decision–making, implementation and evaluation. A model was developed in order to take account, first, of the specific governance structure within the European Union in which the institutions involved at each respective stage were pointed out. Second, it showed that, although governmental authorities and external non–state actors were clearly separated, a number of participation opportunities were offered to the latter.

The institutions to which CSOs were able to gain access were discussed. In addition, the tasks performed by these organizations were shown to be not only determined by the institution but also by the relevant stage of the policy cycle and the institution's respective function therein.

The overview of the literature on formal access and participation opportunities concluded that access to the political institutions of the European Union is, though still subject to selective criticism, fairly well–established and participation and consultation procedures are comparatively transparent and accountable. Support for this assumption in environmental policy was provided by the comparison of the first two pillars of the Aarhus Convention on access to information and participation to decision–making for the public concerned and the respective provisions of European legislation currently in force. The finding was that, overall, the obligations were complied with on EU as well as Member State level.

Shortcomings have, however, been identified in the ability of environmental CSOs to gain access to the General Court and the Court of Justice of the European Union in order to enforce their rights under the first two Aarhus pillars and to have the legality of EU Institutions' (in–)actions reviewed. Particularly with regard to the latter, the criticism on the requirement of an applicant's individual concern has been substantiated thoroughly and placed into the specific context of the paradox concerning the protection of the environment.

This criterion determining whether or not an association of interest representatives is granted *locus standi* was identified as constituting the greatest obstacle to the ability of this type of litigants to pursue a litigation strategy, either in combination with tactical lobbying or exclusively. Of course, many other factors determine whether an interest group seeks redress before a court or chooses open lobbying of political decision–makers. Yet, it has nonetheless been found that the risk of not being granted standing as an association is the most severe hindrance.

This finding is evidenced by the examination of environmental cases of the European Court of Justice. Not only were few direct actions initiated before the Court and the vast majority of the cases were infringement proceedings followed by preliminary references by national courts, but also most of these direct actions were dismissed on grounds of lack of standing because the applicant did not fulfill the condition of direct or individual concern (cf. chapter 13). In addition, the case statistics and the comparative study undertaken by Milieu Ltd. have shown that rules on *locus standi* for individuals and groups greatly differ between the legal systems of the Member States and only one–third were classified as having "good" access to courts (cf. chapter 11). Neither reforms of the relevant Treaty provisions nor a reconsideration of the interpretation of the individual concern requirement by the ECJ can be expected in the near future. Hence, an alternative method to ensure the objective control of the (in–)action of EU Institutions, bodies, offices and agencies in environmental matters, as well as to guarantee effective legal protection to individuals who would be affected in an adverse manner, had to be found.

The Proposal: Introducing Environmental *Amici Curiae*

In response to the strict *locus standi* requirements for non–privileged applicants that have a particular adverse impact on litigation in environmental disputes, the introduction of the *amicus curiae* concept at the ECJ has been proposed.

After a thorough examination of potential gains and disadvantages, both from the perspective of judges and the legal system as such as well as that from potential *amici*, the concept has been found to offer an innovative alternative to the status quo. The EU legal system could be an appropriate framework for such an extension of access to justice. Despite the fact that several Member States strictly adhere to the continental systems of law of civil law tradition, some aspects of common law (where *amici curiae* are established) have been included at EU level. Additionally, the office of the Advocate–General as an influential advisor to the judges already includes an *amicus curiae* aspect (cf. below).

Although the concept of *amicus curiae* as such is welcomed, it is suggested that its introduction should not be without rules and limitations. Regulations of *who* could qualify as an *amicus* to the ECJ, deadlines, and formal requirements concerning the content, and the way of submission have been formulated. These rules will ensure that *amicus curiae* briefs are indeed helpful to the Court and may not become a burden by increasing the latter's workload substantially. These rules further help to prevent inappropriate influence on judges via judicial lobbying by demanding the disclosure of all information and relations and increasing the transparency of the working process that leads to the final decision.

Political Participation Rights and Amici Curiae

Throughout the policy cycle, external stakeholders have been identified as a valuable and appreciated source of information and democratic legitimacy. Although both forms of legitimacy still remain very important within European policy–making, a shift in focus has been identified from *output* to *input* legitimacy. The premises and assumptions of the various participatory and deliberative democracy approaches have been discussed in the context of political and administrative decision–making processes. However, the proposal on the introduction of *amici curiae* has transferred some of these prerequisites to the stage of judicial evaluation.

It was stated that political participation by CSOs increases public awareness of a specific problem as well as the the public's monitoring ability of the responding behavior of decision–makers. Increased engagement and activism by civil society in turn also informs politicians about the level of a public interest. The same can be presumed for judicial proceedings, where a large number of *amicus curiae* briefs indicates great public concern to the judges.

Whereas the function of civil society in providing an additional legitimatizing source for political institutions does not apply to the ECJ *mutatis mutandis*, the former's role as a provider of scientific evidence, technical data and information about the cultural and societal value might be appreciated as much.

In addition, *sine qua non* is that access and participation should be granted with an open end, i.e. that institutions and authorities should be receptive to the input offered by external stakeholders. Although the mere right to participate within a formal decision–making process does not guarantee that the effort results in a specific outcome, of course, the greatest possible consideration and reflection of the arguments and evidence provided by environmental CSOs is the goal. This applies as much to administrative consultation processes as to *amicus curiae* briefs in judicial proceedings.

Finally, in administrative decision–making processes, participation – and control – by external actors makes internal working procedures more transparent and accountable. In a similar manner, the submissions of *amici curiae* might aid in making judicial proceedings more transparent to the public. This, of course, is only the case, when formal requirements are met and rules of procedure are adhered to. Thus, many of the criteria qualifying environmental CSOs as *amici curiae* in the proposal have been taken from the rules for institutionalized consultation procedures of the Commission. The rules and standards must be high and demanding in order to ensure a credible representation of the interests of the vast majority of the European population.

Amended EU Participatory Policy Cycle

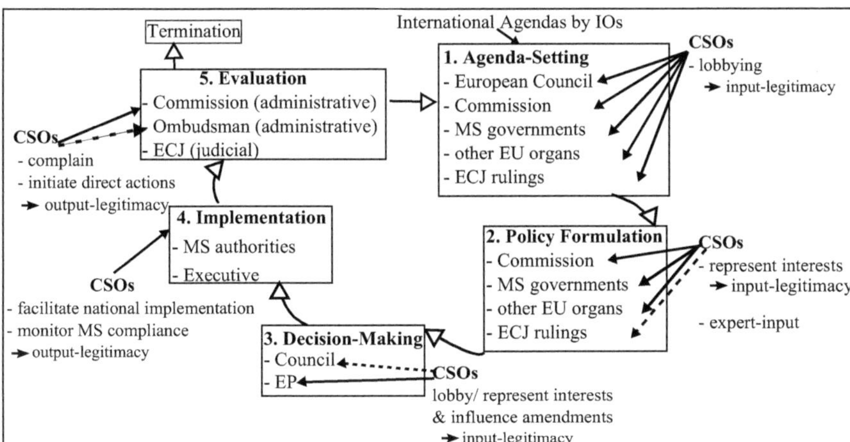

Figure 15: Amended EU Participatory Policy Cycle

While participation opportunities during the first four stages remain so far unchanged, the admission of *amici curiae* would improve access opportunities to the ECJ and its General Court and thereby enhance the judicial evaluation of policies adopted, decisions taken, acts executed or not executed by an EU Institution, body, office or agency.

Although environmental CSOs would still not be able to initiate direct actions and would not enjoy the same rights as *amici* as they would as a litigating party, access to the EU judiciary would substantially be facilitated for participation in disputes that have already been filed with the Court. The improved access opportunities are illustrated by the fact that the arrow has been thickened as compared with the model in chapter 6.

When *amici curiae* abide by the formal rules laid down in the proposed Article of the Court's Rules of Procedure and bear the strategies for successful litigation (cf. chapter 8) and the findings on successful *amici curiae* submissions (cf. chapter 14) in mind, the

ECJ should, in most instances, be receptive to the content of their briefs. In addition, reference to previous case–law, as well as a pro–European argumentation style, may well increase a brief's likelihood to be admitted and considered by the judges (cf. chapter 7 on the modes of interpretation as employed by the ECJ).

The Advocate–General as an opportunity structure Special attention could be paid also to the office of the Advocate–General. As mentioned before, the Advocate–General submits his or her opinion to a given case with a recommendation to the Court on how to interpret and solve the legal dispute between the parties.

Amici could therefore become a valuable source of information to the Advocate–General in preliminary references, infringement proceedings, or appeal cases of direct actions that are adjudicated before the European Court of Justice. Acting as an advisor to the judges, whose opinions are based on thorough research, an intensive examination of the arguments put forward by the parties to the dispute placed in the context of the relevant legal text, and a well–reflected balance of legal and factual considerations, he or she serves as a real ***amicus curiae***, a counselor, indeed.

The Advocate–General might become an efficient, alternative opportunity structure and target of *amicus curiae* submissions, given that, although the ECJ is not obligated to do so, the Court at times follows the conclusions drawn in the Advocate–General's opinion.

Political Scientific Results and Practical Significance

The author submits this dissertation as a contribution to the debate on the democratic structure and working processes within the EU. It aims at reforming the approach of European governance through a re–interpretation – and new application – of the concept of *participation by the public concerned.*

Overall, the reasoning that access to participation should be granted by the courts in order to complement the participation opportunities throughout the policy cycle as a whole is, although probably not incontestable, innovative and the dissertation has provided a number of cogent arguments in favor of this suggestion.

This work establishes a clear link between political science and legal studies.
Political science has innumerable connecting points with other areas of the humanities and social sciences. Clearly, political science touches upon sociology, communication science, social psychology and even economics, depending on the respective focus of the research undertaken. Moreover, the affinity of politics and law is not new, neither is the connection of the two sciences in governance studies. However, political scientists have only recently (approximately during the last two decades) discovered the European Court of Justice as a politically significant actor in the European integration process. Yet, the Court is not an institution in which the judges take politically sensitive and groundbreaking decisions by themselves, in isolation of any external influence. Quite to the contrary, this dissertation offers sufficient arguments and evidence to identify the Court

even as a political opportunity structure to which civil society aims at gaining access in order to contribute to the process of hading down final judgments.

Of course, courts have, in the traditional understanding of Montesquieu's concept of the separation of powers, always been a controlling factor in order to ensure an equilibrium of power. The judiciary has also always been clearly distinguished from the political branches of government, namely the legislative and the executive. Although this work honors the independence and impartiality of the judicial branch, it nonetheless attempts to widen the closed cycle of the persons involved in a particular court proceeding. This openness and receptiveness is proposed exclusively for cases in which the public interest of environmental protection is at stake and to those persons that are in a position to represent and defend such interests.

The dissertation has contributed to the academic debate on how governance should be structured within the European Union in a number of ways.

The importance attributed to participation opportunities of non–state actors in European policy–making has been pointed out with reference not only to the academia but to political practitioners as well. The benefits of participatory democracy in combination with the multi–level governance structure of the EU have been described and enable conclusions to be drawn that are specific to the *sui generis* system of the European Union.

In addition, only few studies on EU governance and democracy have combined the methodological model of the policy cycle with only one specific type of non–governmental actors; namely environmental civil society organizations. The manner in which this 'participatory component' was added to the policy cycle and the responsible government authorities clearly depicted them outside the current internal working processes but also indicted their potential influence.

Moreover, the political scientific understanding of *participation* of non–governmental stakeholders acting in the general interest has been extended from administrative or political decision–making processes to the judicial arena. It is this very understanding of participation as "grace" rather than a legally enforceable "right"[54] that is innovative and ambitious. Hence, participation would be offered on similar conditions throughout the policy cycle as a whole, including the stage of judicial evaluation.

Outlook – potential further studies

This work has intentionally focused on the examination and interpretation of primary legal sources; first and foremost the Treaties as the 'constitutional' documents of the European Union, as well as the Statute and Rules of Procedure of the Court of Justice of the European Union. The Aarhus Convention served as an example of a regional agreement into which the EU and its Member States have entered as a legal commitment. Although the work also considered the position, i.e. primarily through a comparison of

54 Ala'i, 2000, p.85

the benefits and losses, of CSOs, the focus was placed upon a top–down perspective and includes an institutional aspect.

Empirical field research was omitted on purpose because the primary aim was to find out what *could be possible* under the *current* legal system and institutional framework in the EU – subject to suggested minor amendments. The various opinions of selected staff members of the bureaucracy or NGOs would, without doubt, offer additional and worthy insights. Yet, this approach would not have supported the primary intention of this work as they would certainly only have included a number of estimations and assumptions as subjective as those of the author. The case is truly different, where events are studied that have actually taken place and the experts could provide a 'witnessing observation' simply because they have participated in or observed a particular process.

Nevertheless, a different approach toward the very same topic is still possible. Studies building upon the, mainly theoretical, findings of this dissertation project that focus on the practical implications are certainly numerous and are not restricted to the following examples.

An empirical feasibility study could be undertaken prior to a potential introduction of *amicus curiae* briefs in legal disputes affecting the environment. This could possibly be executed via qualitative interviews with experts from the legal staff of the EU branches of environmental CSOs (for instance the G10) and administrative staff of the Court of Justice. Whether Advocates–General and Judges would be available for qualitative interviews is questionable. It might, however, be possible to draw up a questionnaire with prepared multiple–choice answers, although this method has its own flaws. The most pressing questions to be answered by such a study concern the possible time delay, the extent of the additional workload for both, ECJ staff and CSO members, and the estimated likelihood that such briefs could actually be considered by Advocates–General and Judges.

Evidently, *if* environmental *amici curiae* were to be introduced at the ECJ, an evaluation of the goals, the implementation and the problems possibly incurred, and its effects should be undertaken. Such a study could be executed on the basis of data collected on the number of cases whose merits affected the environment as opposed to those, in which *amicus curiae* briefs were filed. The latter would then have to be assessed with regard to whether these briefs were admitted or refused. If admitted, data would be needed to show, whether the parties allowed them or to what percentage the President granted leave. The final outcome of the decision would have to be compared with the content of the brief and data would also be needed to determine if the published reasoning of the GC or the ECJ referred to an *amicus curiae* brief and, if so, with what frequency. Again, qualitative interviews may aid to compare the goals that were sought by the *amici* with their personal feeling about success or failure.

A third study could be broader research into the feasibility of extending the concept of the *amicus curiae* into all or other specific policy areas, in which *locus standi* for non–privileged applicants might be similarly restricted and problematic when defending the general interest of a society; e.g. public health or aspects of social policy. However, the author's advice would be not to extend the admission of *amici curiae* to any policy area for the reasons given in chapter fifteen.

Of course, not only the stage of judicial evaluation deserves closer examination and further study. It is therefore suggested that theoretical and empirical research is also undertaken with regard to the changing access and participation opportunities for environmental CSOs at the political EU Institutions and each corresponding policy stage. The fact that this work has presented those opportunities rather positively results from a comparison of the less than full inclusion of non–state actors in judicial proceedings. It should not give a false impression and negate that improvements are still desirable, if not even necessary. Thus, continuous monitoring of participation opportunity structures throughout the policy cycle, as a whole, is essential to the further development of EU policy–making.

This dissertation has contributed a proposal on how to improve access to European justice for environmental civil society organizations and attempted to thereby enhance overall policy participation in an area of great public interest.

Bibliography

Literature

Books

Alter, Karen Jane
2001, *Establishing the Supremacy of European law*, New York: Oxford University Press.

Anheier, Helmut; Glasius, Marlies & Kaldor, Mary
2001, *Introducing Global Civil Society*, in: Helmut Anheier, Marlies Glasius & Mary Kaldor (eds.), "Yearbook of Global Civil Society 2001" (pp.3–22), The Centre for the Study of Global Governance, retrieved 09/21/2010 from the WWW: http://www.lse.ac.uk/Depts/global/Publications/Yearbooks/2001/2001chapter1.pdf

Anheier, Helmut & Themudo, Nuno
2002, *Organisational Forms of Global Civil Society: Implications of Going Global*, in: Helmut Anheier, Marlies Glasius & Mary Kaldor (eds.), "Yearbook of Global Civil Society 2002" (pp.191–216), The Centre for the Study of Global Governance, retrieved 09/21/2010 from the WWW: http://www.lse.ac.uk/Depts/global/Publications/Yearbooks/2002/2002chapter8.pdf

Anheier, Helmut
2004, *Civil Society, Measurement, Evaluation, Policy*, London: Earthscan Publications Ltd.

Andrusevych, Andriy
2003, *Access to justice on the international level: Citizen enforcement under theNorth American Agreement on Environmental Cooperation*, in: Stephen Stec (ed.), "Handbook on Access to Justice under the Aarhus Convention" (pp.79–80), Szentendre: The Regional Environmental Center for Central and Eastern Europe. Retrieved 10/17/2010 from the WWW: http://www.unece.org/env/pp/a.to.j/handbook.final.pdf

Bauer, Lukas
2008, *Der Europäische Gerichtshof als Verfassungsgericht?*, in Reihe: "Schriften zum internationalen und vergleichenden öffentlichen Recht", Band 6, Baden–Baden: Nomos.

Beetham, David & Lord, Christopher
1998, *Legitimacy and the European Union*, in: Michael Nentwich & Albert Weale (eds.), "Theory and the European Union: Legitimacy, Constitutional Choice and Citizenship" (pp.15–34), London: Routledge.

Bellier, Irène
1997, *The Commission as an Actor: An Anthropologist's View*, in: Helen Wallace & Alasdair Young (eds.), "Participation and Policy–Making in the European Union" (pp.91–115), Oxford: Oxford University Press.

Bieber, Roland, Epiney, Astrid & Haag, Marcel
2005, *Die Europäische Union. Europarecht und Politik*, 6. Auflage, Baden–Baden: Nomos.

Blum, Sonja & Schubert, Klaus
2009, *Politikfeldanalyse*, Wiesbaden: VS Verlag für Sozialwissenschaften.

Chandhoke, Neera
2002, *The Limits of Global Civil Society*, in: Helmut Anheier, Marlies Glasius & Mary Kaldor (eds.), "Yearbook of Global Civil Society 2002" (pp.35–53), The Centre for the Study of Global Governance, retrieved 09/21/2010 from the WWW: http://www.lse.ac.uk/Depts/global/Publications/Yearbooks/2002/2002chapter2.pdf

Charrad, Kristina
2008, *Lobbying and European Civil Society: Problems and Perspectives of Civil Society Actors from Visegrád Countries*, in: Freise (ed.), "European Civil Society on the Road to Success?" (pp.109–128), Baden–Baden: Nomos.

Cichowski, Rachel A.
2007, *The European Court and Civil Society. Litigation, Mobilization and Governance*, Cambridge: Cambridge University Press.

Craig, Paul
2008, *Fundamental rights*, in: Philip Moser & Katrine Sawyer (eds.), "Making Community Law. The Legacy of Advocate General Jacobs at the European Court of Justice" (pp.54-76), Cheltenham: Edwards Elgar Publishing Limited.

de Bùrca, Graínne
2003, *The European Court of Justice and the Evolution of EU Law*, in: Tanja A. Börzel & Rachel A. Cichowski (eds.), "The State of the European Union. Law, Politics, and Society", Vol. 6 (pp.48–75), Oxford: Oxford University Press.

Dobler, Philipp
2008, *Legitimation und Grenzen der Rechtsfortbildung durch den EuGH*, in: Peter Hilpold & Günther H. Roth (eds.), "Der EuGH und die Souveränität der Mitgliedstaaten. Eine kritische Analyse richterlicher Rechtsschöpfung auf ausgewählten Rechtsgebieten" (pp.509-559), Wien: Linde Verlag.

Eisele, Gudrun
2008, *Towards Visibility and Representativeness? Perspectives of the European Economic and Social Committee*, in: Matthias Freise (ed.), "European Civil Society on the Road to Success?" (pp.87–108), Baden–Baden: Nomos.

Freise, Matthias
2008a, *Introduction: European Civil Society on the Road to success?* (pp.9–22) and *The Civil Society Discourse in Brussels. Between Societal Grievances and Utopian Ideas* (pp.23–44) in: Matthias Freise (eds.), "European Civil Society on the Road to Success?", Baden-Baden: Nomos.

Friedrich, Dawid
2008, *Actual and Potential Contributions of Civil Society Organisations to Democratic EU Governance*, in: Freise (ed.) "European Civil Society on the Road to Success?" (pp.67–86), Baden–Baden: Nomos.

Gbikpi, Bernard & Grote, Jürgen, R.
2002, *From Democratic Government to Participatory Governance*, in: Bernard Gbikpi

& Jürgen, R. Grote (eds.), "Participatory Governance. Political and Social Implications" (pp.1–34), Opladen: Leske + Budrich.

Glasius, Marlies
2002, *Expertise in the Cause of Justice: Global Civil Society Influence on the Statute for an International Criminal Court*, in: Helmut Anheier, Marlies Glasius & Mary Kaldor (eds.), "Yearbook of Global Civil Society 2002" (pp.137–168), The Centre for the Study of Global Governance, retrieved 09/21/2010 from the WWW: http://www.lse.ac.uk/Depts/global/Publications/Yearbooks/2002/2002chapter6.pdf

Greenwood, Justin
2007a, *Interest Representation in the European Union*, Second Edition, Basingstoke: Palgrave Macmillan.

Greenwood, Justin
2007b, *Organized Civil Society and Input Legitimacy in the EU*, in: Joan De Bardeleben & Achim Hurrelman (eds.), "Democratic Dilemmas of Multilevel Governance – Legitimacy, Representation and Accountability in the European Union" (pp.174–193), Hampshire: Macmillan Publishers Ltd.

Harratsch, Andreas; Koenig, Christian & Pechstein, Matthias
2009, *Europarecht*, 6. Auflage, Tübingen: Mohr Siebeck.

Heinrich, Finn
2008, *Assessing Civil Society in Europe: Comparative Findings of the CIVICUS Civil Society Index* in: Freise (ed.), "European Civil Society on the Road to Success?" (pp.45-66), Baden–Baden: Nomos.

Hilger, Peter
2008, *Engagement Policies in European Governance*, in: Freise (ed.), "European Civil Society on the Road to Success?" (pp.181–200), Baden–Baden: Nomos.

Holzinger, Katharina
2005, *Institutionen und Entscheidungsprozesse der EU*, in: Katharina Holzinger, Christoph Knill, Dirk Peters, Berthold Rittberger, Frank Schimmelfennig & Wolfgang Wagner (eds.), "Die Europäische Union. Theorien und Analysekonzepte" (pp.81–152), Paderborn: Schöningh UTB Verlag.

Howlett, Michael & Ramesh, M.
2003, *Studying Public Policy: Policy Cycles and Policy Subsystems*, Oxford: Oxford University Press.

Jann, Werner & Wegrich, Kai
2003, *Phasenmodelle und Politikprozesse: Der Policy Cycle*, in: Klaus Schubert & Nils Bandelow (eds.), "Lehrbuch der Politikfeldanalyse" (pp.71–104), München: Oldenbourg Wissenschaftsverlag.

Jans, Jan H.
2003, *EU Environmental Policy and the Civil Society*, in: Jan H. Jans (ed.), "The European Convention and the Future of European Environmental Law" (pp.53–66), Groningen: Europa Law Publishing

Knill, Christoph
2005, *Die Politiken der EU*, in: Katharina Holzinger, Christoph Knill, Dirk Peters, Berthold Rittberger, Frank Schimmelfennig & Wolfgang Wagner (eds.), "Die Europäische Union. Theorien und Analysekonzepte" (pp.81–152), Paderborn: Schöningh UTB Verlag.

Knodt, Michèle & Große Hüttmann, Martin
2006, *Der Multi–Level Governance–Ansatz*, in: Hans–Jürgen Bieling & Marika Lerch (eds.), "Theorien der europäischen Integration", 2. Auflage (pp.223–247), Wiesbaden: VS Verlag für Sozialwissenschaften.

Kohler–Koch, Beate
1997, *Organized Interests in European Integration: The Evolution of a New Type of Governance?*, in: Helen Wallace & Alasdair Young (eds.), "Participation and Policy–Making in the European Union" (pp.42–68), Oxford: Clarendon Press.

Kohler–Koch, Beate
2008, *Does Participatory Governance Hold its Promises?* in: Beate Kohler–Koch, Fabrice Larat (eds.), "Efficient and Democratic Governance in the European Union", CONNEX Report Series Vol. 9 (pp.265–295), Mannheim.

Kravchenko, S., Skrylnikov, D. & Bonine, J.
2003, *Access to Justice in cases involving public participation in decision–making*, in: Stephen Stec (ed.) "Handbook on Access to Justice under the Aarhus Convention" (pp.27–30), Szentendre: The Regional Environmental Center for Central and Eastern Europe. Retrieved 10/17/2010 from the WWW: http://www.unece.org/env/pp/a.to.j/handbook.final.pdf

Lasok, Paul; Millet, Timothy & Howard, Anneli (eds.)
2004, *Judicial control in the EU - procedures and principles*, Richmond: Richmond Law and Tax.

Lenaerts, Koen & van Nuffel, Piet
2005, *Constitutional Law of the European Union*, second edition (edited by Robert Bray), London: Thomson Sweet & Maxwell.

Lovan, Robert W.; Murray, Michael & Shaffer, Ron
2004, *Participatory Democracy in a Changing World*, in: Robert W. Lovan, Michael Murray & Ron Shaffer (eds.), "Participatory Democracy: Planning, Conflict Mediation and Public Decision-Making in Civil Society" (pp.1-22), Aldershot: Ashgate Publishing Ltd.

Mahoney, Christine
2008, *The role of interest groups in fostering citizen engagement: the determinants of outside lobbying*, in: William A. Maloney & Jan Van Deth (eds.), "Civil Society and Governance in Europe. From National to International Linkages" (pp.170–192), Cheltenham: Edward Elgar Publishing Limited.

Maloney, William A. & Van Deth, Jan
2008, *Introduction: from bottom-up and top-down towards multi-level governance in Europe* (pp.3–18) and *Conclusion: Europeanization, multi–level governance and civil society* (pp.241–252), in: William A. Maloney & Jan Van Deth (eds.), "Civil Society and Governance in Europe. From National to International Linkages", Cheltenham: Edward Elgar Publishing Limited.

Mazey, Sonia & Richardson, Jeremy
2006, *Interest groups and EU policy–making: organisational logic and venue shopping*, in: Jeremy Richardson (ed.), "European Union: Power and Policy–Making", third edition (pp.239-260), London: Routledge.

McCown, Margaret
2006, *Judicial law–making and European integration*, in: Jeremy Richardson (ed.), "European Union: Power and Policy Making", third edition (pp.171–186), London: Routledge.

Meyer–Ohlendorf, Nils
2004, *Strategien europäischer Umweltverbände zur Interessendurchsetzung*, in: Carola Ensslen, Doris König & W. Rainer Walz (eds.), "Interessenvermittlung durch NGOs auf EU–Ebene. Beiträge zum Symposium am 11. Juni 2004 an der Bucerius Law School" (pp.97–102), Hamburg: Mauke–Verlag.

Michalowitz, Irene
2005, *Assessing Conditions for Influence of Interest Groups in the EU*, Wien: Institut für Höhere Studien (HIS).

Nentwich, Michael
1998, *Opportunity structures for citizens' participation. The case of the European Union*, in: Michael Nentwich & Albert Weale (eds.), "Theory and the European Union: Legitimacy, Constitutional Choice and Citizenship" (pp.125–140), London: Routledge

Nölke, Andreas
2006, *Supranationalismus*, in: Hans–Jürgen Bieling & Marika Lerch (eds.), "Theorien der europäischen Integration", 2. Auflage (pp.145-168), Wiesbaden: VS Verlag für Sozialwissenschaften.

Oppermann, Thomas, Classen, Claus Dieter & Nettesheim, Martin
2009, *Europarecht*, 4. Auflage, München: C.H. Beck.

Randzio–Plath, Christa
2004, *Interessenvertretung durch NGOs auf EU–Ebene*, in: Carola Ensslen, Doris König & W. Rainer Walz (eds.), "Interessenvermittlung durch NGOs auf EU–Ebene. Beiträge zum Symposium am 11. Juni 2004 an der Bucerius Law School" (pp.3–13), Hamburg: Mauke–Verlag.

Richardson, Jeremy
2006, *Policy Making in the EU: interests, ideas and garbage cans of primeval soup*, in: Richardson, Jeremy (ed.), "European Union: Power and Policy Making", third edition (pp.2–29), London: Routledge.

Rohan, Brian & Jacobstein, David
2003, *Remedies*, in: Stephen Stec (ed.), "Handbook on Access to Justice under the Aarhus Convention" (pp.49–54), Szentendre: The Regional Environmental Center for Central and Eastern Europe. Retrieved 10/17/2010 from the WWW: http://www.unece.org/env/pp/a.to.j/handbook.final.pdf

Rosamond, Ben
2000, *Theories of European Integration*, Basingstoke: Macmillan

Rust, Ursula
2004, *Der rechtliche Rahmen des Dialogs mit der Zivilgesellschaft auf EU–Ebene*, in: Carola Ensslen, Doris König & W. Rainer Walz (eds.), "Interessenvermittlung durch NGOs auf EU–Ebene. Beiträge zum Symposium am 11. Juni 2004 an der Bucerius Law School" (pp.97–102), Hamburg: Mauke–Verlag.

Savoia, Remo
2003, *Administrative, judicial and other means for access to justice*, in: Stephen Stec (ed.) "Handbook on Access to Justice under the Aarhus Convention (pp.39–41), Szentendre:

The Regional Environmental Center for Central and Eastern Europe. Retrieved 10/17/2010 from the WWW: http://www.unece.org/env/pp/a.to.j/handbook.final.pdf

Savoia, Remo & Skrylnikov, Dmitry
2003, *Access to Justice in cases involving access to environmental information*, in: Stephen Stec (ed.) "Handbook on Access to Justice under the Aarhus Convention" (pp.23–25), Szentendre: The Regional Environmental Center for Central and Eastern Europe. Retrieved 10/17/2010 from the WWW: http://www.unece.org/env/pp/a.to.j/handbook.final.pdf

Scharpf, Fritz W.
2009, *Legitimacy in the multilevel European polity*, Köln: Max–Planck–Institut für Gesellschaftsforschung.

Schmidt, Manfred G.
2008, *Demokratietheorien. Eine Einführung*, 4. Auflage, Wiesbaden: VS Verlag für Sozialwissenschaften.

Schneider, Volker & Janning, Frank
2006, *Politikfeldanalyse. Akteure, Diskurse und Netzwerke in der öffentlichen Politik*, Wiesbaden: VS Verlag für Sozialwissenschaften.

Senior Nello, Susan
2005, *The European Union. Economics, Policies and History*, Berkshire: McGraw Hill Education.

Stec, Stephen
2003, *Rights and duties towards a healthy environment*, in: Stephen Stec (ed.), Handbook on Access to Justice under the Aarhus Convention" (pp.73–75), Szentendre: The Regional Environmental Center for Central and Eastern Europe. Retrieved 10/17/2010 from the WWW: http://www.unece.org/env/ pp/a.to.j/handbook.final.pdf

Thiele, Alexander
2007, *Europäisches Prozessrecht*, Reihe: Juristische Kurz–Lehrbücher. Müchen: C.H. Beck.

Tridimas, Takis & Poli, Sara
2008, *Locus standi of individuals under Article 230(4)EC: the return of Euridice?*, in: Moser, Philip & Sawyer, Katrine (eds.), "Making Community Law. The Legacy of Advocate General Jacobs at the European Court of Justice" (pp.77–99), Cheltenham: Edwards Elgar Publishing Limited.

Wainwright, Hilary
2004–5, *Civil Society, Democracy and Power: Global Connections*, in: Helmut Anheier, Marlies Glasius & Mary Kaldor (eds.), "Yearbook of Global Civil Society 2004–5" (pp.95–119), The Centre for the Study of Global Governance, retrieved 09/21/2010 from the WWW: http://www.lse.ac.uk/Depts/global/Publications/Yearbooks/2004/Chapter504.pdf

Weale, Albert
1998, *Between representation and constitutionalism in the European Union*, in: Michael Nentwich & Albert Weale (eds.), "Theory and the European Union: Legitimacy, Constitutional Choice and Citizenship" (pp.51–64), London: Routledge.

Weber, Karl unter Mitarbeit von Engel, Christopher & Wasserer, Simone
2008, *Der Transitverkehr in der Judikatur des EuGH: Spannungsfeld zwischen Warenverkehrsfreiheit und Umweltschutz*, in: Peter Hilpold & Günther H. Roth (eds.), "Der

EuGH und die Souveränität der Mitgliedstaaten. Eine kritische Analyse richterlicher Rechtsschöpfung auf ausgewählten Rechtsgebieten" (pp.395-426), Wien: Linde Verlag.

Wessels, Wolfgang
1997, *The Growth and Differentiation of Multi–Level Networks: A Corporatist Mega–Bureaucracy or an Open City?*, in: Helen Wallace & Alasdair R. Young (eds.), "Participation and Policy–Making in the European Union" (pp.17–41), Oxford: Clarendon Press.

Wolf, Klaus Dieter
2002, *Contextualizing Normative Standards for Legitimate Governance beyond the State*, in: Bernhard Gbikpi & Jürgen R. Grote (eds.), "Participatory Governance. Political and Social Implications" (pp.36–49), Opladen: Leske + Budrich.

Zimmer, Annette & Sittermann, Birgit
2004, *Brussels Civil Society–Definition of NGOs und ihre Mitwirkung in den Politikprozessen der EU*, in: Carola Ensslen; Doris König & W. Rainer Walz (eds.), "Interessenvermittlung durch NGOs auf EU–Ebene. Beiträge zum Symposium am 11. Juni 2004 an der Bucerius Law School", Hamburg: Mauke–Verlag.

Zimmer, Annette & Freise, Matthias
2008, *Bringing Society Back In: Civil Society, Social Capital, and Third Sector*,in: William A. Maloney & Jan Van Deth (eds.) "Civil Society and Governance in Europe" (pp.19–42), Cheltenham: Edward Elgar.

Zittel, Thomas
2007, *Participatory democracy and political participation*, in: Thomas Zittel Dieter Fuchs (eds.), "Participatory Democracy and Political Participation. Can participatory engineering bring citizens back in?" (pp.9–28), London: Routledge.

Dissertations

Busse–Muskala, Dominika
2007, *Normenkontrolle in der Europäischen Union. Zu den Direktklagemöglichkeiten von Individuen gegen EU-/EG-Normativakte*, Dissertation: Frankfurt/Oder, Europäische Hochschulschriften: Reihe 2, Rechtswissenschaft, Frankfurt/Main: Lang.

Dederichs, Mariele
2004, *Die Methodik des EuGH. Häufigkeit und Bedeutung methodischer Argumente in den Begründungen des Gerichtshofes der Europäischen Gemeinschaften*, Dissertation: Münster (Westf.), Schriftenreihe Europäisches Recht, Politik und Wirtschaft, Baden–Baden: Nomos.

Kwanka, Siegfried
2006, *Die Einwirkungen des Europarechts auf den vorläufigen Rechtsschutz im nationalen Verwaltungsprozess*, Dissertation: Passau, Frankfurt/Main: *Studien und Materialien zum Öffentlichen Recht*, Band 27, Peter Lang Europäischer Verlag der Wissenschaften.

Neugärtner, Ilka
2002, *Die actio popularis in der WTO*, Dissertation: Hamburg, retrieved 09/08/2010 from the WWW: http://deposit.ddb.de/cgi–bin/dokserv?idn=965588009&dok_var=d1&dok_ext=pdf&filename=965588009.pdf

Sloot, Lars
2005, *Die Lehre von den implied powers im Recht der Europäischen Gemeinschaften*, Dissertation: Köln, Aachen: Shaker.

Thiele, Alexander
2006, *Individualrechtsschutz vor dem Europäischen Gerichtshof durch die Nichtigkeitsklage*, Dissertation: Göttingen, Schriften des Europa–Instituts der Universität des Saarlandes–Rechtswissenschaft, Band 68, Baden–Baden: Nomos.

Tohidipur, Timo
2008, *Europäische Gerichtsbarkeit im Institutionensystem der EU. Zu Genese und Zustand justizieller Konstitutionalisierung*, Dissertation: Frankfurt/Main, Nomos Universitätsschriften, Recht, Band. 571, Baden–Baden: Nomos.

Journal Articles

Ala'i, Padideh
2000, *Judicial Lobbying at the WTO: The Debate over the Use of Amicus Curiae Briefs and The U.S. Experience*, in: *Fordham International Law Journal*, Vol.24, No.1 (pp.62–94), New York: Fordham University School of Law. Retrieved 10/13/2010 from the WWW: http://ssrn.com/abstract=1557893

Albors–Llorens, Albertina
1999, *Locus Standi of Private Parties in Environmental Cases*, in: *The Cambridge Law Journal*, Vol.58, No.1 (pp. 33–36), Cambridge: Cambridge University Press. Retrieved 01/02/2010 from the WWW: http://www.jstor.org/stable/4508523

Albors–Llorens, Albertina
2003, *The Standing of Private Parties to Challenge Community Measures: Has the European Court Missed the Boat?*, in: *The Cambridge Law Journal*, Vol.62, No.1 (pp.72-92), Cambridge: Cambridge University Press. Retrieved 01/02/2010 from the WWW: http://www.jstor.org/stable/4508970

Alter, Karen J.
2000, *The European Union's Legal System and Domestic Policy: Spillover or Backlash?*, in: *International Organization*, Vol.54 No.3 (pp.489–518), Cambridge Journals Online: Cambridge University Press. Retrieved 10/13/2010 from the WWW, doi: 10.1162/002081800551307.

Alter, Karen J. & Vargas, Jeannette
2000, *Explaining Variation in the Use of European Litigation Strategies: European Community Law and British Gender Equality Law*, in: *Comparative Political Studies*, Vol.33 No.4 (pp.452–482), Sage. Retrieved 01/12/2009 from the WWW, doi: 10.1177/0010414005283216

Angell, Ernest
1967, *The Amicus Curiae American Development of English Institutions*, in: *International and Comparative Law Quarterly*, Vol.16 (pp.1017–1044), Cambridge Journals, Cambridge: Cambridge University Press. Retrieved 10/13/2010 from the WWW, doi: 10.1093/iclqaj/16.4.1017

Armstrong, Kenneth A.
2002, *Rediscovering Civil Society: The European Union and the White Paper on Governance*, in: *European Law Journal*, Vol.8, No.1 (pp.102–132), Blackwell Publishers Ltd. Retrieved 10/13/2010 from the WWW: http://web.ebscohost.com /ehost/pdfviewer/pdfviewer?vid=2&hid=105&sid=1dc99e42-9585-4d1c-affb-1036ddae a620%40sessionmgr111

Baumeister, Peter
2005, *Effektiver Individualrechtsschutz im Gemeinschaftsrecht*, in: *Europarecht (EuR)*, Heft 1, (pp.1–35), Baden–Baden: Nomos.

Bilder, Richard B.
1989, *International Third Party Dispute Settlement*, in: *Denver Journal of International Law & Policy*, Vol.17, No.3 (pp.471–503), Denver: University of Denver College of Law. Retrieved 10/13/2010 from the WWW: http://ssrn.com/abstract=1641166

Bouwen, Pieter & McCown, Margaret
2007, *Lobbying versus litigation: political and legal strategies of interest representation in the European Union*, in: *Journal of European Public Policy*, Vol.14, No.3 (pp.422–443), London: Routledge. Retrieved 07/24/2010 from the WWW, doi: 10.1080/13501760701243798

Börzel, Tanja A.
2006, *Participation Through Law Enforcement: The Case of the European Union*, in: *Comparative Political Studies*, Vol.39 (pp.128–152), Sage Journals Online. Retrieved 01/12/2009 from the WWW, doi:10.1177/0010414005283220

Caldeira, Gregory A. & Wright, John R.
1990, *Amici Curiae before the Supreme Court: Who Participates, When, and How Much?*, in: *The Journal of Politics*, Vol.52, No.3 (pp.782-806), Cambridge: Cambridge University Press. Retrieved 02/03/2010 from the WWW: http://www.jstor.org/stable/2131827

Charnovitz, Steve
2000, *Opening the WTO to Non-Governmental Interests*, in: *Fordham International Law Journal*, Vol.24 (pp.1–35), New York: Fordham University School of Law. Retrieved 10/20/2010 from the WWW: http://www.worldtradelaw.net/articles/charnovitzngos.pdf

Cichowski, Rachel A.
1998, *Integrating the environment: the European Court and the construction of supranational policy*, in: *Journal of European Public Policy* Vol.5, No.3 (pp.387–405), London: Routledge. Retrieved 10/13/2010 from the WWW, doi: 10.1080/135017698343884

Cichowski, Rachel A.
2006, *Courts, Rights and Democratic Participation*, in: *Comparative Political Studies*, Vol.39 (pp.50–75), Sage Journals Online. Retrieved 01/12/2009 from the WWW, doi: 10.1177/0010414005283217

Collins, Paul M. Jr.
2004, *Friends of the Court: Examining the Influence of Amicus Curiae Participation in U.S. Supreme Court Litigation*, in: *Law & Society Review*, Vol.38 No.4 (pp.807–832), Blackwell Publishing. Retrieved 02/03/2010 from the WWW: http://www.jstor.org/stable/1555091

Costa, Olivier
2003, *The European Court of Justice and democratic control in the European Union*, in: *Journal of European Public Policy*, Vol.10, No.5 (pp.740–761), Routledge. Retrieved 01/24/2009 from the WWW, doi: 10.1080/1350176032000124069

Crossen, Teall & Niessen, Veronique
2007, *NGO standing in the European Court of Justice Does the Aarhus regulation open the door?*, in: *Review of European Community and International Environmental Law* (RECIEL), Vol.16, No.33 (pp.332-341), Oxford: Wiley Blackwell. Retrieved 10/13/2010 from the WWW, doi: 10.1111/j.1467–9388.2007.00569.x

de Bùrca, Graínne
1996, *The Quest for Legitimacy in the European Union*, in: *The Modern Law Review*, Vol.59, No.3 (pp.349–376), Blackwell Publishing. Retrieved 07/22/2009 from the WWW: http://www.jstor.org/stable/1097363

Dougan, Michael
2008, *The Treaty of Lisbon 2007: Winning Minds, not Hearts*, in: *Common Market Law Review*, Vol.45, No.3 (pp.617–703), Kluwer Law International. Retrieved 10/13/2010 from the WWW: http://www.kluwerlawonline.com/document.php?id=COLA2008047&type=toc&num=2&PHPSESSID=896j7paopd70gf6r215gaq7ct4

Dür, Andreas
2008, *Interest Groups in the European Union: How Powerful Are They?*, in: *West European Politics*, Vol.31, No.6 (pp.1212–1230), London: Routledge. Retrieved 07/24/2010 from the WWW, doi: 10.1080/01402380802372662

Finke, Barbara
2007, *Civil society participation in EU governance*, in: *Living Reviews in European Governance* (Online Article), Vol.2, No.2. Retrieved 07/24/2010 from the WWW: http://www.livingreviews.org/lreg–2007–2

Flango, Victor E., Bross, Donald C. & Corbally, Sarah
2006, *Amicus Curiae Briefs: The Court's Perspective*, in: *The Justice System Journal*, Vol.27, No.2 (pp.180–190) HeinOnline. Retrieved 10/13/2010 from the WWW: http://www.hein online.org/HOL/Page?handle=hein.journals/jusj27& id=1& size=2 & collection=journals& index=journals/jusj 206

Freise, Matthias
2008b, *Mehr als bloß ein Feigenblatt? Der Zivilgesellschaftsdiskurs in Brüssel*, retrieved 10/17/2010 from the WWW: http://nez.uni-muenster.de/download/Freise_mehr_als_bloss_ein_feigenblatt.pdf

Geddes, Andrew
1992, *Locus Standi and EEC Environmental measures*, in: *Journal of Environmental Law*, Vol.4, No.1 (pp.29–39), Oxford: Oxford University Press. Retrieved 10/13/2010 from the WWW, doi: 10.1093/jel/4.1.29

Gérard, Nicole
1996, *Access to Justice on Environmental Matters - a case of Double Standards?: Greepeace and Others v Commission of the European Communities*, in: *Journal of Environmental Law*, Vol.8 No.1 (pp.139–157), Oxford: Oxford University Press. Retrieved 09/03/2008 from the WWW, doi: 10.1093/jel/8.1.139

Gérard, Nicole
1998, *Access to the European Court of Justice: A Lost Opportunity Stichting Greenpeace Council (Greenpeace International) and Others v Commission*, in: *Journal of Environmental Law*, Vol.10, No.2 (pp.331–346), Oxford: Oxford University Press. Retrieved 09/03/2008 from the WWW, doi: 10.1093/jel/10.2.331

Greenwood, Justin
2007c, *Review Article: Organized Civil Society and Democratic Legitimacy in the European Union* in: *British Journal of Political Science* Vol.37 (pp.333–357), Cambridge University Press. Retrieved 10/13/2010 from the WWW, doi: 10.1017/S0007123407000166

Hansford, Thomas G.
2004, *Information Provision, Organizational Constraints, and the Decision to Submit an Amicus Curiae Brief in a U.S. Supreme Court Case*, in: *Political Research Quarterly*, Vol.57, No.2 (pp.219–230), Sage Journals Online. Retrieved 03/02/2010 from the WWW, doi: 10.1177/106591290405700204

Harlow, Carol
1992, *A Community of Interests? Making the Most of European Law*, in: *The Modern Law Review*, Vol.55, No.3 (pp.331–350), Blackwell Publishing. Retrieved 02/21/2009 from the WWW: http://www.jstor.org/stable/1096405

Harlow, Carol
2002, *Public Law and Popular Justice*, in: *The Modern Law Review*, Vol.65, No.1, Blackwell Publisher Ltd. Retrieved 10/13/2010 from the WWW: http://www.jstor.org/pss/1097514

Hedman, Susan
1991, *Friends of the Earth and Friends of the Court: Assessing the Impact of Interest Group Amici Curiae in Environmental Cases Decided by the Supreme Court* in: *Virginia Environmental Law Journal*, Vol.10 (pp.187–212), HeinOnline. Retrieved 10/13/2010 from the WWW: http://www.heinonline.org/HOL/Page?page=187&handle=hein.journals%2Fvelj10&colle ction=journals

Hilson, Chris
2002, *New social movements: the role of legal opportunity*, in: *Journal of European Public Policy*, Vol.9, No.2 (pp.238-255), Routledge. Retrieved 10/13/2010 from the WWW, doi: 10.1080/13501760110120246

Hollis, Duncan B.
2002, *Private Actors in Public International Law: Amicus Curiae and the Case for the Retention of State Sovereignty*, in: *Boston College International & Comparative Law Review*, Vol.25 (pp.235–255), Boston: Boston College Law School. Retrieved 10/13/2010 from the WWW: http://www.heinonline.org/HOL/Page?page=235&handle=hein.journals%2Fbcic25&collection=journals

Howse, Robert
2003, *Membership and its Privileges: the WTO, Civil Society, and the Amicus Brief Controversy*, in: *European Law Journal*, Vol.9, No.4 (pp.496–510), Blackwell Publishing. Retrieved 10/13/2010 from the WWW, doi: 10.1111/14680386.00188

Jacobs, Francis
2006, *The role of the European Court of Justice in the protection of the environment*, in: *Journal of Environmental Law*, Vol.18, No 2 (pp.185-205), Oxford: Oxford University Press. Retrieved 10/13/2010 from the WWW, doi: 10.1093/jel/eql012.

Kohler–Koch, Beate & Finke, Barbara
2007, *The Institutional Shaping of EU-Society Relations: A Contribution to Democracy via Participation?* in: *Journal of Civil Society*, Vol.3, No.3 (pp.205–219), London: Routledge. Retrieved 07/24/2010 from the WWW, doi: 10.1080/17448680701775630

Kohler–Koch, Beate
2010, *Civil society and EU democracy: 'astroturf' representation?* in: *Journal of European Public Policy*, Vol.17, No.1 (pp.100–116), London: Routledge. Retrieved 07/21/2010 from the WWW, doi: 10.1080/13501760903464986

Krämer, Ludwig
1996, *Public interest litigation in environmental matters before European courts*, in: *Journal of Environmental Law*, Vol.8 (pp.1–18), Oxford Journals, Oxford: Oxford University Press.

Krämer, Ludwig
2006, *Statistics on Environmental Judgments by the EC Court of Justice*, in: *Journal of Environmental Law*, Vol.18, No.3 (pp.407–421), Oxford: Oxford University Press. Retrieved 10/13/2010 from the WWW, doi: 10.1093/jel/eql019.

Krislov, Samuel
1963, *The Amicus Curiae Brief: From Friendship to Advocacy* in: *Yale Law Journal*, Vol.72, No.4 (pp.694–721). Retrieved 03/02/2010 from the WWW: http://www.jstor.org/stable/794698

Lee, Maria & Abbott, Carolyn
2003, *The Usual Suspects? Public Participation Under the Aarhus Convention*, in: *The Modern Law Review Limited*, Vol.66, No.1, (pp.80–108), Oxford: Blackwell Publishing Ltd. Retrieved 10/13/2010 from the WWW, doi: 10.1111/j.1467–9388.2007.00569.x

Mattli, Walter & Burley, Anne–Marie
1993, *Europe before the Court: A Political Theory of Legal Integration*, in: *International Organizations* Vol.47, No.1 (pp.47–76), Cambridge Journals. Retrieved 10/13/2010 from the WWW, doi: 10.1017/S0020818300004707

Mattli, Walter & Slaughter, Anne–Marie
1998, *Revisiting the European Court of Justice*, in: *International Organizations*, Vol.52, No.1 (pp.177-209). Retrieved 10/13/2010 from the WWW: http://www.jstor.org/stable/2601331

Marceau, Gabrielle & Stilwell, Mathew
2001, *Practical Suggestions for Amicus Curiae Briefs before WTO Adjudicating Bodies*, in: *Journal of International Economic Law*, Vol.4, No.1 (pp.155–187), Oxford: Oxford University Press. Retrieved 10/13/2010 from the WWW, doi: 10.1093/jiel/4.1.155

McGuire, Kevin T.
1994, *Amici Curiae and Strategies for Gaining Access to the Supreme Court*, in: *Political Research Quarterly*, Vol.47, No.4 (pp.821–837), Sage Journals Online. Retrieved 03/02/2010 from the WWW, doi: 10.1177/106591299404700402

Morgera, Elisa
2005, *An Update on the Aarhus Convention and its Continued Global Relevance*, in: *Review of European Community and International Environmental Law*, Vol. 14, No.2 (pp.138-147), Oxford: Blackwell Publishing. Retrieved 10/13/2010 from the WWW, doi: 10.1111/j.1467-9388.2005.00434.x

Munford, Luther, T.
1999, *When does the Curiae need an Amicus?*, in: *The Journal of Appellate Practice and Process*, Vol.1, No.2 (pp.279–284), University of Arkansas at Little Rock. Retrieved 10/13/2010 from the WWW: http://heinonline.org/HOL/Landing Page?collection=journals&handle=hein.journals/jappp 1&div=24&id=&page=

Nentwich, Michael
1996, *Opportunity Structures for Citizens' Participation: The Case of the European Union*, European Integration Online Papers (EIOP) Vol.0, No.1 (pp.1–21). Retrieved 10/13/2010 from the WWW, doi: 10.2139/ssrn.302082

O'Connor, Karen & Epstein, Lee
1983, *Court Rules and Workload: A Case Study of Rules Governing Amicus Curiae Participation*, in: *The Justice System Journal*, Vol.8, No.1 (pp.35–45). Retrieved 10/13/2010 from the WWW: http://www.heinonline.org/HOL/Page?page=35&handle=hein.journals%2Fjusj8&collection=journals

Princen, Sebastiaan & Kerremans, Bart
2008, *Opportunity Structures in the EU Multi–Level System* in: *West European Politics*, Vol.31, No.6 (pp.1129–1146), London: Routledge. Retrieved 07/24/2010 from the WWW, doi: 10.1080/01402380802370484

Rodenhoff, Vera
2002, *The Aarhus Convention and its Implications for the 'Institutions' of the European Community*, in: *Review of European Community and International Environmental Law (RECIEL)* Vol.11, No.3 (pp.343-357), Blackwell Publishers Ltd. Retrieved 10/13/2010 from the WWW: http://web.ebscohost.com/ehost/pdfviewer/pdfviewer?vid=2&hid=105&sid=4b6832f1-ea95-40e4-ac9a-ab9a4aea2c6b%40sessionmgr104

Saurugger, Sabine
2008, *Interest Groups and Democracy in the European Union* in: *West European Politics* Vol.31, No.6 (pp.1274–1291), London: Routledge. Retrieved 07/22/2009 from the WWW, doi: 10.1080/01402380802374288

Schmitter, Philippe C.
2005, *Ernst B. Haas and the legacy of neofunctionalism*, in: *Journal of European Public Policy*, Vol.12, No.2 (pp.255–272), London: Routledge. Retrieved 07/08/2008 from the WWW, doi: 10.1080/13501760500043951

Shelton, Dinah
1994, *The Participation of Nongovernmental Organizations in International Judicial Proceedings*, in: *The American Journal of International Law*, Vol.88, No.4 (pp.611–642), American Society of International Law. Retrieved 03/08/2010 from the WWW: http://www.jstor.org/stable/2204133

Smismans, Stijn
2003, *European Civil Society: Shaped by Discourses and Institutional Interests*, in; *European Law Journal*, Vol.9, No.4 (pp.473–495), Blackwell Publishers Ltd. Retrieved 10/13/2010 from the WWW, doi: 10.1111/1468-0386.00187

Songer, Donald R. & Sheehan, Reginald, S.
1993, *Interest Group Success in the Courts: Amicus Participation in the Supreme Court*,

in: *Political Research Quarterly*, Vol.46, No.2 (pp.339–354), Sage Journals Online. Retrieved 03/15/2010 from the WWW, doi: 10.1177/106591299304600207

Spagnuolo, Francesca
2009, *Beyond Participation: Administrative–Law Type Mechanisms in Global Environmental Governance. Toward a New Basis of Legitimacy?*, in: *European Public Law*, Vol.15, No.1 (pp.49–62), Kluwer Law International. Retrieved 10/13/2010 from the WWW: http://www.kluwerlawonline.com/document.php?id=EURO2009004&type=toc&num=4&

Spriggs, James F. & Wahlbeck, Paul J.
1997, *Amicus Curiae and the Role of Information at the Supreme Court*, in: *Political Research Quarterly*, Vol.50, No.2 (pp.365–386), Sage Journals Online. Retrieved 03/02/2010 from the WWW, doi: 10.1177/106591299705000206

Stone Sweet, Alec
2010, *The European Court of Justice and the judicialization of EU governance*, in: *Living Reviews in European Governance*, Vol.5, No.2. Retrieved 07/24/2010 from the WWW: http://www.livingreviews.org/lreg-2010-2.

Umbricht, Georg C.
2001, *An 'Amicus Curiae Brief' on Amicus Curiae Briefs at the WTO*, in: *Journal of International Economic Law* Vol.4, No.4 (pp.773–794), Oxford: Oxford University Press. Retrieved 10/13/2010 from the WWW, doi: 10.1093/jiel/4.4.773

Wates, Jeremy
2005, *The Aarhus Convention: a Driving Force for Environmental Democracy*, in: Journal for European Environmental and Planning Law, Vol.2, No.1 (pp.2–11), Martinus Nijhoff Publishers. Retrieved 10/13/2010 from the WWW: http://www.estig.ipbeja.pt/ãc_direito/JEEPL_1_2005.pdf

Warleigh, Alex
2001, *'Europeanizing' Civil Society: NGOs as Agents of Political Socialization*, in: *Journal of Common Market Studies*, Vol.39, No.4 (pp.619–39), Blackwell Publishers Ltd. Retrieved 10/13/2001 from the WWW: http://web.ebscohost.com/ehost/pdfviewer/pdfviewer?vid=2&hid=105&sid=d79f3aff-8baa-44a8-81c7-e5e8e118fdb6%40sessionmgr113

Papers Presented at Conferences

Hallo, Ralph
2006, *Access to environmental information held by EU institutions and bodies. The Aarhus Regulation: New Opportunities for Citizens in the EU and Beyond?*, Report of the ECOSPHERE Forum held in Brussels, 27 October 2006 with the support of the Brussels Capital Region (pp.7–10). Retrieved 10/17/2010 from the WWW: http://ecosphere.be/pdfflyers/ReportForumOct2006.pdf

Rose–Ackermann, Susan & Halpaap, Achim A.
2001, *The Aarhus Convention and the Politics of Process: The Political Economy of Procedural Environmental Rights*, Draft paper for *The Law and Economics of Environmental Policy: A Symposium*, Faculty of Laws, University College London, September 5–7, 2001. Forthcoming in Timothy Swanson, ed., Research in Law and Economics (pp.1–42),

July 13, 2001. Retrieved 10/17/2010 from the WWW: http://www.ucl.ac.uk/cserge/ Ackerman_and_Halpaap.pdf

Sands, Philippe QC
2008, *Rethinking environmental rights - climate change, conservation and the European Court of Justice* presented on 11 June 2008: The Professor David Hall Memorial Lecture Environmental Law Foundation in association with the Law Society, Published in: *Environmental Law & Management*, 20 (pp.117–123), by: Lawtext Publishing Limited. Retrieved 10/19/2010 from the WWW: http://www.lawtext.com/pdfs/sampleArticles/ELM-20-3-Sands-final-07-07-08.pdf

Comparative Research Study

Milieu Ltd.
2007, *Inventory of EU Member States' measures on access to justice in environmental matters*, Brussels: Milieu Ltd, ordered by the Commission of the European Union. Retrieved 10/17/2010 from the WWW: http://ec.europa.eu/environment/aarhus/study_access.htm

Report

Hallo, Ralph
2007, *How far has the EU applied the Aarhus Convention?*, Report prepared for the European Environmental Bureau, Brussels: EEB (EEB Publication No.: 2007/010). Retrieved 10/17/2010 from the WWW: http://www.eeb.org/index.cfm/lib rary/index.cfm?month=10&year=2007

HM Treasury
2006, *Stern Review Report on the Economics of Climate Change*. Retrieved 09/09/2010 from the WWW: http://webarchive.nationalarchives.gov.uk/+/http://www.hm–treasury.gov.uk/sternreview_index.htm

Working Paper

Bignami, Francesca
2005, *Creating European Rights: National Values and Supranational Interests*, forthcoming in *11 Columbia Journal of European Law*, retrieved 08/09/2010 from the WWW: http://eprints.law.duke.edu/705/1/11_Colum._J._Eur._L._draft_4-2005.pdf

Dyevre, Arthur
2008/2009, *Making Sense of Judicial Lawmaking: A Theory of Theories of Adjudication. EUI Working Papers, Max Weber Programme*, European University Institute. Retrieved 10/17/2010 from the WWW: http://cadmus.iue.it/dspace/handle/1814/8510

Sandholtz, Wayne & Stone Sweet, Alec
2010, *Neo–functionalism and Supranational Governance*, forthcoming in the Oxford Handbook of the European Union, Oxford University Press, retrieved 09/06/2010 from the WWW: http://works.bepress.com/alec_stone_sweet/38

Stone Sweet, Alec & Brunell, Thomas
2010, *How the Legal System of the European Union Works – and Does Not Work: Response to Carruba, Gabel, and Hankla* (pp.1–40). Retrieved 10/17/2010 from the WWW: http://works.bepress.com/alec_stone_sweet/36/

Official Documents

African Union
African Charter on Human and Peoples' Rights, retrieved 09/13/2010 from the WWW: http://www.africa–union.org/official_documents/Treaties_Conventions_ProtocolsBanjul Charter.pdf

African Commission on Human and People's Rights
Protocol to the African Charter on Human and Peoples' Rights on the establishment of an African Court on Human and Peoples' Rights, retrieved 09/13/2010 from the WWW: http://www.achpr.org/english/_info/court_en.html

African Court on Human and Peoples' Rights
Interim Rules of Court, retrieved 09/13/2010 from the WWW: http://www.african–court.org/fileadmin/documents/Court/Interim%20Rules%20of%20Court/Interim%20Rul es%20of%20Court.pdf

Council of Europe
1950, *Convention for the Protection of Human Rights and Fundamental Freedoms (European Convention on Human Rights)*, retrieved 09/17/2010 from the WWW: http://conventions.coe.int/treaty/en/Treaties/Html/005.htm

Council of Europe
2003a, *Resolution Res(2003)8. Participatory status for international non–governmental organisations with the Council of Europe*, retrieved 09/21/2010 from the WWW: https://wcd.coe.int/ViewDoc.jsp?id=88953&Site=CM

Council of Europe
2003b, *Resolution Res(2003)9. Status of partnership between the Council of Europe and national non–governmental organisations*, retrieved 09/21/2010 from the WWW: https://wcd.coe.int/ViewDoc.jsp?id=88997&Site=CM

Council of Europe
2004, *Protocol No. 14 to the Convention for the Protection of Human Rights and Fundamental Freedoms, amending the control system of the Convention*, retrieved 10/18/2010 from the WWW: http://conventions.coe.int/Treaty/EN/Treaties/html/194.htm

European Free Trade Association
1993, *Agreement on the European Economic Area*, retrieved 10/20/2010 from the WWW: http://www.efta.int/eea/~media/Documents/legal-texts/eea/the-eea-agreement/Main %20Text%20of%20the%20Agreement/EEAagreement.ashx

International Court of Justice
Statute of the Court, retrieved 10/05/2010 from the WWW: http://www.icj–cij.org/docu ments/index.php?p1=4&p2=2&p3=0

International Court of Justice
1978, *Rules of Court* (last amended 14 April 2005), retrieved 10/05/2010 from the WWW: http://www.icj–cij.org/documents/index.php?p1=4&p2=3&p3=0&PHPSESSI D=cddcff975ce751e1529687ef7e1ebc48

International Criminal Court
2002 *Rules of Procedure and Evidence*, retrieved 10/05/2010 from the WWW: http://www.icc–cpi.int/NR/rdonlyres/F1E0AC1C–A3F3–4A3C–B9A7–B3E8B115E886/ 140164/Rules_of_procedure_and_Evidence_English.pdf

International Criminal Tribunal for Rwanda (ICTR)
1996, *Rules of Procedure and Evidence* (last amended 1 October 2009), retrieved 09/13/2010 from the WWW: http://69.94.11.53/ENGLISH/rules/080314/080314.pdf

International Tribunal for the Prosecution of Persons Responsible for Serious Violations of International Humanitarian Law Committed in the Territory of the Former Yugoslavia
1994, *Rules of Procedure and Evidence* (last amended 10 December 2009), retrieved 09/13/2010 from the WWW: http://www.icty.org/x/file/Legal%20Library/Rules_procedure_evidence/IT032_rev44_en.pdf

Secretariat of the Commission for Environmental Cooperation
1993, *North American Agreement on Environmental Cooperation*, retrieved 09/13/2010 from the WWW: http://www.worldtradelaw.net/nafta/naaec.pdf

Supreme Court of the United States
2010, *Rules of the Supreme Court of the United States*, retrieved 04/08/2010 from the WWW: http://www.supremecourt.gov/ctrules/2010RulesoftheCourt.pdf

United Nations
1948, *The Universal Declaration of Human Rights*, retrieved 09/17/2010 from the WWW: http://www.un.org/en/documents/udhr/index.shtml

United Nations Treaty Collection
1969, *Vienna Convention on the Law of Treaties*, retrieved 10/05/2010 from the WWW: http://untreaty.un.org/ilc/texts/instruments/english/conventions/1_1_1969.pdf

United Nations Environment Programme
1992, *Rio Declaration on Environment and Development*, retrieved 09/14/2010 from the WWW: http://www.unep.org/Documents.Multilingual/Default.asp?documentid =78&articleid=1163

United Nations Economic Commission for Europe
1998, *Convention on Access to Information, Public Participation in Decision–Making and Access to Justice in Environmental Matters (Aarhus Convention)*, retrieved 10/05/2010 from the WWW: http://www.unece.org/env/pp/documents/cep43e.pdf

United Nations Treaty Collection
Aarhus Convention, Parties & Declarations, Website (last visited: 07/16/2010): http://treaties.un.org/Pages/ViewDetails.aspx?src=TREATY&mtdsg_no=XXVII–13&chapter=27&lang=en

United Nations
2009, *ICTY Rules of Procedure and Evidence* Rev.44, retrieved 10/05/2010 from the WWW: http://www.icty.org/x/file/LegalLibrary/Rules_procedure_evidence/IT032_rev44_en.pdf

United Nations
2010, *ICTR Rules of Procedure and Evidence*, retrieved 10/05/2010 from: the WWW: http://www.unictr.org/Portals/0/English%5CLegal%5CROP%5C100209.pdf

World Trade Organization
Additional Procedure, retrieved 10/18/2010 from the WWW: http://www.wto.org/english/tratop_e/dispu_e/repertory_e/a2_e.htm#A.2.3

World Trade Organization
Understanding on rules and procedures governing the settlement of disputes, retrieved 10/19/2010 from the WWW: http://www.wto.org/english/tratop_e/dispu_e/dsu_e.htm

National Constitutions

Deutscher Bundestag
2010, *Basic Law for the Federal Republic of Germany*, retrieved 09/16/2010 from the WWW: https://www.btg–bestellservice.de/pdf/80201000.pdf

Senado de España
1992, *Spanish Constitution*, retrieved 09/16/2010 from the WWW: http://www.senado.es/constitu_i/indices/consti_ing.pdf

Tribunal Constitucional Portugal
2005, *Constitution of the Portuguese Republic* (seventh revision), retrieved 09/28/2010 from the WWW: http://www.tribunalconstitucional.pt/tc/conteudo/files/constituicaoingles.pdf

Ustavno sodišče (Constitutional Court of the Republic of Slovenia)
2006, *Constitution*, retrieved 09/16/2010 from the WWW: http://www.us–rs.si/media/full.text.of.the.constitution.pdf

Seijm Rzeczypospolitej Polskiej (Seijm of the Republic of Poland)
1997, *The Constitution of the Republic of Poland*, retrieved 09/16/2010 from the WWW: http://www.sejm.gov.pl/prawo/konst/angielski/kon1.htm

Official EU Documents

European Union
2008, *Treaty on European Union*, retrieved 10/05/2010 from the WWW: http://eur-lex.europa.eu/LexUriServ/LexUriServ.do?uri=OJ:C:2008:115:0013:0045:EN:PDF

European Union
2008, *Treaty on the Functioning of the European Union*, retrieved 10/05/2010 from the WWW: http://eur–lex.europa.eu/LexUriServ/LexUriServ.do?uri=OJ:C:2008:115:0047:0199:EN:PDF

Council of the European Union
1985, Directive 85/337/EEC of 27 June 1985 *on the assessment of the effects of certain public and private projects on the environment*, retrieved 10/05/2010 from the WWW: http://ec.europa.eu/environment/eia/full–legal–text/85337.htm

Council of the European Union
1990, Council Regulation (EEC) No 1210/90 of 7 May 1990 *on the establishment of the European Environment Agency and the European Environment Information and Observation Network*, retrieved 09/16/2010 from the WWW: http://eur–lex.europa.eu/ LexUriServ/LexUriServ.do?uri=CELEX:31990R1210:EN:HTML

Council of the European Union
1996, Directive 96/61/EC of 24 September 1996 *concerning integrated pollution prevention and control*, retrieved 10/05/2010 from the WWW: http://eur–lex.europa.eu/ LexUriServ/LexUriServ.do?uri=CELEX:31996L0061:en:HTML

Council of the European Union
2005, Council Decision of 17 February 2005 *on the conclusion, on behalf of the European Community, of the Convention on access to information, public participation in decision–*

making and access to justice in environmental matters, retrieved 09/15/2010 from the WWW: http://eur–lex.europa.eu/LexUriServ/LexUriServ.do?uri=OJ:L:2005:124:0001:00 03:EN:PDF

Court of the European Union
2008a, *Annual Report 2008*, retrieved 09/28/2010 from the WWW: http://curia.europa.eu/jcms/upload/docs/application/pdf/2009–03/ra08_en_cj_stat.pdf

Court of the European Union
2008b, *The Statute of the Court of Justice of the European Union* (Protocol No.3), retrieved 06/10/2010 from the WWW: http://curia.europa.eu/jcms/upload/docs/appli cation/pdf/2008-09/statut_2008–09–25_17–29–58_783.pdf

Court of the European Union
2009, *Tables alphabétique de matières (Volumes 1985 —2009)*, retrieved 09/13/2010 from the WWW: http://curia.europa.eu/jcms/upload/docs/application/pdf/2009–05/tm.pdf

Court of the European Union
2010, *Rules of Procedure of the European Court of Justice* (consolidated version), retrieved 06/10/2010 from the WWW: http://curia.europa.eu/jcms/upload/docs/application/pdf/2010–04/rp.en.pdf

European Commission
2001, COM(2001) 428 final, *European Governance. A White Paper*, retrieved 09/13/2010 from the WWW: http://eur–lex.europa.eu/LexUriServ/site/en/com/2001/com2001_0 428en01.pdf

European Commission
2002a, COM 2002/141/final, *Communication on relations with the complainant in respect of infringements of Community law*, retrieved 10/05/2010 from the WWW: http://eur–lex.europa.eu/LexUriServ/LexUriServ.do?uri=COM:2002:0141:FIN:EN:PDF

European Commission
2002b, COM(2002)725 final/4, *Communication: Better monitoring of the application of Community law*, retrieved 10/18/2010 from the WWW: http://eur-lex.europa.eu/ LexUriServ/LexUriServ.do?uri=COM:2002:0725:FIN:en:PDF

European Commission
2003, COM(2003) 624 final – *Proposal for a Directive of the European Parliament and of the Council on access to justice in environmental matters* retrieved 06/10/2010 from the WWW: http://eur–lex.europa.eu/LexUriServ/site/en/com/2003/com2003_0624en01.pdf

European Commission
2005, Communication SEC(2005) 1658 – *Application of Article 228 of the EC Treaty [now: Article 260 TFEU]*, retrieved 09/13/2010 from the WWW: http://eur–lex.euro pa.eu/LexUriServ/LexUriServ.do?uri=CELEX:52005SC1658:EN:HTML

European Commission
2006, COM(2006) 194 final, *Green Paper. European Transparency Initiative*, retrieved 10/19/2010 from the WWW: http://eur-lex.europa.eu/LexUriServ/LexUriServ.do?uri=CO M:2006:0194:FIN:EN:PDF

European Commission
2007a, COM(2007) 502 final, *Communication: A Europe of Results – Applying Commu–*

nity Law, retrieved 10/05/2010 from the WWW: http://ec.europa.eu/community_law/infringements/application_monitoring_en.htm

European Commission
2007b, COM(2007) 412 final, Communication from the Commission to the Council, *Reforming Europe for the 21st Century*, retrieved 09/17/2010 from the WWW: http://eur–lex.europa.eu/LexUriServ/site/en/com/2007/com2007_0412en01.pdf

European Commission
2008, SEC(2008) 556, *Aarhus Convention Implementation Report – European Community*, retrieved 10/05/2010 from the WWW: http://ec.europa.eu/environment/aarhus/pdf/sec_2008_556_en.pdf

European Commission
2009, *General budget of the European Union for the financial year 2009*, retrieved 10/05/2010 from the WWW: http://ec.europa.eu/budget/library/publications/budget_in_fig/syntchif_2009_en.pdf

European Economic and Social Committee
1999, *Opinion of the Economic and Social Committee on The Role and Contribution of Civil Society Organisations in the building of Europe*, retrieved 10/05/2010 from the WWW: http://www.eesc.europa.eu/resources/docs/ces851–1999_ac_en.pdf

European Economic and Social Committee
2002, *Rules of Procedure of the European Economic and Social Committee* [codified version in force 12 March 2008], retrieved 09/16/2010 from the WWW: http://www.ena.lu/rules_procedure_european_economic_social_committee_july_2002_consolidated_version_2006–020008178.html

European Parliament
1994, *Decision of the European Parliament on the regulations and general conditions governing the performance of the Ombudsman's duties* (as amended 18 June 2008), retrieved 10/05/2010 from the WWW: http://www.ombudsman.europa.eu/resources/statute.faces;jsessionid=F343D57D42A1049836F513F1854BAFB8

European Parliament
2000, *Charter of Fundamental Rights of the European Union*, retrieved 09/17/2010 from the WWW: http://www.europarl.europa.eu/charter/pdf/text_en.pdf

European Parliament
2001, *European Parliament resolution on the Commission White Paper on European governance* (COM(2001) 428–C5–0454/2001–2001/2181(COS)), retrieved 09/16/2010 from the WWW: http://www.europarl.europa.eu/sides/getDoc.do?type=TA&reference=P5–TA–2001–0643&format=XML&language=EN

European Parliament
2010, *Rules of Procedure of the European Parliament*, retrieved 09/16/2010 from the WWW: http://www.europarl.europa.eu/sides/getLastRules.do?language=EN&reference=TOC#GAX1

European Parliament & Council of the European Union
2000, Regulation 45/2001/EC of 18 December 2000 *on the protection of individuals with regard to the processing of personal data by the Community institutions and bodies and on*

the free movement of such data, retrieved 09/13/2010 from the WWW: http://eur–lex.europa.eu/LexUriServ/LexUriServ.do?uri=OJ:L:2001:008:0001:0022:EN:PDF

European Parliament & Council of the European Union
2001, Regulation 1049/2001/EC of 30 May 2001 *regarding public access to European Parliament, Council and Commission documents*, retrieved 09/13/2010 from the WWW: http://www.europarl.europa.eu/RegData/PDF/r1049_en.pdf

European Parliament & Council of the European Union
2003, Directive 2003/4/EC of 28 January 2003 *on public access to environmental information and repealing Council Directive 90/313/EEC*, retrieved 10/05/2010 from the WWW: http://eur–lex.europa.eu/LexUriServ/LexUriServ.do?uri=OJ:L:2003:041:0026:0032:EN:PDF

European Parliament & Council of the European Union
2003, Directive 2003/35/EC of 26 May 2003 *providing for public participation in respect of the drawing up of certain plans and programmes relating to the environment and amending with regard to public participation and access to justice Council Directives 85/337/EEC and 96/61/EC*, retrieved 10/05/2010 from the WWW: http://eur–lex.europa.eu/LexUriServ/LexUriServ.do?uri=OJ:L:2003:156:0017:0024:EN:PDF

European Parliament & Council of the European Union
2006, Regulation 1367/2006/EC of 6 September 2006 *on the application of the provisions of the Aarhus Convention on Access to Information, Public Participation in Decision–making and Access to Justice in Environmental Matters to Community institutions and bodies*, retrieved 10/05/2010 from the WWW: http://eur–lex.europa.eu/LexUriServ/LexUriServ.do?uri=OJ:L:2006:264:0013:0013:EN:PDF

Online Sources

United Nations Department of Economic and Social Affairs
1992, *Agenda 21, Section III - Strengthening the role of major groups, Chapter 23, Preamble 23.2*, adopted at Rio de Janerio, Brazil, 3 to 14 June 1992, Website (last visited: 06/28/2010): http://www.un.org/esa/dsd/agenda21/res_agenda21_23.shtml

United Nations Department of Economic and Social Affairs
NGO Branch. Consultative Status, Website (last visited: 09/10/2010): http://esango.un.org/civilsociety/consultativeStatusSummary.do?method=applyForConsultativeSt&session Check=false

Websites of the European Union

european navigator (ena)
The Tindemans Report, Website (last visited: 09/13/2010) http://www.ena.lu/the_tindemans_report–020100267.html

Europa
27 Member Countries, Website (last visited: 07/16/2010): http://europa.eu/about–eu/27–member–countries/index_en.htm

Europa,
Agencies of the European Union – Community Agencies, Website (last visited: 07/16/2010): http://europa.eu/agencies/community_agencies/index_en.htm

European Commission
Infringements of EU law, Website (last update: 05/18/2010; last visited: 09/12/2010): http://ec.europa.eu/community_law/infringements/infringements_en.htm

European Commission
Exercise your rights, Website (last update: 05/18/2010; last visited: 07/22/2010): http://ec.europa.eu/community_law/your_rights/your_rights_en.htm

European Commission
1. Methods of submitting a complaint, Website (last update: 05/18/2010; last visited: 07/22/2010): http://ec.europa.eu/community_law/your_rights/your__en.htm#1depot

European Commission
2.1 Information gathering; *2.2. Opening of an infringement procedure: formal contacts between the Commission and the Member State concerned*; *2.3. Referral to the European Court of Justice*, Website (last update: 05/18/2010; last visited: 07/22/2010): http://ec.europa.eu/community_law/your_rights/your_rights_en.htm#2traitement

European Commission
3. National means of redress, Website (last update: 05/18/2010; last visited: 07/22/2010): http://ec.europa.eu/community_law/your_rights/your_rights_en.htm#3voies

European Commission
4(b) Administrative guarantees; *4 (c) Administrative guarantees*; *4(d) Administrative guarantees*, Website (last update: 05/18/2010; last visited: 07/22/2010): http://ec.europa.eu/community_law/your_rights/your_rights_en.htm#4garanties

European Commission
5. Protection of the complainant and personal data, Website (last update: 05/18/2010; last visited: 07/22/2010): http://ec.europa.eu/community_law/your_rights/your_rights_en.htm#5protection

European Commission
Complaint to the European Ombudsman, Website (last update: 05/18/2010; last visited: 07/22/2010): http://ec.europa.eu/community_law/your_rights/your_rights_en.htm#6recours

European Commission
Action under Article 260 TFEU, Website (last update: 05/18/2010; last visited: 07/22/2010): http://ec.europa.eu/community_law/infringements/infringements_260_en.htm

European Commission
Better monitoring. New! EU Pilot, (Website last update: 05/18/2010; last visited: 07/22/2010): http://ec.europa.eu/community_law/infringements/application_moni toring_en.htm

Case Selection

(The case–law was retrieved online from Eur–lex)

1950s

ECJ, Case 6/54 *Netherlands v High Authority* [1955] ECR 103
ECJ, Case 8/55 *Fédération Charbonnière de Belgique v. High Authority* [1956] ECR 245
ECJ, Case 9/56 *Meroni & Co, Industrie Metallurgiche, SpA v High Authority* [1958] ECR 133
ECJ, Joined Cases 42 & 49/59 *Société Nouvelle des Usines de Pontlieue-Aciéries du Temple v High Authority* [1961] ECR 53

1960s

ECJ, Joined Cases 16/62 & 17/62 *CNPFL et al v Council* [1962] ECR 471
ECJ, Joined Cases 19 to 22/62 *Fédération Nationale de la Boucherie en Gros et du Commerce en Gros des Viandes and Others v Council* [1962] ECR 491
ECJ, Case 24/62 *Germany v. EEC Commission* [1963] ECR 63
ECJ, Case 25/62 *Plaumann v Commission* [1963] ECR 95
ECJ, Case 26/62 *NV Algemene Transport- en Expeditie Onderneming van Gend & Loos v Netherlands Inland Revenue Administration* [1963] ECR 1
ECJ, Joined Cases 28-30/62 *Da Costa (Da Costa en Schaake NV, Jacob Meijer NV, Hoechst–Holland NV v Netherlands Inland Revenue Adminis.)* [1963] ECR 31
ECJ, Case 32/62 *M. Maurice Alvis v Council* [1963] ECR 49
ECJ, Case 66/63 *Netherlands v. High Authority* [1964] ECR 533
ECJ, Joined Cases 106 & 107/63 *Toepfer v Commission* [1965] ECR 405
ECJ, Case 6/64 *Flaminio Costa v E.N.E.L.* [1964] ECR 585
ECJ, Case 14/68 *Walt Wilhelm and Others v Bundeskartellamt* [1969] ECR 1

1970s

ECJ, Case 9/70 *Franz Grad v Finanzamt Traunstein* [1970] ECR 825
ECJ, Case 11/70 *Internationale Handelsgesellschaft* [1970] ECR 1125
ECJ, Case 22/70 *Commission of the European Communities v Council of the European Communities (ERTA)* [1971] ECR 263
ECJ, Joined Cases 41-44/70, *International Fruit Co NV v. Commission* [1971] ECR 411
ECJ, Case 59/70 *Netherlands v Commission* [1971] ECR 639
ECJ, Case 62/70 *Bock v Commission* [1971] ECR 897
ECJ, Case 8/71 *Komponistenverband e.V. v Commission* [1971] ECR 705
ECJ, Joined Cases 21-24/72 *International Fruit Company* [1972] ECR 1219
ECJ, Case 81/72 *Commission v. Council* [1973] ECR 575
ECJ, Case 9/73 *Schlüter v Hauptzollamt Lörrach* [1973] ECR 1135
ECJ, Case 134/73 *Holtz & Willemsen GmbH v Council* [1974] ECR 1
ECJ, Case 181/73 *Haegemann* [1974] ECR 449
ECJ, Case 8/74 *Procureur du Roi v Benoît and Gustave Dassonville* [1974] ECR 837
ECJ, Case 41/74 *Yvonne Van Duyn v Home Office* [1974] ECR 1337
ECJ, Case 72/74 *Union Syndicale v Council* [1975] ECR 401

ECJ, Case 26/76 *Metro v Commission* [1977] ECR 1875

ECJ, Case 33/76 *Rewe–Zentralfinanz eG et Rewe-Zentral AG v Landwirtschaftskammer für das Saarland* [1976] ECR 1989

ECJ, Case 112/76 *Manzoni v Fonds National de Retraite des Ouvriers Mineurs* [1977] ECR 1647

ECJ, Case 106/77 *Simmenthal II (Amministrazione delle Finanze dello Stato v Simmenthal SpA.)* [1978] ECR 629

ECJ, Case 125/77 *Koninklijke Scholten–Honig NV and De Verenigde Zetmeelbedrijven "De Bi–jenkorf" BV v Hoofdproduktschap voor Akkerbouwprodukten* [1978] ECR 1991

ECJ, Case 92/78 *Simmenthal v Commission* [1979] ECR 777

ECJ, Case 4/79 *Société coopérative "Providence agricole de la Champagne" v Office national interprofessionnel des céréales* [1980] ECR 2823

ECJ, Joined Cases 33 & 75/79 *Richard Kuhner v Commission* [1980] ECR 1677

ECJ, Case 60/79 *Producteurs de Vins de Table et Vins de Pays v Commission* [1979] ECR 2429

ECJ, Case 104/79 *Foglia v. Novella I* [1980] ECR 745

1980s

ECJ, Case 126/80 *Maria Salonia v Giorgio Poidomani and Franca Baglieri, née Giglio* [1981] ECR 1563

ECJ, Case 8/81 *Becker v Finanzamt Münster-Innenstadt* [1982] ECR 53

ECJ, Case 60/81 *IBM v Commission* [1981] ECR 2639

ECJ, Case 246/81 *Nicholas William, Lord Bethell, v Commission* [1982] ECR 2277

ECJ, Case 283/81 *CILFIT (Srl CILFIT and Lanificio di Gavardo SpA v Ministry of Health)* [1982] ECR 3415

ECJ, Case 11/82 *Piraiki-Patraiki* [1985] ECR 207

ECJ, Case 191/82 *Fediol v Commission* [1983] ECR 2913

ECJ, Joined Cases 239 and 275/82 *Allied Corporation v Commission* [1984] ECR 1005

ECJ, Case 264/82 *Timex v Council* [1985] ECR 849

ECJ, Case 13/83 *EP v Council* [1985] ECR 1513

ECJ, Case 112/83 *Produits de mais v Adm. des douances et droits indirects* [1985] ECR 719

ECJ, Case 240/83 *Procureur de la République v Association de défense des brûleurs d'huiles usagées (ADBHU)* [1985] ECR 531

ECJ, Case 294/83 *Parti écologiste "Les Verts" v European Parliament* [1986] ECR 1339

ECJ, Case 169/84 *Compagnie frančaise de l'azote (Cofaz) SA v Commission* [1986] ECR 391

ECJ, Case 179/84 *Piercarlo Bozzetti v Invernizzi SpA and Ministero del Tesoro* [1985] ECR 2301

ECJ, Case 222/84 *Marguerite Johnston v Chief Constable of the Royal Ulster Constabulary* [1986] ECR 1651

ECJ, Case 35/85 *Procureur de la République v Tissier* [1986] ECR 1207

ECJ, Joined Cases 67/85, 68/85 and 70/85 *Van der Kooy and Others v Commission* [1988] ECR 219

ECJ, Case 69/85 *Wünsche Handelsgesellschaft v Germany* [1986] ECR 947

ECJ, Case 223/85 *Rijn–Schelde-Verolme (RSV) Maschinefabrieken en Scheepwerven v Commis–sion* [1987] ECR 4617

ECJ, Case 282/85 *DEFI v Commission* [1986] ECR 2469
ECJ, Case 314/85 *Foto–Frost v Hauptzollamt Lübeck-Ost* [1987] ECR 4199
ECJ, Case 12/86 *Demirel* [1987] ECR 3719
ECJ, Case 117/86 *UFADE v Council and Commission* [1986] ECR 2483
ECJ, Case 119/86 *Spain v Council and Commission* [1987] ECR 4121
ECJ, Case 222/86 *UNECTEF v Heylens and Others* [1987] ECR 4097
ECJ, Case 302/86 *Commission v Denmark* [1988] ECR 4607
ECJ, Case C–262/88 *Barber v Guardian Royal Exchange Assurance* [1990] ECR I–1889
ECJ, Joined Cases C–143/88 and C–92/89 *Zuckerfabrik Suederdithmarschen and Zuckerfabrik Soest* [1991] ECR I–415
ECJ, Case C–320/88 *Staatssecretaris van Financiën v Shipping and Forwarding Enterprise Safe* [1990] ECR I–285
ECJ, Case C–106/89 *Marleasing* [1990] ECR I–4135
ECJ, Case C–221/89 *The Queen v Secretary of State for Transport, ex parte: Factortame Ltd and others (Factortame)* [1991] ECR I–3905
ECJ, Case C–298/89 *Government of Gibraltar v Council* [1993] ECR I–3605
ECJ, Case C–309/89 *Codorníu SA v Council* [1994] ECR I–1853
ECJ, Case C–358/89 *Extramet v Council* [1991] ECR I–2501

1990s

ECJ, Case C–313/90 *CIRFS and Others v Commission* [1993] ECR I–1125
ECJ, Case C–316/91 *EP v Council* [1994] ECR I–625
ECJ, Case C–188/92 *TWD v Germany* [1994] ECR I–833
ECJ, Case C–359/92 *Germany v Council* [1994] ECR I–3681
ECJ, Case C–415/93 *Bosman* [1995] ECR I–4921
ECJ, Case C–465/93 *Atlanta II (Atlanta Fruchthandelsgesellschaft mbH and others v Bundesamt für Ernährung und Forstwirtschaft)* [1995] ECR I–3761
CFI, Joined Cases T–447/93, T–448/93 and T–449/93 *AITEC and Others v Commission* [1995] ECR II–1971
CFI, Joined Cases T–480/93 and T–483/93 *Antillean Rice Mills and Others v Commission* [1995] ECR II–2305
CFI, Joined Cases T–481/93 and T–484/93 *Vereniging van Exporteurs in Levende Varkens and others and Nederlandse Bond van Waaghouders van Levend Vee and others v Commission* [1995] ECR II–2941
CFI, Case T–585/93 *Greenpeace & Others v Commission* [1995] ECR II–2205
ECJ, Case C–21/94 *EP v Council* [1995] ECR I–1827
ECJ, Case C–61/94 *Commission v Germany* [1996] ECR I–3989
ECJ, Case C–206/94 *Brennet AG v Paletta* [1996] ECR I–2357
Opinion of the Advocate General Cosmas in: Case C–321/95P *Greenpeace and Others v Com–mission* [1998] ECR I–1651
ECJ, Case C–321/95P *Greenpeace and Others v Commission*[1998] ECR I–1651
ECJ, Case C–106/96 *UK v Commission* [1998] ECR I–2729
CFI, Case T–122/96 *Federolio v Commission* [1997] ECR II–1559
CFI, Case T–135/96 *UEAPME v Council* [1997] ECR II–373

ECJ, Case C–379/97 *Pharmacia & Upjohn SA v Paranova A/S* [1999] ECR I–6927

CFI, Case T–173/98 *Unión de Pequeños Agricultores v Council* [1999] ECR II–3357

ECJ, Case C–407/98 *Katarina Abrahamsson & Leif Anderson v Elisabet Fogelqvist* [2000] ECR I–5539

ECJ, Case C-6/99 *Greenpeace v Ministère de l'Agriculture et de la Pêche* [2000] ECR I-1651

2000s

Opinion of the Advocate General Jacobs in: Case C-50/00P *Unión de Pequeños Agricultores v Council* [2002] ECR I-6677

ECJ, Case C-50/00P *Unión de Pequeños Agricultores v Council* [2002] ECR I-6677

ECJ, Case C-453/00 *Kühne & Heitz NV v Produktschap voor Pluimvee en Eieren* [2004]

ECJ, Case C-463/01 *Commission v Germany* [2004]

CFI, Case T-177/01 *Jégo-Quéré v Commission* [2002] ECR II-2365

ECJ, Case C–263/02P *Commission v Jégo-Quéré* [2004]

ECJ, Joined Cases C-453/02 & C-462/02 *Finanzamt Gladbeck v Edith Linneweber and Finanz–amt Herne–Westcontre Savvas Akritidis* [2005]

CFI, Case T–137/04 *Mayer and Others v Commission* [2006]

European Court of Human Rights

(Cases retrieved from HUDOC Search Portal)

Zander v. Sweden, application 14282/88 (case 45/1992/390/468) [25.11.1993]

López Ostra v. Spain, application 16798/90 (case 41/1993/436/515) [9.12.1994]

Guerra and Others v. Italy, application 14967/89 (case 116/1996/735/932) [19.02.1998]

Bundesverfassungsgericht

BVerfG, BVerfGE 89, 155 vom 12. Oktober 1993 (2 BvR 2134, 2159/92), retrieved 10/17/2010 from the WWW: http://sorminiserv.unibe.ch:8080/tools/ainfo.exe?Command=ShowPrint Text&Name=bv089155